Alexis Smith

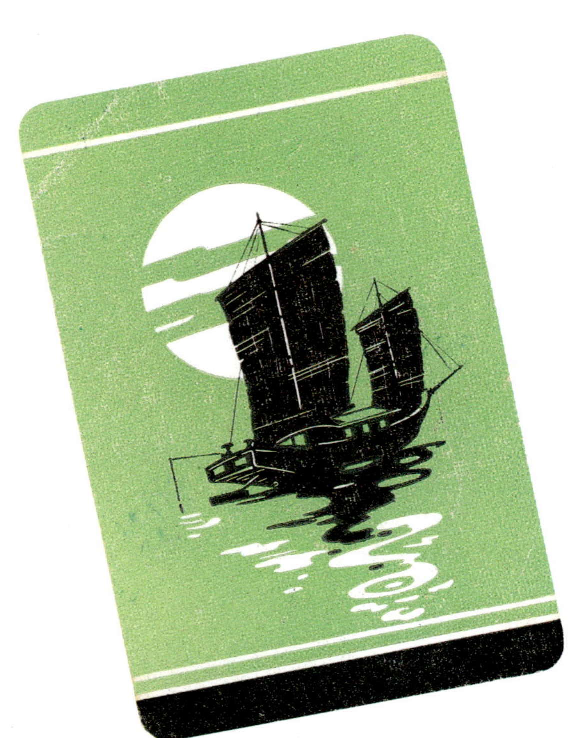

Alexis Smith

by Richard Armstrong

Whitney Museum of American Art, New York

Rizzoli, New York

This catalogue was published in conjunction with the exhibition "Alexis Smith."
Whitney Museum of American Art, New York
November 22, 1991–February 29, 1992

The Museum of Contemporary Art, Los Angeles
March 29–July 5, 1992

This exhibition is supported by a generous grant from The Bohen Foundation with additional funding from the National Committee of the Whitney Museum, the National Endowment for the Arts, and an anonymous donor.

Research for this exhibition and publication was supported by income from an endowment established by Henry and Elaine Kaufman, The Lauder Foundation, Mrs. William A. Marsteller, The Andrew W. Mellon Foundation, Mrs. Donald Petrie, the Primerica Foundation, the Samuel and May Rudin Foundation, Inc., The Simon Foundation, and Nancy Brown Wellin.

Trade edition distributed by Rizzoli International Publications, Inc.
300 Park Avenue South, New York, New York 10010

ISBN 0-87427-076-6 softcover edition
ISBN 0-8478-1446-7 hardcover edition

Printed in Hong Kong by South China Printing Company

The appropriated passages from literary sources that constitute a major component of Alexis Smith's work are not intended to be exact transcriptions.

Endleaves: **Alexis Smith Playing Cards, Made in USA,** 1981 (press sheet detail)
Cover: based on **Wild Life,** 1985 (p. 153)

Contents

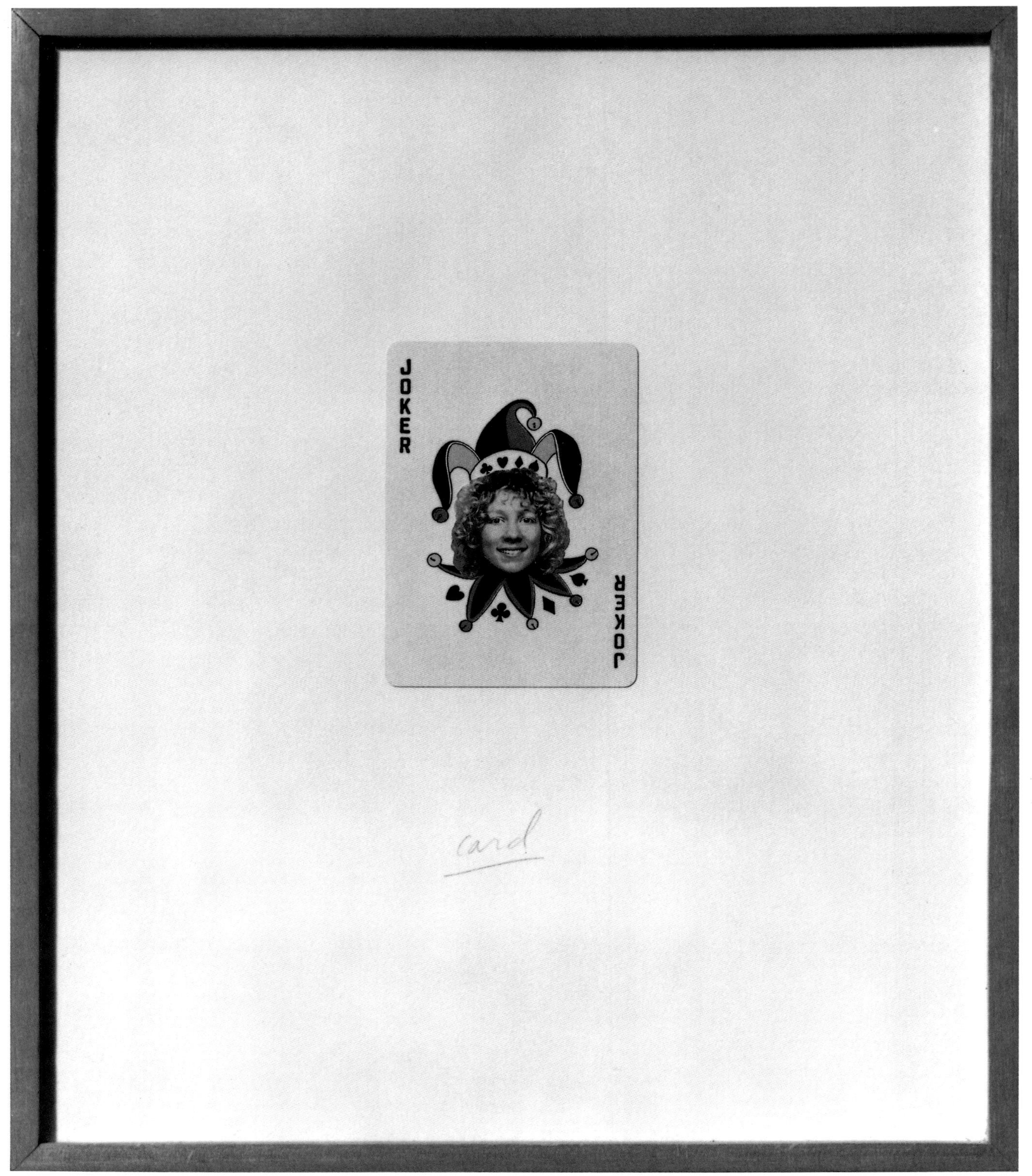

Card, 1978
Paper collage, 11¾ × 9¼ inches
Collection of the artist, courtesy Margo Leavin Gallery, Los Angeles

Foreword

Working from inside American popular culture, Alexis Smith makes direct use of our shared values, fears, and aspirations to create an art that is both extremely private and remarkably plain-speaking. This is no simple matter, for Smith's art is deeply rooted in the narrative forms of Conceptualism —a genre that led many others to produce a cynical, hermetic art primarily addressing either the impossibility of communication or postmodern concerns such as the death of the author and the near miracle of meaning.

Not that Smith's work is without an edge, or that it lacks a point of view. To the contrary, Smith produces a profoundly moral art confronting social issues from a psychologically charged perspective. As Richard Armstrong notes in his essay on Smith's development, the artist is best understood in the Symbolist tradition, and it is that quality, served well by her dry wit, that elevates her unique constructions above most common narrative work. That she often draws her themes from Hollywood film culture and the pulp fiction universe only adds to the lure of legibility which underscores Smith's desire to include her reader-viewer in her compelling vision.

In presenting this exhibition of Alexis Smith's work, the Whitney Museum continues to recognize the vitality and significance of California art and, by extension, the art of other regions of the United States, which together construct those unique traditions and idioms that epitomize the rich complexity of the American scene.

The Museum is grateful to Richard Armstrong for his thoughtful and thorough survey of Smith's work, and for his perceptive introductory essay and catalogue texts. In a style that perfectly reflects Smith's sensibility, author, poet (and sometime Smith-collaborator) Amy Gerstler has provided a provocative and thoroughly delightful biographical sketch of the artist. We thank her for asking the question on so many minds today—"just who is Alexis Smith?"

The exhibition was funded by The Bohen Foundation with additional funding from the National Committee of the Whitney Museum, the National Endowment for the Arts, and an anonymous donor. We are grateful for their generosity, matched only by the generosity of the exhibition's numerous lenders, who have selflessly agreed to part with their works for the duration of the exhibition's tour.

Finally, the Whitney Museum would like to express its profound gratitude to the artist herself. Working with Alexis Smith has been a pleasure and privilege for all of us, and we offer her our thanks.

David A. Ross
Director

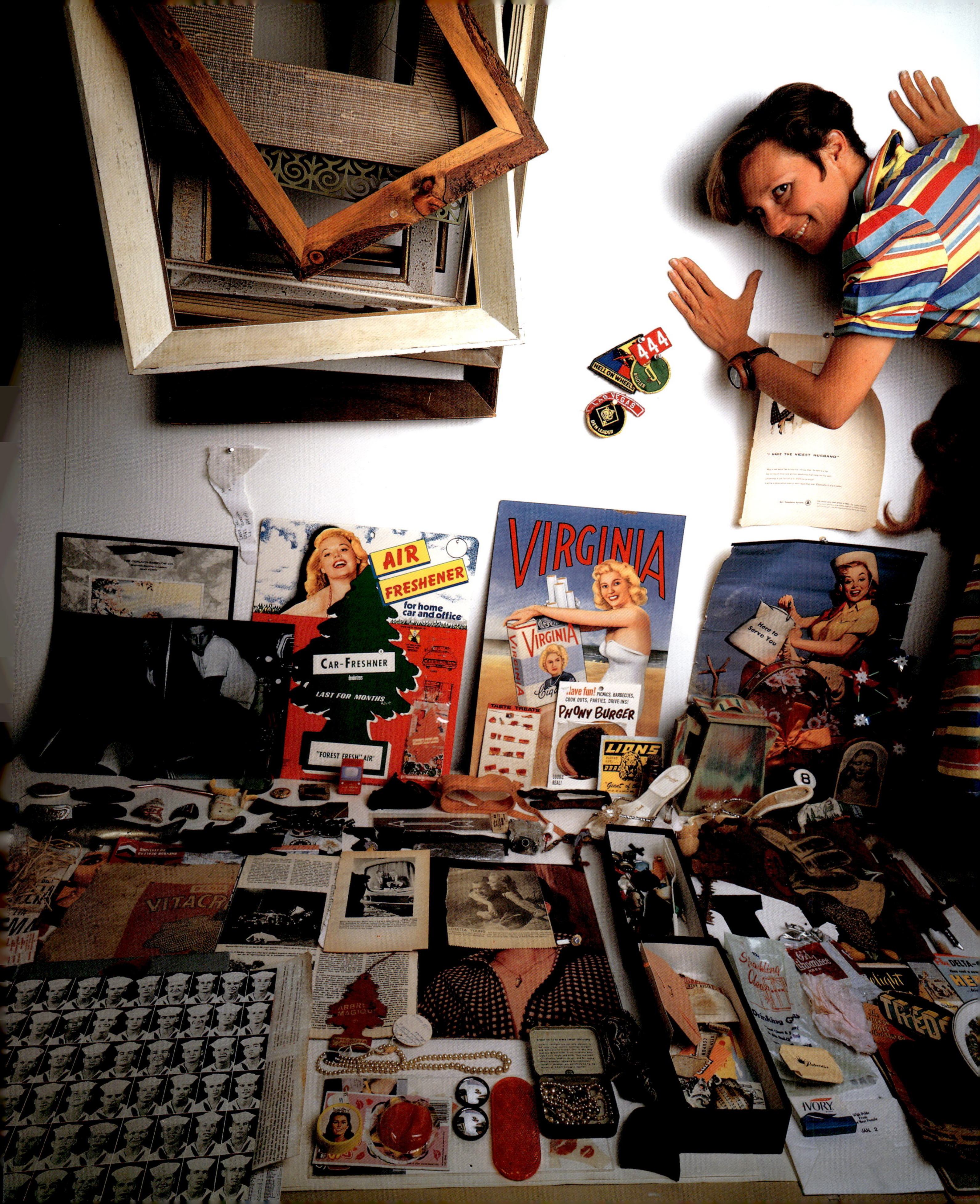
AIR
FRESHENER
for home
car and office
CAR-FRESHNER
LAST FOR MONTHS
"FOREST FRESH" AIR
VIRGINIA
Have fun!
PHONY BURGER
LIONS
Here to Serve You
HELL ON WHEELS
444
LAS VEGAS
DEN LEADER
"I HAVE THE NICEST HUSBAND"
VITACR
IVORY

Interview

Richard Armstrong: You were born Patricia Anne Smith. When and why did you become Alexis Smith?

Alexis Smith: I became Alexis Smith at seventeen, when I went to college. Previously I had been Patti Anne Smith, which was not very appealing. I guess I had the desire to be somebody different, to reinvent myself. I first picked the name Alex arbitrarily from a person in a movie as sort of a nice, androgynous nickname. Then it turned out that there was an Alexis Smith who was a movie star. So I lengthened the nickname, and Alexis became my pseudonym.

RA: Let's talk about the personalities and circumstances of your childhood that may have led you to become an artist and when that decision was made.

AS: I wasn't the kind of person who always knew I was going to be an artist, but I always did what I do now in some form—making things, collecting things. I used to chop words out of magazines and put them together or try to coerce the neighborhood kids into putting on plays that I wrote. I was an only child, and I had a lot of time to fill. I grew up on the grounds of a mental hospital, where my father was assistant superintendent. The hospital was a very peculiar environment, but it was also an extremely protected one because it was a walled city. It had very small, manageable versions of all the things you find in a real city. I think that probably made my life a little bit different.

RA: Where was the hospital?

AS: It was Metropolitan State Hospital in Norwalk, California. Norwalk is on the east side of Los Angeles County, and Los Angeles County was more rural than it is now. Before moving to the hospital grounds, we had a citrus ranch in Charter Oaks, out by Claremont. In the 1950s, there were still orange groves. Norwalk was near Santa Fe Springs, where there were lots of oil wells—lots of smog and oil wells.

RA: Your father was a psychiatrist?

AS: Yes. In a way, a lot of the source material that I ultimately used in my work came from my father. He was born in 1906, and so he was two generations older than I. He sort of grew up with the century. He was born in Ogden, Utah, and he used to ride around in his grandfather's horse and buggy under a buffalo robe while Grandpa Driver, the only doctor around in those times, made house calls in rural Utah. My father lived through World War I, the Depression, and World War II. He told me the whole history of the century through his own experiences because he was a big talker.

RA: What about your mother?

AS: My mother was a very vivacious, entertaining person. But she died when I was eleven, and we weren't that close, so she had less impact on me.

RA: Was she from Utah?

AS: She was from San Diego. I probably got my initial interest in making things and decorating from my mother. She was very keen on interior decoration and making

Alexis Smith in her studio, 1985

clothes and reupholstering furniture. Right before she died, we left the hospital in Norwalk and moved to Whittier, where I went to junior high and high school. It was a very middle class, suburban area, a little better than Norwalk. We also had a house in Palm Springs during my childhood and spent most weekends in the desert.

RA: Did that have an effect on you?

AS: It was very high kitsch—Palm Springs in the 1950s with the Gabor sisters—and the enormity of the desert landscape was very powerful.

RA: Do you think that Los Angeles has molded your vision?

AS: I think the West helped me form a sense of self. I have assimilated so much of its history from my father and his family: its traditional pioneer values of individuality—being who you want and changing your life and doing what you please. I also think that Los Angeles is such a different kind of place from the rest of the country in terms of its climate and relative newness and, until very recently, its lack of European culture.

RA: Why did you decide to go to the University of California, Irvine?

AS: I had applied to a few places, but UC, Irvine, was a brand-new school. I had some friends who were going there. There was a high proportion of men to women, and it was much less expensive than any of the private schools that I had applied to. It was a fateful non-decision.

RA: What did you intend to study?

AS: I arrived there in 1966 with the intention of being a humanities major. My field was French, but after a couple of summers in France I could see that the field was a dead end for me. Mostly, my intentions were to have a good time and get away from home.

RA: What made you decide to study art?

AS: A friend of mine in my dorm, an art major, talked me into taking some art classes. I was always making things—cutting words and pictures out of magazines, collaging them together, and giving them to people as gifts. She was convinced that they were something; that I should take some art classes.

The Irvine art department turned out to be a unique place. It had no facilities and no equipment and hardly any classrooms. So what they did was bring in the best faculty they could find—working artists and critics from all over the country. And for the students who found their way into that program it was an extraordinary experience. It was just hanging out and talking and making things, but it galvanized us, and a lot of artists came out of that program.

RA: Who at Irvine had the greatest impact on you?

AS: Bob Irwin and Vija Celmins, who were my professors as well as my friends and mentors. Bob was an extremely charismatic teacher, really passionate about art, and his ideas about art as a personal investigation, almost a spiritual pursuit, were very seductive, especially in the 1960s. Vija was sort of a role model for me because she was really good and really respected by the male artists. She and I became close friends, and she helped me get a job with Frank Gehry when I got out of school. And then I met Barbara Haskell, and Vija and Barbara and I were in a women's group together for a couple of years. That was about 1972 or so.

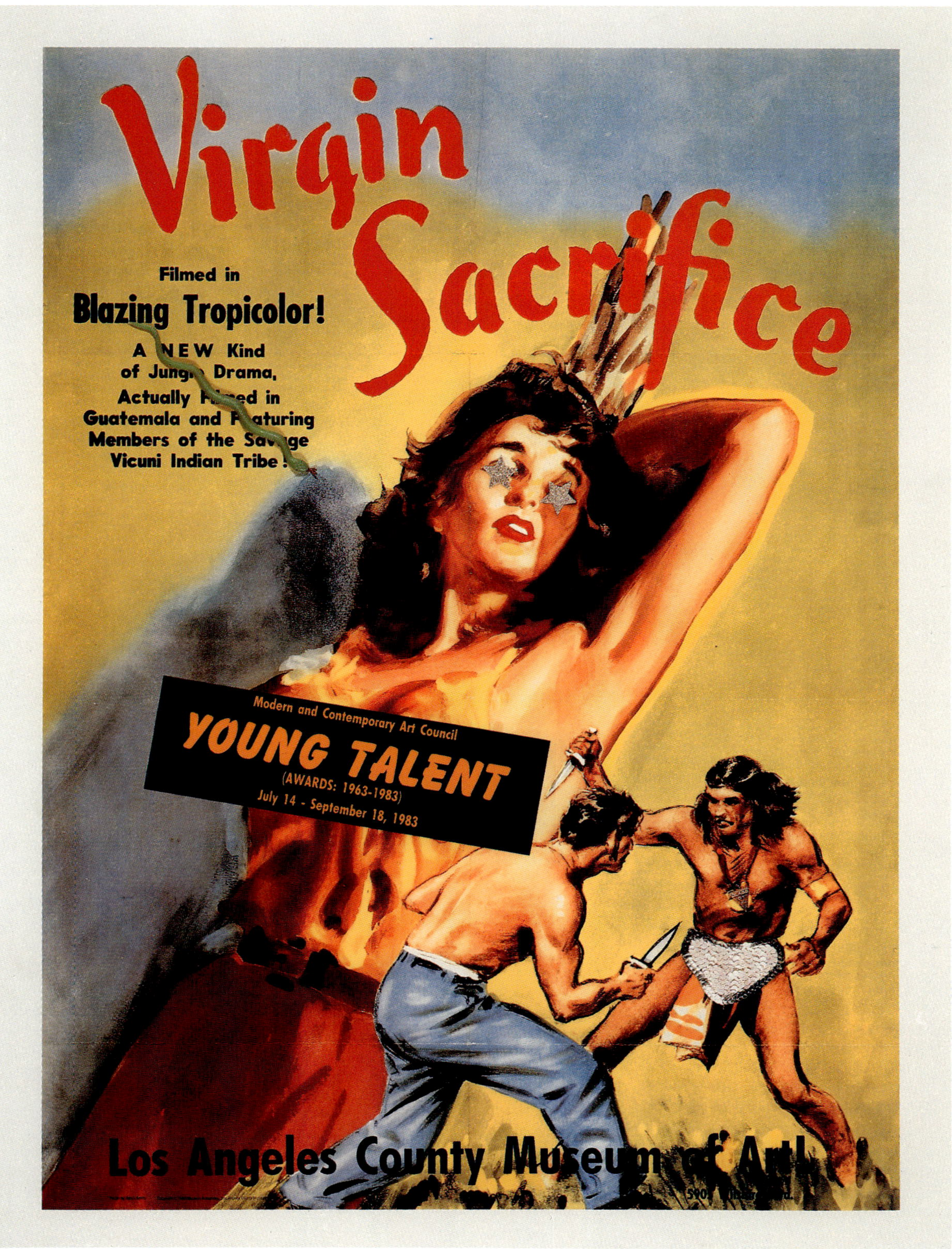

Virgin Sacrifice, 1983
Poster, 24 × 18 inches
Commissioned by Los Angeles County Museum of Art

RA: Would you say that at the beginning of your career you were repeatedly concerned with women who are determined to be successful and somehow survive?

AS: I don't really think that my work has that much female imagery in it. It sometimes has female voices, although if you go back and look at my early work you find that the voice that's the most commonly used is Borges, who wasn't female. Occasionally, I've used female voices as ciphers for myself when there was something special about the female experience that I wanted to concentrate on. Later, when I got into the *Jane* images, I started to play on what I consider to be the inherent irony between traditional female images and who I am and who I would have to be in order to make these pieces. There's a kind of tension there between the ideal and the real.

The female imagery I've particularly wanted to deal with at times involved the conflict between trying to reconcile two roles—being a success and also having a love relationship. You know that famous Bette Davis soliloquy from *All About Eve*.

RA: There are symbolic continuities in your work—exemplified by, say, the repeating motifs of playing cards, the stars, or the snake. What do they mean? Is the idea of continuity intentional?

AS: I think that continuity is sometimes almost accidental. For example, if you take the playing cards in early works and, more recently, the snake: in each case, I was first attracted to the image and only then started seeing potential meanings for it or other ways to use it.

RA: Is this related to your early interest in double entendres?

AS: Once you start working with an image or a metaphor, you have it in your mind, and then you just keep seeing other things it could mean. Then you are not only punning or playing against the different meanings that the object could have, but you're playing against the different meanings that you've assigned it in the past—a dialogue within the work.

RA: You want that shifting signification.

AS: Yes, I like the idea that these elements of meaning are not static, that they shift around according to the context.

RA: Can you be specific about the symbolic development of the playing cards, stars, and snake?

AS: The playing cards started out as a symbol of fate. If you look at my early work, you'll see that I was particularly preoccupied with ideas of fate and destiny. It makes sense in a way because I was a young person trying to find out what I was supposed to be doing with my life. I felt that I really hadn't planned on being an artist but somehow it came along and got me. Against all odds, considering my background. So I was curious to examine the theme of fate as it affected other people.

I think the "star" struck me as a rather curious symbol because it has the obvious meaning of the heavens and the guiding star, but for some reason it's the word that people used to describe celebrities. That's a very curious double symbolism.

RA: Is the star the intersection of your deep passion for Hollywood and the idea of fate?

AS: Those two things did come together. In the same piece, I could use the repeated imagery of the star, but change the meaning from one connotation to another; that had a lot of appeal. In the case of the snake, its appeal was not just its meaning, but its serpentine form. The snake necklace (*Sidewinder*) exploits that sinuousness; it's a streamliner train that wraps around your neck to become a snake's tail. Or in *Same Old Paradise*, where it's a road that twists around and becomes a coiled snake. These are plays on the snake's slippery, serpentine form. On the other hand, the snake can be seen as a sexual image—as the evil of the Garden of Eden. In the piece *Jack*, it has the obvious historical connection to the "Don't Tread On Me" flag, but you also have the snake as a menacing creature, the archetypal symbol of forbidden things.

RA: Would it be accurate to say that from the beginning of your career, your art has been generated by the need to tell a story? If so, why do you think this concern puts you outside the mainstream of modernism?

AS: The last question is hard to answer because it's not easy to place yourself in a perspective of modernism or postmodernism or anything else. The idea that my primary motivation is storytelling has some truth to it, but the impulse to tell stories is generated more by a search for meanings than by a narrative need.

RA: How so?

AS: For me, stories are an extended series of meanings. I think I can look at things and see relatedness, that is, see instinctually how something could be a metaphor for something else—how images and objects fit together or how people generate stories, words, and objects. All these things are extensions of how people experience the world.

When I started working, I put together pieces of other people's writing with objects and images. I was using all of it as found material—taking things that other people had said more eloquently than I could say myself. I figured that if other people thought these things, and I thought them too, they must be somehow universal. I sought to show people the connection between the physical things that they make and the stories that they tell—how the same impulses that generate the language and the stories generate the objects. For me everything is related, and I think it always has been. When I was younger, I just couldn't articulate the connections as well.

As a child—and to some extent even to this day—I felt more comfortable in the world of the inanimate, just as some people feel more comfortable with animals or plants. I have a feel for the everyday objects of the physical universe.

As soon as I fell into the art world, I ceased to exist in a vacuum. I realized that mine was a natural, innate impulse, but I also had to assess all the formal issues of composition, color, and materials. I began to learn and became more sophisticated about both the history of art and its materials. There's no way you can undo that.

RA: Do you now feel connected with some sort of cycle or sequence inside the story of modern art?

AS: I think you could justifiably make a case for me as some kind of eccentric like Cornell—somebody really driven by a particular cosmology and the attempt to articulate it. But, on the other hand, you could make an equally good case for me as one of a contingent of humorous L.A. Conceptual artists who are tongue-in-cheek and irreverent, yet still serious or intellectual, like Ed Ruscha or Mike Kelley, John Baldessari or Al Ruppersberg. I'm just as tied to that group of people as I am to the world of the inanimate.

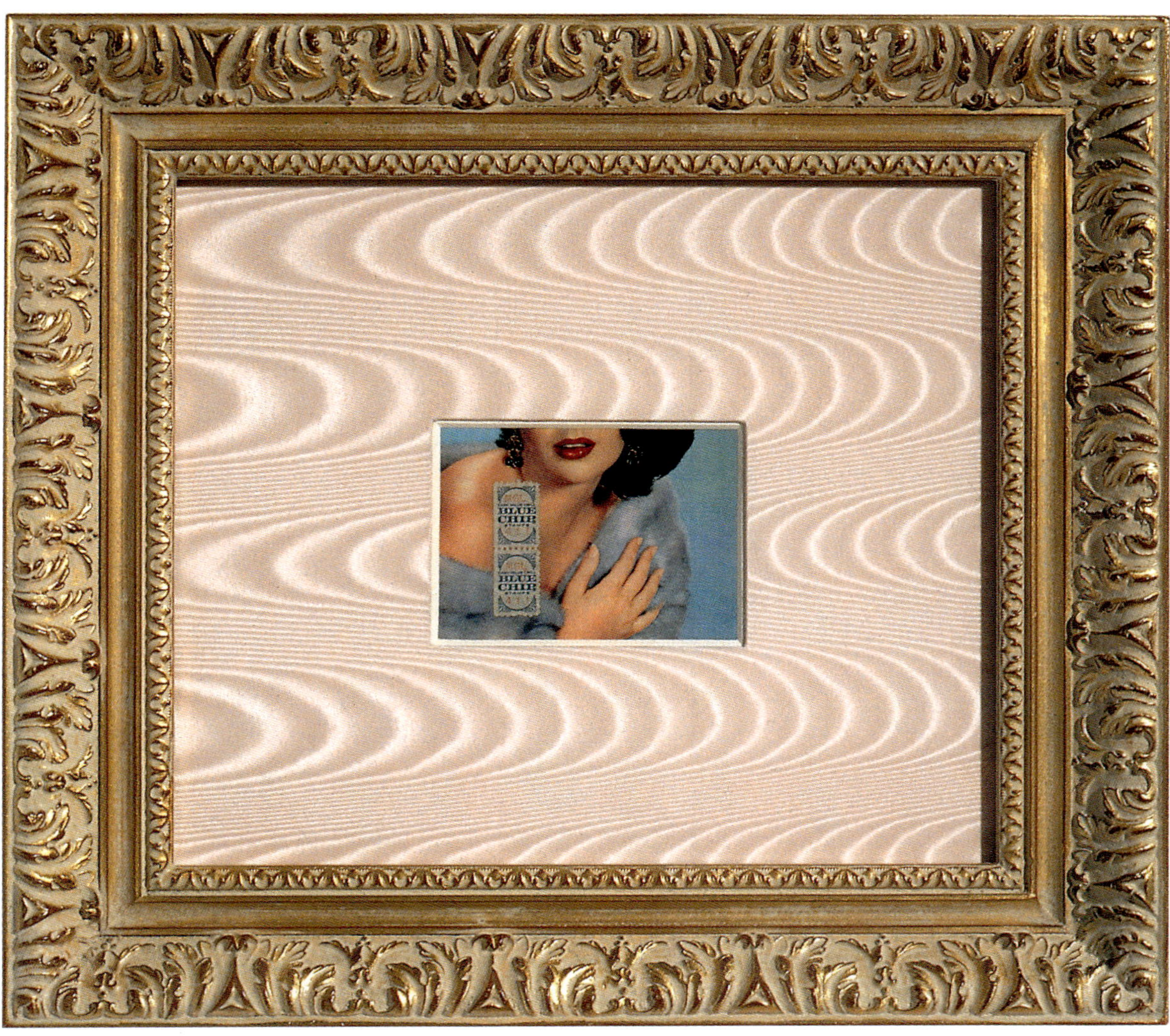

Blue Chip, 1989
Paper collage,
$14\frac{3}{16} \times 12\frac{7}{8}$ inches
Collection of James and Linda Burrows

RA: The concept of postmodernism really doesn't have much validity for you and your work?

AS: I think that collage is a modernist device. In that sense, my work may be an extension of an early twentieth-century idea with some Pop overlays. I certainly don't have a lot truck with people like Foucault. I think I'm too sentimental and connected to people's real passionate experience of life to be very interested in deconstruction.

RA: When did your work stop being about yourself and assume a wider ambition?

AS: As I got more confident, I began to project my own life into a sort of prototypical American experience. My father's accounts of his own experience of the century were really helpful. I put them together with the things I had read for myself and I did a sort of humanization of history—some creative anthropology about the texture of the way things looked and felt. I found that there's a kind of mythology that's peculiarly American and is outside standard history and traditional, European academic culture. I became extremely fascinated with that. For example, I like the democratic point of view of Walt Whitman probably because he's so anti-academic, and I have a perverse sort of antagonism to the European academic tradition and the tyranny it has exercised over the art schools and non-archival forms and materials. There's a whole hierarchy that places painting and bronzes at the top of the aesthetic heap, and you can't do what I do without feeling a certain amount of antagonism toward this system.

RA: Is Isadora Duncan another model of the freedom you seek?

AS: Yes. The artists whom I really relate to or feel strongly about are not visual artists. Rather they're quirky American geniuses like Isadora Duncan, Frank Lloyd Wright, Thomas Edison, Gershwin, and Whitman. For me, they represent values of courage and originality and personal vision: they reinvented their forms because they refused to accept the traditional definitions of the things they wanted to do. They did their work through a weird hybrid of ignorance and naiveté and chutzpah and imagination. That's what I respond to, and that's a peculiarly American tradition.

RA: What metaphorical role does Hollywood play in your work? Is it still as operative as it was in the collages of the seventies and early eighties?

AS: Hollywood is a fantasy place that has a real locale—here, L.A., where I live. It's also a place of the imagination; for decades people have been talking about going to Hollywood. It's the fantasy that one day you're working in a gas station or as a waitress, and the next day you're under contract to MGM. It's the quintessential American transformation myth—a nobody one day, and a somebody the next. Initially, it was a fertile territory for my work. But it's been pretty well mined in the last twenty years; now I've shifted away from Hollywood to the Garden of Eden. When I was doing *On the Road*, I needed a metaphor for California and I went back to the Garden of Eden—a paradise of lush plants and opulence that harbors the extremes of good and evil, where ignorance is bliss.

There's also another aspect of my connection with Hollywood, but it's more formal than thematic. It began in 1980 when I started to make the frames relate to the content of the pieces. For example, in the *Chandlerisms*, you have the Baroque gold frame on the "blonde to make a bishop kick a hole in a stained glass window" or the rough wood frame for "a farm boy at a Latin lesson." My first forays into relating the frames, and images were a little tentative; but later, in *Christmas Eve, 1943* and *Satan's Satellites*, they became more integral. In the *Janes*, the frames actually became a major sculptural element and a large part of the content. Two things made this possible.

About 1975, I began working with the people at Jerry Solomon's, a framing company in Los Angeles, and over the years I developed a personal rapport with them. By the early eighties I was working with the guys directly in the shop. They had tremendous resources in terms of creating a variety of finishes and making things look old. They could make things look like the fifties or as if they had paint peeling off them. In other words, I could suddenly get a look that wasn't part of traditional picture-framing—the look of found, weather-beaten objects.

Another key to my involvement with Hollywood illusionism was that I started working with Richard Sedivy, an artist who supported himself for years as a scenic painter at CBS. He helped me paint the big *Satan's Satellites* wall paintings I exhibited at Rosamund Felsen in 1982 and he helped me do the wall paintings at Grand Rapids. Through him I learned a lot of scenic painting techniques and hung out a little at CBS and on some of the sets. I began to see that not only could I do faux finishes, but also that if I couldn't find the objects I wanted, I could make representations of them—as they do on a Hollywood set. I realized that the look of "real" is a standard Hollywood set-decorating technique—where you can't tell the difference between the found and the made—and that this technology was literally at my disposal.

RA: Do you think that working on large-scale commissions like the *Snake Path* or, earlier, *The Grand* in Grand Rapids, or the L.A. Convention Center has had an effect on your studio work, either materially or intellectually?

AS: Those experiences have increased my comfort and self-confidence with materials. I came to art without knowing how to do anything and didn't have any proper art school training. Thus my early work is very ephemeral, primarily because I was so afraid to do anything with materials. But when you're imagining gigantic things on an architectural scale out of stone and terrazzo and bronze you have to get over this fear, an effort that of necessity extends into the studio work.

RA: How do the large-scale pieces summarize or extend your concepts?

AS: In terms of the individual pieces, *The Grand*, which I did in 1983, fit into my anthropological, historical tour of the century. It was my exploration of the interiors of 1920s and 1930s movie theaters as escapist entertainment palaces during the Depression. The L.A. Convention Center, being done now, is a nonverbal, cross-cultural piece where the imagery is about relationships among design motifs of other cultures. It has a universal quality that's really outside of American experience. The snake piece at UCSD is interesting because the form and the content of the piece are the same: every scale is a piece of slate, and the form of the snake is the pathway itself. The possible congruence of form and content may ultimately push me in the direction of real, three-dimensional sculpture.

RA: Do you think Los Angeles still plays a central role in your sensibility?

AS: I don't think that I'm specifically interested in Southern California, but I'm a product of it. The place in my work is not so much here but everywhere. I want the everyman-everywhere sensibility of American culture. Lately, I have given myself permission to take the words out of some of the pieces because the images don't always require a text. Initially, I used the words as an infrastructure from which to free associate; they generated the pieces. Now, the public pieces and the installations are often generated by the people who are going to see them and the places where the works are situated. The words are secondary.

RA: Are your symbols now so overpowering that there's no necessity for verbal direction?

AS: I now use the words more as an irritating subtext than as associative catalysts. I don't feel as constricted by the format I developed as I used to, because I work in so many different formats these days. But I do think that something of me comes through whether there are words or not.

RA: Your work seems to have evolved from literature to cliché to the abandonment of words altogether?

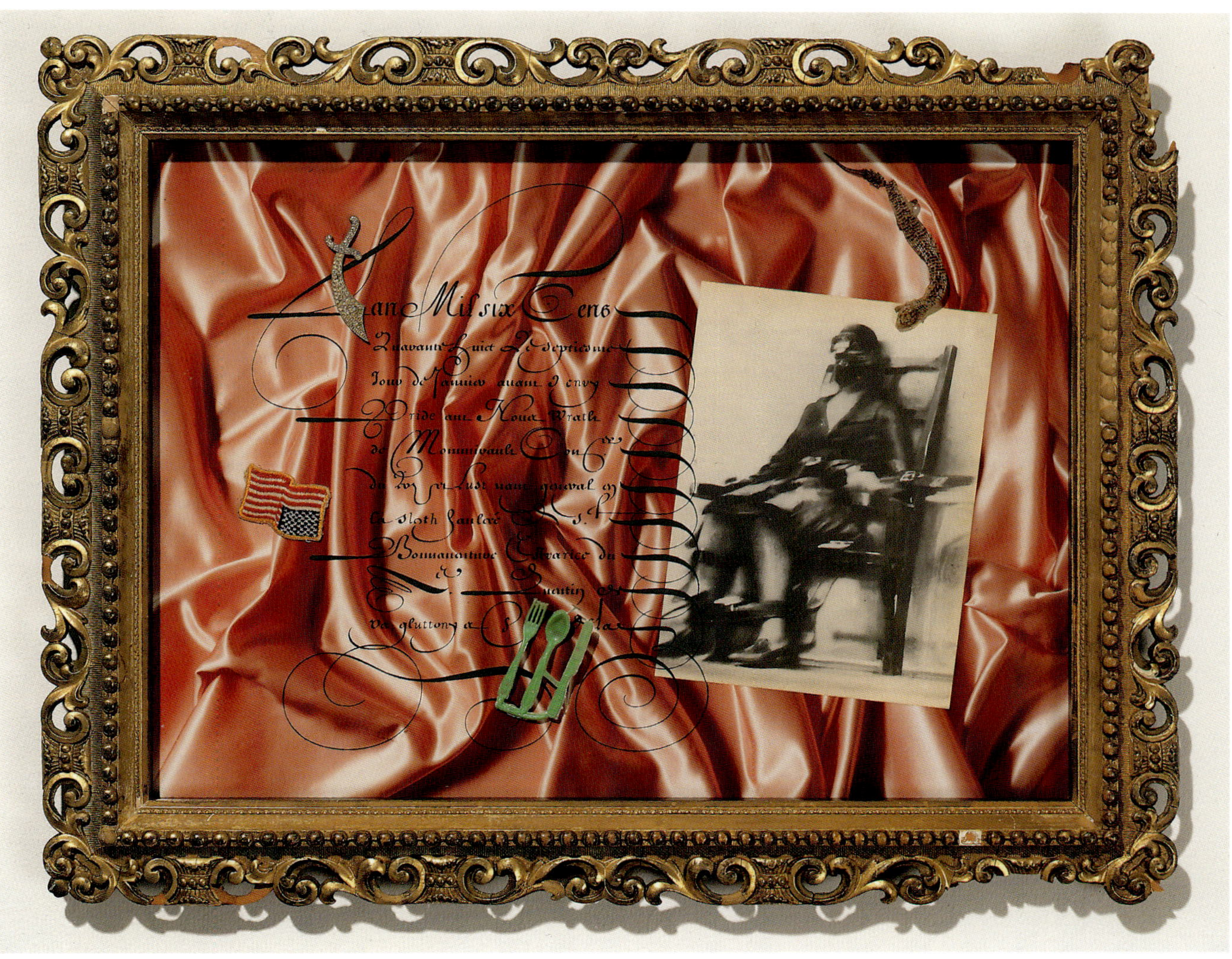

AS: It's not so much a question of abandoning words—but I think my focus has gradually shifted from literature to cliché, to whatever images and impulses are underneath the clichés. Most people think that thought structures language, but in my experience, the reverse is true. People learn to think using the words and word-images, or metaphors, that their culture provides them with. There are just certain patterns of thought and certain images that are built right into the language and which we all seem to share. When you start to use those patterns, and to isolate their underlying images and impulses, then sometimes words are useful, and sometimes they are unnecessary. Images are enough.

RA: Is that your new ambition, to make your work even more pictorial and less language oriented?

AS: I think when you start following that impulse you've got to be free enough to go where it leads you.

June 16, 1991
Venice, California

Karma, 1990
Mixed-media collage,
26 × 33 inches
Collection of Lari Pittman and Roy Dowell

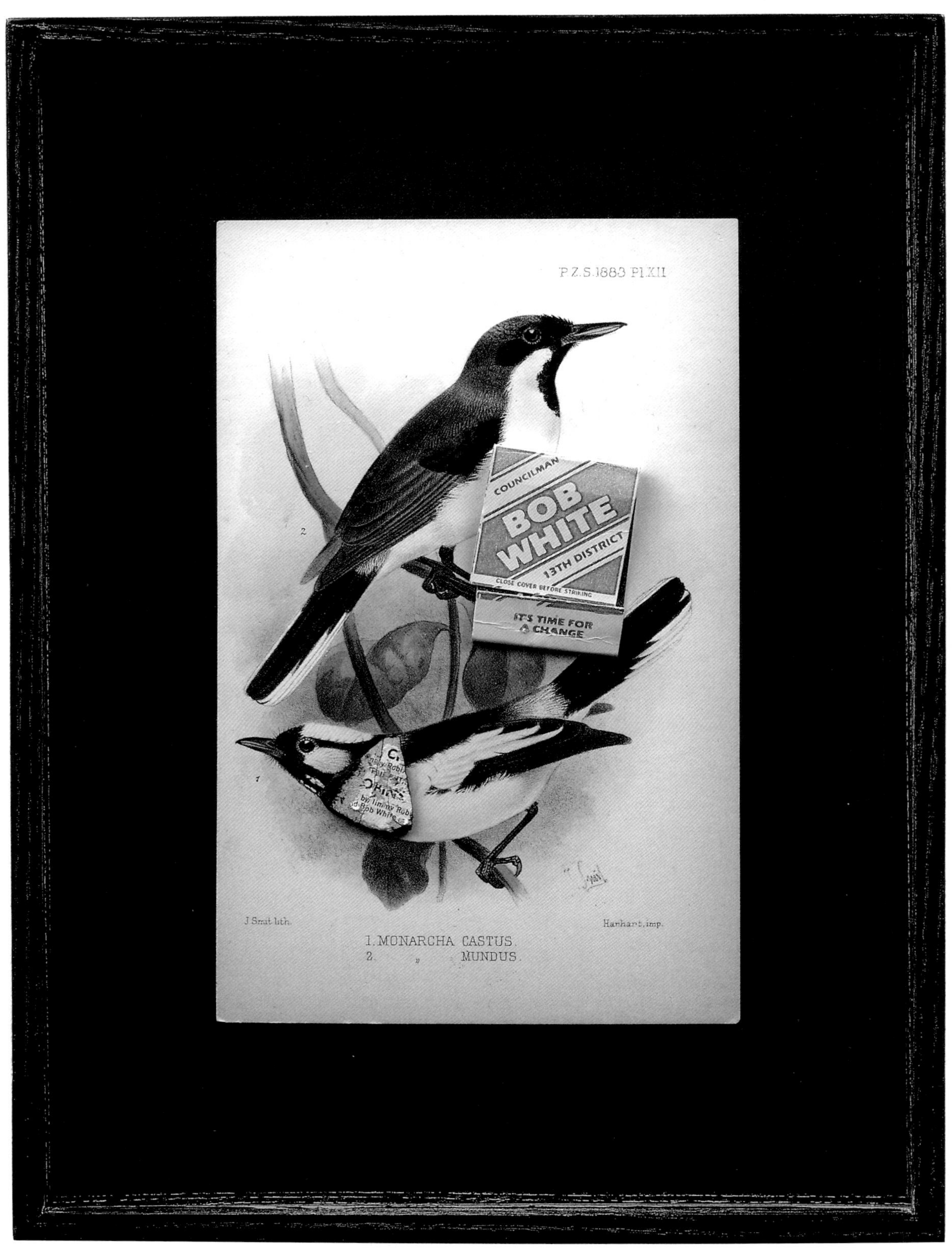

Bobwhite, 1986
Mixed-media collage, 12⅞ × 10¾ inches
Collection of Margo Leavin

Introduction

"Any Dream Is Better Than No Dream"
—Alexis Smith, *Stardust*

For Alexis Smith, in the beginning there was the word and there was the object. Both spoke to her with uncommon intensity and she understood them as conjoined halves of a common vocabulary, part conceptual and part physical. When she began her search for meaning by recounting stories, her narratives came from what she had read and thought, seen and touched. Seeking to make sense, literally, of the physical world, she employs elements she finds in the surfeit of words and images that surrounds us. Because she is a person for whom vision is paramount, she became an artist, but of a particular sort. Neither painter nor sculptor, her works employ illusions of both media—and of writing. To accommodate this hybrid form, she refined a practice she had first taken up as a child, and in the last twenty years her work has redefined the meaning of collage.

Inspired by found texts as well as found images, Smith evokes a state between idea and sensation. Reading and seeing are harnessed into a single, synaesthetic activity. What she puts before us acts first as a catalyst to recollection and then, if necessary, as an object for formal delectation. Her work exists in the gap between text and image, past and present, word and thing, ordinary and extraordinary. She unites thought and physical perception, relying on the eye and memory to make the synthesis. Smith is most successful when otherwise unrelated thoughts and objects are seamlessly melded together, when fragments from our mental and physical lives are "reunited." Collectively, the stories that Smith has reconstructed over the past twenty years form a history of twentieth-century America; individually, each is a forceful aide-mémoire.

The look and outlook of Smith's works have changed since her first book collages of the early 1970s, with their emphasis on self-analysis and self-invention. Around 1972, concerned with making her work more public, she began presenting sequential texts—passages of fiction—on 8 ½ x 11-inch typing paper. Small, discrete found objects were applied to the pages of typed texts. Distinctly narrative, these pieces were heralded as part of a wider development within Conceptual Art that favored storytelling. Smith reiterated the metaphoric power of a given passage by juxtaposing it with some piquant bit of consonant flotsam. She wanted to provoke common memory by exploiting the associative powers inherent in each of the timeworn objects in her collages—to conjure up Proust's madeleine as often as she could. The multiple meanings generated by her frequent double entendres lent her work a humorous air which, along with its precise but handmade composition and light touch, distinguished it from most other narrative art of the moment. While attracted to the verbal logic of Conceptualism, she was far too romantic to adhere to its analytic strictures.

Smith refined her technique and enlarged her ambitions around 1975. With *Madame Butterfly* (1975), she recognized that to paraphrase a work of art another work of equal genius was necessary—as Puccini's operatic adaption of an existing play demonstrated. Henceforth Smith's use of text became both more eclectic in its sources and more pointed as she edited it to her own purposes. She also complicated the format by adding more collage elements and altering the frames encasing the work. Moving beyond literature, she began to employ popular Hollywood myths, seeing in them reflections of the myths of modern American fiction and of our own media-generated identities. Moreover, as the physical characteristics of the works were enriched, the found objects and images gradually assumed equal, sometimes even greater, visual strength than the found words. By the late 1970s, Smith was reaching out to encompass everyman and everywoman.

Smith's work entered a second stage of development around 1980 with such large-scale installations as *Raymond Chandler's L.A.* and *U.S.A.* In both presentations, she decorated the galleries to amplify the significance of the wall-bound collages. These efforts entailed abstract and representational wall paintings that provided an atmospheric surround for each collage and highlighted the traditional wall-art relationship, proposing it as a kind of meta-collage. The content and context of Smith's collages would frequently intermingle, as she employed all available illusions whether inside or outside the frame. These gallery installations reached an apogee of artifice with *Cathay* (1981). Here Smith filled a large, built-to-order gallery with disjunctive images—Orientalist texts and three-dimensional objects—in her most exotic and least traditionally literary piece to that moment. It was the finale of an exotic strain of Smith's art that had begun with her repeated use of Jorge Luis Borges' writings and, among other sources, *The Thousand and One Nights*. After *Cathay*, Smith limited herself to the work of American authors and other sources in popular culture—the same culture that had long supplied her with images and objects.

The Big Sleep (Requiem for Raymond Chandler) (1978) is an early example of the new contentual complexity Smith imposed on her frames. Its trompe l'oeil wallpaper-covered frame suggests the ratty hotel rooms of Raymond Chandler's prose, infusing the piece with richly associative inferences. From there Smith quickly expanded her frames and supports; the process culminated in the made-to-order faux antiques of so many of the component parts of *Christmas Eve, 1943* (1982) and the *Janes* (1985). With the elaboration and signification of the frames, her work became less dependent on the found object. Its physicality had gradually overcome its written messages, so that each piece now existed principally as an artifact inscribed with multiple meanings rather than as embellished literature.

For the remainder of the decade, Smith focused on large groups of related collages. Having explored the 1920s in *U.S.A.* and the 1930s in *Raymond Chandler's L.A.*, she moved on to the 1940s in *Christmas Eve, 1943*, and the *Jane* series exuded a 1950s air. Two more recent groups, *On the Road* (1988) and *Eldorado* (1990), although drawn from Jack Kerouac's 1957 *On the Road*, addressed a culture that lingered through the 1960s and 1970s. This decade-by-decade consideration of the century mirrors Smith's understanding of and profound attachment to Los Angeles as both source and inspiration. As she has noted, "The thing that makes L.A. unique is that . . . it continues to be supplanted on an ongoing basis. You can see what was 1920, 1930, 1950. They exist as independent styles and architectural vignettes as you drive along

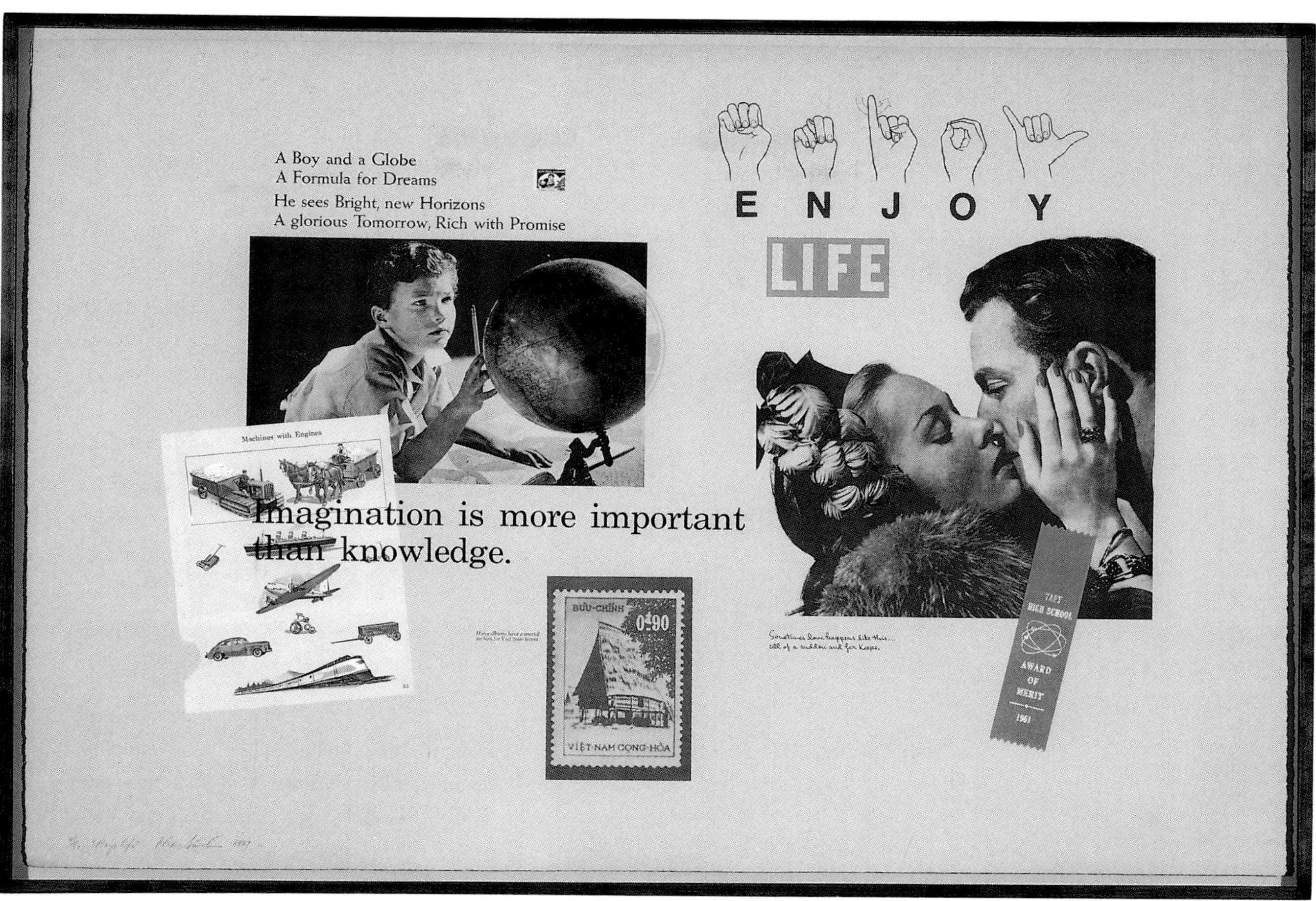

Boy's Life, 1989
Lithograph with collage,
30×44¼ inches
Margo Leavin Gallery,
Los Angeles

the boulevard. The enormous differences in patterns . . . are quickly manifest in the popular culture."

Los Angeles as an environment as well as the values of the entertainment industry have shaped Smith's sensibility. That films (and, later, advertising in general) should play so large a role in her work owes something to her birth and upbringing there. Her chosen name, appropriated from the well-known actress, reflects that attachment, as does her frequent incorporation of movie detritus and screenplays. Her sense of narrative is largely filmic, and for the first ten years of her career the typing-paper format of her art even resembled a script.

Smith is typical of the generation born after World War II, which matured in a consumer society whose self-interpretation was largely proposed and elaborated by mass media. Growing up in and around Los Angeles, she lived her life at the epicenter of this emerging culture, in which vision is prized above all other senses. Like its post-war population, she experienced Los Angeles as a continuous dialogue between the visual pandemonium of the "buy, sell, act, do" advertisements that effectively obliterate its commercial landscape of two- and three-story storefronts and the commercial-studded cacophony and ceaseless replays of popular music on AM radio. As the only child of older parents, she found an imaginative solace from this assault in reading and being read to. Books became her principal playthings. She wrote plays and made

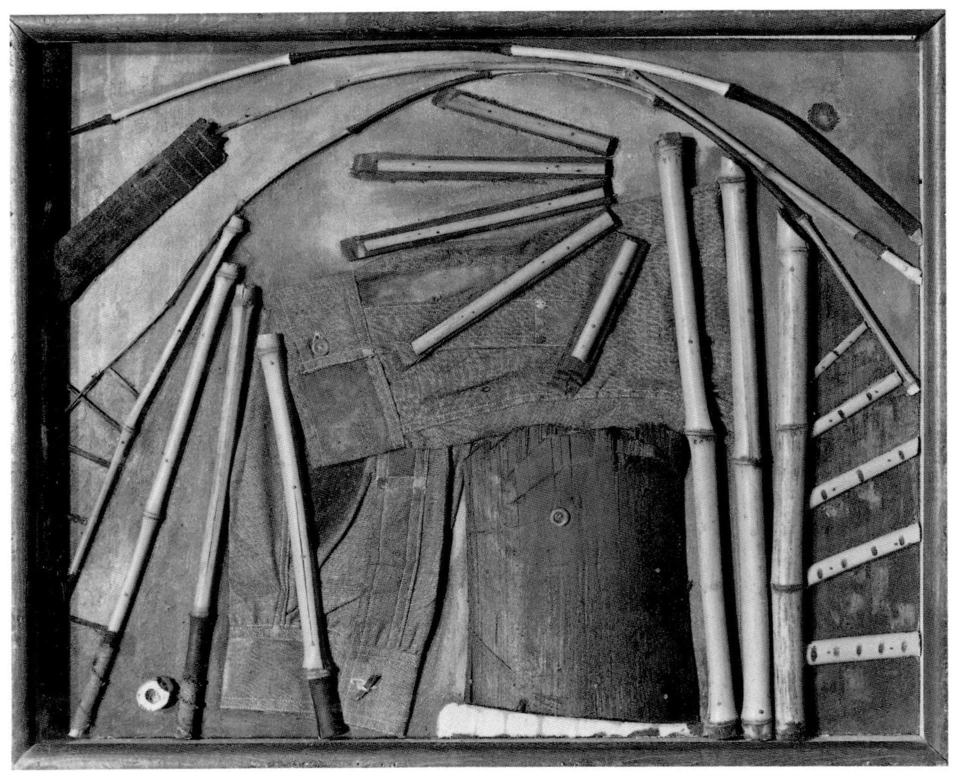

Arthur G. Dove
Goin' Fishin', 1925
Collage on wood panel,
19½ × 24 inches
The Phillips Collection,
Washington, D.C.

magazine-derived textual collages through childhood and adolescence. After her mother's death in 1960, Smith was raised by her father, who regaled her with stories of growing up in the West during the first half of the twentieth century. Later, her narratives would respond, if only subconsciously, to his.

At the University of California, Irvine, a newly established Orange County extension of the state system, Smith began as a French major after having spent parts of two summers in France. A friend convinced her to take classes with the especially charismatic art faculty then assembled at Irvine; overnight, her life changed. The literary collages she had made for years assumed significance as vehicles of self-expression. The fledgling department was composed of such iconoclasts as Robert Irwin, Craig Kauffman, and Vija Celmins—none of them inclined to disabuse Smith of her collagism.

By structuring her newly valued compositions around redolent passages from literature rather than inventing the phrases from cutout words, as she had done previously, she could retell significant stories. In piece after piece, she speaks through others, restoring the universality of their work, reinvesting it with mystery, shared sentiments, and talismanic truths. From behind this mask, she could cast a new and revelatory light on the story at hand. The voice could be male or female, but the perspective was necessarily that of a woman. An early feminist who frequently cites a women's group she joined in the early 1970s as an important factor in her maturation, Smith has been drawn to female subjects throughout her career.

Among the precedents for Smith's kind of obliquely autobiographical pieces were the collages of Arthur Dove. Dove's deep attachment to nature was profoundly symbolic rather than narrative, though it was expressed primarily in his paintings. But in such playful collages as *Grandmother* (1925) or *Goin' Fishin'* (1925) Dove sought to represent biographical moments with the kind of physical detritus later so attractive to Smith. His collage-assemblages, which unabashedly retain their identity as found objects, were evocations of places and people, with a distinctly American forthrightness about them. Guided by Yankee pragmatism, Dove eschewed the mostly formal concerns found in collages of the School of Paris or Kurt Schwitters.

The work of H.C. Westermann is chronologically and conceptually closer to Smith's enterprise, both because of its humor and its familiarity in Los Angeles. His quixotic combination of found and crafted objects and images with descriptive, often punning, titles was especially influential among that city's artists, inspiring the sardonic wit of, among others, John Baldessari and Edward Ruscha.

A related taste for storytelling and humor was widespread in the Los Angeles art scene Smith entered when she moved to Venice in 1971. Proponents of the genre such as Allen Ruppersberg and William Wegman were her friends. She valued Ruppersberg's kindred dependence on found texts no less than Wegman's quirky humor. But her proclivity for found, visibly used imagery and texts of a certain epic sort, combined with a technical precision bordering on the fussy, separated their more casually rendered work from hers. But all these artists profited from an aesthetic climate hospitable to narrative art, a climate that had developed as a reaction against the bombastic, anti-verbal stance of Minimalist sculpture and painting.

The traditions of collage and assemblage were especially well-established in California. San Francisco artists had long been involved in various manifestations of the assemblage aesthetic, partly in response to the hyperbole that accompanied Abstract Expressionism as it developed in their city. By the 1960s this work became known as "funk art." Painters and sculptors such as Roy De Forest, Robert Hudson, and William Wiley extravagantly combined found and fashioned things. This material hedonism, a willingness to incorporate and decorate all kinds of objects, frequently distinguished northern California collage-assemblage from its counterpart to the south. In Los Angeles, the genre assumed many forms but in general was more restrained in imagery and treatment than its San Francisco equivalent. From Wallace Berman's obsessive graffiti to the more constructed works of such artists as Tony Berlant, George Herms, and Llyn Foulkes, a penchant for structuring logic prevailed.

Because of her desire to configure her pieces around texts, Smith looked to other

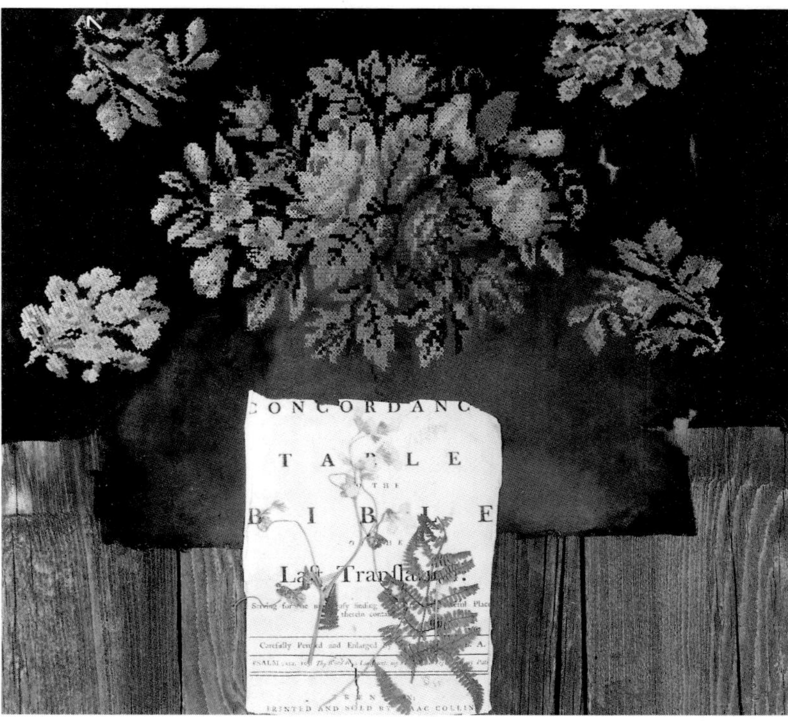

Arthur G. Dove
Grandmother, 1925
Collage of shingles, page from the Concordance, pressed flowers, and ferns, 20×21¼ inches
Collection, The Museum of Modern Art, New York; Gift of Philip L. Goodwin (by exchange)

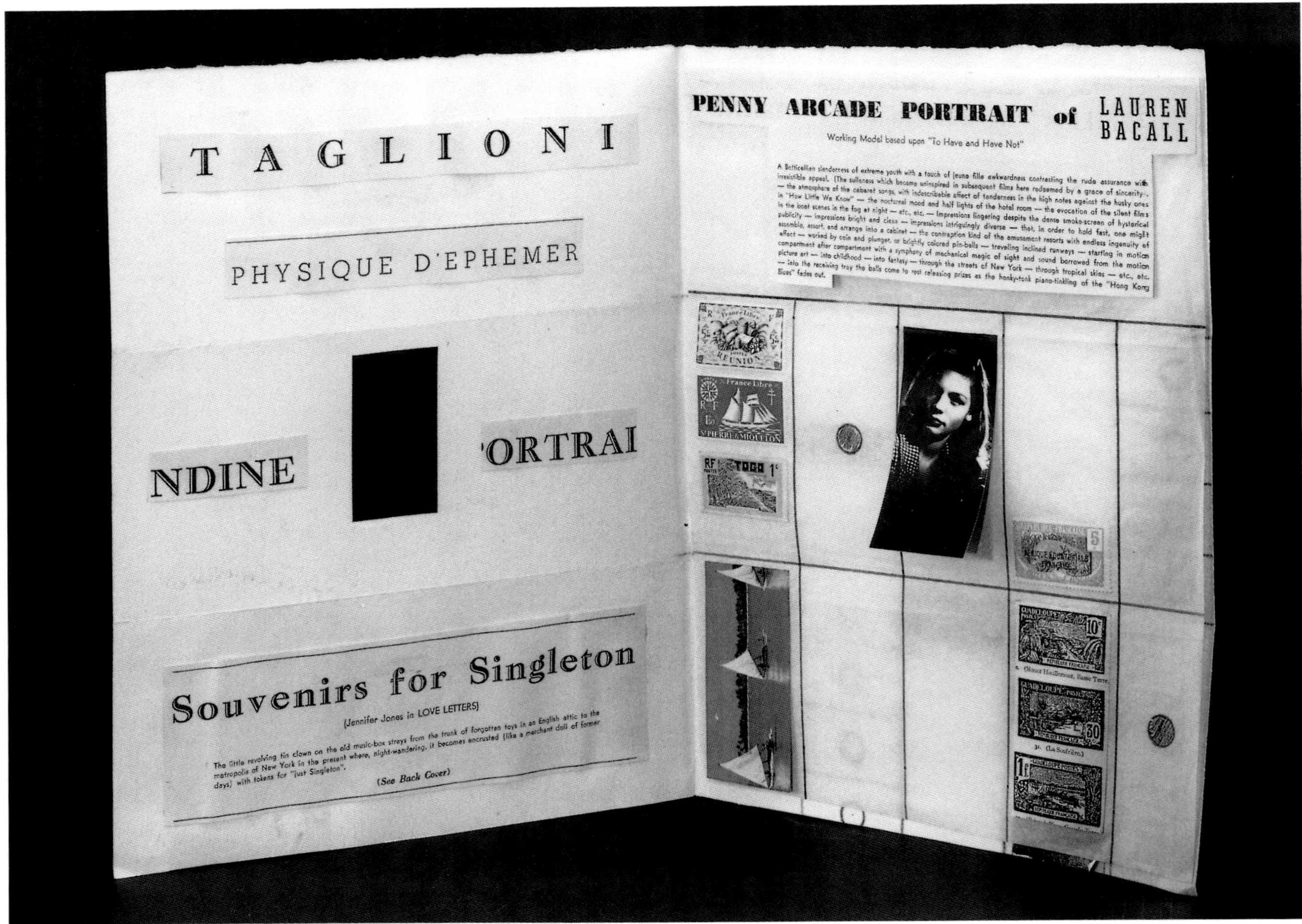

Joseph Cornell
Untitled (Penny Arcade Portrait of Lauren Bacall), 1945–46
Dossier, $11\frac{15}{16} \times 8\frac{11}{16}$ inches
The Art Institute of Chicago;
Lent by Lindy Bergman

like-minded artists within the Los Angeles community. John Baldessari's skill in inventing a visual logic made exclusively of found and recombined photographs and Edward Ruscha's commingling of enigmatic words and representational imagery were particularly instructive. Both artists not only had a taste for puns, but also exhibited a deadpan humor Smith found naturally appealing, as she did their technical finesse.

The first public exhibition of Smith's work, in a group show at the Pasadena Art Museum, consciously simulated the atmosphere and activities of a reading room—the morphological model for many Conceptual artists. But Smith varied the usual, analytic use of texts in Conceptualism by incorporating imagery. Ideas and their verbal form, words, could substitute for imagery since in Smith's system they are but half of an inseparable voice. For Smith, the stories of life reside not only in the written word but also in the things around us. Their symbiosis, obvious to her, had been broken by inattention, fragmentation, and the exclusion of all sensory data save that gained through sight. She meant to reintegrate word and object in a format that provoked multiple interpretations and a simultaneous perception through as many senses as she could engage. This profound connection to both literary sources and the array of inanimate objects she finds, collects, and eventually redeploys *obliged* Smith to become a collagist.

An obligation to a so-called minor medium is but one of the many connections Smith shares with Joseph Cornell, whose work she studied on the advice of Robert Irwin. Both the art and certain aspects of the lives of Smith and Cornell have similarities. Their work represents a universe in miniature, created mostly with flotsam. Both stand outside the mainstream of modernist art despite ties to important historical groups—his to the Surrealists, hers to the narrative arm of Conceptualism. Both traffic in nostalgia but supersede the sentimental. As Cornell was drawn to nineteenth-century French culture via the second-hand bookstores of Third Avenue, Smith sees the world via the silver screen of classic Hollywood. Movie myths as well as literature have inspired both artists. Cornell's devotion to Nerval, Mallarmé, Verlaine, and Rimbaud is matched by Smith's to Raymond Chandler, John Dos Passos, the romantic pulp novel, and Jack Kerouac. Each transforms an immediate past—Cornell by reconstituting a late nineteenth-century New York to Symbolist ends, Smith by considering the twentieth-century as lived in Los Angeles from a Conceptualist vantage. Moreover, they reinvent narration so that the most ordinary things around us become transcendental souvenirs.

Because Smith's work can bring forth a narrative from the most modest of things, it stands in direct succession to the symbolic collages of Joseph Cornell. Smith updates and extends the genre, but abandons Cornell's preciousness of means and scale in favor of a public position. As she has gained assurance in popular idioms, her work has assumed a more confident, even brazen stance. She has replaced Cornell's eternal and engaging introversion with an extroversion that, in time, has become less verbal and more and more monumental. Like all *bricoleurs,* Smith wants to retrieve catalytic evidence from the past. She is fascinated by the mass-produced detritus that finds its way into successive ownership by means of yard sales, thrift shops, and that most Californian of flea markets, the swap meet. Through the physical and emotional tenacity of these castoffs, she celebrates the human narrative that is the saga of our times.

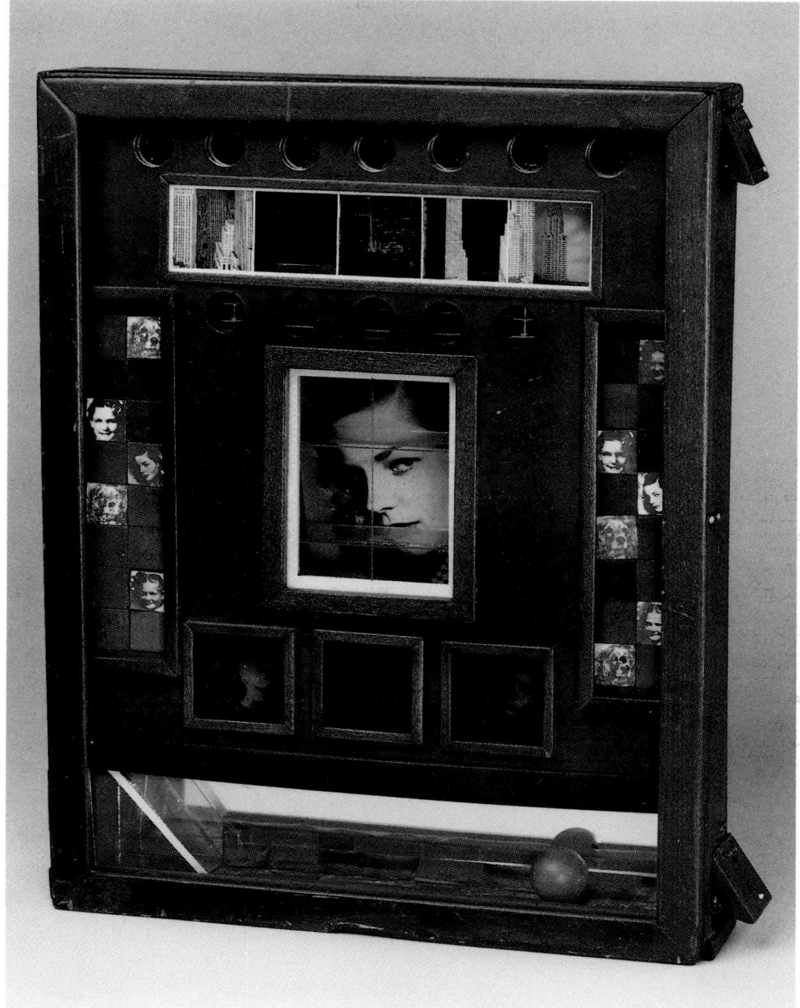

Joseph Cornell
Untitled (Penny Arcade Portrait of Lauren Bacall), 1945–46
Mixed-media construction,
20½ × 16 × 3½ inches
The Art Institute of Chicago;
Lent by Lindy Bergman

Works

Alexis Smith has been an avid reader since childhood and, since adolescence, a maker of collage drawings. Her earliest work combined these two activities in the form of fabricated narratives bound together as books. A confirmed Angeleno, she moved to Venice, California, after graduating from the University of California, Irvine, in 1970. There she rented a storefront on Washington Boulevard, took a part-time job as an assistant to the architect Frank Gehry, and began to work as an artist. *Ma-cheesma* (1971) is one of her first efforts and remains significant for the message of its title and its choice of imagery. Smith, born Patricia Anne, had styled her first name "Alex," then "Alexis" at age seventeen. The cropped photo of a glamorous woman luxuriating in bed is that of the movie star Alexis Smith, whose name the young artist had knowingly appropriated. It is cut to fit into a standard-size white envelope on which Smith has faintly inscribed "ma-chees-ma" in pencil. A phonetic, feminine form of the Spanish noun *machismo*, the title simultaneously alludes to the wiles—here eroticized—of female movie stars and to Smith's declaration of independence in converting herself from Patricia Anne to Alexis. This small celebration of both her new identity and of Hollywood as an inexhaustible dream factory foretold much about Smith's central fascination with female survivors.

More typical of this early period was a series of bound or boxed books presented in her first public exhibition, a group show organized by Barbara Haskell for the Pasadena Art Museum in 1972. Smith recalls that she wanted her section of the show to function as a reading room, physically and metaphorically. Her ritualized and fetishized elevation of reading connects her intentions to contemporaneous installations by such Conceptualists as Joseph Kosuth. But in contrast to most Conceptual artists' preoccupation with linguistics, Smith operates from a romantic model that emphasizes sensation, especially tactility, and consciously exploits sentiment.

Colorado (1971), a wood-encased photo album, its cover decorated with the raised letters "Colorado," is the fullest exposition of Smith's early techniques and ambitions. The action of turning the pages punctuates an ambiguous and spare narrative. The words "hiss, clang, sizzle, crackle, pop," stenciled on various individual pages, introduce an aural component to Smith's story. A double-page spread marked "Ars Longa" features postcards of the Eiffel Tower, the Taj Mahal, and one of the great pyramids. An ordinary yearbook photograph of schoolboys and girls follows, then a spread with the words "Ars Longa, Vita Brevis." A De Stijl painting has been altered to resemble a waste receptacle; on a later page the joke is reiterated by the word "guffaw" stenciled sideways. A subsequent publicity shot of the ever glamorous actress Alexis Smith, adorned with the two artists' interchangeable autograph, prepares us for a final exhortation: "clap." Ending the piece with this stage direction reinforces the cinematic quality of the book. Like all film animation, it is a series of conjoined stills, and it haughtily declares in Latin its relative immortality—an unlikely gesture for a girl from suburban Los Angeles. Part souvenir—the class photo—and part prediction—behold the new likeness of Alexis Smith!—the piece is a charming aggrandizement of her artistic personality-in-formation.

Such subsequent pieces as *Flatland* (1972), *Hiawatha* (1972), and *Braille Book* (1973) show Smith expanding her subject beyond the confines of self-identification to explore various modes of perception. The words of *Flatland* are taken from the book *Flatland*, a charming parable of life among the inhabitants of a strictly two-dimensional world by Edwin A. Abbott, a noted Shakespearean scholar in Victorian England. Each segment of the Flatland society is shaped differently: members of the middle class are equilateral triangles, gentlemen are squares or pentagons, the lowest nobility are hexagons, and the most exalted are polygons who, at their highest evolution, become circular or priests. Similarly, from Longfellow's poem "Hiawatha," Smith isolates a passage from the chapter called "Picture Writing," which concerns the creation of a communicable alphabet. She illustrates it with small cutout shapes and a photo of two hands on piano keys to reinforce the connection of hand to sound. The *Braille Book* is a braille copy of *Reader's Digest* with a rectangular section cut out of the middle. In this hidden compartment are paper silhouettes whose forms refer to the word black: blackbird, blackface, blackmail, black magic, etc. In varied but related ways, Smith seems to be underscoring the importance of touch in her otherwise essentially visual world.

Larger themes, all filtered through Hollywood narration, occupied Smith for the next few years. From the otherness of Charlie Chan and the tragic fates of Orpheus and Beauty and the Beast, to the operatic melodramas of *Madame Butterfly* and *The Red Shoes*, Smith worked with an array of screenplay narratives that enabled her to outgrow her preoccupation with self and look to a wider social scope.

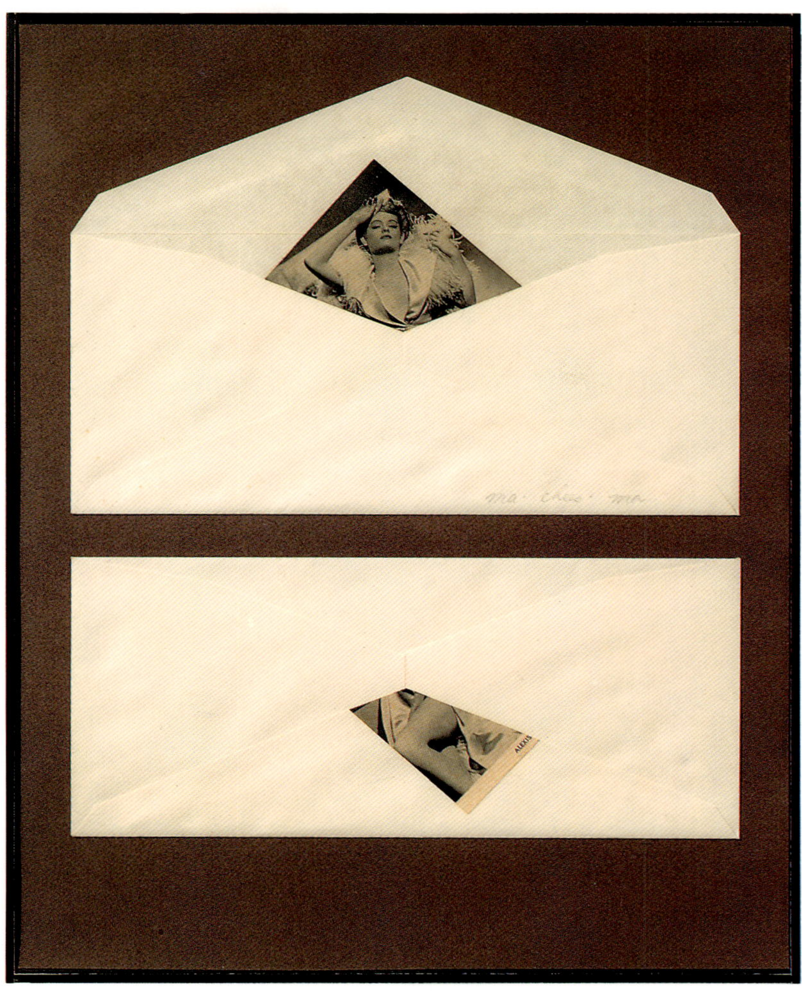

Ma-chees-ma, 1971
Paper collage, 14 × 11 inches
Collection of the actress Alexis Smith

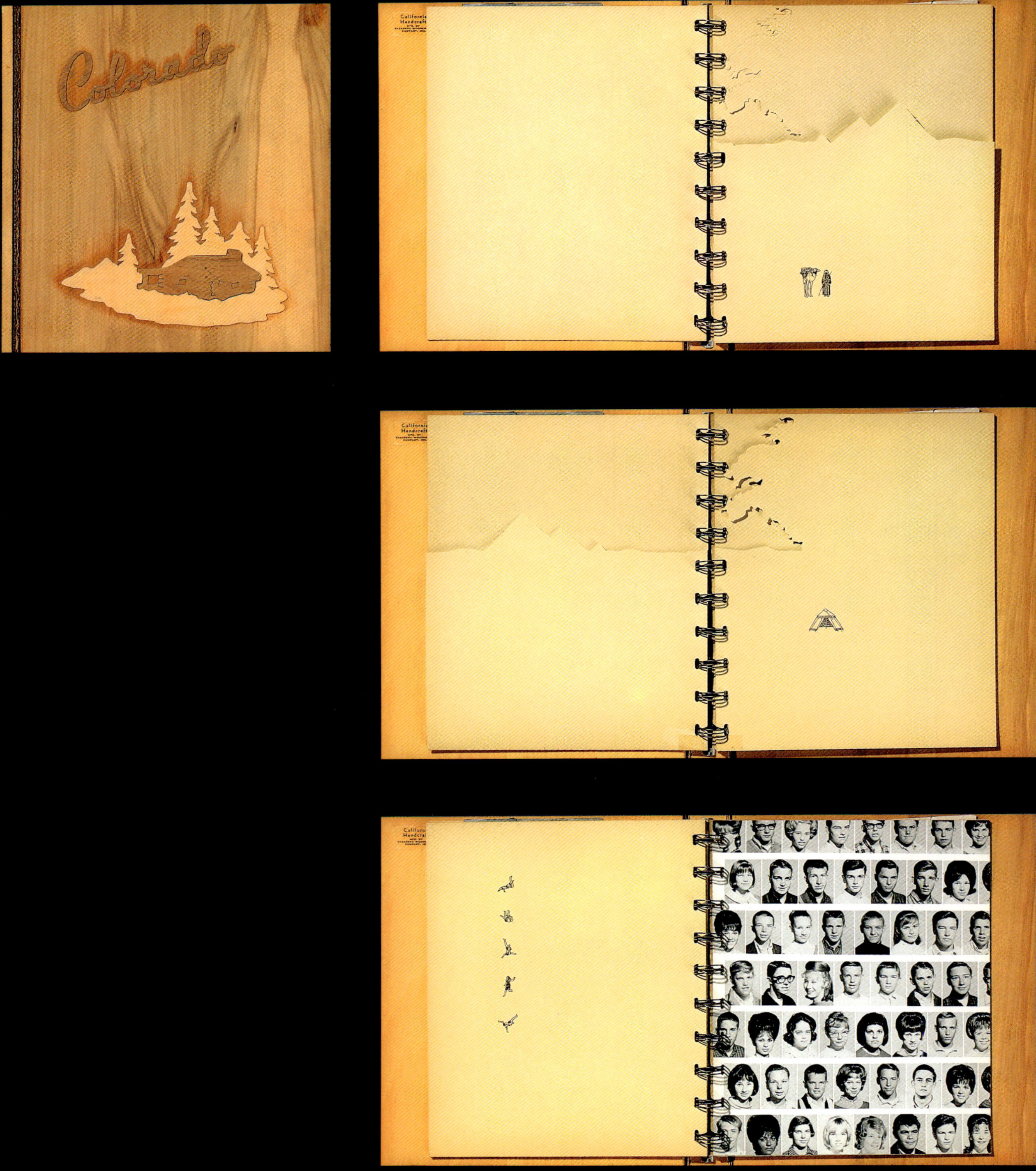

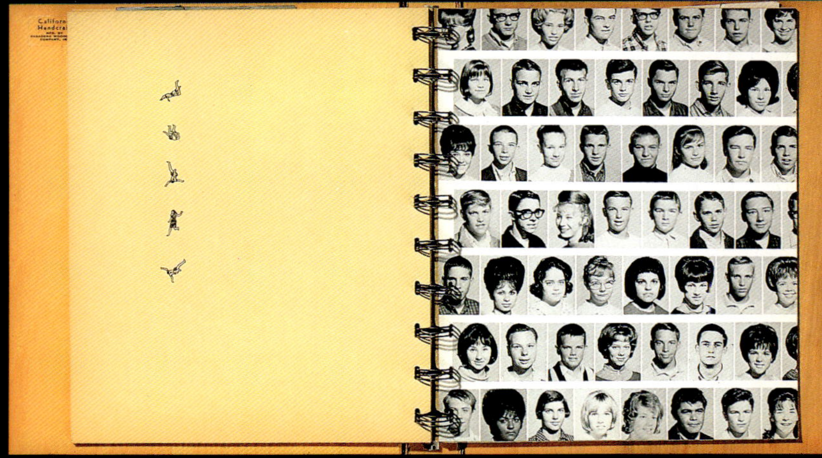

Colorado, 1971
Loose-leaf book with collage pages, 11 × 10½ inches each
Collection of the artist

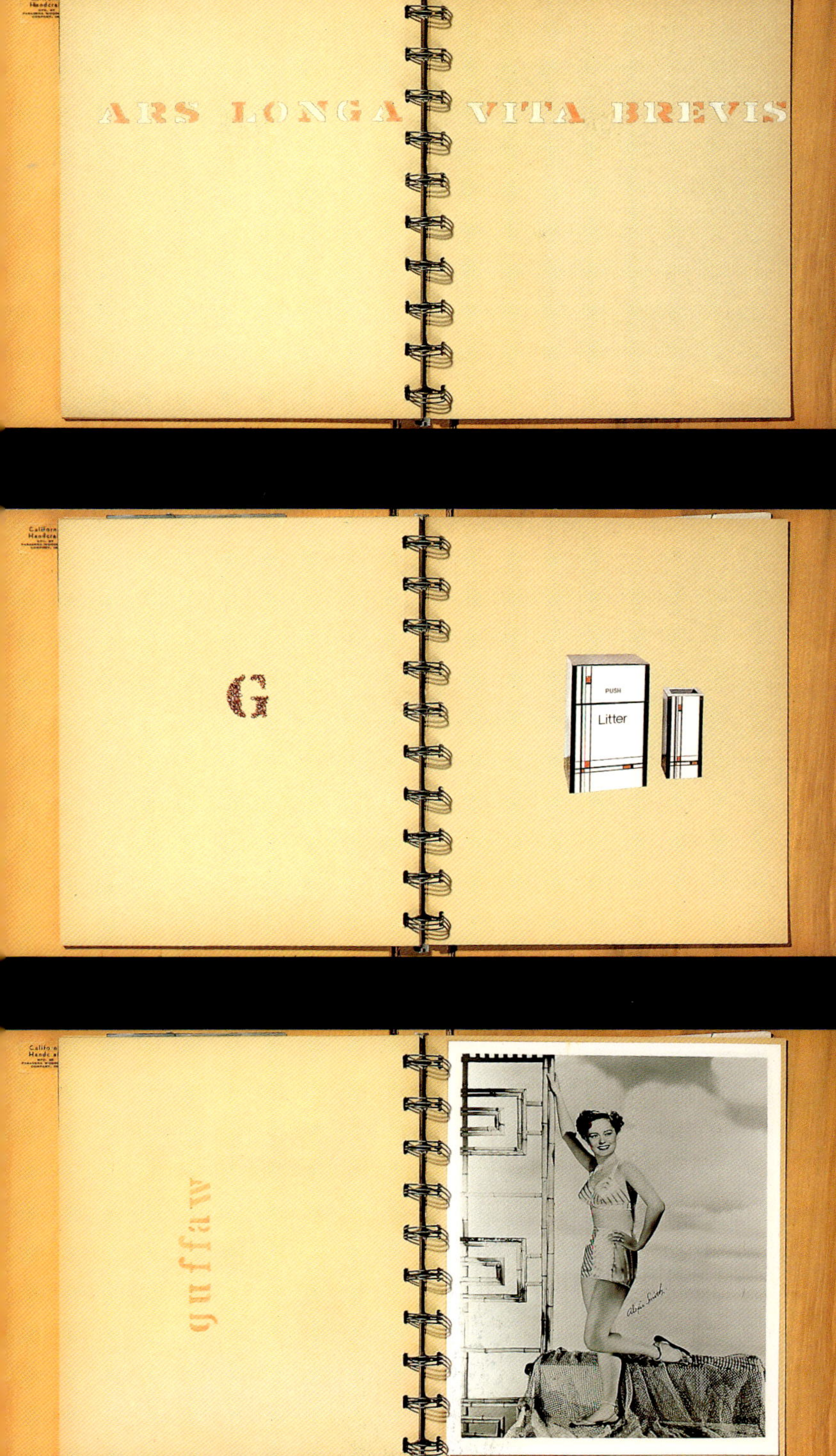
ARS LONGA VITA BREVIS
G
PUSH
Litter
guffaw

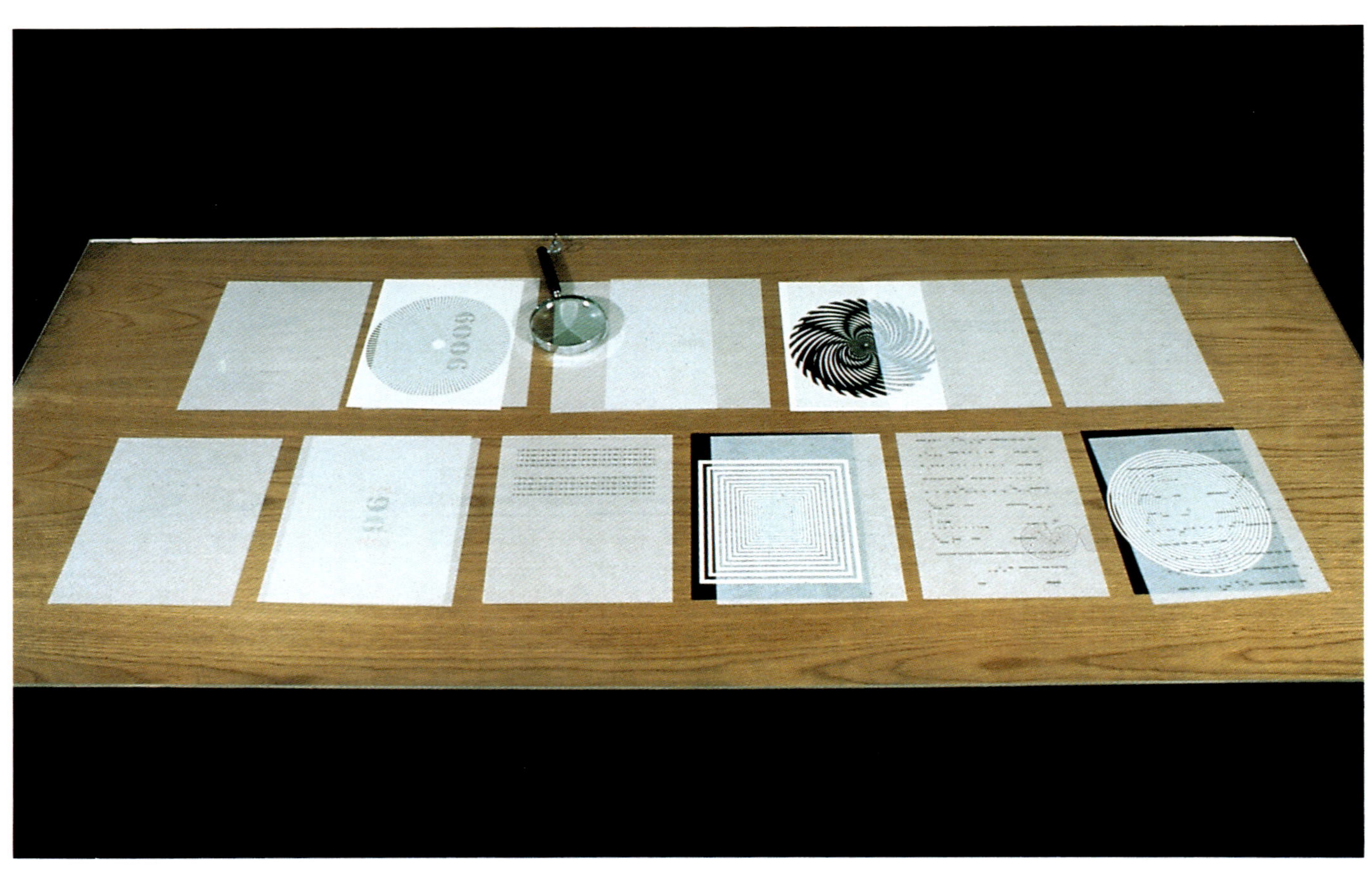

Untitled Book, 1971
Loose leaf paper pages, 11 × 8½ inches each
Collection of the artist

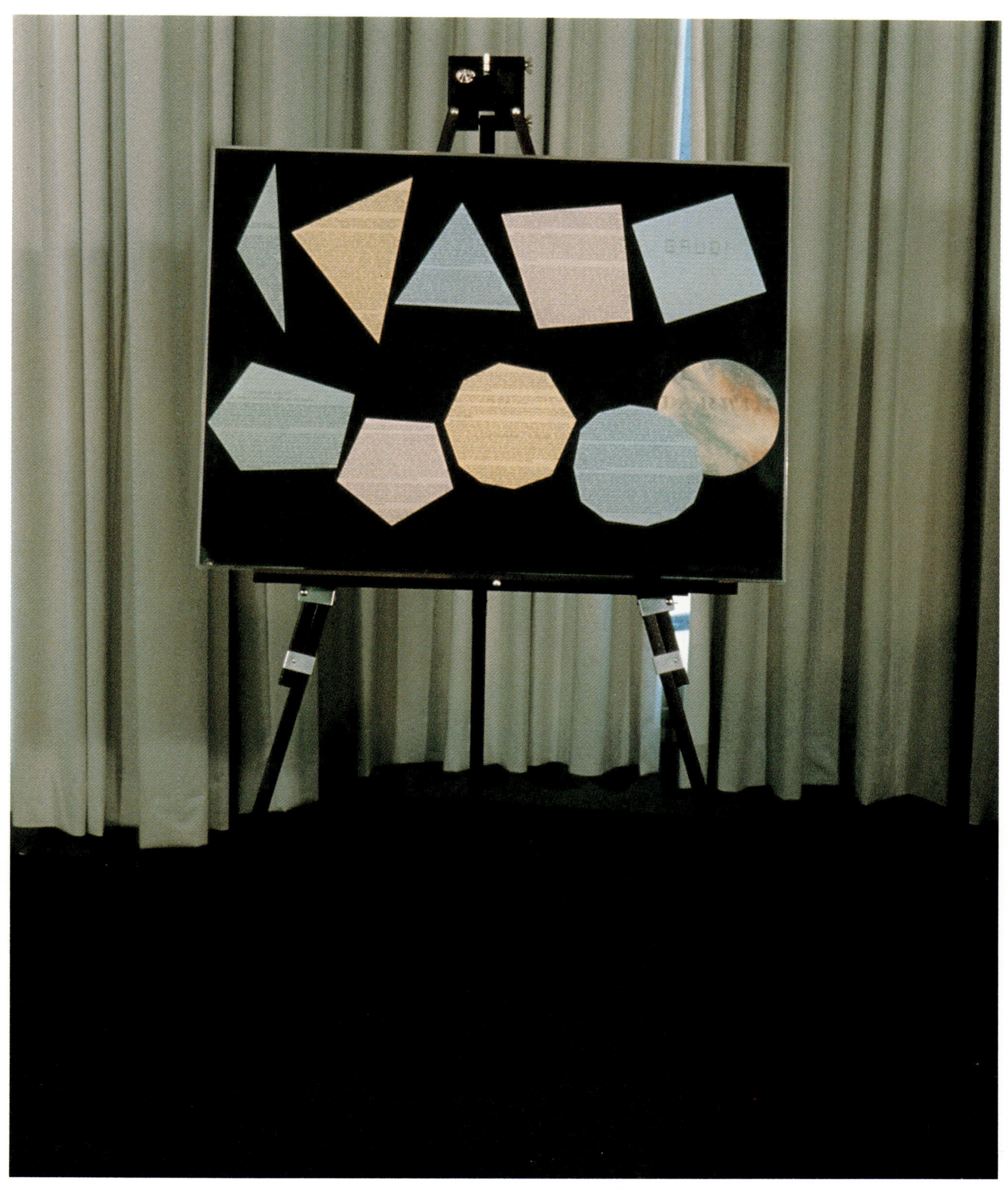

Flatland, 1972
Paper collage, 24 × 32 inches
Laguna Art Museum, Laguna Beach, California;
Gift of Herbert Hirsh from the Estate of Pauline Hirsh

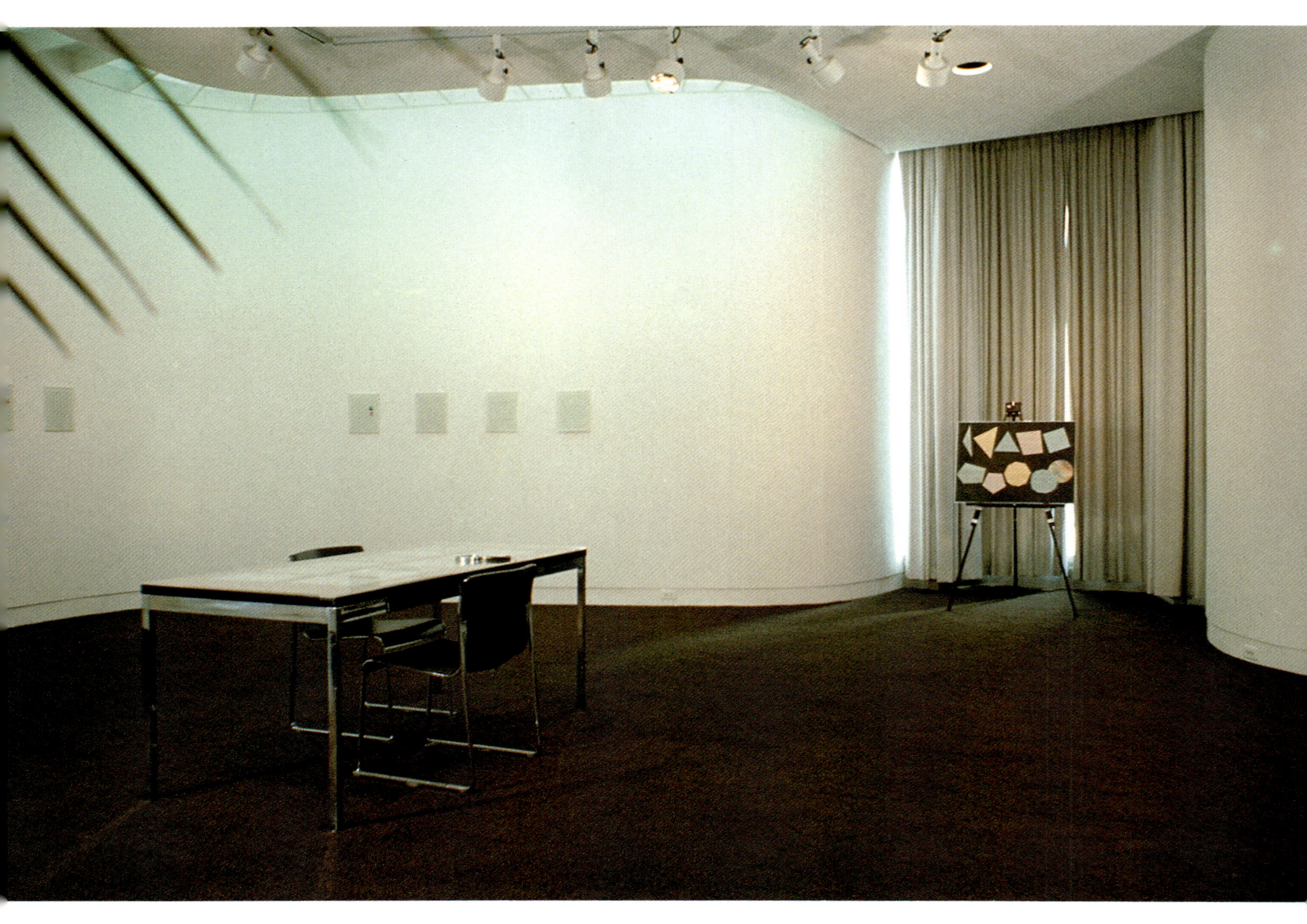

"Southern California Attitudes," 1972, Pasadena Art Museum

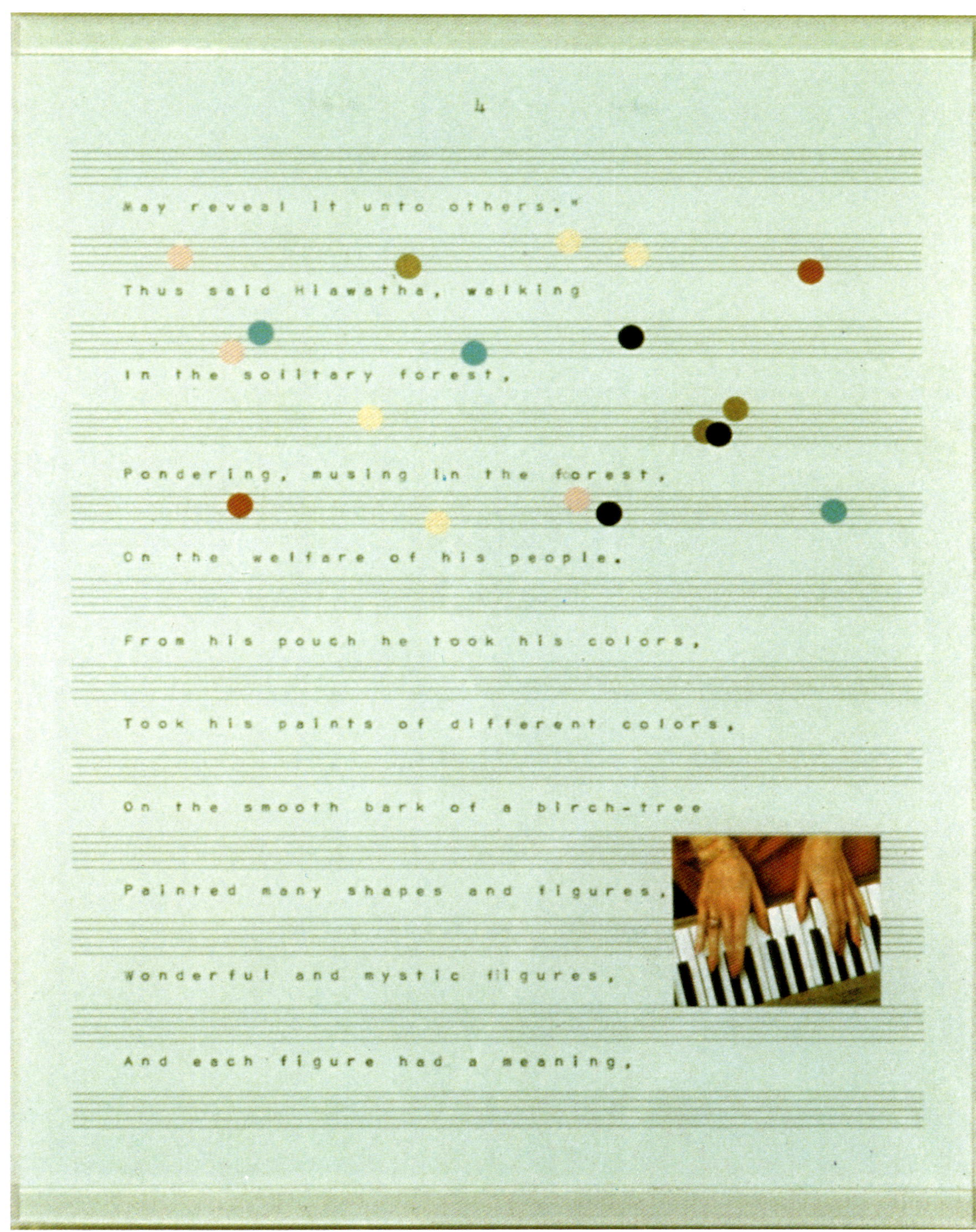

Hiawatha, 1972 (detail)
Paper collage, twelve panels, 12 × 9¼ inches each
Collection of Anne and Patrick Lannan

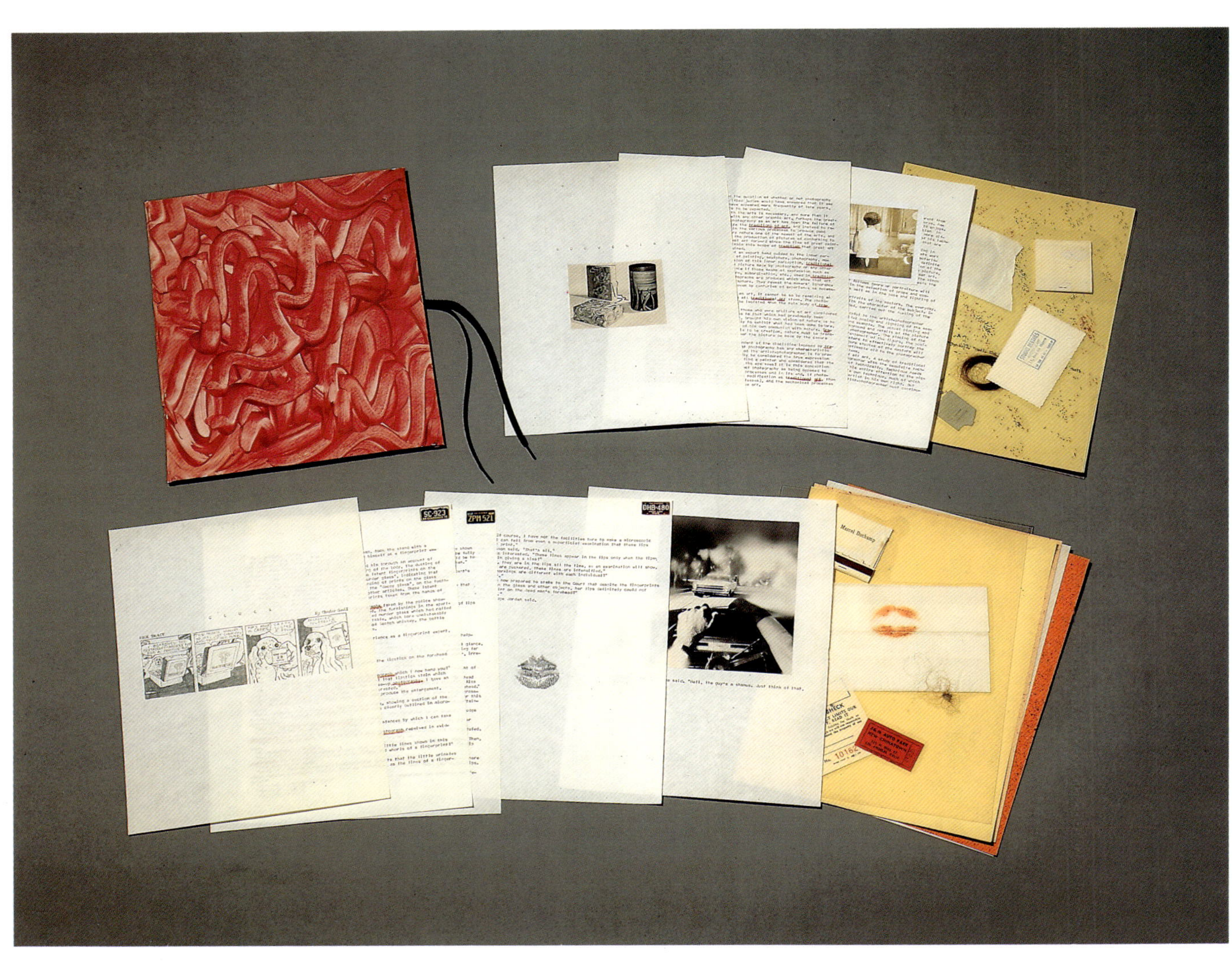

Clues and Souvenirs, 1971-72
Loose leaf book with collage, 11½ × 9½ inches (closed)
Collection of the artist

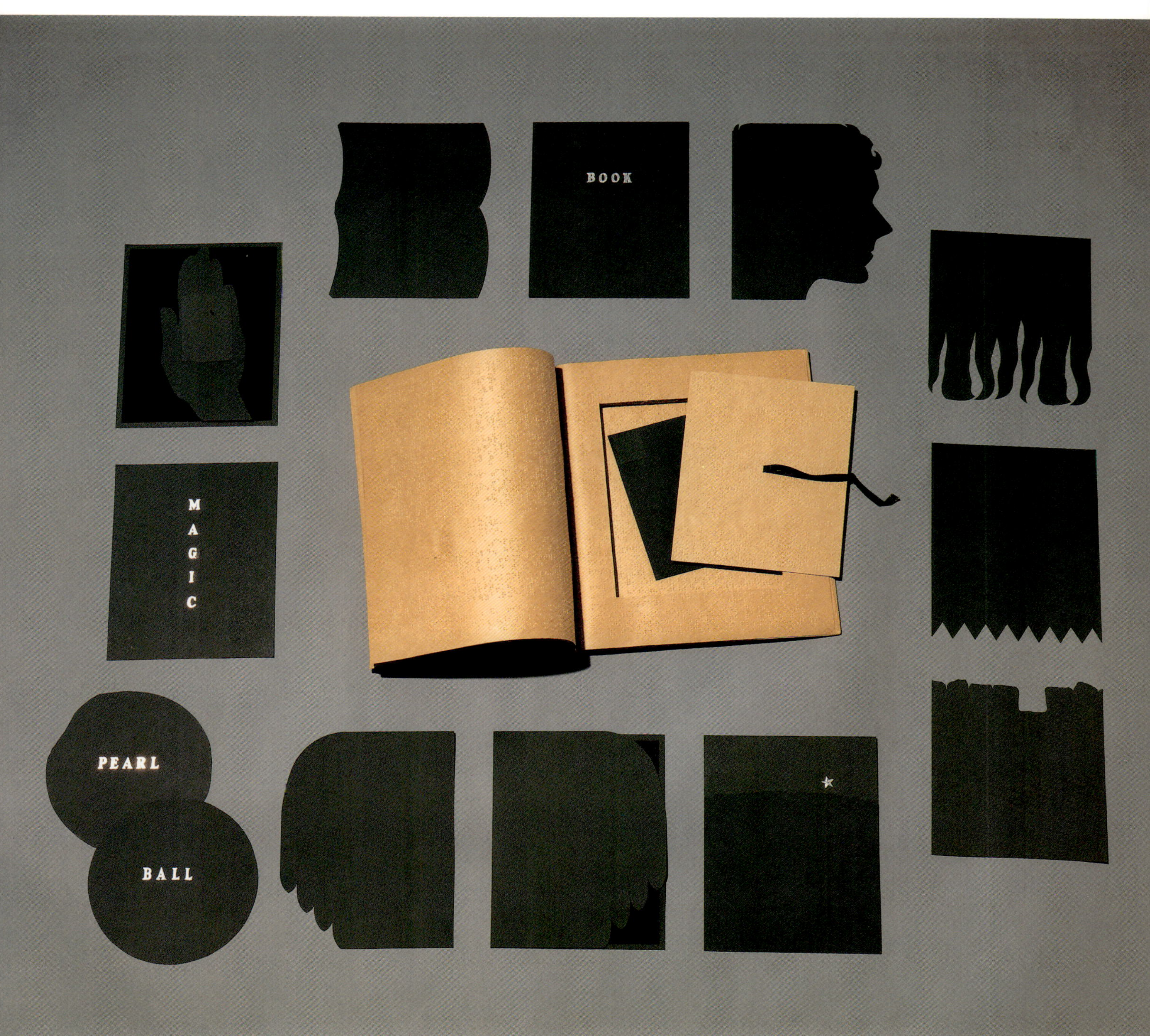

Braille Book, 1973
Loose leaf book with collage cutouts, 21½ × 13½ × 1 inches (closed)
Margo Leavin Gallery, Los Angeles

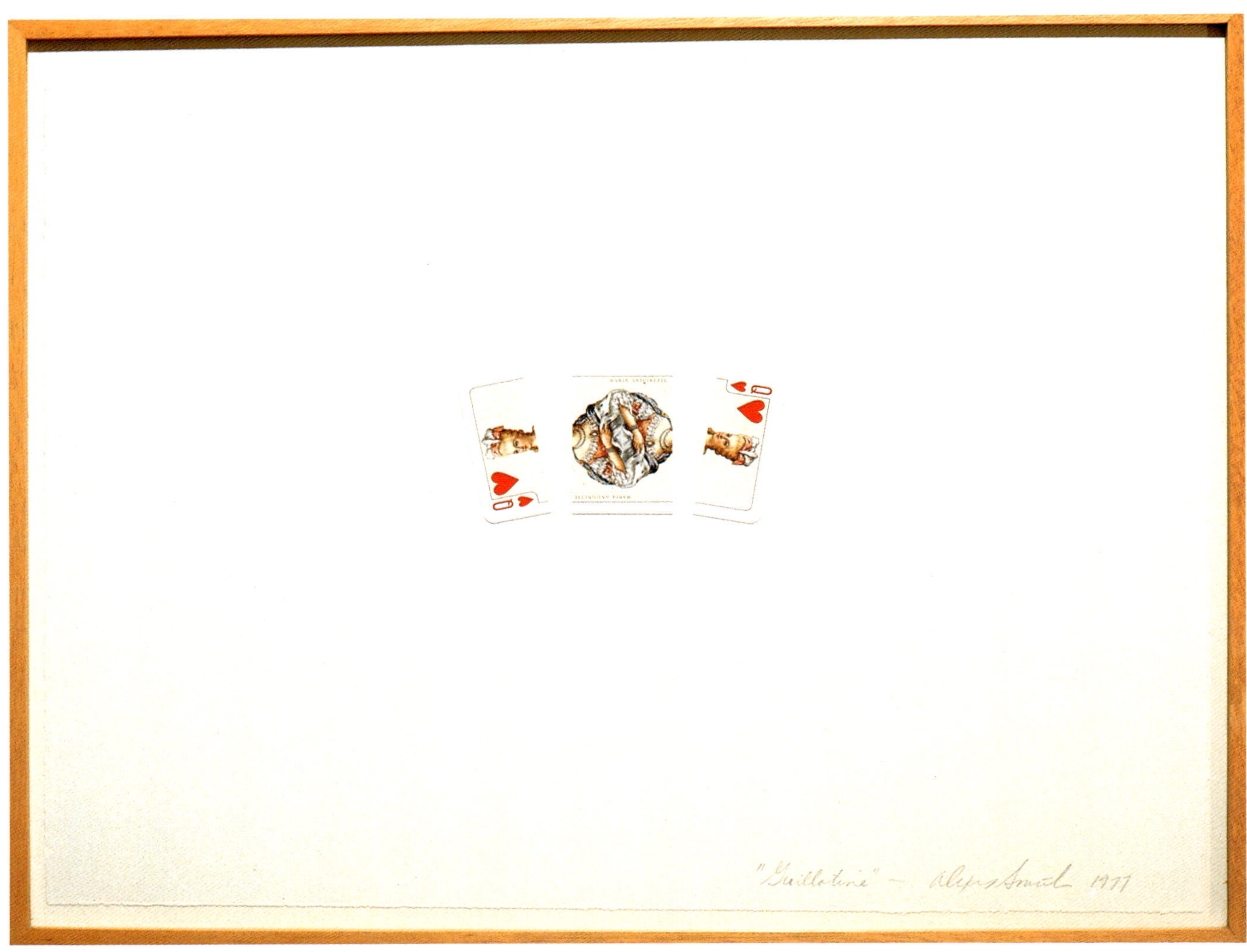

Guillotine, 1977
Paper collage, 13 × 17 inches
Collection of Deborah Bonnier

By 1974 Smith had adopted a new, more confrontational format for her work. She arranged stationery in long, lateral suites of five or more sheets, which she mounted inside a single rectangular frame. The narration is read left to right, as the viewer takes in Smith's collaged elements and the typed script.

In *Charlie Chan* (1973-74), Smith grapples with the artistic ego. In its first panel, she quotes Chan, a stereotypical Oriental sage, as he equates madness and genius. Smith had spent her childhood on the grounds of a mental hospital, where her father was a psychiatrist and administrator, so that determinations of relative sanity had an autobiographical resonance. Smith inserts her persona with snapshots of herself and citations from a study about "creative people." The authors found successful creators to be as schizophrenic as certain institutionalized people, the difference residing only in the size of the ego. "The *successful* creators differ from the institutionalized unfortunates in that they have learned the disguises and dissimulations required by the world-as-it-is." Smith seems in this way to be granting herself permission to be both

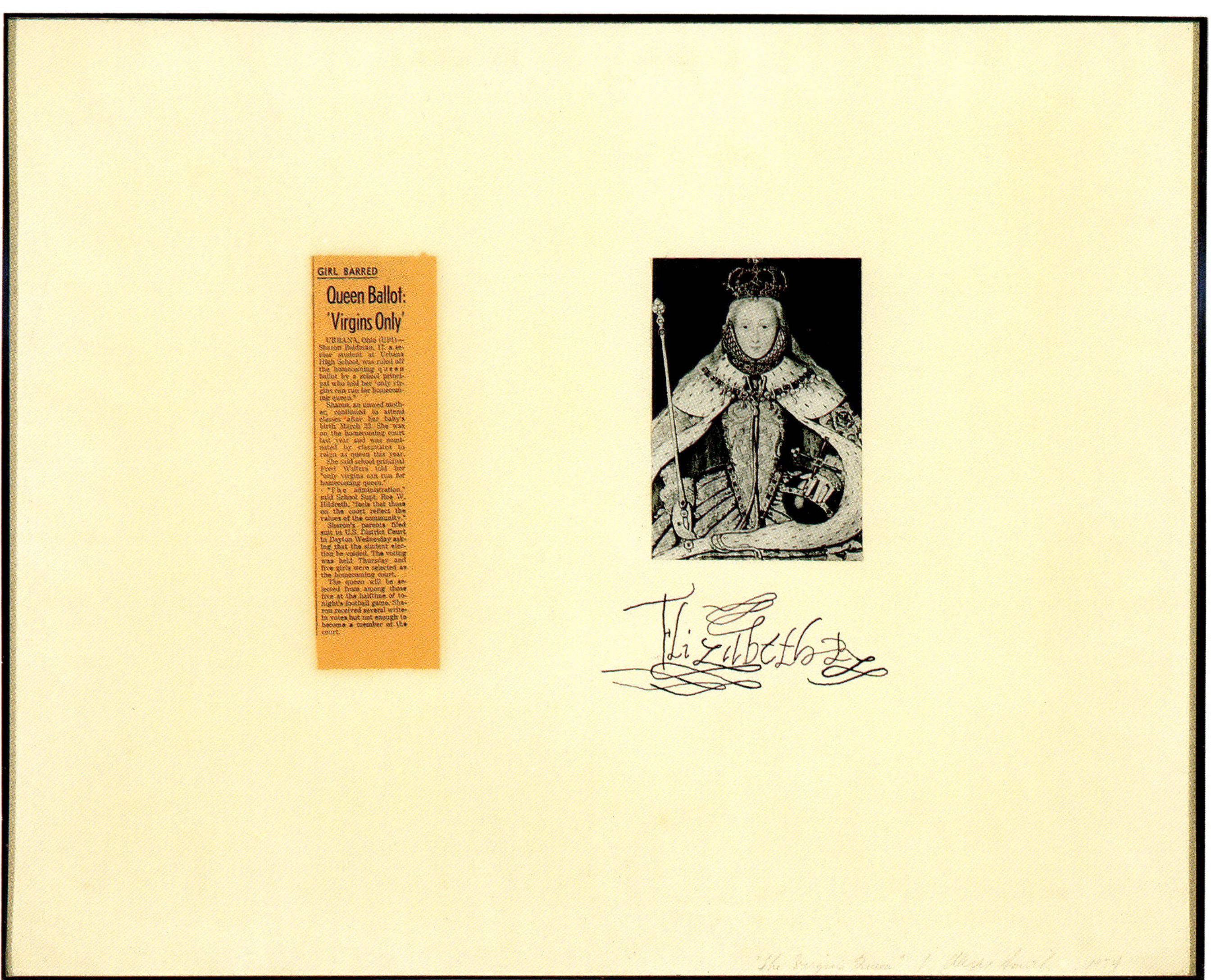

The Virgin Queen, 1974
Paper collage, 18 × 21¾ inches
Margo Leavin Gallery,
Los Angeles

creative and to adopt the protective coloration of normalcy. This critical step in self-justification marks a turning point in her maturity.

Juvenile fantasies lie behind *The Red Shoes* (1975) and *Beauty and the Beast* (1977), but each is altered to heighten aspects of female endurance—professional and emotional—important to Smith. In the former, she interweaves bits of the original tale and a screenplay (as well as a *Time* magazine cover of Alexis Smith in *Follies*). The story begins with the pronouncement, "Carry this vain and foolish child to the ends of the earth," which once again signals Smith's serious intent to succeed as a woman artist. In *Beauty and the Beast*, the quoted Cocteau screenplay includes the note, "My method is simple: not to aim at poetry. That must come of its own accord." Another tale of the triumph of a long-suffering woman, the piece again expresses Smith's determination. The Cocteau quote reflects Smith's recognition that the success of her work depends in large part on a seamless and ultimately catalytic conjunction of text and image. Her poetry, like his, must appear effortless.

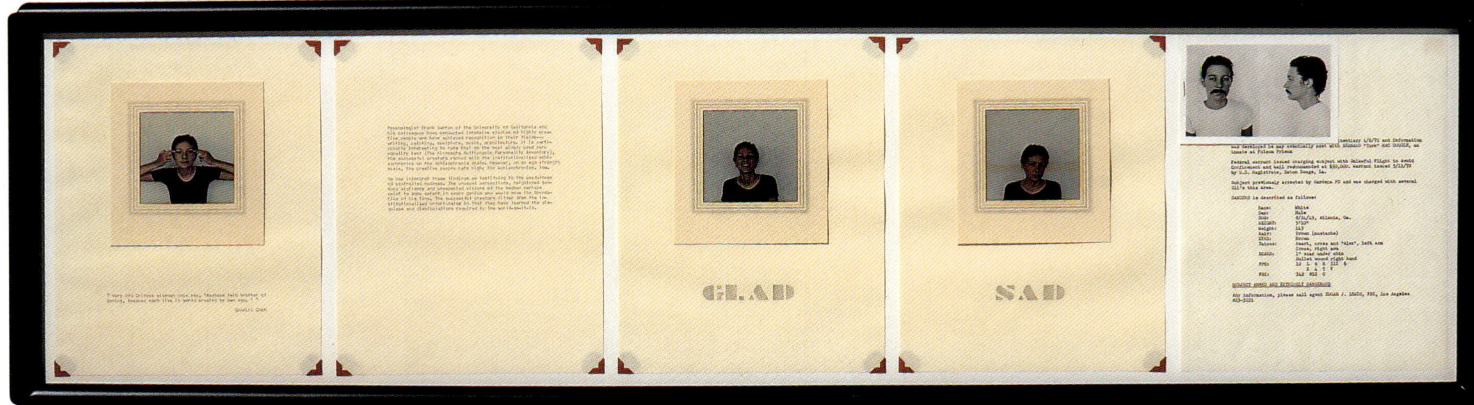

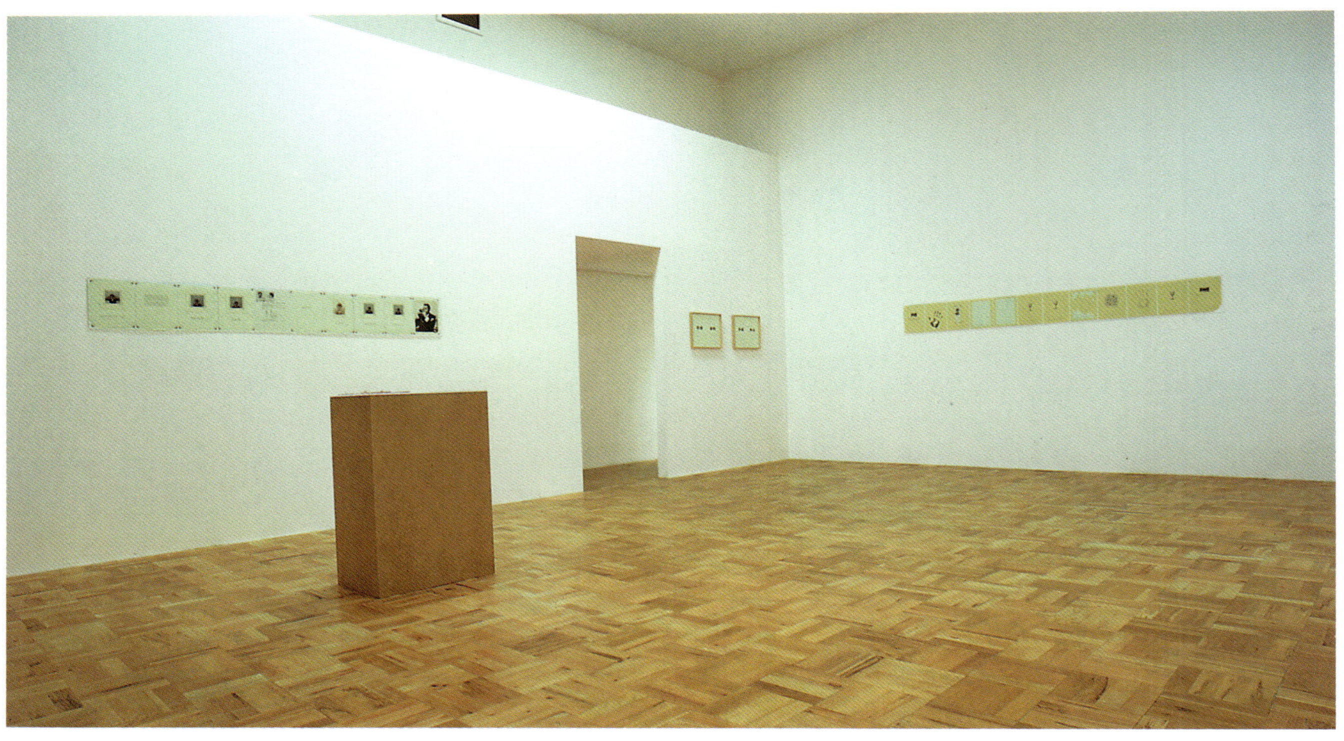

Installation view, Riko Mizuno Gallery, Los Angeles, 1974

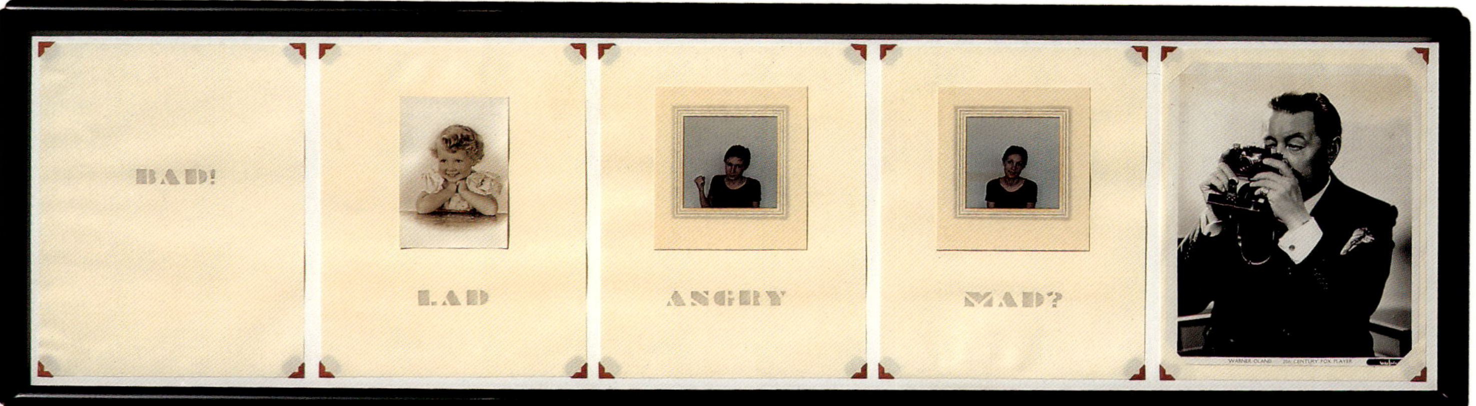

"Very old Chinese wiseman once say,
'Madman twin brother of Genius.
Both live in world created by own ego.'"
—Charlie Chan

Psychologist Frank Barron of the University of California and his colleagues have conducted intensive studies of highly creative people who have achieved recognition in their fields—writing, painting, sculpture, music, architecture. It is particularly interesting to note that, on the most widely used personality test, the successful creators ranked with the institutionalized schizophrenics on the Schizophrenia Scale. However, on an ego strength scale, the creative people rate high; the schizophrenics, low.

We may interpret these findings as testifying to the usefulness of controlled madness. The unusual perceptions, heightened sensory vigilance and unexpected visions of the madman perhaps exist to some extent in every genius who would move the boundaries of his time. The *successful* creators differ from the institutionalized unfortunates in that they have learned the disguises and dissimulations required by the world-as-it-is.

Charlie Chan, 1973-74
Mixed-media collage, two panels, 12 × 45½ inches each
The Museum of Contemporary Art, Los Angeles;
Gift of Frank and Berta Gehry, Santa Monica

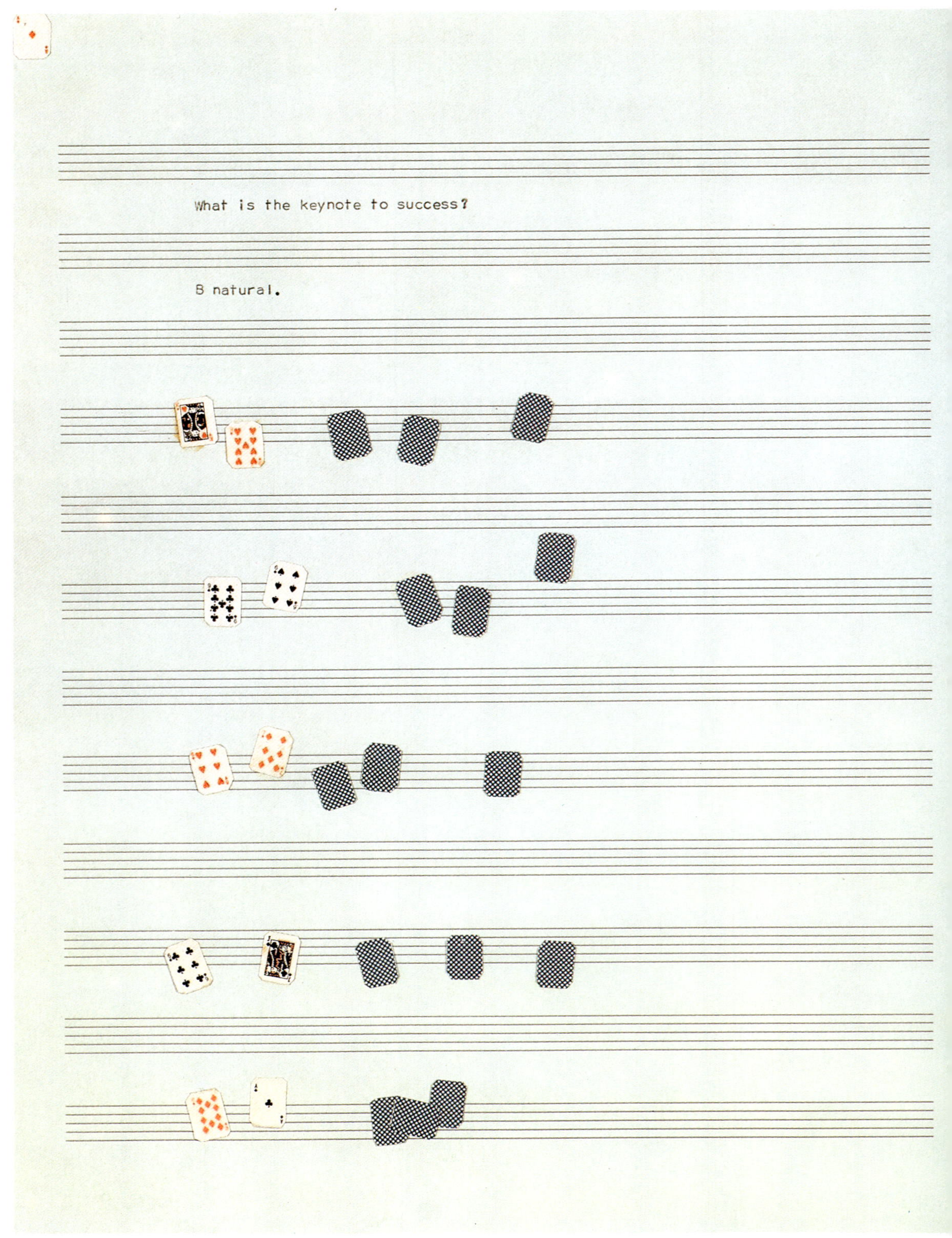

The Keynote to Success, 1974
Paper collage, 12½ × 18½ inches
Collection of James and Linda Burrows

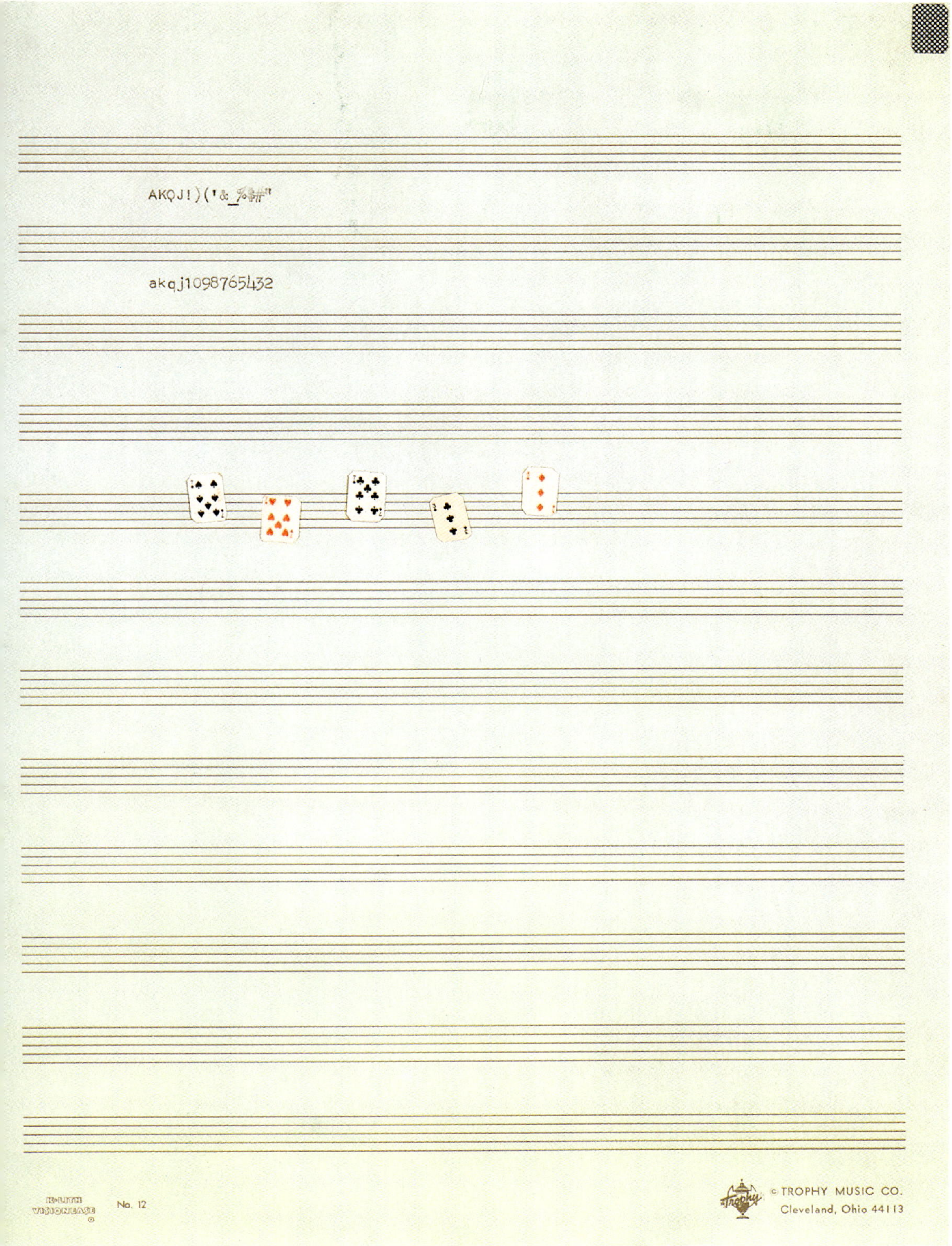

AKQJ!)('&_%$#"

akqj1098765432

HI-LITH VISIONEASE ©

No. 12

© TROPHY MUSIC CO.
Cleveland, Ohio 44113

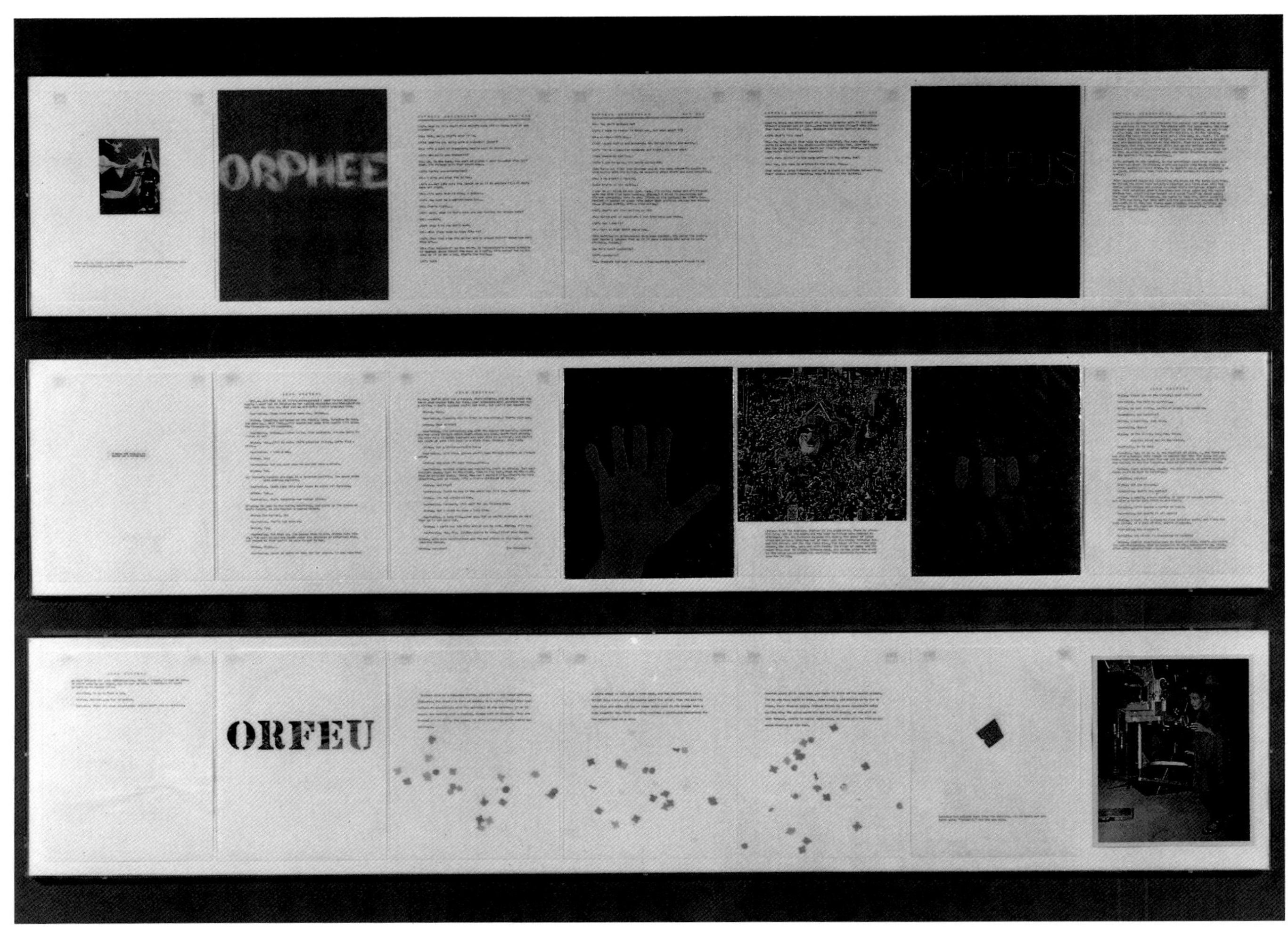

Orpheus: Three Movies, 1974
Paper collage, three panels, 12¾ × 62¾ inches each
Los Angeles County Museum of Art;
Modern and Contemporary Art Council, New Talent Purchase Award

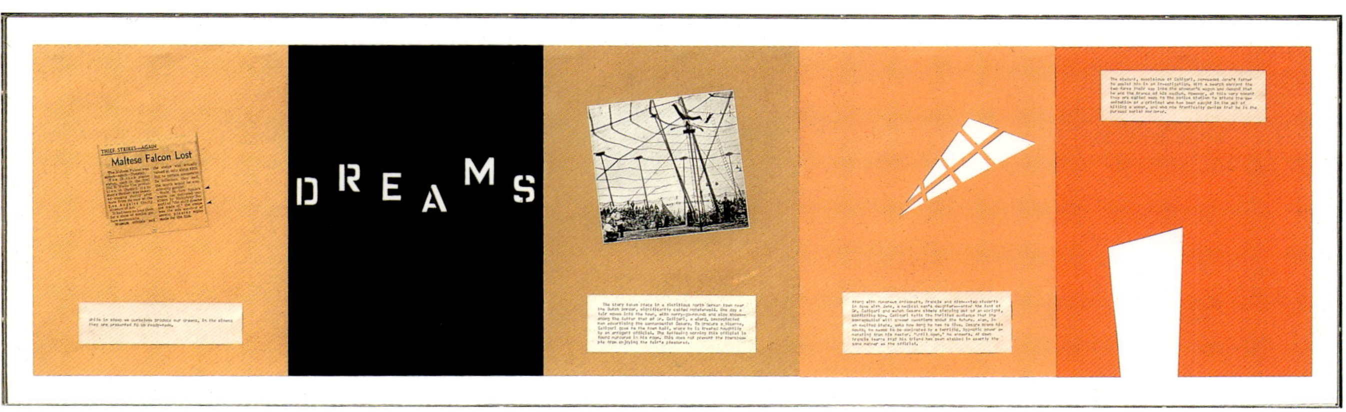

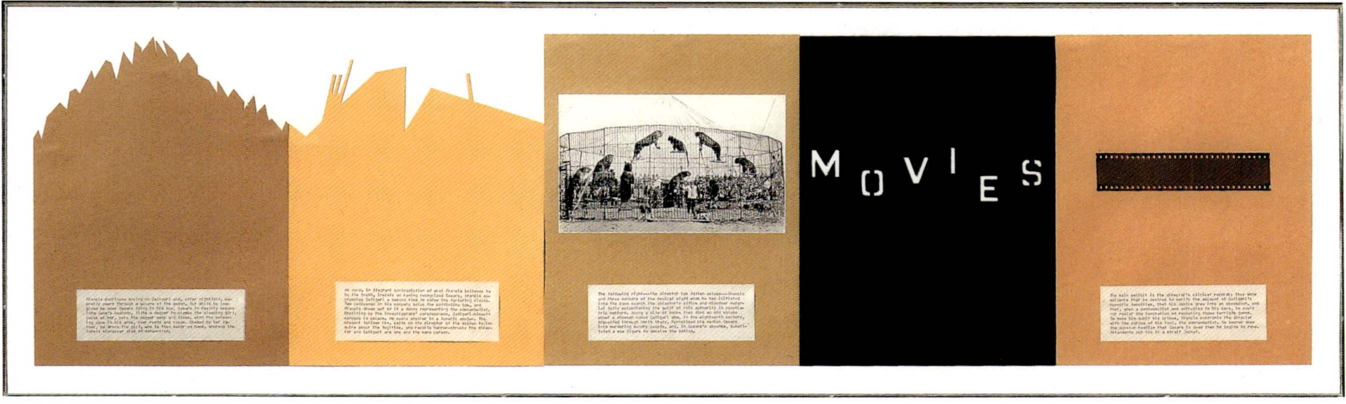

Movies and Dreams, 1974-75
Paper collage, two panels, 14¼ × 47¼ inches each
Collection of Bette Hirsh

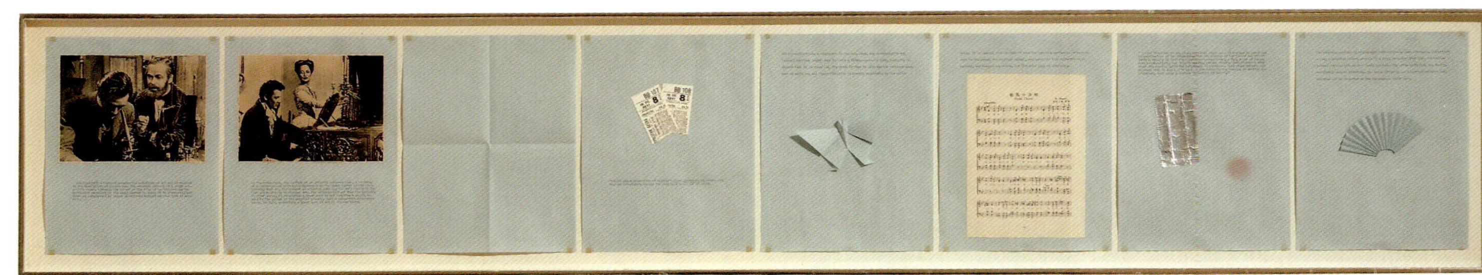

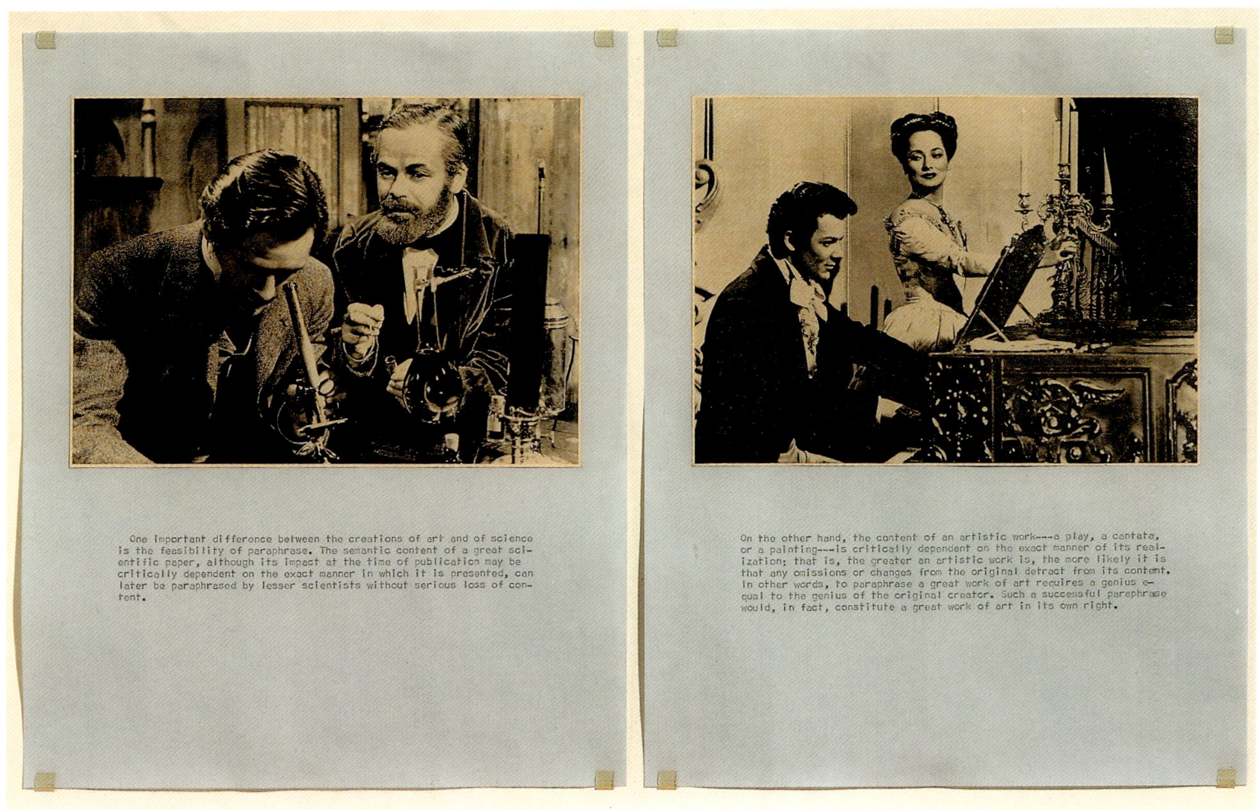

Madame Butterfly, 1975
Mixed-media collage, two panels, 12½ × 71 inches each
Collection of Patricia Faure

Panel 1, detail

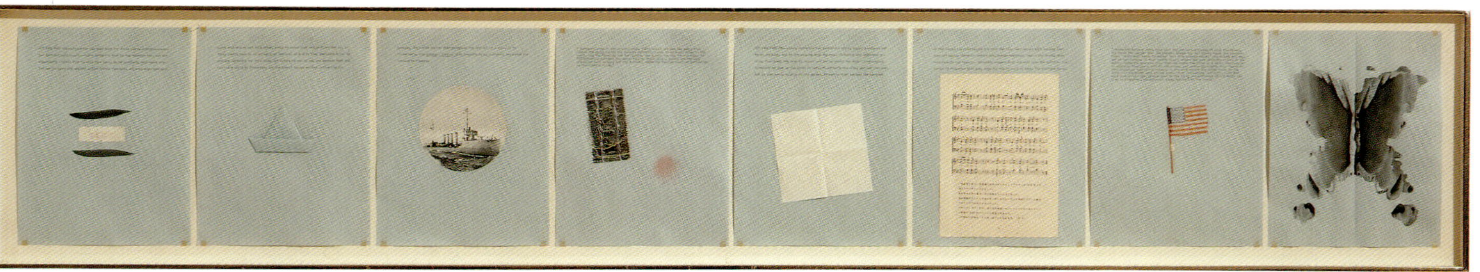

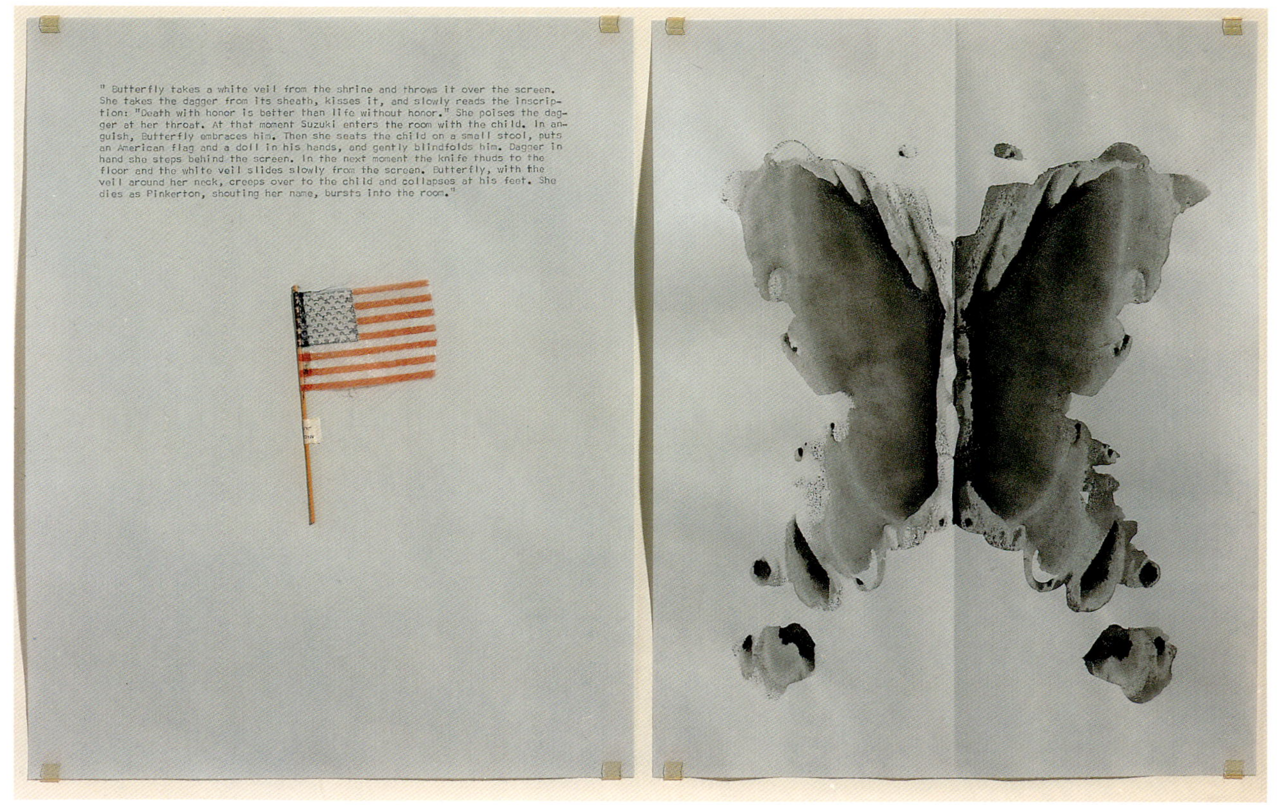

Panel 2, detail

The Red Shoes, 1975
Mixed-media collage, two panels, 13½ × 63; 13½ × 54½ inches
Collection of the Grinstein Family

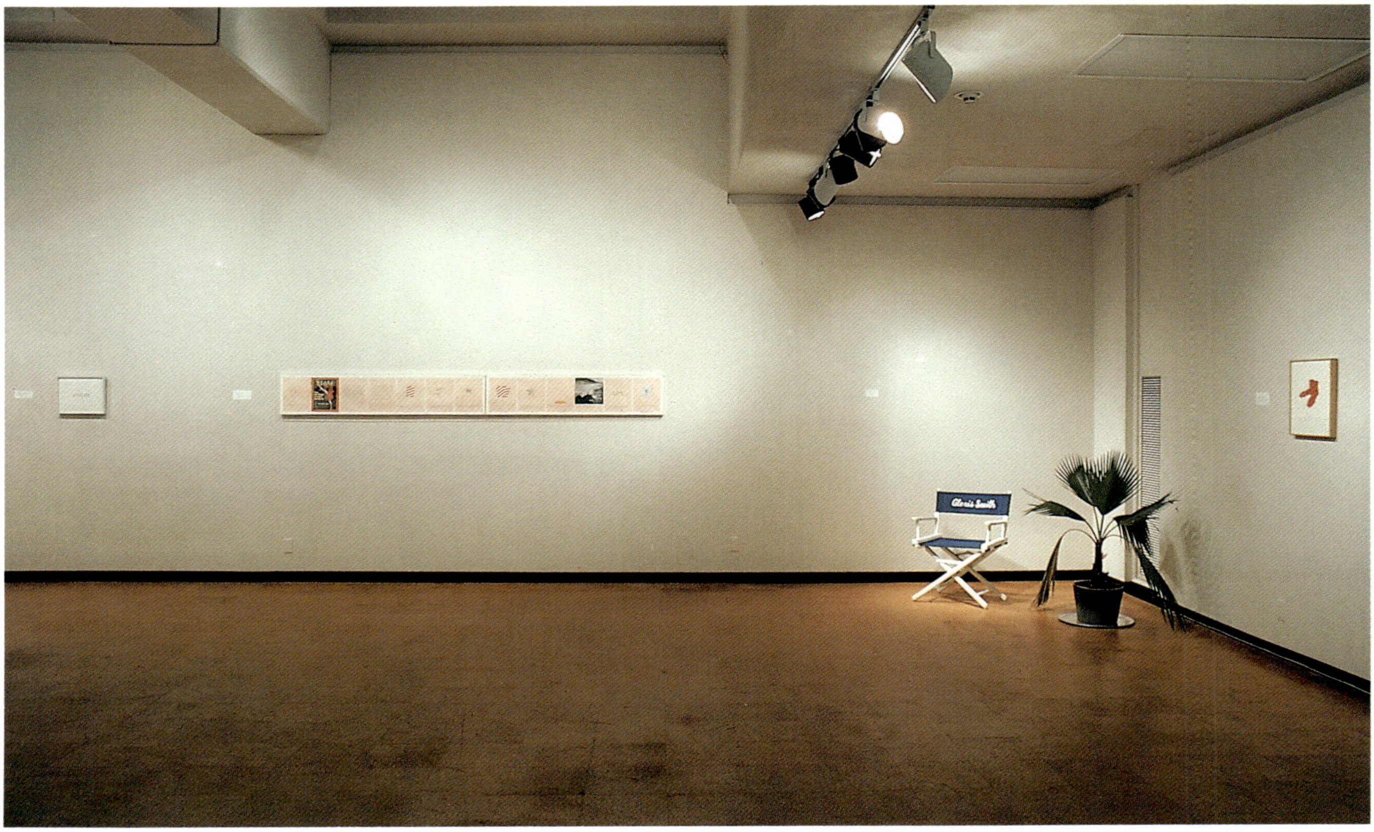

Installation view, Mandeville Art Gallery,
University of California, San Diego, 1976

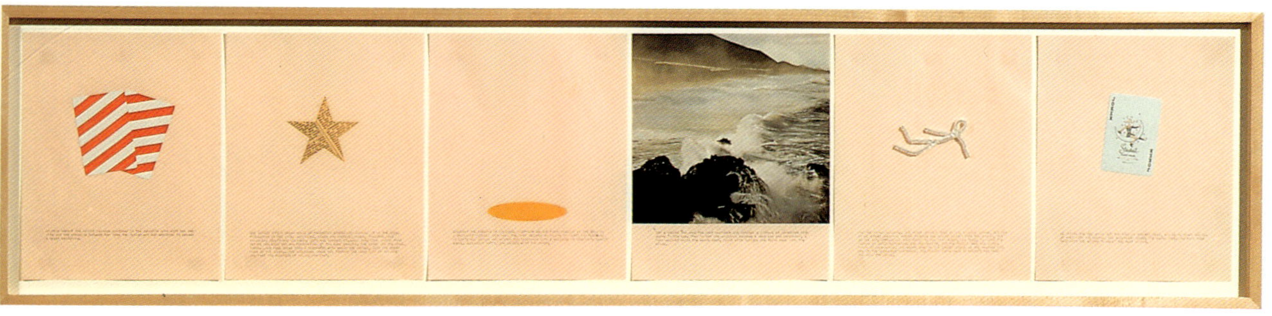

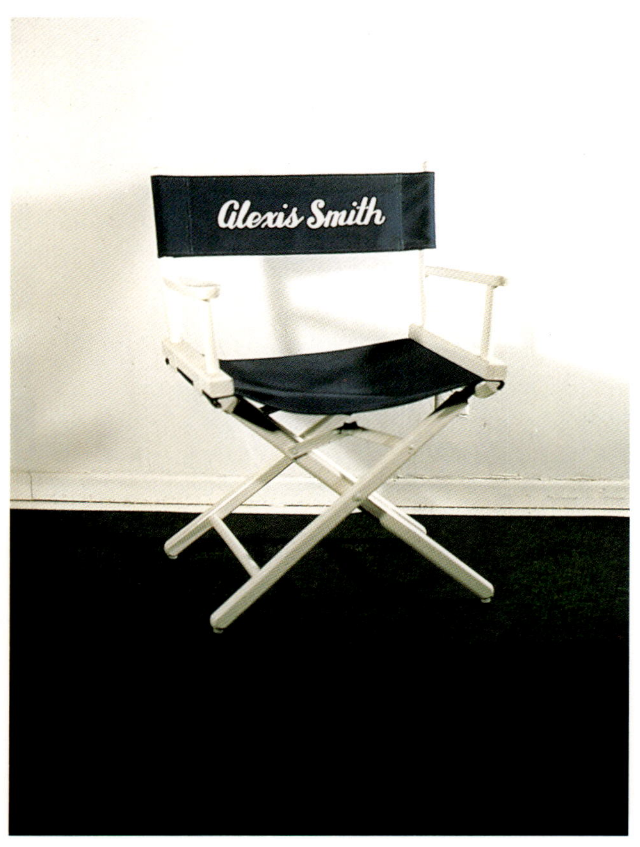

Your Name Here, 1975
Mixed media, 34 × 22 × 20 inches
Collection of the artist

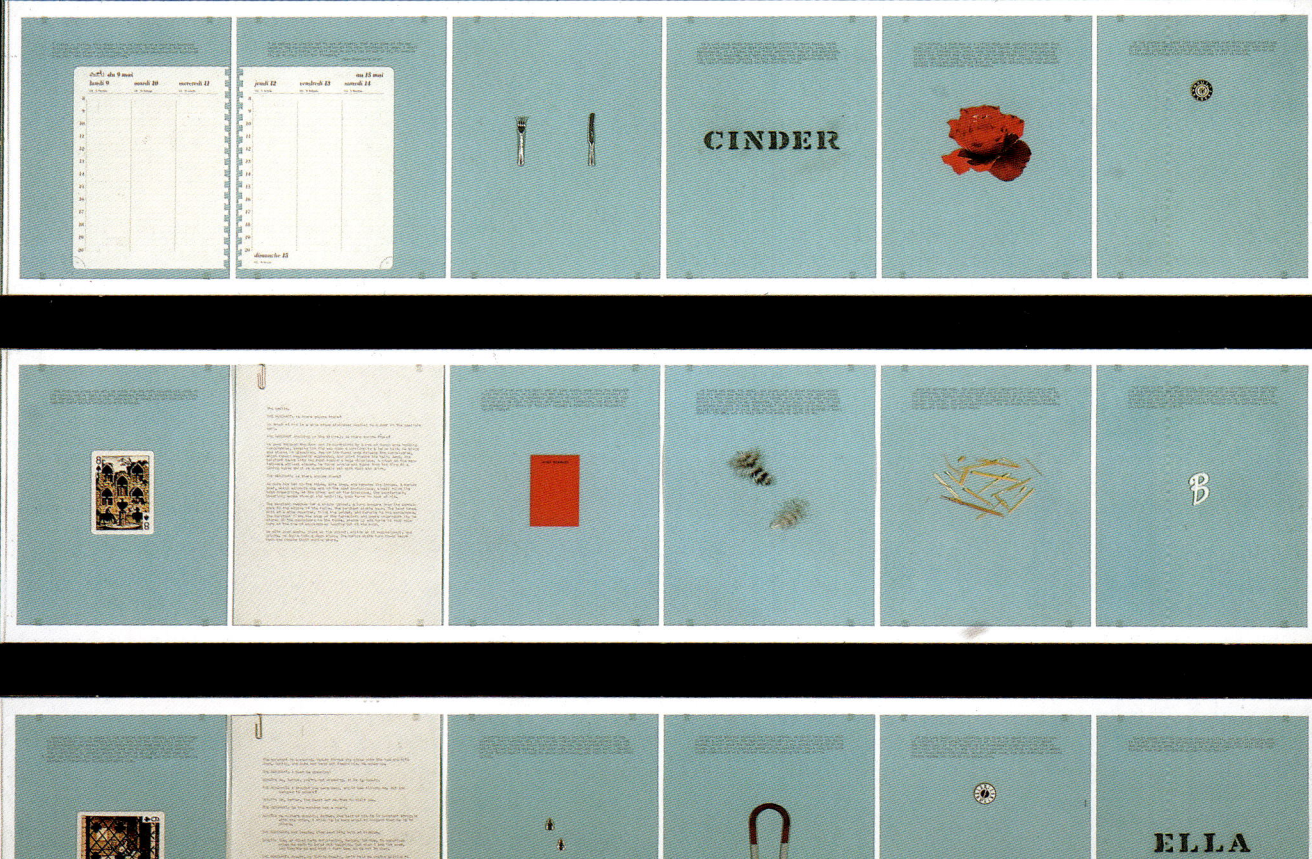

Beauty and the Beast, 1977
Mixed-media collage, three panels, 12½ × 53¾ inches each
Whitney Museum of American Art, New York;
Purchase, with funds from Mr. and Mrs. William A. Marsteller   78.30

BEAUTY'S RICH CLOTHES AND EXPENSIVE JEWELS EXCITE THE JEALOUSY OF HER SISTERS. THEY FLATTER HER, TELLING HER HOW MUCH THEY HAVE MISSED HER, AND FEIGN TEARS BY RUBBING THEIR EYES WITH ONIONS. HER SISTERS PLEAD WITH HER NOT TO RETURN TO THE CASTLE, FOR THEY HOPE TO TURN HER BACK INTO A SERVANT. BY THIS TRICK BEAUTY IS MADE TO BREAK HER PROMISE, AND THEN NO LONGER DARES RETURN.

MAGNIFICENT ARRIVES BEARING THE MAGIC MIRROR. NO DOUBT THESE HAVE BEEN SENT AS A LAST APPEAL FOR BEAUTY'S FORSAKEN LOVE. LOOKING INTO THE MAGIC MIRROR, BEAUTY SEES THE BEAST WEEPING. SHE IS ALL ALONE. SHE PUTS ON THE GLOVE. SHE IS AT THE CASTLE. WHERE IS THE BEAST? SHE CALLS HIM, SHE RUNS ABOUT LOOKING FOR HIM, AND SHE FINDS HIM BESIDE THE LAKE DYING.

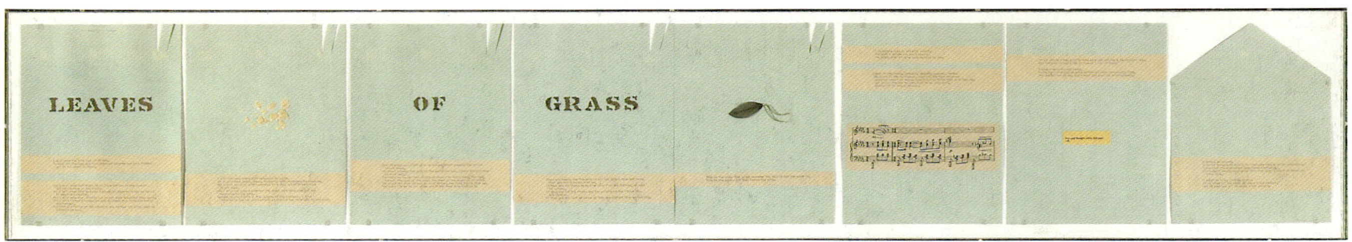

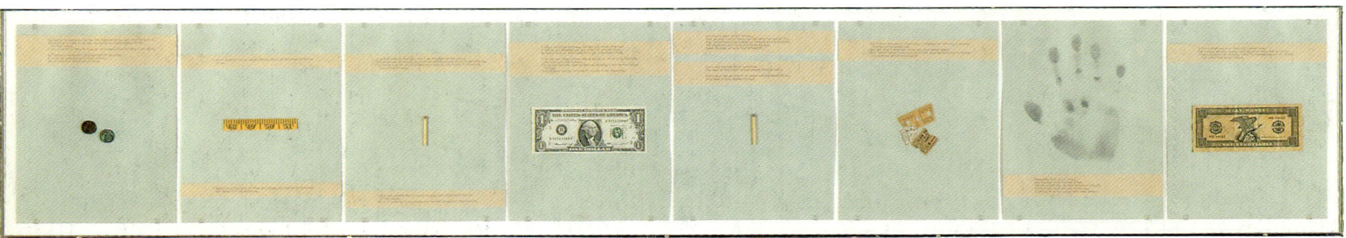

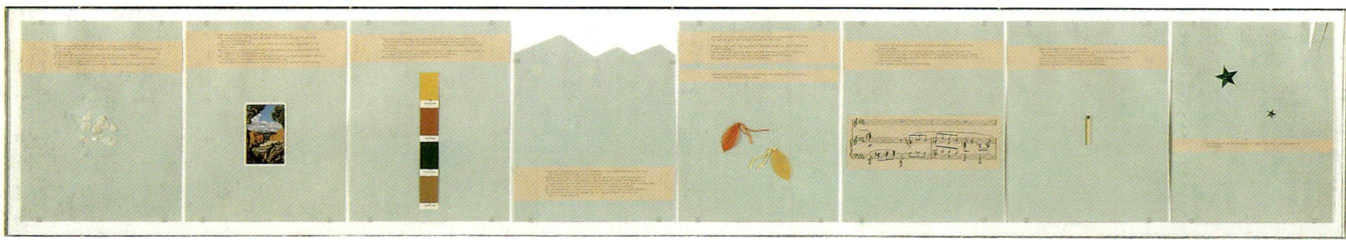

Panel I

I will make the true poem of riches,
To earn for the body and the mind whatever adheres and
  goes forward and is not dropt by death;

And I will show that there is no imperfection in the present,
  and can be none in the future,
And I will show that whatever happens to anybody it may
  be turn'd to beautiful results,
And I will show that nothing can happen more beautiful
  than death,
And I will thread a thread through my poems that time and
  events are compact,
And that all the things of the universe are perfect miracles,
  each as profound as any.

Leaves of Grass, 1977
Mixed-media collage, three panels, 12¾ × 72 inches each
Margo Leavin Gallery, Los Angeles

As Smith's ideas grew in ambition and diversity, her sources broadened. Walt Whitman's sonorous collection of poems to America, *Leaves of Grass*, inspired a similarly titled work in 1977. Smith appropriated lines from Whitman's poems to reassert her respect for egalitarianism, the profundity of the ordinary, the inescapable reality of time, and the interconnection of all things. In a passage such as "to me the converging objects of the universe perpetually flow,/All are written to me, and I must get what the writing means," Smith and Whitman underscore the primacy of the word in their respective universes and the critical role of man's effort to decipher. But, at the same time, both revere the extra-verbal: "There is something that comes to one now and perpetually,/It is not what is printed, preach'd, discussed, it eludes discussion and print,/It is not to be put in a book, it is not in this book,/It is for you whoever you are, it is no farther from you than your hearing and sight are from you,/It is hinted by nearest, commonest, readiest, it is ever provoked by them." The clearest declaration to date of Smith's faith in the transformative power of art—especially as she practices it with "the nearest, commonest, readiest"—these metaphysical statements are illuminated by such ordinary imagery as Smith's handprint and the face and back of a dollar bill.

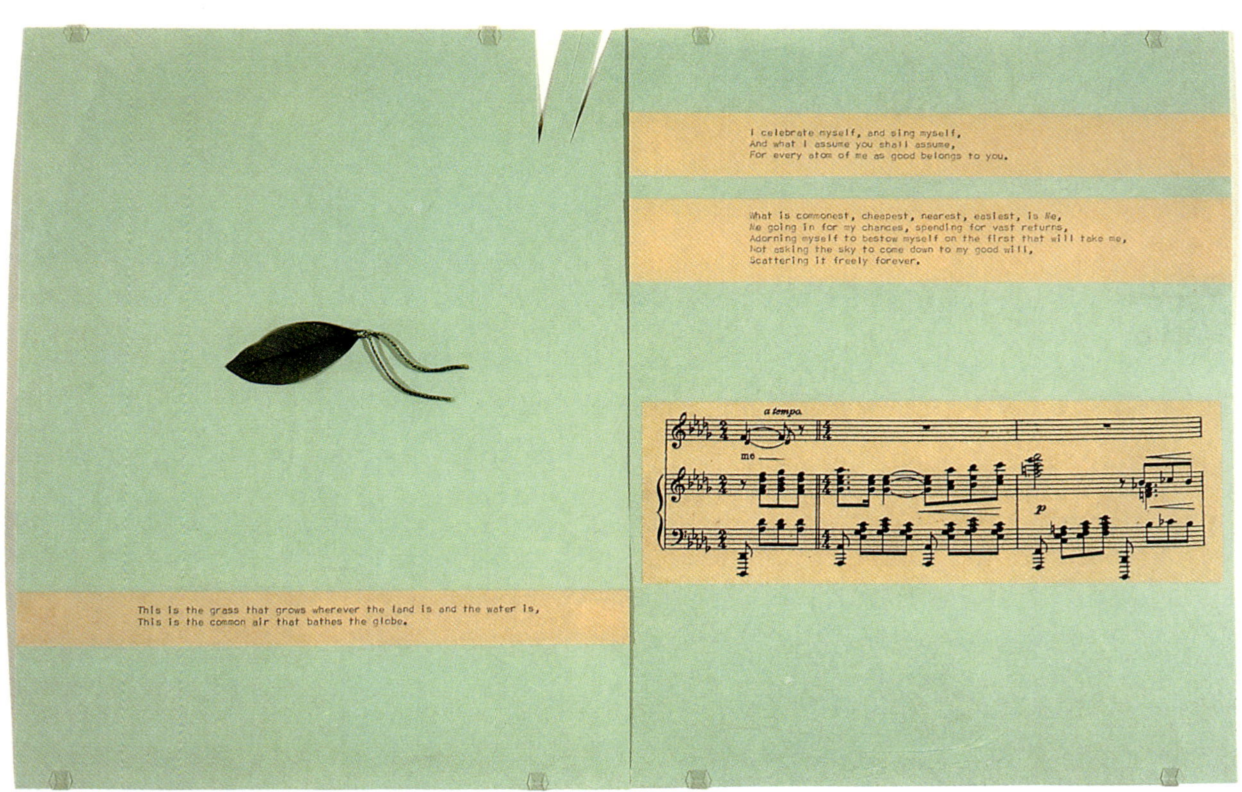

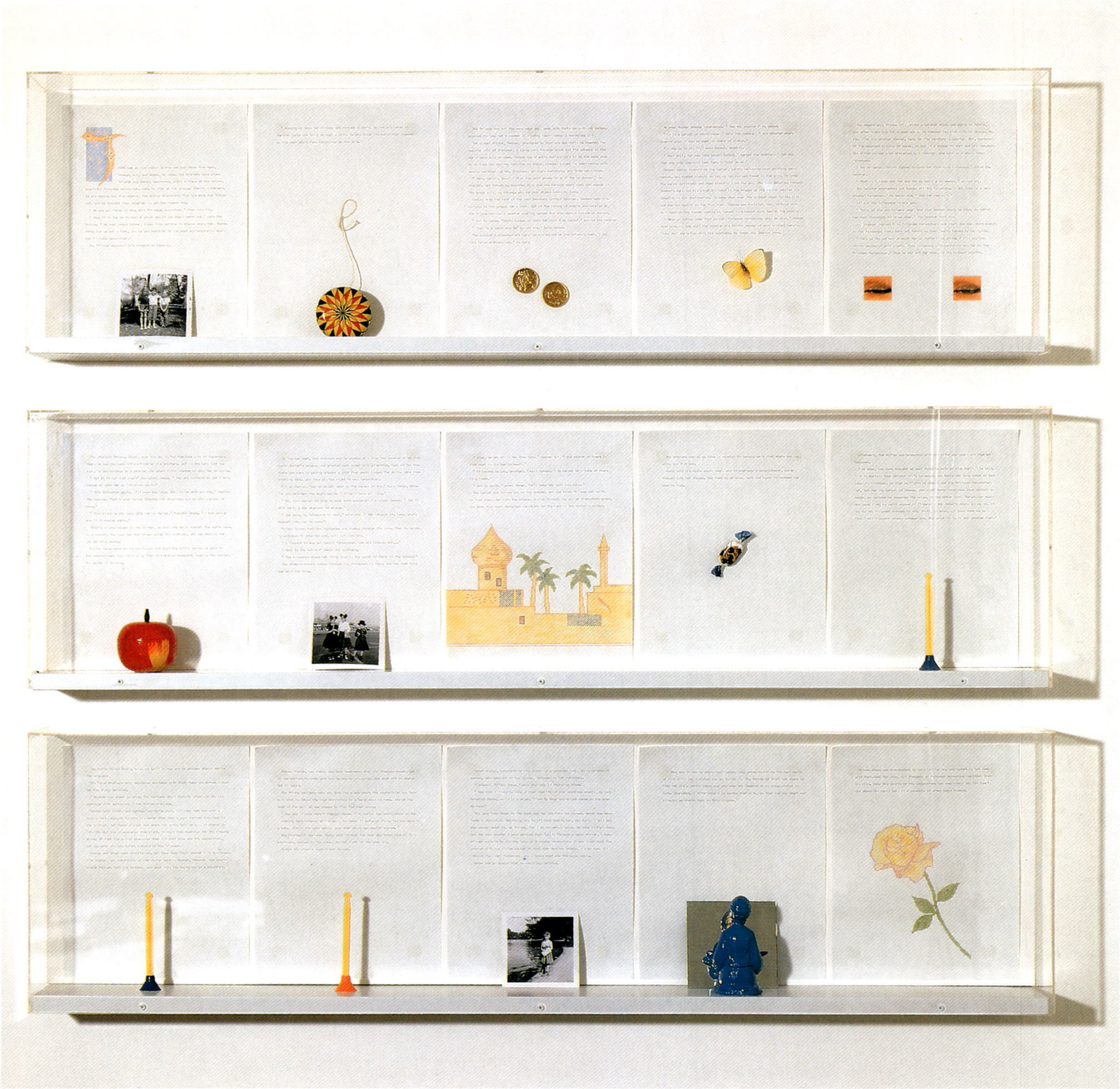

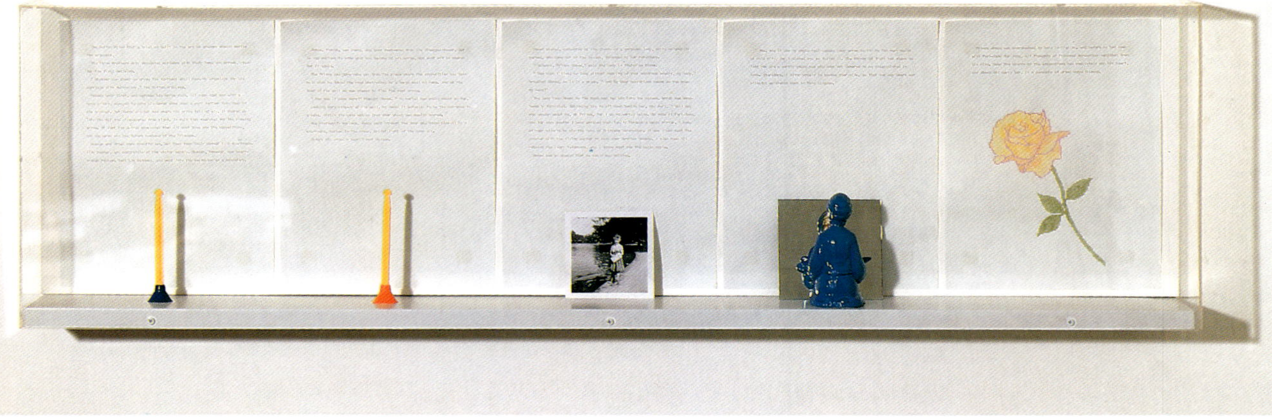

A Story from My Childhood, 1977
Mixed-media collage, three panels, 13 × 45¼ inches each
The Museum of Contemporary Art, Los Angeles;
Gift of Beatrice and Philip Gersh

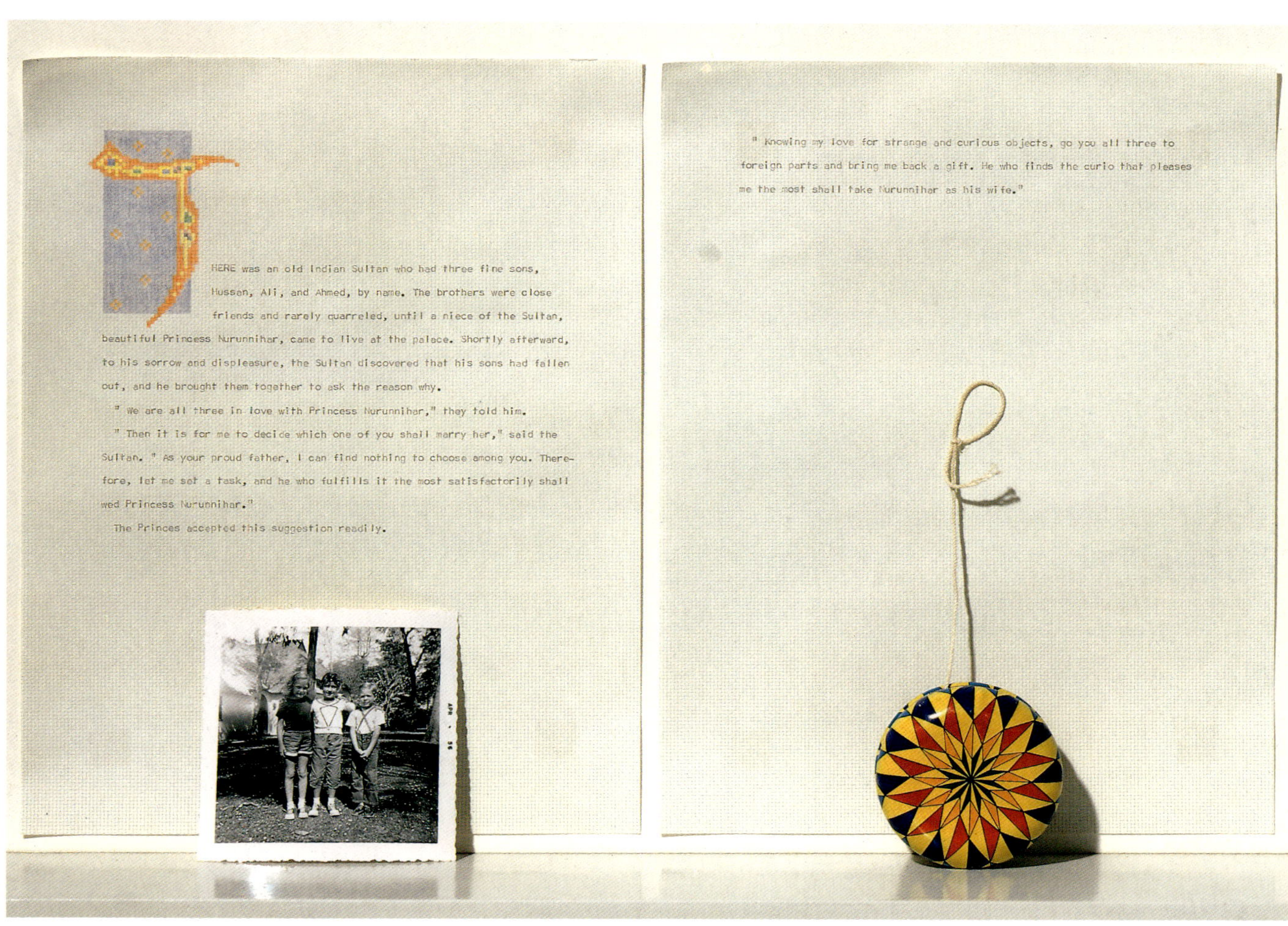

Detail from panel 1

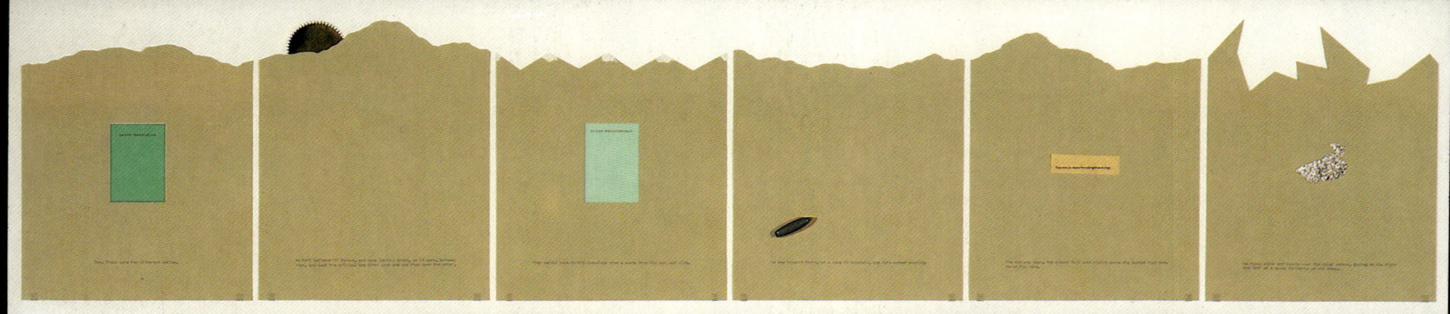

The Magic Mountain, 1978

Yes, these were two different worlds./As Herr Settembrini talked, and Hans Castorp stood, as it were, between them and cast his critical eye first upon one and then upon the other,/they called back to his conscious mind a scene from his own past life./He saw himself rowing on a lake in Holstein, one late summer evening;/the sun was down, the almost full moon rising above the bushes that bordered the lake./He rowed alone and slowly over the quiet waters, gazing to right and left at a scene fantastic as any dream./In the west it was still broad daylight with a fixed and glassy air;/but in the east he looked into a moonlit landscape, wreathed in the magic of rising mists and equally convincing to his bewildered senses./The strange combination lasted some brief quarter-hour before the balance finally settled in favor of night and the moon;/all that time Hans Castorp's dazzled eyes went shifting in lively amazement from one scene to the other;/from day to night and back again

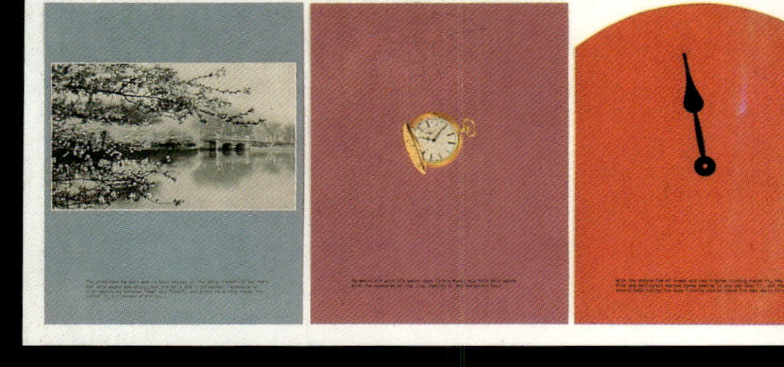

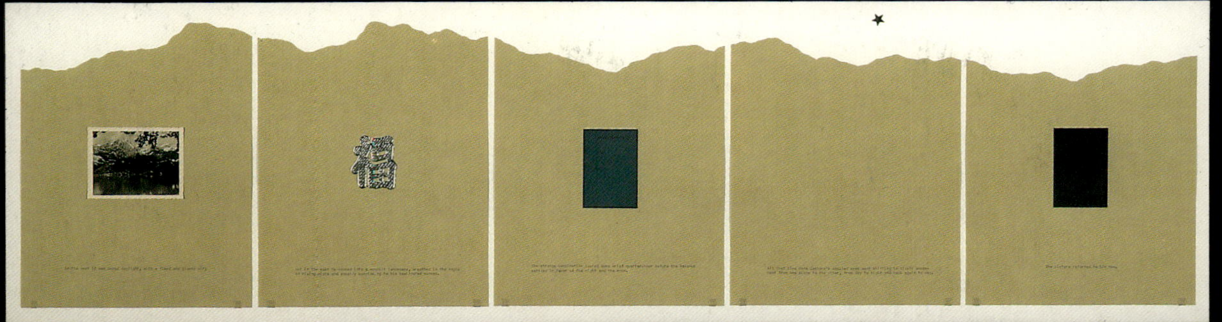

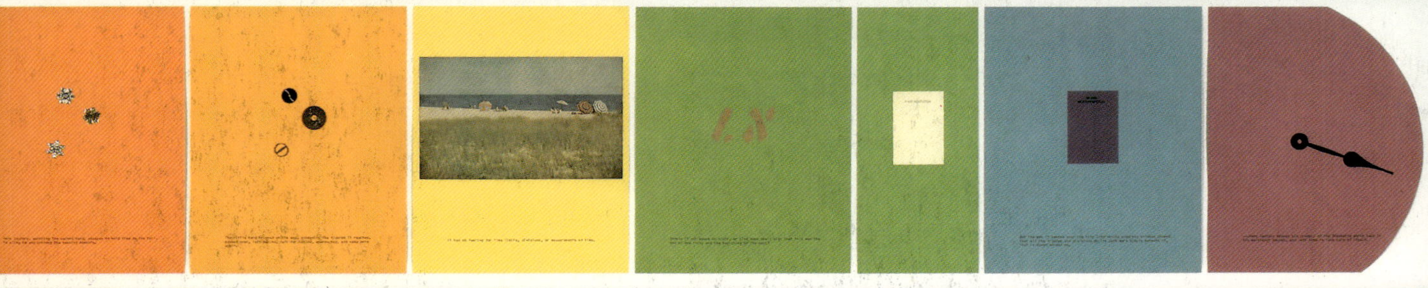

Moto Perpetuo (from *The Magic Mountain*, 1978)

The giddiness he felt was in both senses of the word: rendering our hero not only dazed and dizzy, but flighty and lightheaded, incapable of distinguishing between "now" and "then," and prone to mingle these together in a timeless eternity.../He would sit with his watch open in his hand, his thin gold watch with the monogram on the lid, looking at the porcelain face/with the double row of black and red figures running round it, the two fine and delicately curved hands moving in and out over it, and the little second hand taking its busy ticking course round its own small circle./Hans Castorp, watching the second hand, essayed to hold time by the tail, to cling to and prolong the passing moments./The little hand tripped on its way, unheeding the figures it reached, passed over, left behind, left far behind, approached, and came on to again./It had no feeling for time limits, divisions, or measurements of time./Should it not pause on the sixty, or give some small sign that this was the end of one thing and the beginning of the next?/But the way it passed over the tiny intervening unmarked strokes showed that all the figures and divisions on its path were simply beneath it, that it moved on, and on./—Hans Castorp shoved his product of the Glashutte works back in his waistcoat pocket, and left time to take care of itself.

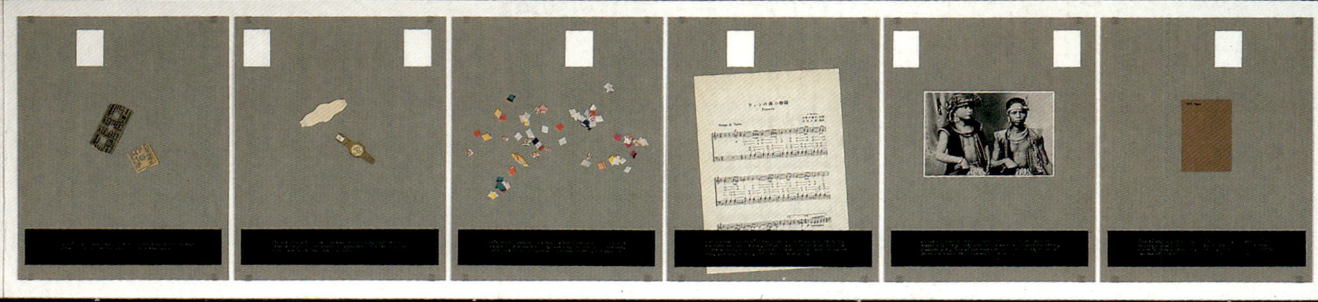

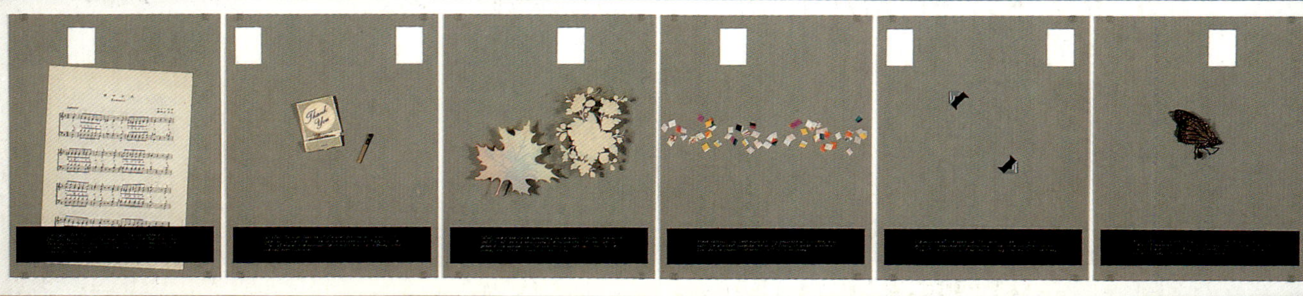

The used quality of most of what Smith employs in her collages suggests the mortality of all physical matter. Smith's fascination with time eloquently manifests itself in works such as *The Magic Mountain* and *Moto Perpetuo* (both 1978), each incorporating the words of part-time Los Angeles resident Thomas Mann. *The Magic Mountain,* with quotes from Mann's protagonist Hans Castorp, focuses on memory's powerful ability to transport us to some suspended midpoint between the past and present—a suspension she often seeks in conjoining found objects with appropriated literary passages. Consciousness of time also animates *Moto Perpetuo*. Smith joins the insides of a broken watch to a text in which Castorp realizes the essential meaninglessness of time. In the next quoted passage, he further confronts its unstoppable movement. Above the quote a purple paint chip called "moto perpetuo" becomes a poignant reminder of time's tyrannical motion.

Both *Moto Perpetuo* and *The Magic Mountain* represent Smith's new willingness to supersede her previously rigid vertical or horizontal formats. She now shaped the page to enhance the typewritten texts: jagged mountain tops charge the general outline of *The Magic Mountain,* while certain sheets of the colored papers of *Moto Perpetuo* echo the circular shape of Castorp's old-fashioned pocket watch.

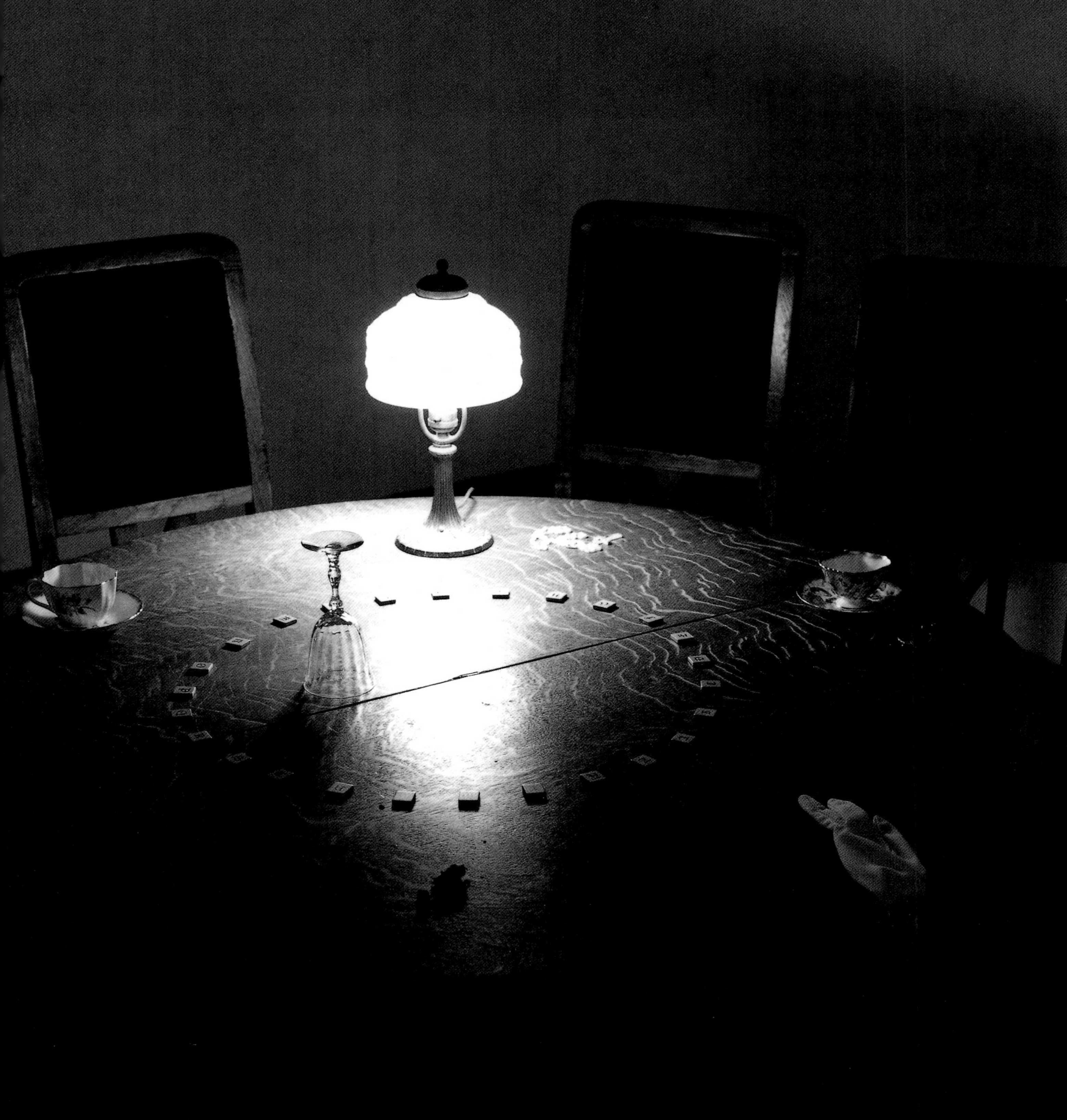

Medium, performance at Rosamund Felsen Gallery, Los Angeles, 1978

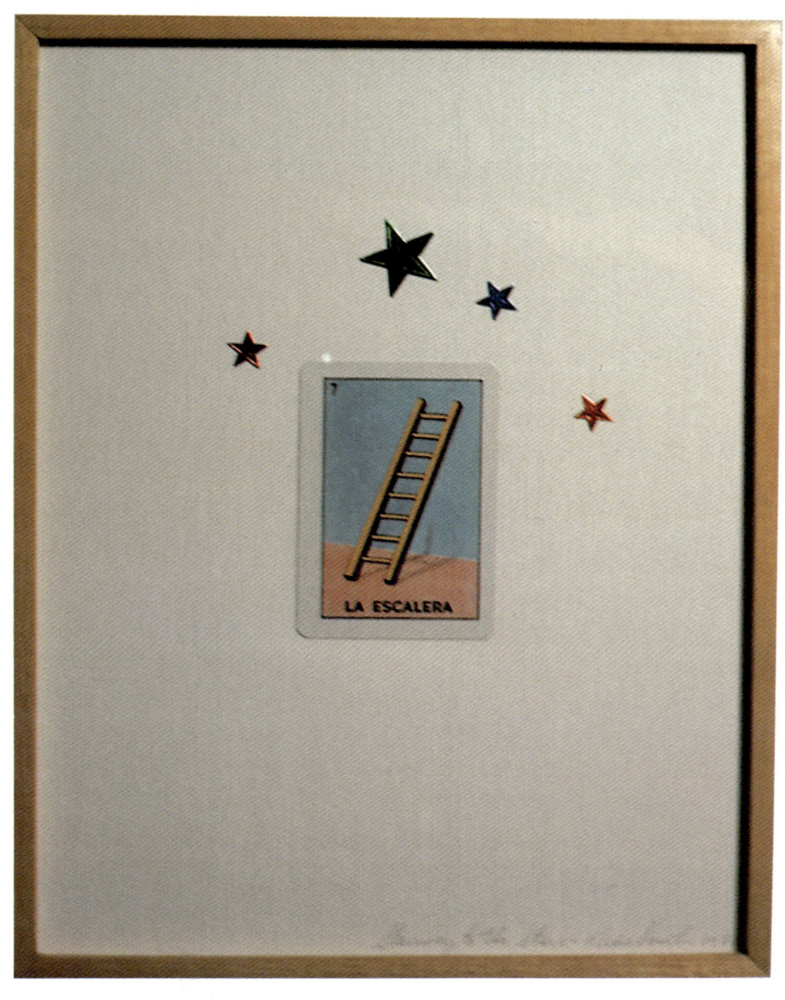

Stairway to the Stars, 1977
Mixed-media collage, 12 × 9 inches
Collection of John Solomon

Stairway to the Stars, 1979
Window installation, Graz, Austria

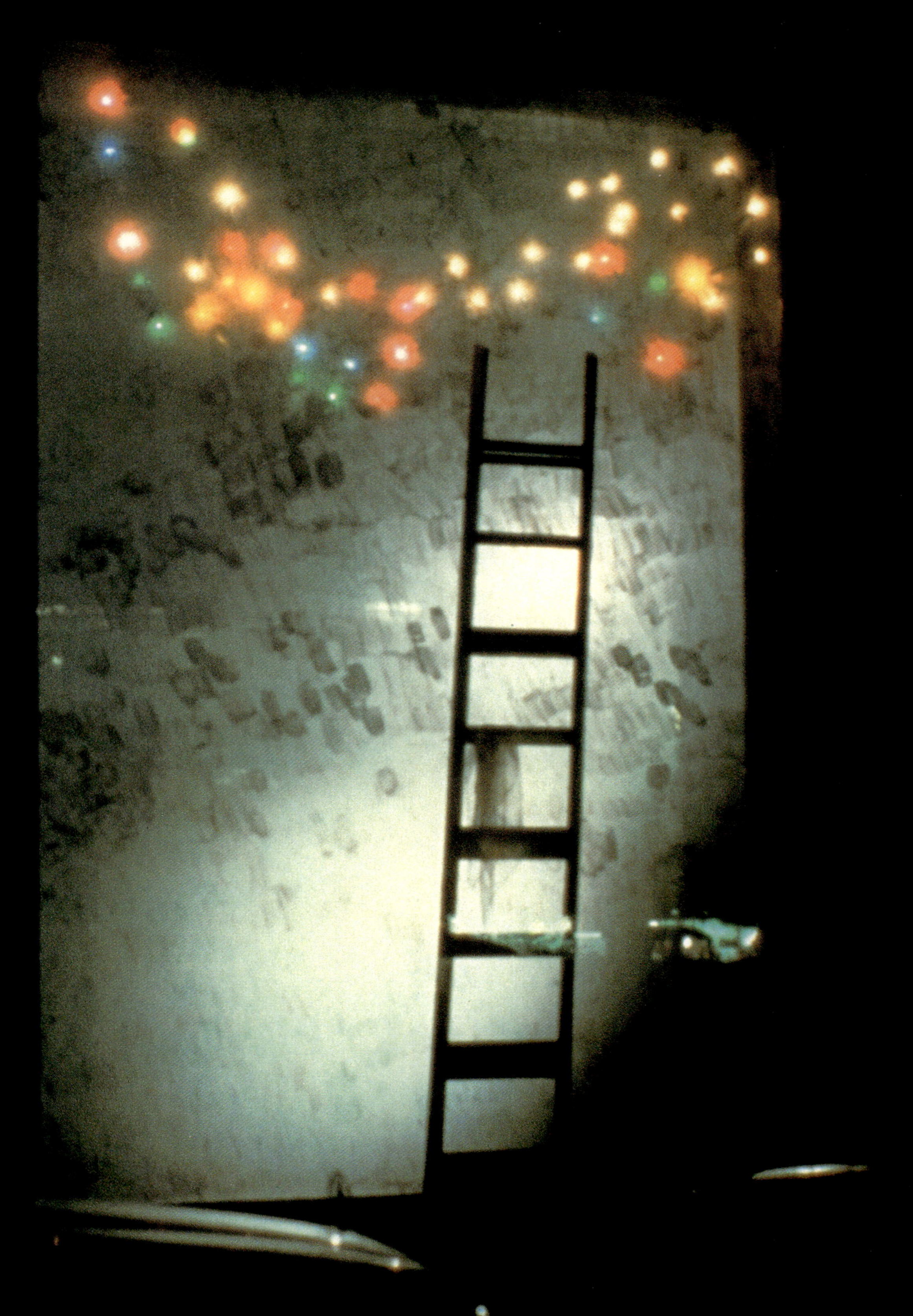

Throughout the 1970s, Smith's work became more public through a series of installations. In 1975 she laid out 190 feet of "n"-gauge miniature railroad track around the art gallery at the University of California, Santa Barbara. As the little train of *Rapido* labored around the room, time and space assumed a miniaturized three-dimensional reality that corresponded to the bits and pieces the artist favored for her two-dimensional collages. A related spatial dislocation distinguished *Anteroom* (1975), in which Smith affixed a chair and lamp to the ceiling of the Los Angeles alternative space CARP. CARP was also the site in 1976 of an evening of readings from *The Thousand and One Nights* by a costumed and bejeweled Smith acting as "Scheherazade the Storyteller."

Smith's belief in the magically transformative power of art was again demonstrated in such performances as *The Art of Magic, Close-Up* (1978). Simple magic tricks, many using playing cards, allude to deceptions of time and space necessary in both the literary and visual arts. That same year, Smith performed *Medium* in an installation at the Rosamund Felsen Gallery during her one-artist show there entitled "The Magic Mountain." In this performance, she read selections from Mann's novel that described a seance.

In a subsequent window installation for a storefront in Graz, Austria, Smith realized a scaled-up version of the small collage *Stairway to the Stars* (1977). The piece, with its twinkling lights and partly obscured, dreamlike atmosphere, translated her vision from two to three dimensions. *Autumn Sonata* (1979) occupied a large display window in downtown Los Angeles. As in Austria, Smith whitewashed the window to near opacity, using it to frame a dancing couple—backlighted cutouts on a revolving base—in another silent ode to erstwhile glamour.

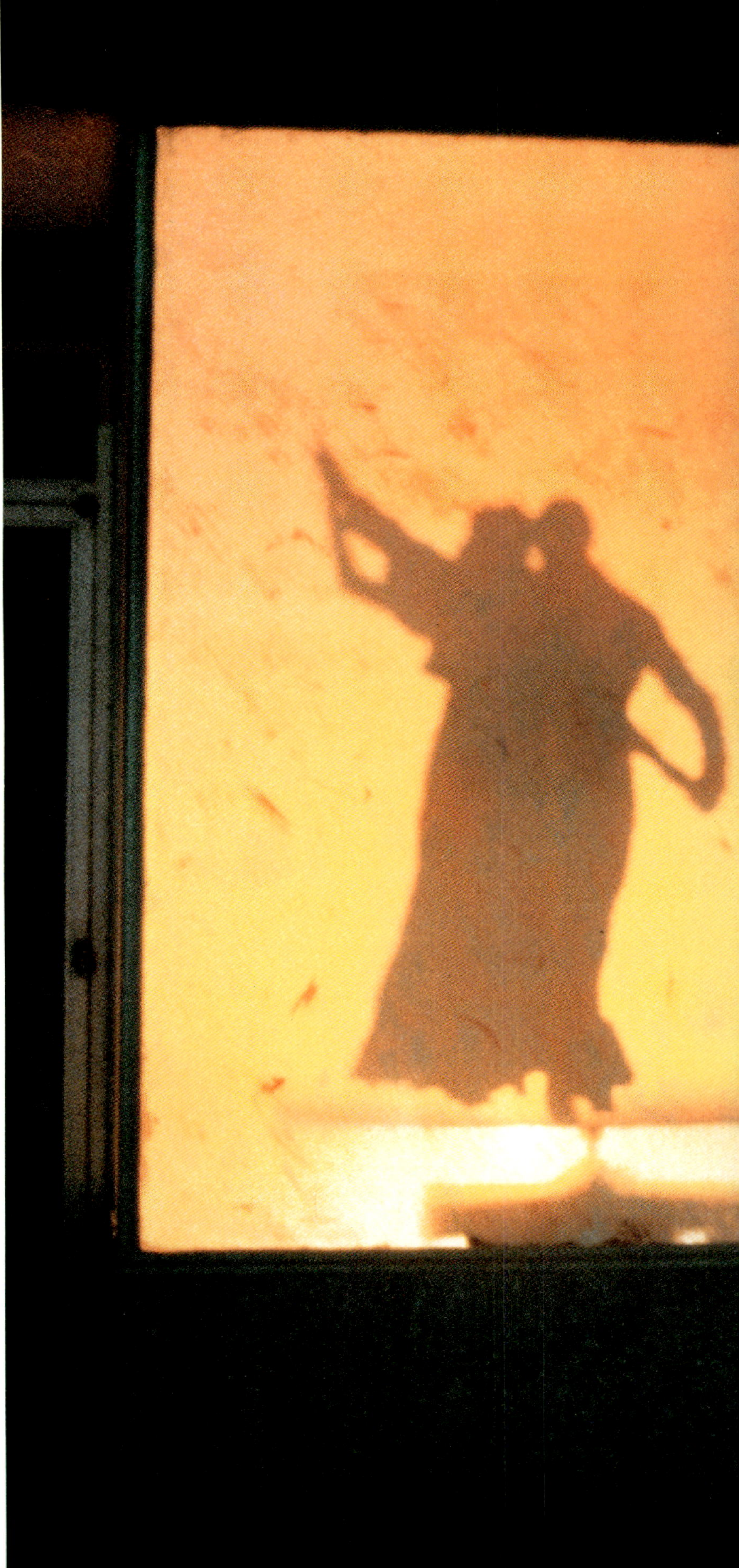

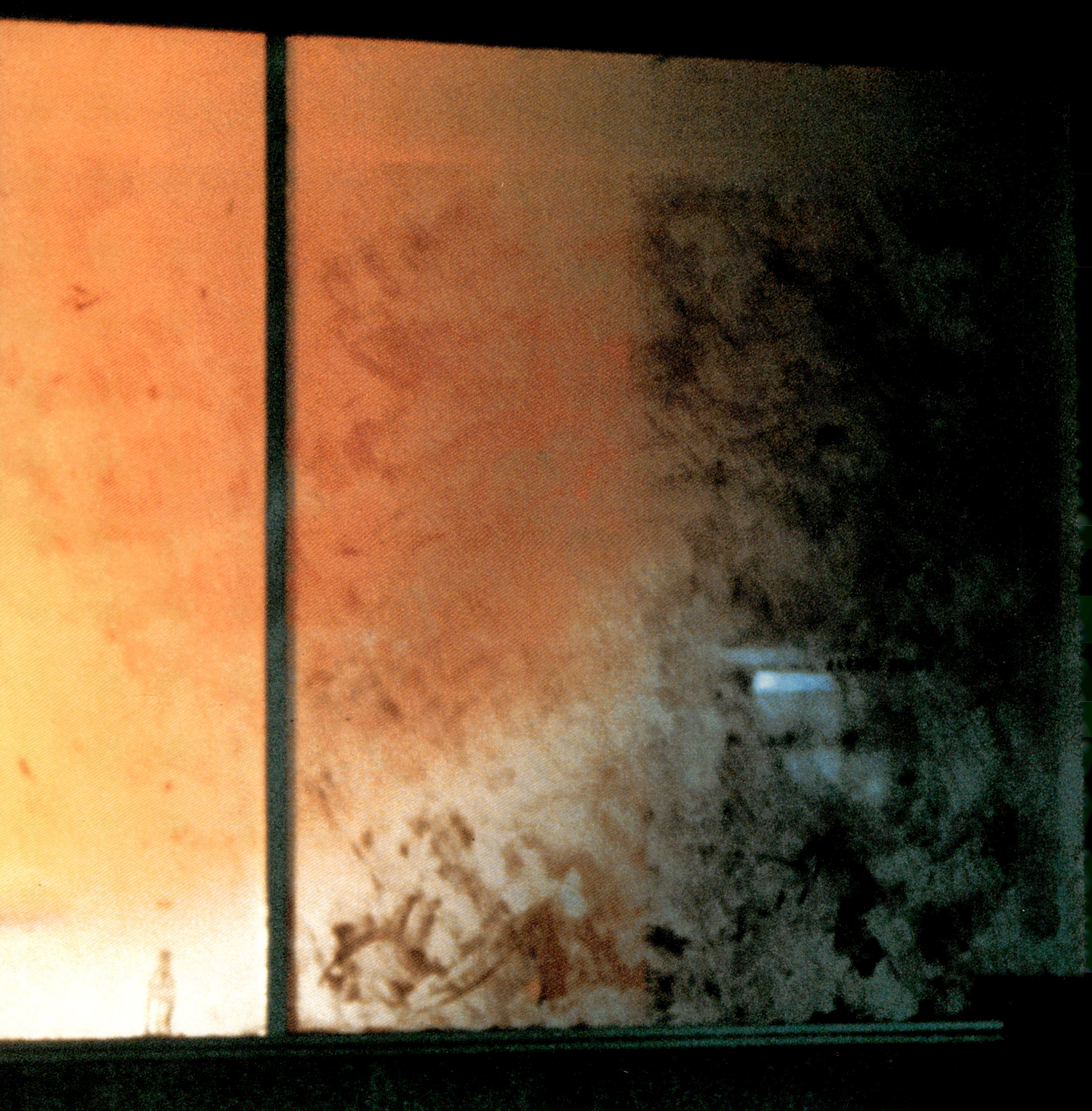

Autumn Sonata, 1979
Window installation, downtown Los Angeles

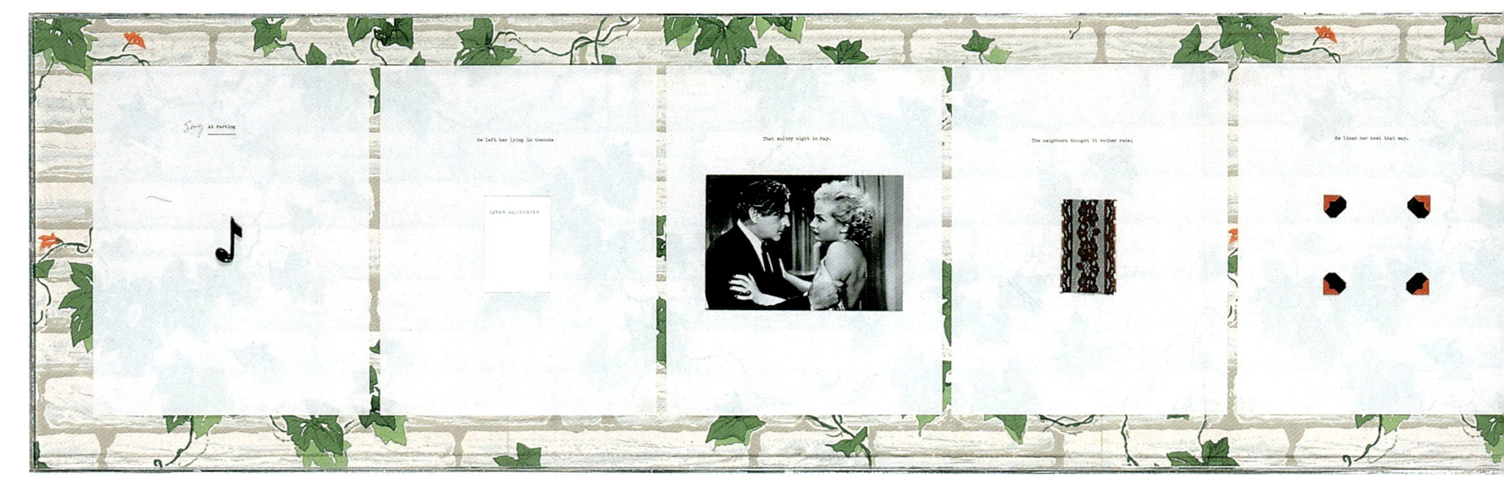

The Big Sleep (Requiem for Raymond Chandler), 1978
Mixed-media collage, 14½ × 83¼ inches
Collection of Richard Levine

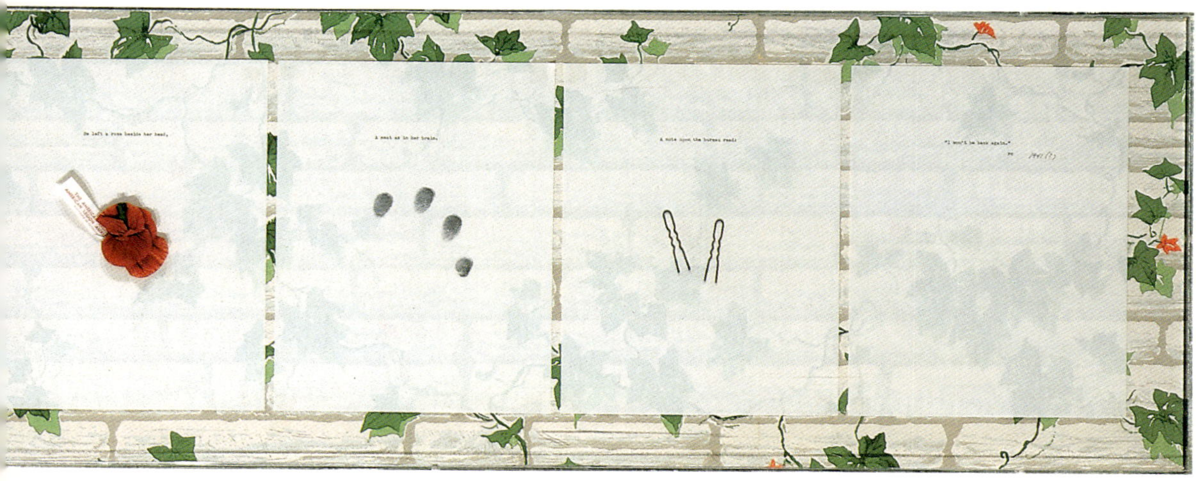

<u>Song at Parting</u>

He left her lying in the nude
That sultry night in May.
The neighbors thought it rather rude;
He liked her best that way.
He left a rose beside her head,
A meat axe in her brain.
A note upon the bureau read:
''I won't be back again.''

—rc 1949?

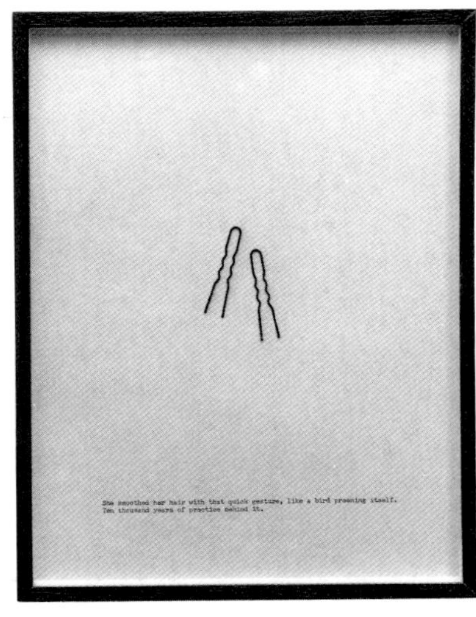

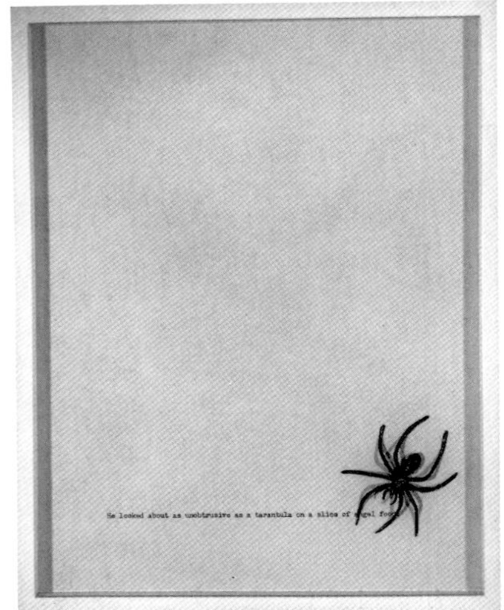

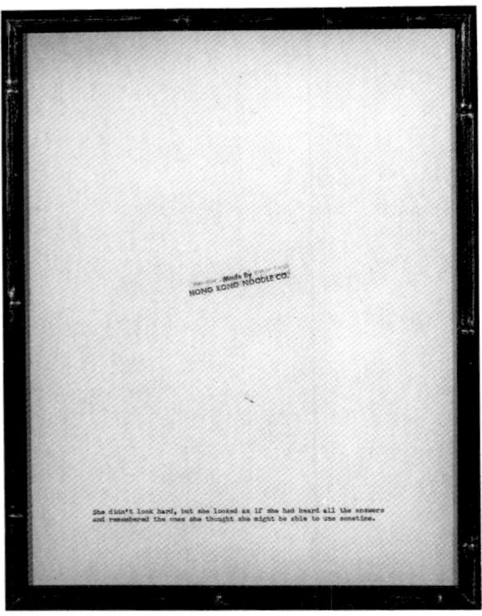

Chandlerism #36, 1978
Mixed-media collage,
12¼ × 9⅜ inches
The Chase Manhattan Bank, NA

Chandlerism #22, 1978
Mixed-media collage,
12¼ × 9½ inches
Private collection

Chandlerism #6, 1978
Mixed-media collage, 12 × 9¼ inches
Collection of Wayne Kuwada

Chandlerism #23, 1978
Mixed-media collage,
12 × 9¼ inches
Collection of Anne Holt

Chandlerism #35, 1978
Mixed-media collage,
12 × 9¼ inches
Collection of J. David Wyles

Chandlerism #29, 1978
Mixed-media collage,
12 × 9¼ inches
Collection of Joy and
Jerry Monkarsh

In Raymond Chandler's writings, Smith found a perfectly pitched melody for the darker, more alto range in her voice. Chandler's sardonic, world-weary tone altered the romantic, soprano strain that had dominated her adopted texts to date. His graphic metaphors readily spawned physical embellishment; his gritty, urban vocabulary was elegantly amplified by the swap-meet detritus always so attractive to Smith. Situated in and around Los Angeles, Chandler's narratives depict the hard-bitten life of Hollywood, the other side of the shiny coin of a perpetually reinventable self. Life as a series of roles, the Hollywood promise, suited Smith's own narrational needs.

The small, rectangular format of the 1978 *Chandlerisms* (roughly 12 × 9 inches) harks back to Smith's earliest narrative appropriations. The short quotations from Chandler—three sentences at most—are typed across the bottom of the page, with an *objet trouvé* collaged above it. All the pages have spare compositions—a single image and a string of words. As always, a dynamic of

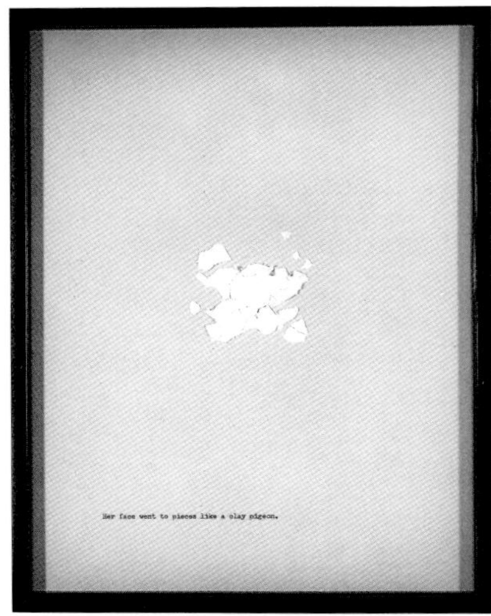

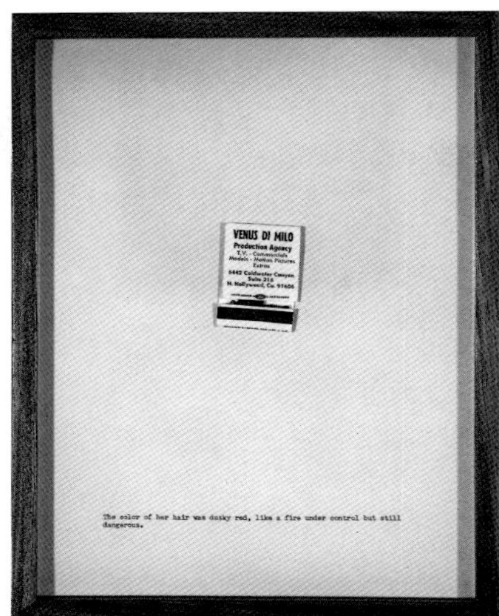

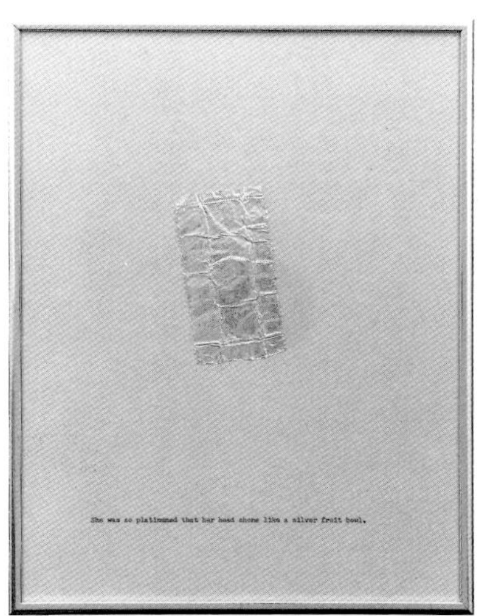

internal composition—one that overcomes the essential modesty of the object—animates each page. In *Chandlerism #22,* the description of Moose Malloy from *The Big Sleep*—"He looked about as unobtrusive as a tarantula on a slice of angel food"—is thus enlivened by a big black plastic spider ominously paused at the right margin of the page.

Chandler's *film noir* dialogue had the added value of embodying a clearly male point of view. His men, as excerpted and reconstructed by Smith, tout their appreciation of women in pool-hall vernacular—"It was a blonde. A blonde to make a bishop kick a hole in a stained glass window" or "She approached me with enough sex appeal to stampede a businessman's lunch." The sexual objectification of the female in Chandler's words perfectly matched what would become Smith's recurrent use of a type of Hollywood woman whose principal role is to look fetching in order to bait and trap men. But, above all, these women are survivors. If not empathetic to women, Chandler often shows them with a wily upper hand—" 'Sweet, isn't he?' she said. 'I'd like eight of him for my cocktail set.' " As distilled by Smith, the *Chandlerisms* are a chorus of sage wisecracks. The range of her quotations in the forty-odd *Chandlerisms* shows a new confidence in adopting either a female or a male voice to further her stories. With the completion of the series in 1978, Smith had added new themes of sexual attraction and violence to her previous fantasies of identity (mostly female) and its transformations. An irreversible drift from the mythic and patriarchal to the ordinary and nonhierarchical was underway.

The *Chandlerisms* are snappy, single-sheet exclamations of allusive virtuosity. In them, Smith's method of marrying idea to thing finds its most minimal realization. These 12×9-inch sheets will survive in enlarged and varied formats in subsequent work, persisting as *sotto voce* assertions of Smith's role as a dispassionate observer and as invocations of old Los Angeles.

Chandlerisms, 1978

1. It was a blonde. A blonde to make a bishop kick a hole in a stained glass window.
2. A little more of that and I'd be falling in love with myself. I might even buy myself a small unpretentious diamond ring.
3. I sipped my drink. I like an effect as well as the next fellow.
4. He came back in softly, holding his pork pie felt under his arm, as debonair as a French count in a college play.
5. She sat in front of her princess dresser trying to paint the suitcases out from under her eyes.
6. She didn't look hard, but she looked as if she heard all the answers and remembered the ones she thought she might be able to use sometime.
7. "Sweet, isn't he?" she said. "I'd like eight of him for my cocktail set."
8. "Listen, Marlowe. You're being a damn fool. I want to tell you—" "Tell yourself. You have a captive audience."
9. He looked at me to see how the show was going over. I had my mouth open and a blank expression on my face, like a farm boy at a Latin lesson.
10. The torn blouse didn't reveal any startling nakedness, merely some skin, and part of a brassiere. You'd see more on the beach, far more, but you wouldn't see it through a torn blouse.
11. His glass eye shown brightly, and was the most lifelike thing about him.
12. "Trouble is my business," I said. "Trouble—" I started to say and stopped. I was tired of that gag for that night.
13. He smiled his first smile of the day. He probably allowed himself four.
14. "My God!" she whispered. "My God!" "You don't have one except money."
15. "How do you feel?" Her voice was soft and lovely, too. "Great," I said. "Except somebody built a filling station on my jaw."
16. She sighed. "All men are the same." "So are all women—after the first nine."
17. Nobody knew what happened except the boys playing pinball games in the drugstore on the corner. They know everything except how to hold a job.
18. We went in so close together that we must've looked like a three-decker sandwich.
19. She had eyes as black and shiny and expressionless as the toes of patent-leather pumps.
20. I gave the front door a heavy shoulder. This was foolish. About the only part of a California house you can't put your foot through is the front door.

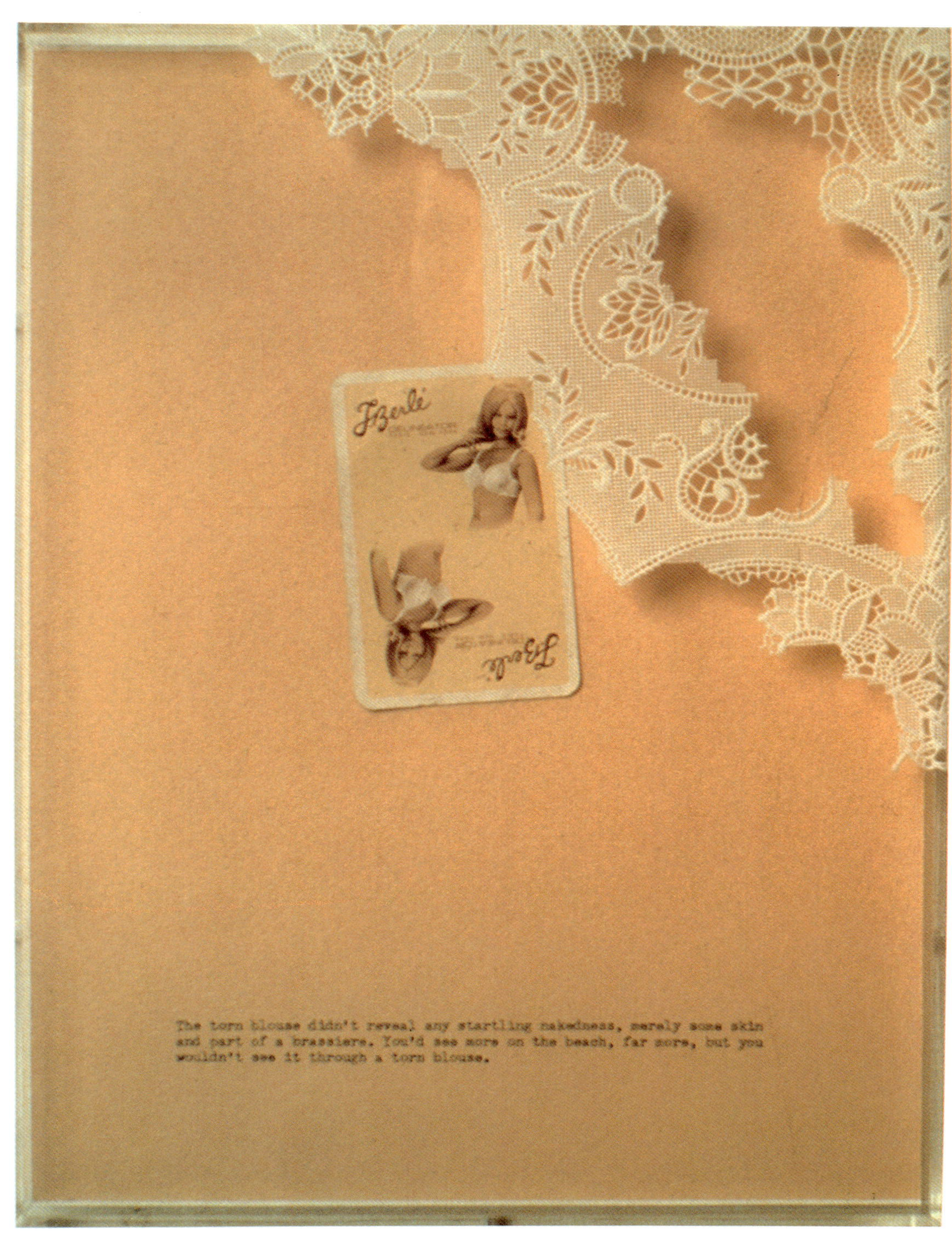

Chandlerism #10, 1978
Mixed-media collage, 12 × 9¼ inches
Collection of Judy and Stuart Spence

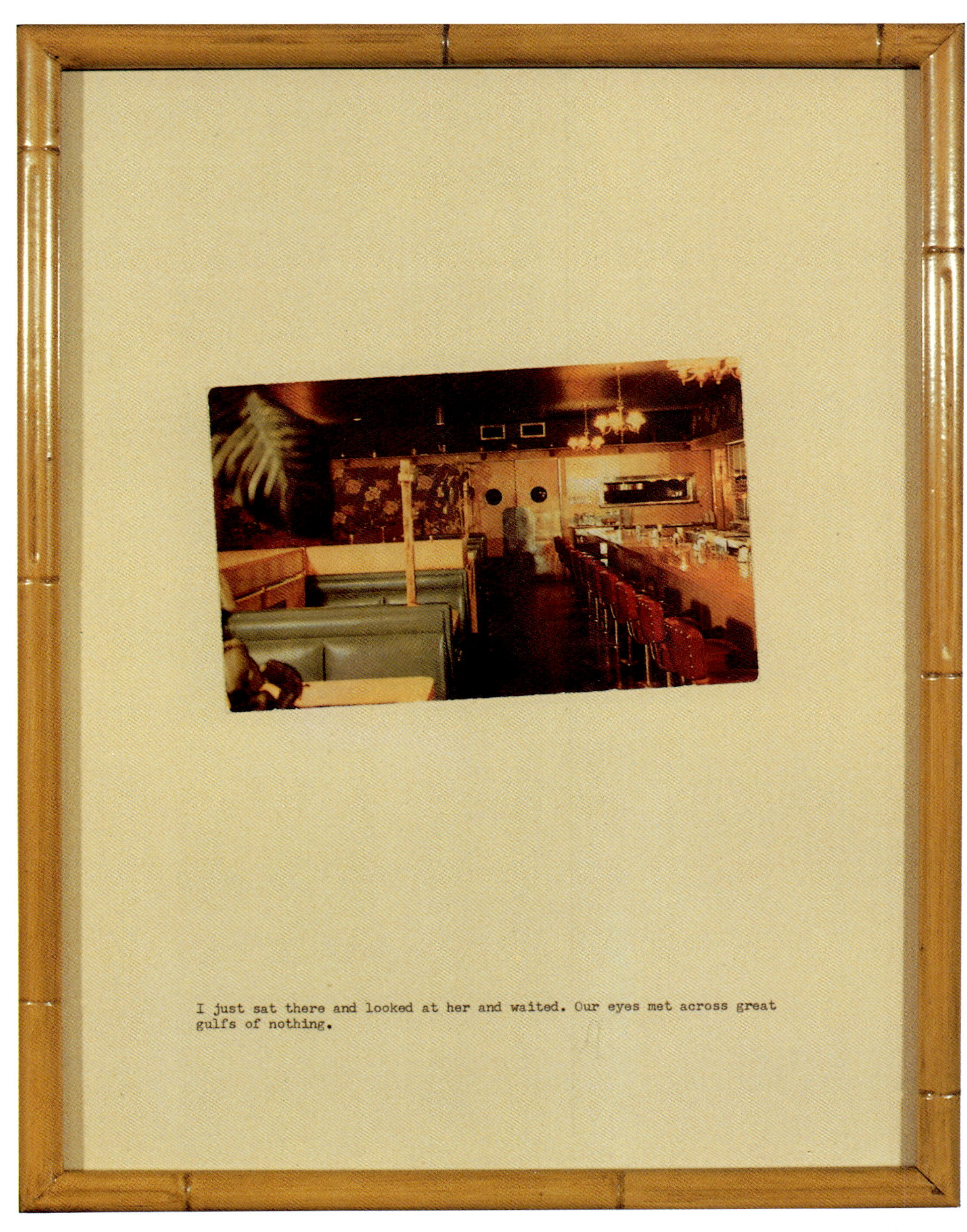

Chandlerism #31, 1978
Mixed-media collage, 12 × 9¼ inches
Collection of the Grinstein Family

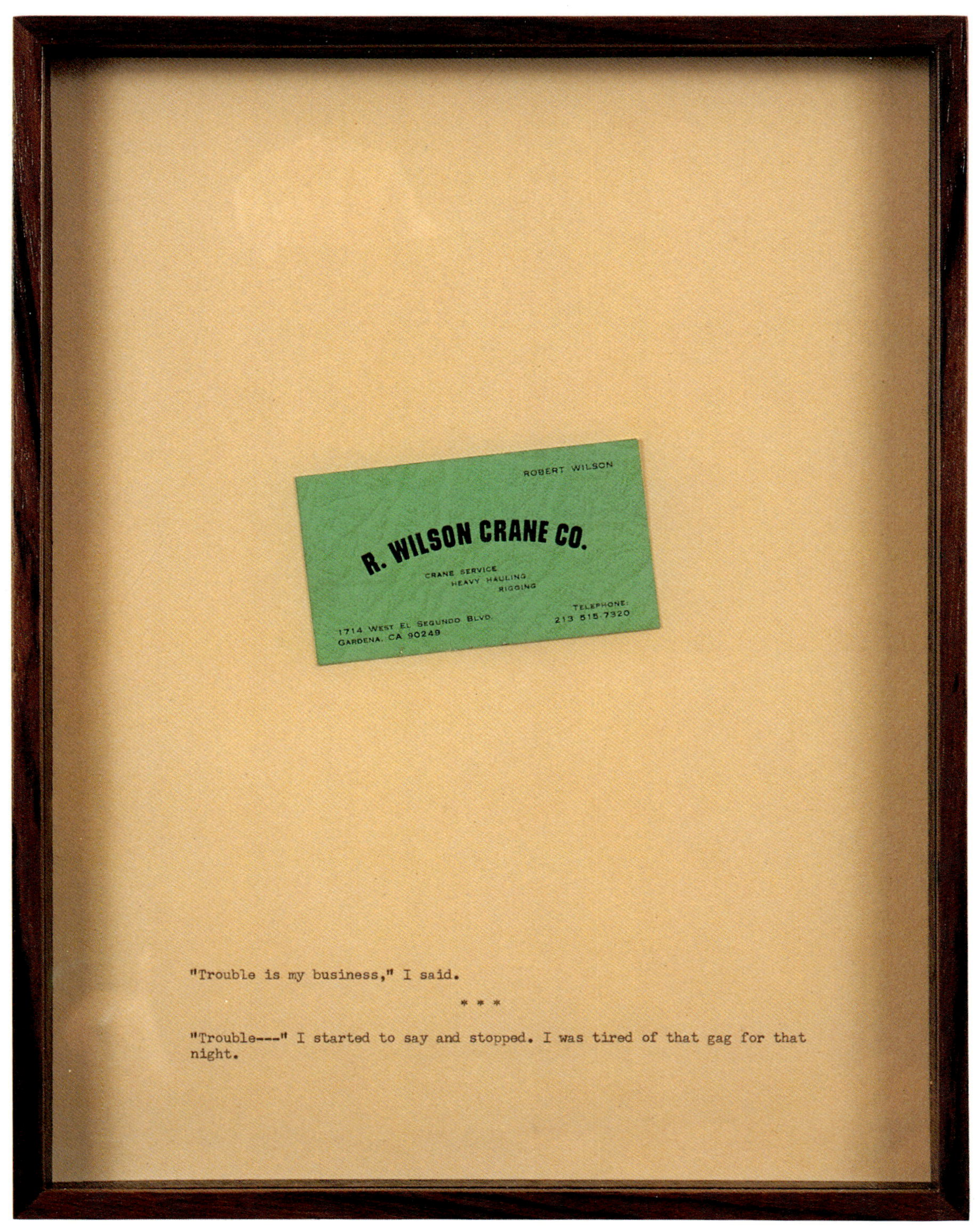

Chandlerism #12, 1978
Mixed-media collage, 12⅜ × 9½ inches
The Chase Manhattan Bank, NA

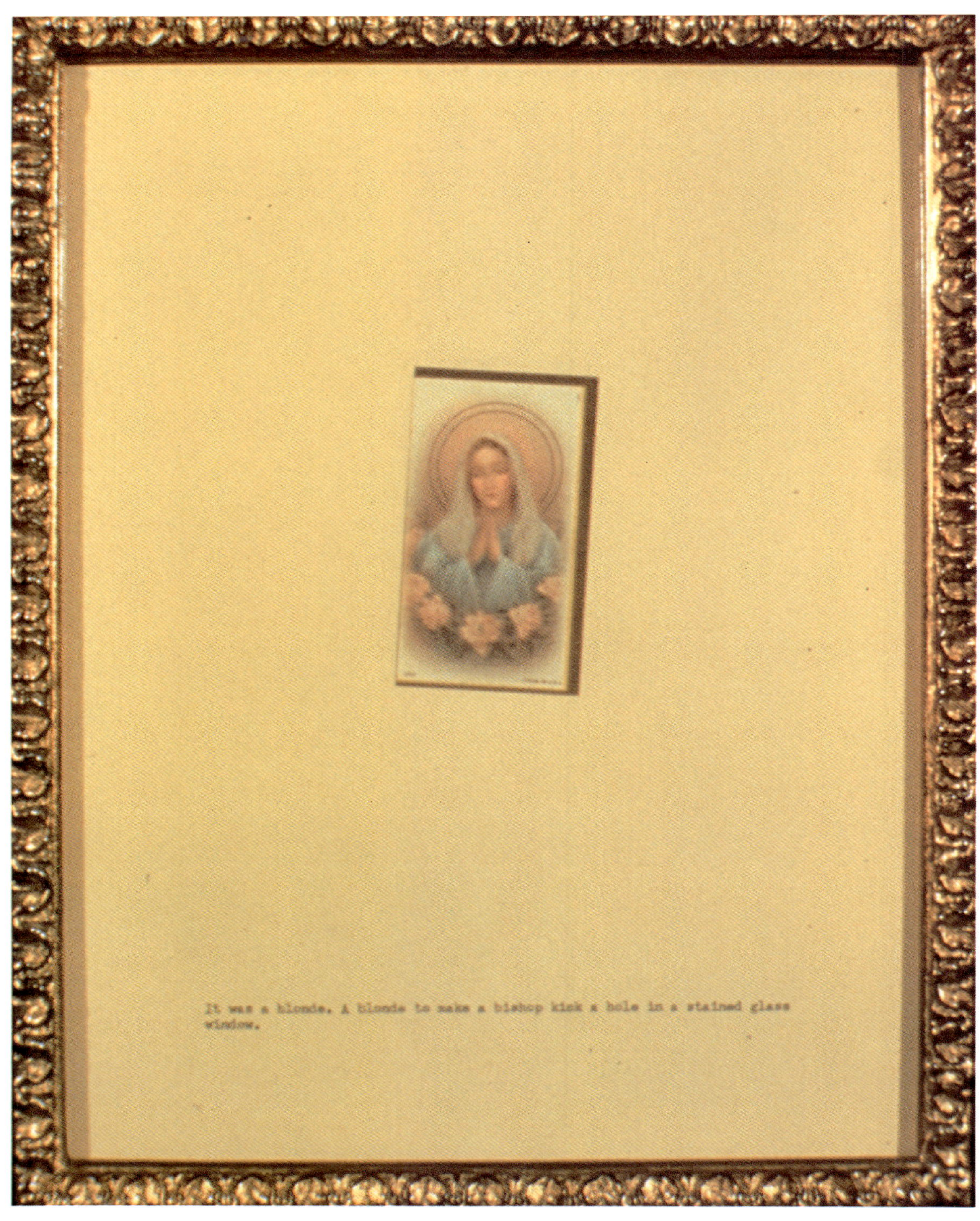

Chandlerism #1, 1978
Mixed-media collage, 12 × 9¼ inches
Collection of the estate of Nancy Yewell

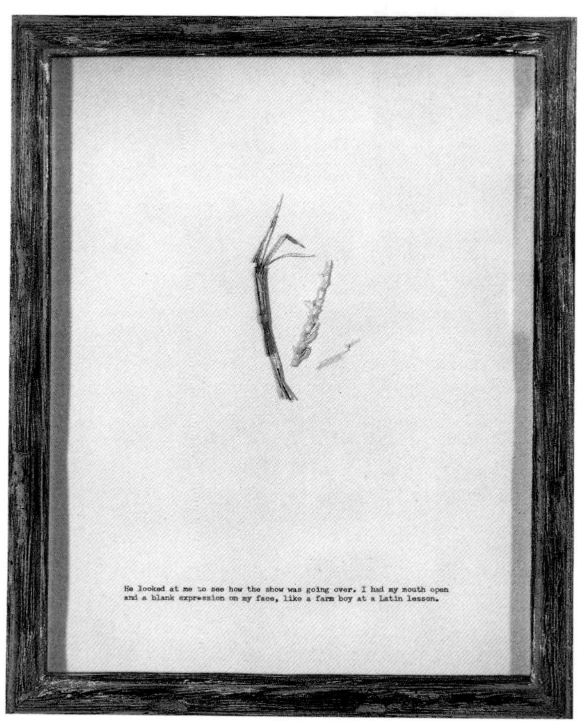

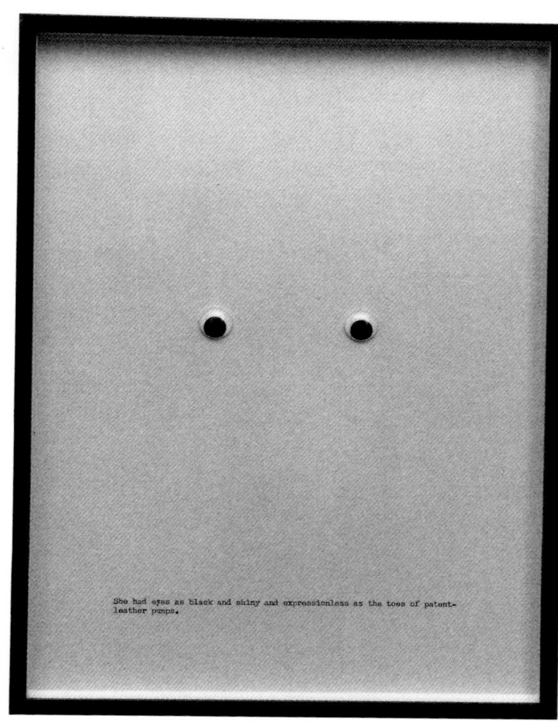

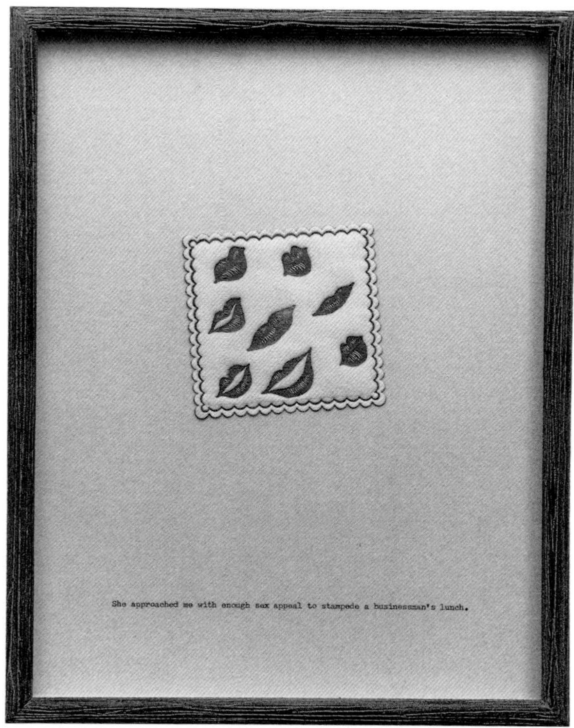

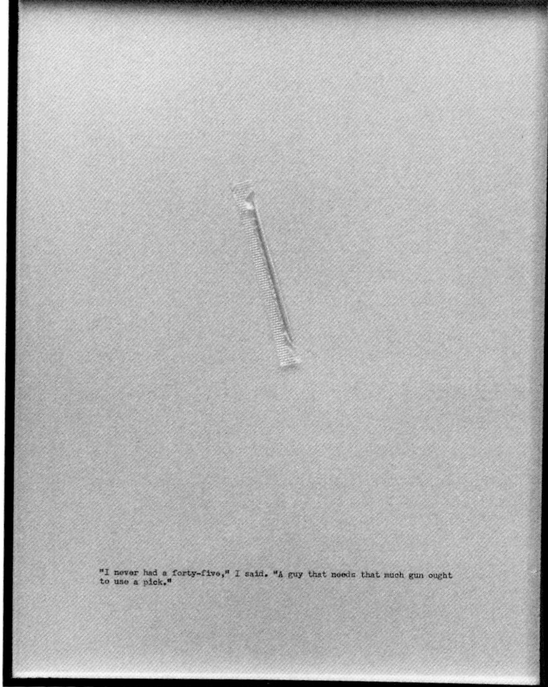

Chandlerism #9, 1978
Mixed-media collage, 12 × 9¼ inches
Collection of Lyn and Norman Lear

Chandlerism #25, 1978
Mixed-media collage, 12 × 9¼ inches
Collection of Richard Wiegand

Chandlerism #19, 1978
Mixed-media collage, 12 × 9¼ inches
Collection of Richard Wiegand

Chandlerism #28, 1978
Mixed-media collage, 12 × 9¼ inches
Private collection

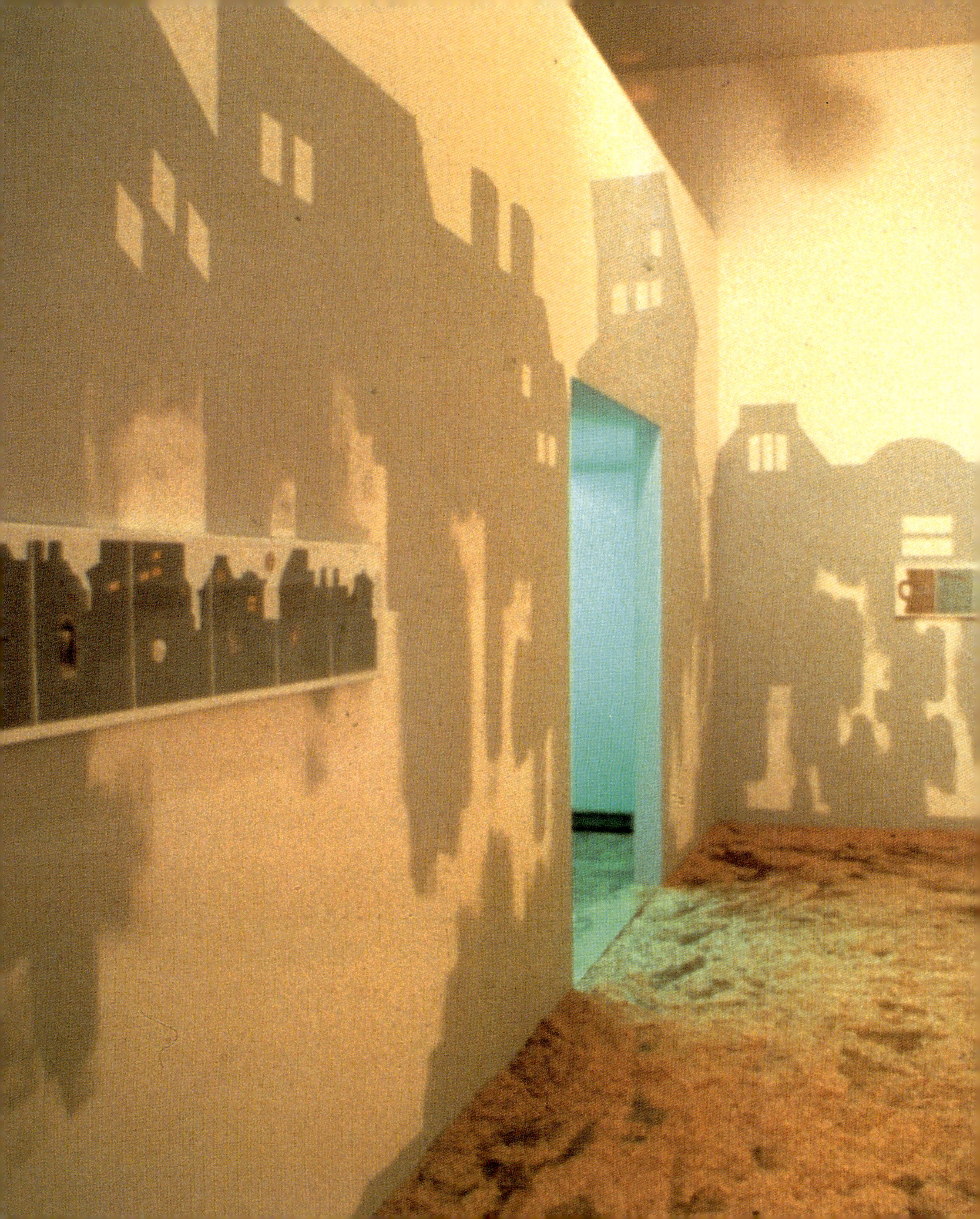

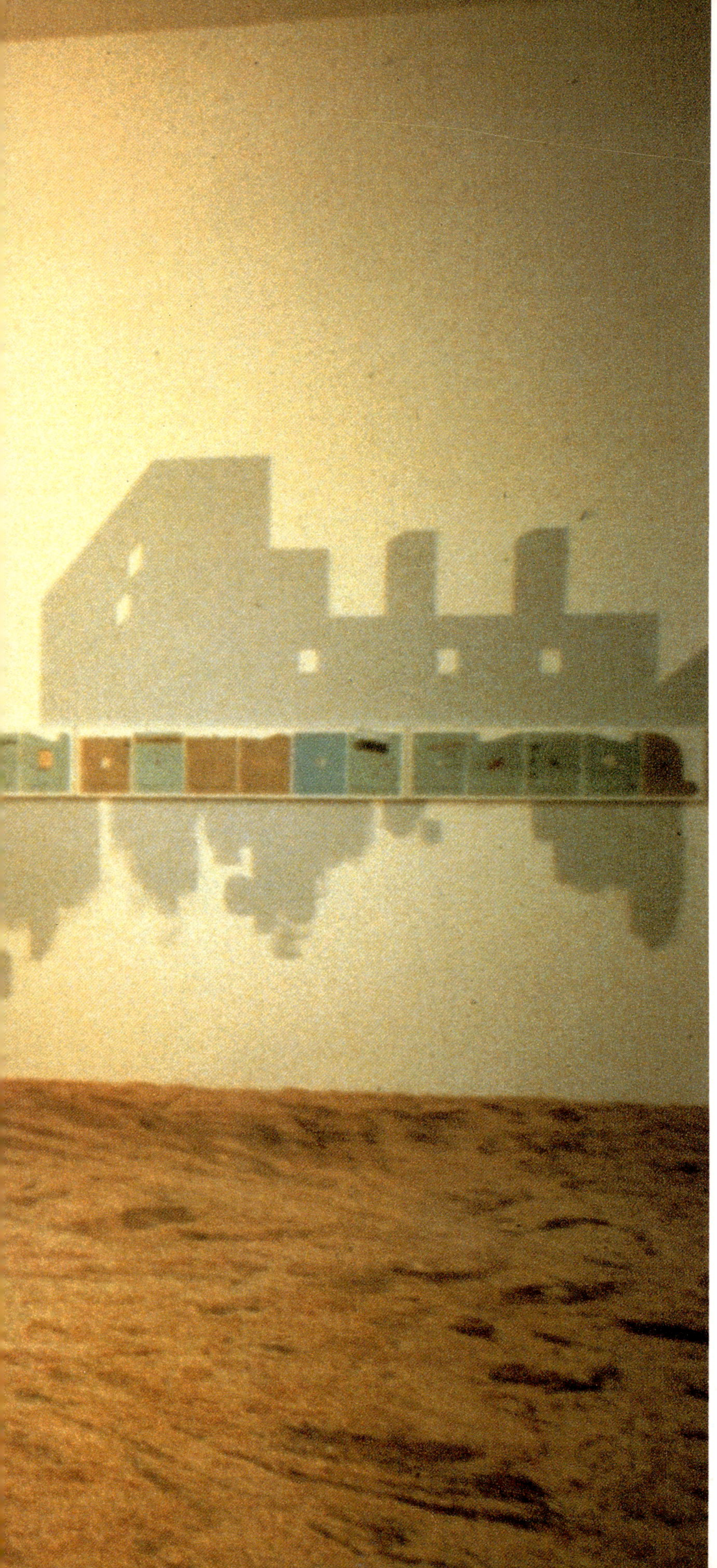

The works that comprised Smith's *Raymond Chandler's L.A.* at Rosamund Felsen Gallery in 1980 were all derived from Chandler's writing. *Downtown, Tightrope*, and *Golden State* followed Smith's formula of lateral, sequential texts and images on rectangular sheets of paper, but in each instance she reconfigured the paper to enhance the narrative. The gruff monologue of *Downtown*, for instance, is typed over pieces of gray paper that read as a cityscape in silhouette. More graphic even is Smith's treatment of the gallery space: by painting its walls as backdrops and strewing sawdust on the floor, she converted it into a three-dimensional ground for her work.

Tightrope hovers over lavender and white painted stripes that simulate a circus tent, while the profiled buildings of *Downtown* are situated on an enlarged rendition of a crowded geometric skyline. The stylized advertisements painted on the wall behind *Golden State* strongly announce the radical advancement of Smith's concept of the relationship between collaged object and ground. The size of the ground is exponentially increased by the decorated wall, so that the framed collage in its entirety becomes another object. The consumerist exhortations on the walls of *Golden State* silently echo the jaded tone of Chandler's tale, with its description of driving over the Cahuenga Pass into the San Fernando Valley and on to the ocean. On the way home, Chandler's protagonist muses, "I smelled Los Angeles before I got to it. It smelled stale and old like a living room that has been closed too long. But the colored lights fooled you. The lights were wonderful. There ought to be a monument to the man who invented neon lights. Fifteen stories high, solid marble. There's a boy who really made something out of nothing."

Raymond Chandler's L.A., 1980
Installation, Rosamund Felsen Gallery, Los Angeles

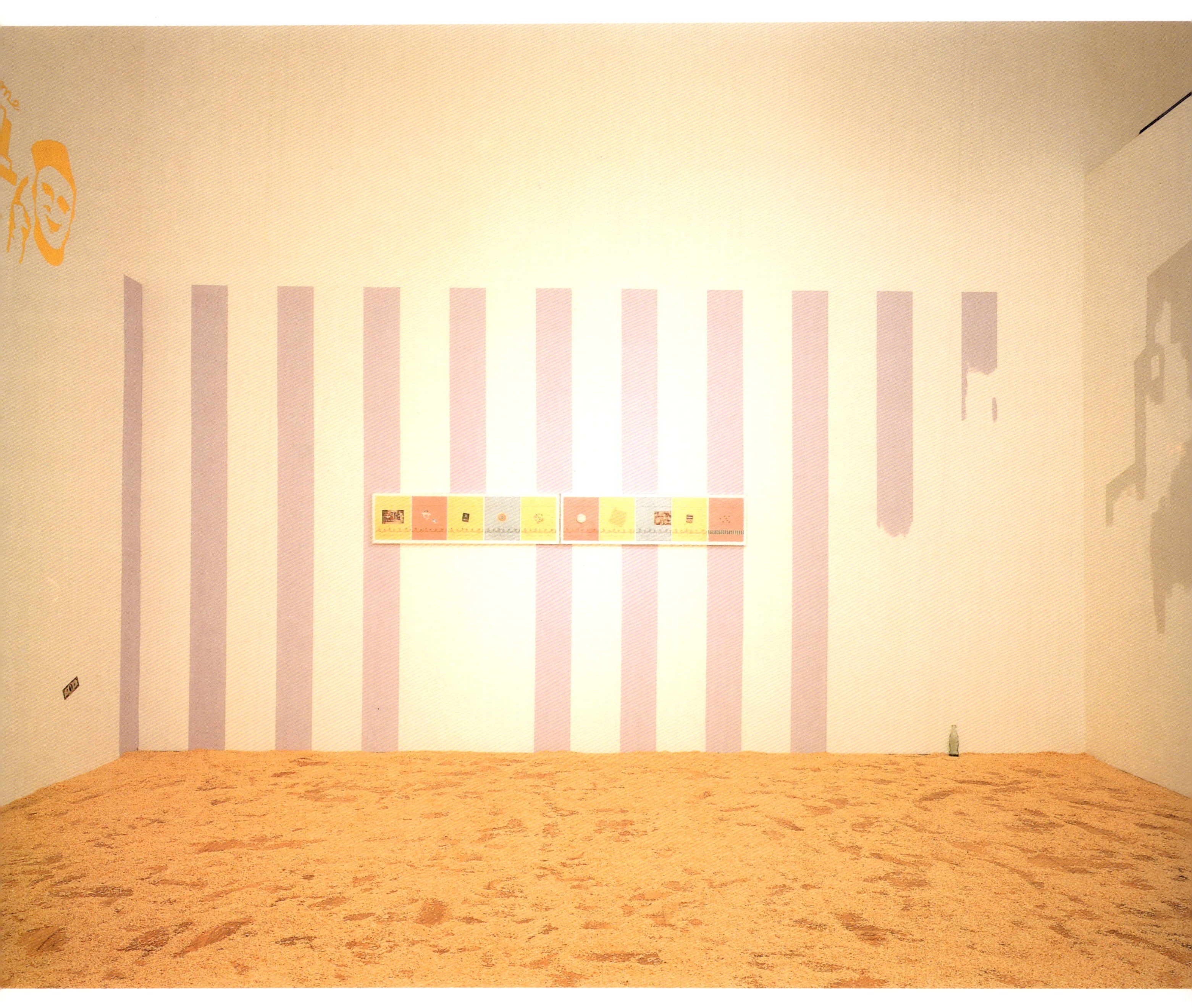

Tightrope, 1980
Installation view
Rosamund Felsen Gallery, Los Angeles

Mixed-media collage, two panels, 12¾ × 45¼ inches each
Courtesy Margo Leavin Gallery, Los Angeles

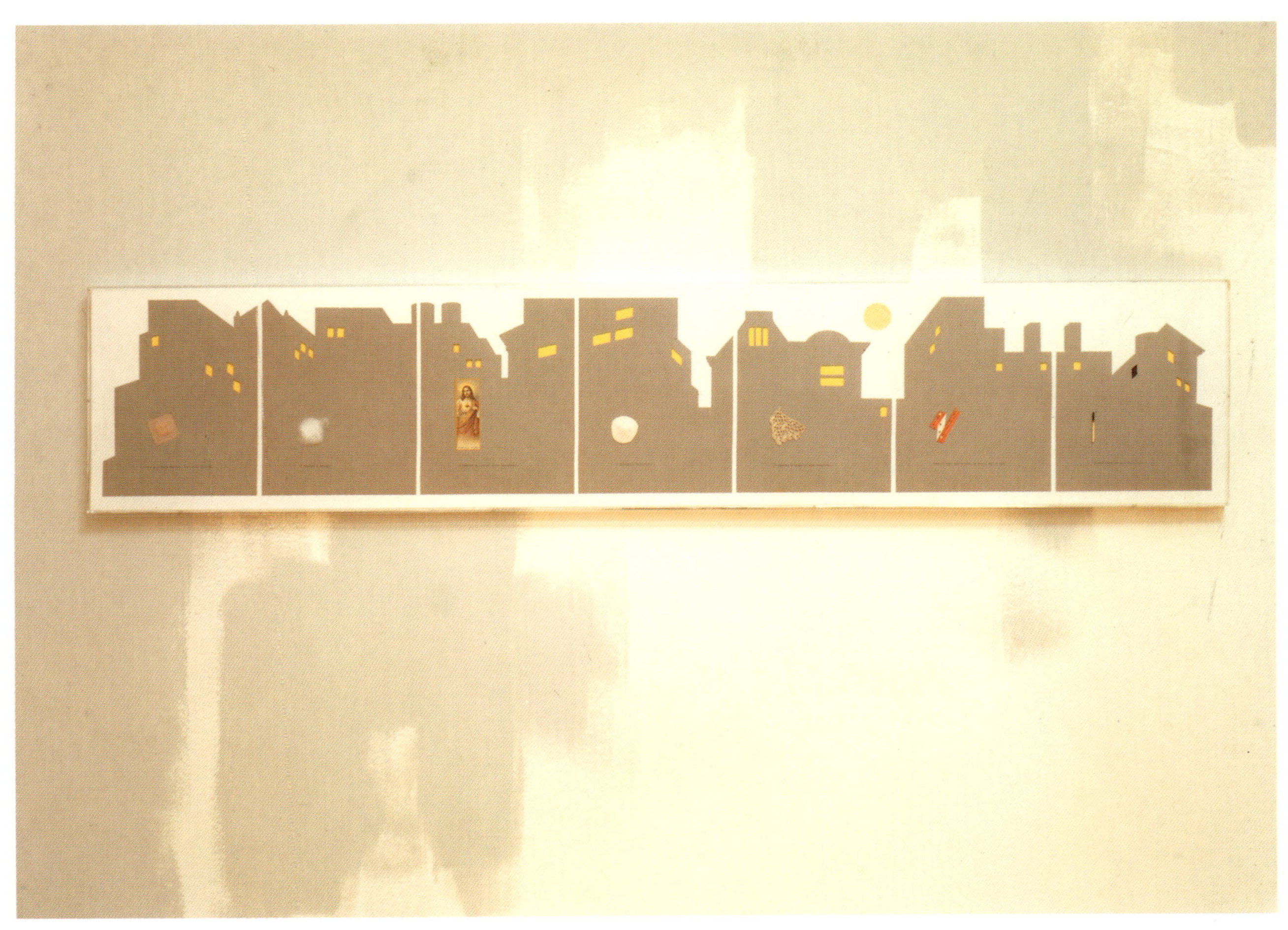

I felt a little better, but very little.
I needed a drink.
I needed a lot of life insurance.
I needed a vacation.
I needed a home in the country.
What I had was a hat, a coat, and a gun.
I put them on and went out.

Downtown, 1980
Mixed-media collage, 12¾ × 60¾ inches
Private collection

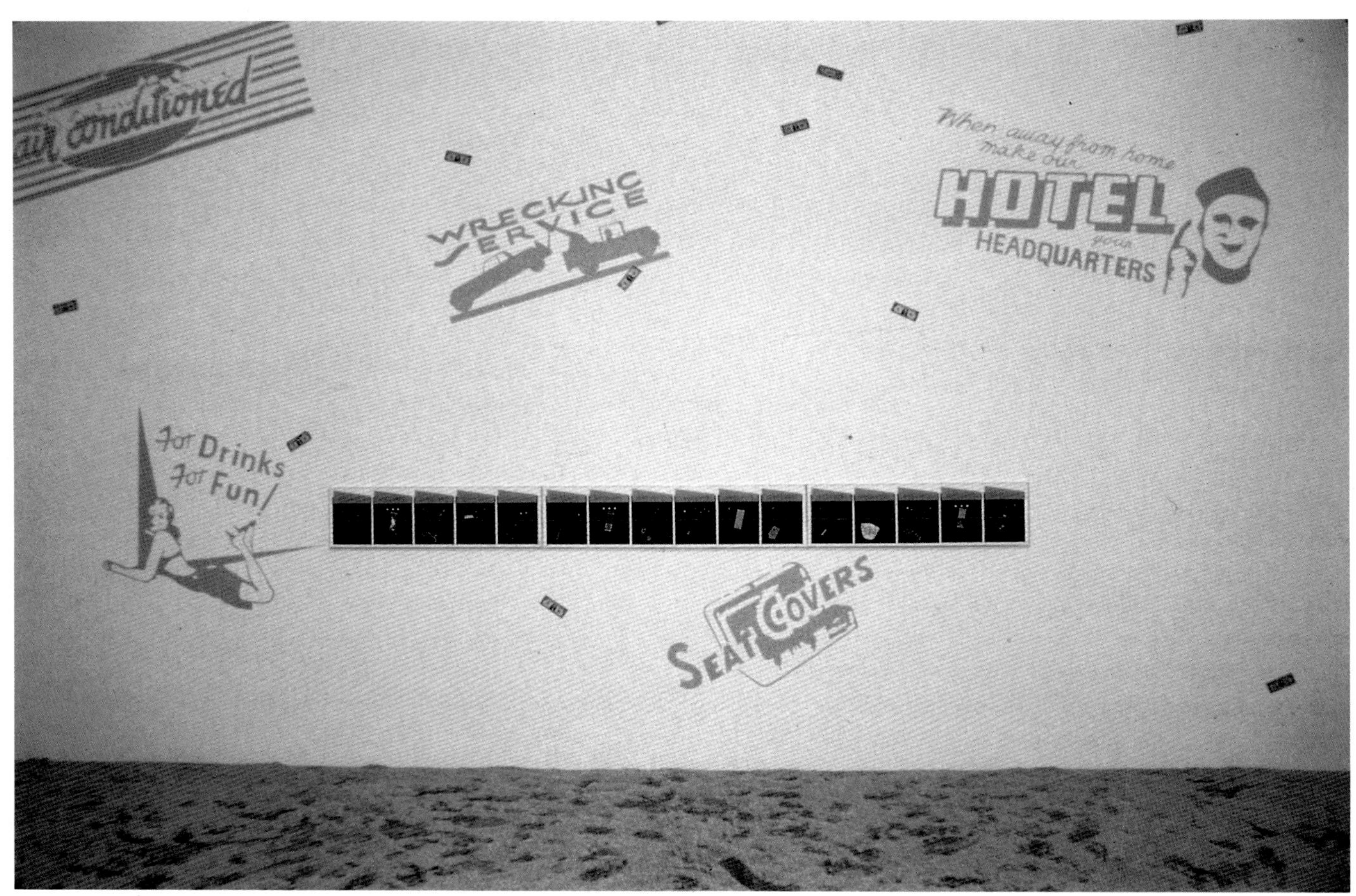

The somewhat more spare *Hello Hollywood* enshrines the roadside advertisements for Burma Shave that dotted America's roads until about thirty-five years ago. Each of the five, wood-framed parallelograms contains one line of the ditty, presented much like the sequential signs that characterized all Burma Shave advertisements. By spacing them across three contiguous walls on top of two rows of palm trees of decreasing height and proximity, Smith played on the steadily receding perspective experienced in driving. A bale of hay reinforces the rural setting of this kind of commercial literature, while infusing the space with the evocatively rich aroma of dried grass—far from the stale smell of Los Angeles.

Golden State, 1980
Mixed-media collage on sandpaper, three panels,
14×48; 14×57; 14×48 inches
Collection of Walker Art Center, Minneapolis;
Gift of Audrey Taylor Pretorius Gonzales, 1986

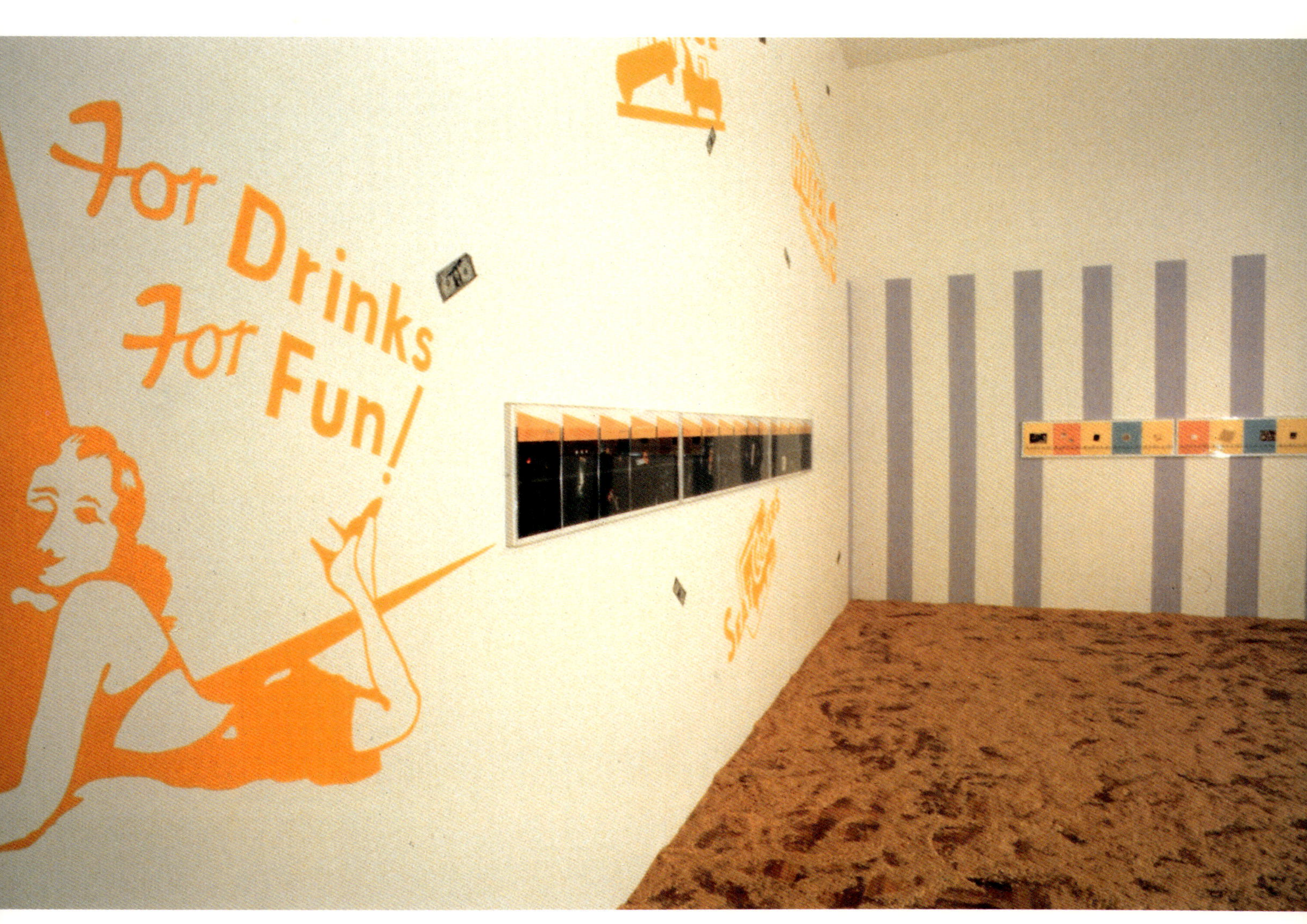

Installation view, 1980
Rosamund Felsen Gallery, Los Angeles

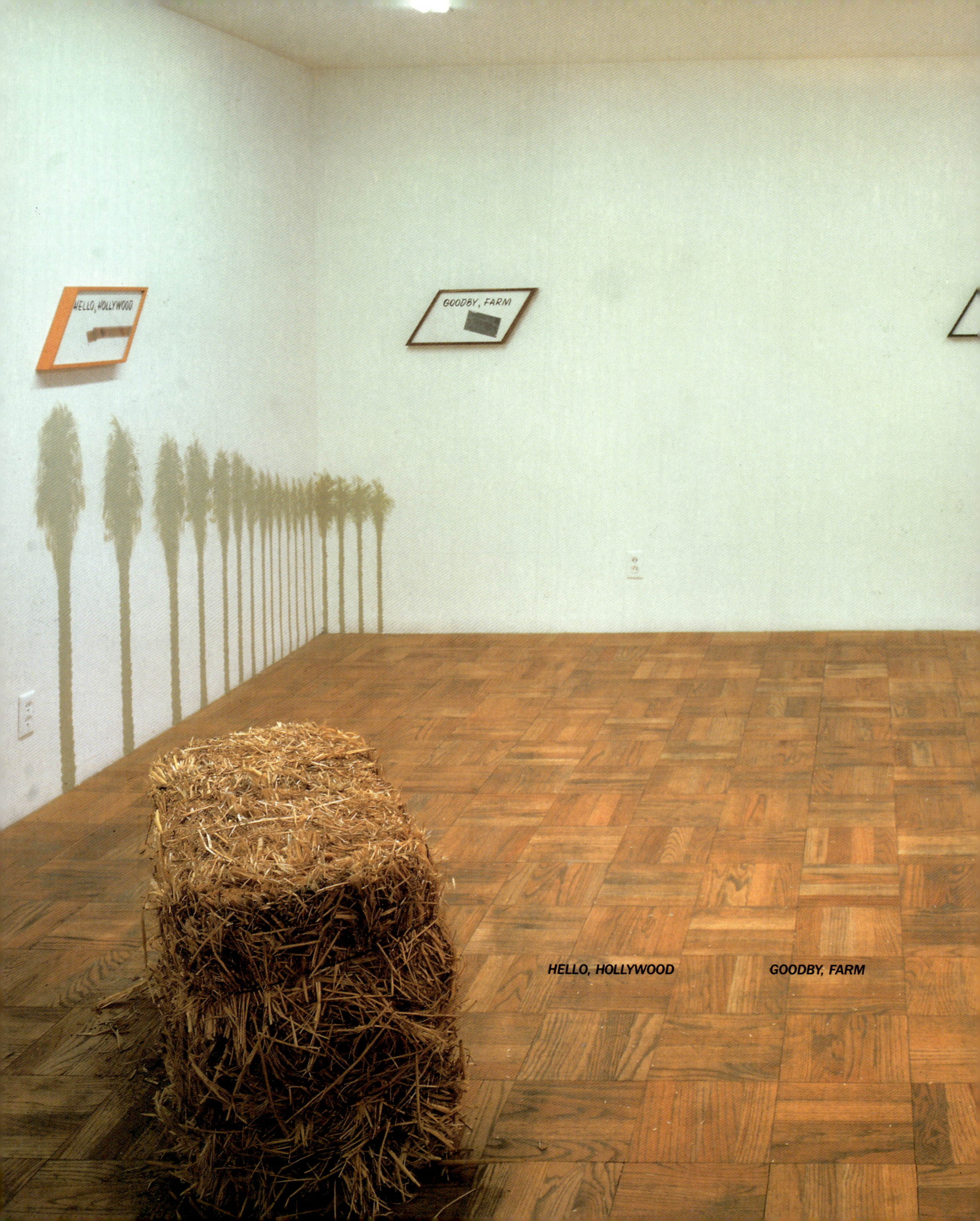

HELLO, HOLLYWOOD GOODBY, FARM

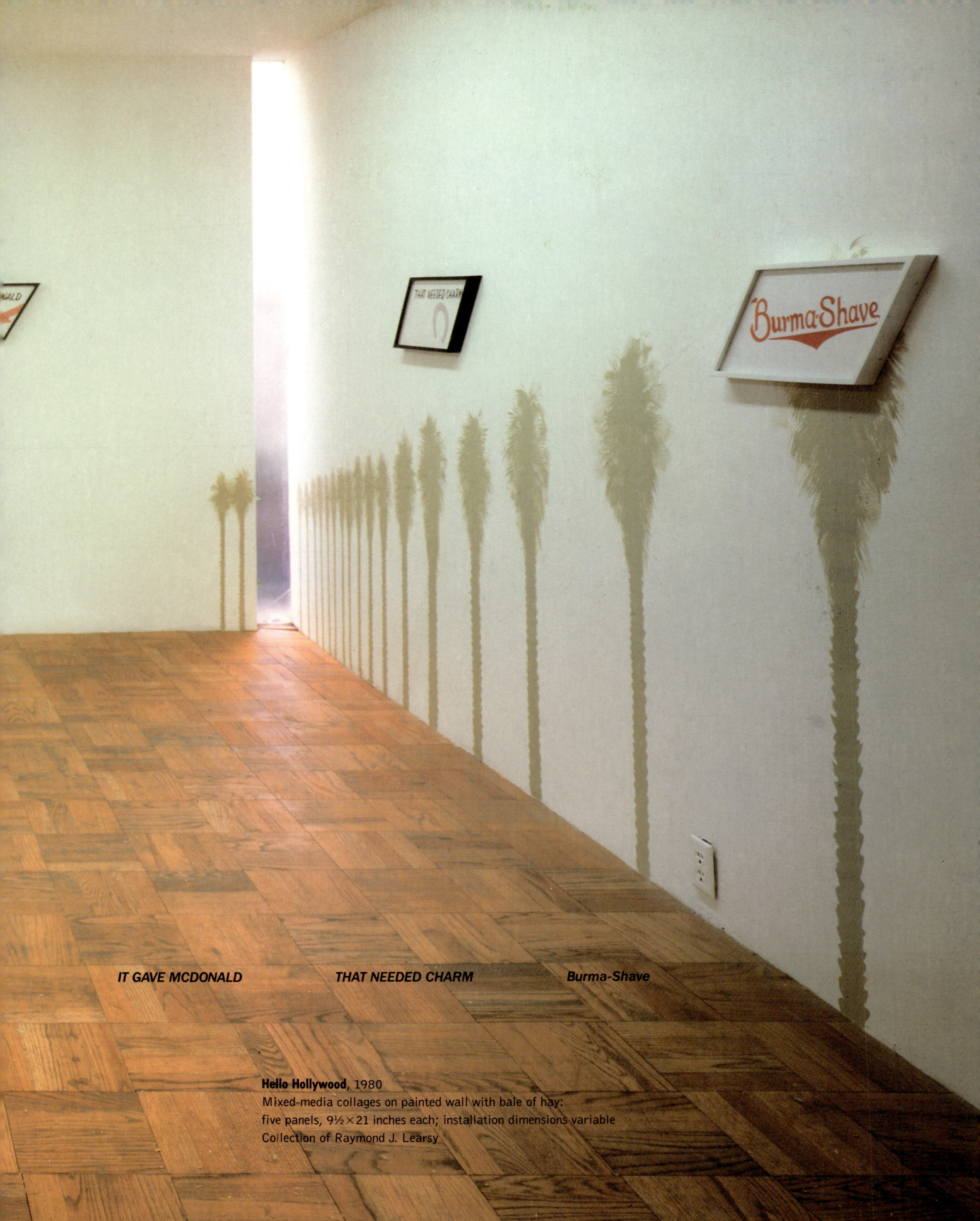

Hello Hollywood, 1980
Mixed-media collages on painted wall with bale of hay:
five panels, 9½ × 21 inches each; installation dimensions variable
Collection of Raymond J. Learsy

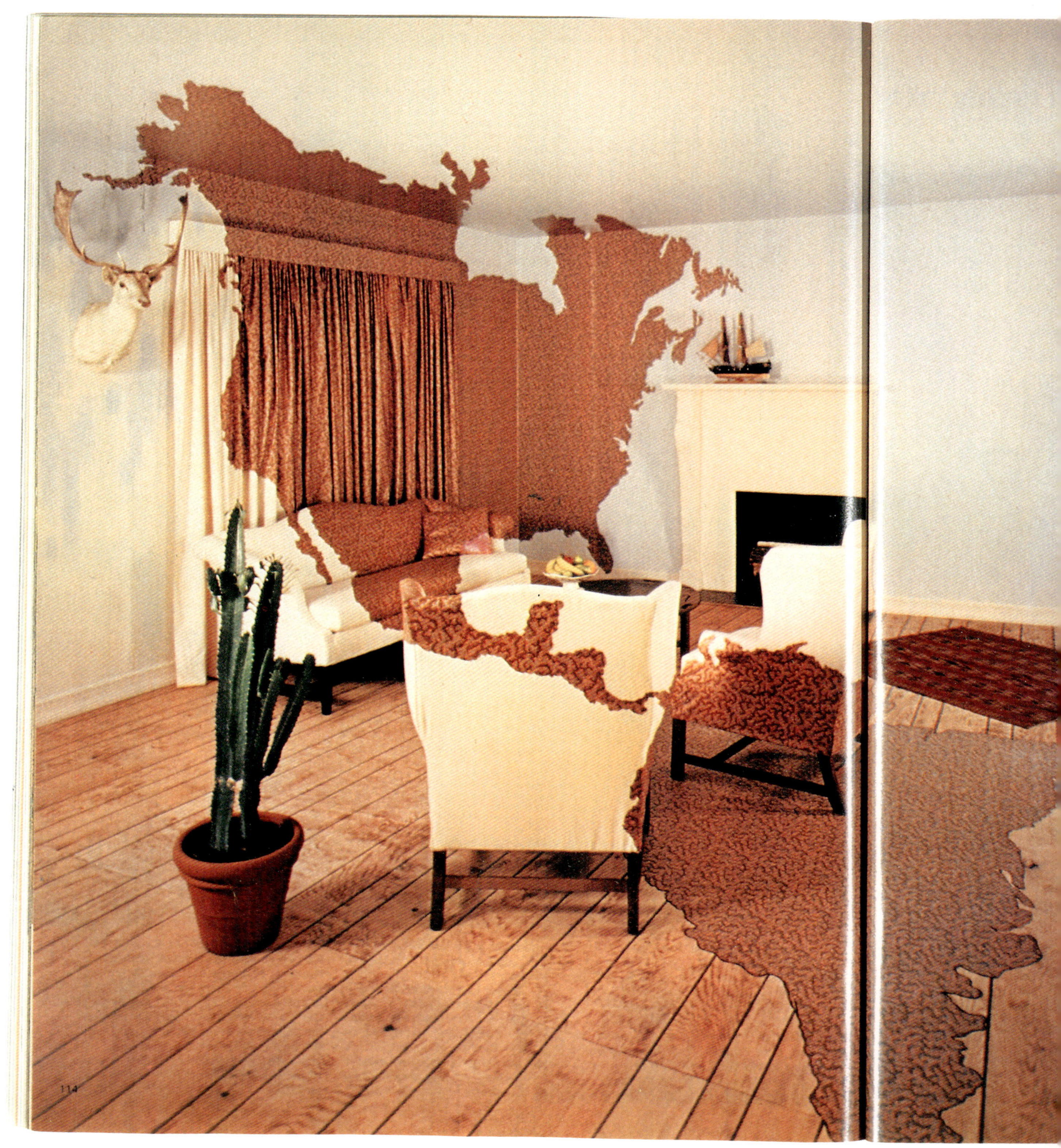

New World, 1980
Commissioned installation for *House & Garden*, Condé Nast studio, New York

REDISCOVERING AMERICA

Artist Alexis Smith creates a room for House & Garden that is both environmental sculpture and conceptual art, proving that the difference between reality and illusion depends above all on how we look at things

By Martin Filler

Editor: Carolyn Sollis

To look and to see are two very different things. The more familiar we are with something, the more likely we are to merely look at it. The less familiar we are with something, the more likely we are to *see* it. To demonstrate the difference between looking and seeing, and to dramatize the role that art can play in uniting those two states of vision, *House & Garden* has commissioned an unusual work, seen on these pages. Entitled *New World,* it was created by the young California artist Alexis Smith (no relation to the movie star of the same name), whose work has been seen in several museum exhibitions and one-woman gallery shows on both coasts.

Working in the Condé Nast Studio in New York (with the help of studio manager Joseph Staiano), Alexis Smith constructed a room that she terms a "perceptual-illusion installation with several levels of meaning." The components she used for this piece were as American as Mom's apple pie: a painted wooden mantel, a pair of wing chairs, a Chippendale-style camelback sofa, a butler's tray table, and wallpaper and cotton fabric in a matching floral print in bittersweet and sage. She added to those basics an unusual, but still typically American, group of accessories: an antique ship model, a stuffed deer head, a porcelain compote, a serape rug, a potted cactus, and a brocade pillow. All normal enough, except for what she did with them.

Over the surfaces of the room meanders a free-form flow of the matching fabric and wallpaper. The flowered cotton was cut and sewn onto the curtains, chairs, sofa, and pillow. The flowered paper was cut and pasted onto the walls, ceiling, and floor. Not in any old shape, though, as the artist explains. "I started out with the idea of a two-dimensional shape superimposed over a three-dimensional room, using the continuous texture of the fabric and wallpaper to underscore the spatial illusion," says Alexis Smith. "But I wanted the room itself and its contents to be rather conventional, so that people could immediately orient themselves. At first I sketched an abstract shape: Then after I thought about it, it looked very much like a map of some imaginary continent. It seemed to me that the dimensional illusion would be more intense if the shape were recognizable, one that is always perceived *(Continued on page 175)*

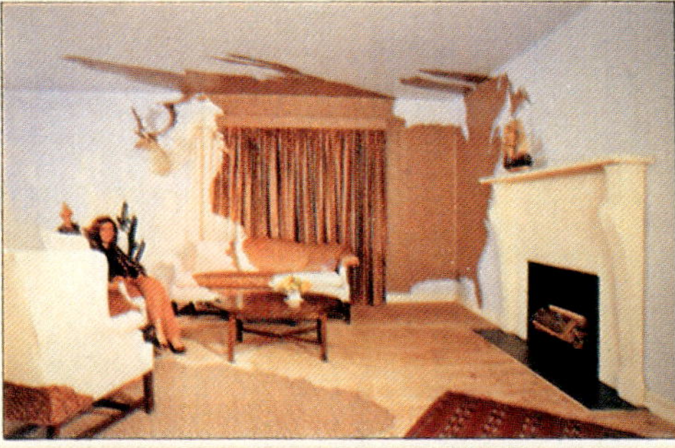

Now you see it, left, and now you don't, above. Illusion is visible from only one point; from other angles it disappears. Seated in room, above, is artist Alexis Smith.

Commissioned by Condé Nast to produce a project for its magazine *House & Garden,* Smith elaborated on the object-ground amplifications within her contemporaneous collages and their relationship to the surrounding space. She filled the empty room she had been given with a typical ensemble—wingback chairs, sofa, fireplace and mantel, drapes, throw rug, and table. A model ship on the mantel, a trophy head, a cactus, a pillow, and a compote with fruit make the room seem inhabited. Intricately superimposed over the ensemble is an outlined map of North and South America, rendered in a floral print sewn to the other fabric surfaces and in wallpaper pasted to the ceiling, walls, and floor. Although she originally conceived them as abstract forms, she quickly saw that maps of continents could evoke reveries of spatial dislocation. The map, unless seen from one fixed point, cannot be read intelligibly. Nor can one comprehend the precise location of the objects: the ship is sailing into Boston Bay; the trophy head is adjacent to Alaska, the cactus to the Southwest; a pink satin corner of the pillow is on top of New Orleans; and the fruit compote is sited by Cuba. The piece suited the static reality of photography and allowed Smith an amusing meditation on the nature of illusion. Her fascination with the two-dimensional world of *Flatland* had clearly borne fruit.

Stardust (1980) was the culmination of Smith's interest in performance, which in turn led to a dramatic change in her narrational collages. Her performances in the late 1970s centered around read-aloud tales. Taken from such sources as *The Thousand and One Nights*, these solo acts allowed Smith to share her genuine delight in the written word and to expose a playful, even exotic side of herself.

Smith's selection and rearrangement of someone else's writing in the collages can be thought of as a kind of ventriloquy. In this sense, *Stardust* reveals her willingness to project her ideas through the literal use of other voices, amalgamated from the words of many American authors. It is especially noteworthy for its disjunctive narrative, here in the form of short quotes from a wide range of sources. Subtitled "a recitation for eight voices," the piece was produced with Heidi Hardin, an art student Smith met while teaching at the University of California, San Diego, whose flatly rendered representational paintings were easily translated to set design. Smith melded quotations from sixteen American authors, including John Dos Passos, Thornton Wilder, Sinclair Lewis, Carson McCullers, and Nathaniel West, with snippets of such popular songs as "Bye Bye, Blackbird," "Sunny Side of the Street," and "Stardust." Eight characters spoke or sang sequentially, their lines building an impressionist mood rather than a story. Dos Passos' biographical comments about the modern dancer Isadora Duncan served as the keystone of this non-narrative about escaping society's confines and growing older and more disillusioned. Hardin painted thirteen flat, upright figures. Eight of them were headless in order to serve as painted two-dimensional costumes for the speakers. They were arranged in front of a backdrop painted to resemble the Jefferson Memorial and tree-lined Tidal Basin in Washington, D.C. Isadora Duncan was never mentioned by name, but her extravagant persona and death provoked commentary from the other characters. Smith's long disquisition on being American in the first half of this century focuses on various female roles: social arbiter, mother, daughter, dreamer, maid.

Amidst this lengthy historical recitation, a strain of clichés, hokum, repetitiveness, and skepticism, dilutes the sense of nostalgia. As in her collages, Smith does not long for the good old days. Rather, she disconnects and rearranges past and present so that time becomes associative rather than chronological.

As performed, the piece consciously recalled productions at community playhouses, complete with whispered cues and a cute little girl whose role was principally to smile at her adoring parents. Amateur values are reinforced by the cheerily painted backdrop and costumes—all evoking the props of old-fashioned itinerant photography. The script, concluding with the death of the unnamed Isadora Duncan, infers the inescapable tragedies of life. America may be a land of incomparable plenty—the character called the black lady emphatically proclaims as the piece opens, "Cheap motorcars, telephones, readymade clothes, silos, alfalfa, Kodaks, phonographs." But there is still sadness. The tension between what we have and who we are, a tension that may have propelled Isadora Duncan on her high-flying illusory trajectory, animates *Stardust*.

An aural collage, *Stardust* was Smith's sole script. It represented a new status for words as *objets trouvés*, as disconnected and fruitfully rejoined as Smith's objects had always been. As a mélange of voices, it augured a new approach to her use of found narrations, one more willful, freer, and more complex.

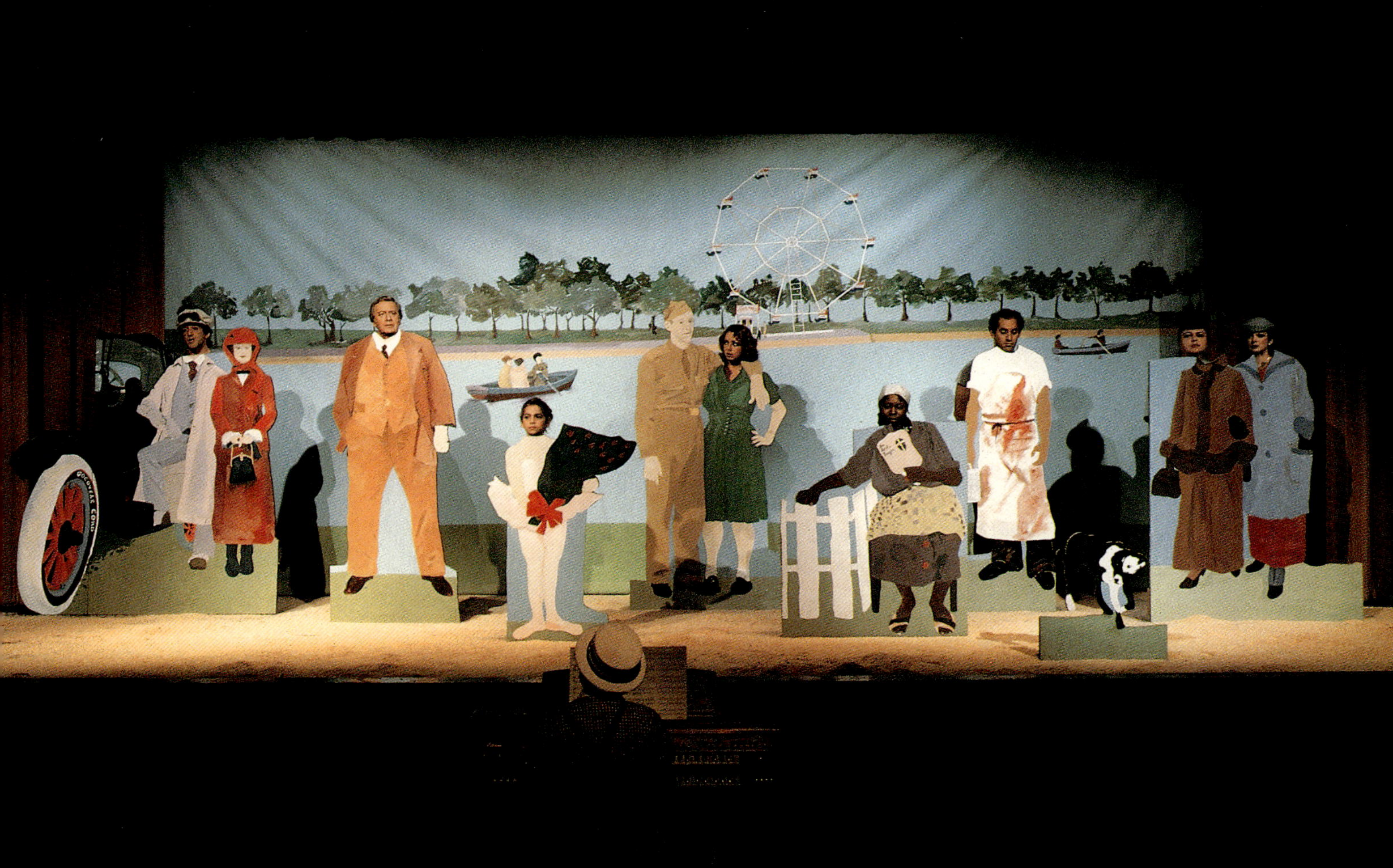

In *Stardust*, the performance Smith wrote and directed with dialogue from many sources, eight characters spoke and sang. The subject was Isadora Duncan, whose name was never spoken, but whose disillusionment served as a symbol for the culture. Smith identified the characters (from left to right): "the man at the wheel, the narrator, Isadora's effete confidant and biographer; historically, her brother, also a dancer"; "the landlord, the millionaire; the guilt-ridden false promiser, and manipulator of $ and minds, a spokesman for American free enterprise"; "the little girl, an aspiring ballerina with a tomboy side; idolizes Isadora Duncan, sometimes Isadora as a child"; "the sailor's girl; a naive, starry-eyed American dreamer, the central character, Isadora Duncan, generous and uninhibited"; "the black lady; Isadora's maid or nanny; her earthy, crude side; she shows great wisdom, humor, and wistful acceptance of reality"; "the butcher, a 'worker' with the soul of a poet, a veneer of callous humor covers his basic idealism, possibly a jilted lover"; "the society ladies, representing the attitudes of the American upper middle class, striving for culture and refinement, but basically Puritanical and unimaginative . . ."

Stardust, performance at Los Angeles County Museum of Art, 1982; originally performed at LACE, 1980

The high, boxy volume of Holly Solomon's gallery on West Broadway lent itself well to the panoramic installation Alexis Smith envisioned there in 1981. Entitled *U.S.A.*, it was filled with old musical lyrics and quotations from her wide-ranging readings of such early twentieth-century American authors as John Dos Passos, Thornton Wilder, Nathaniel West, and Sinclair Lewis. *U.S.A.* formed a visual counterpart to the spoken and sung *Stardust*, produced the year before.

For *U.S.A.*, Smith enriched the genre of wall paintings that had served as backdrops in her installation *Raymond Chandler's L.A.* of the previous year. She gave narrational order to the densely decorated space by constructing a white picket fence and arched trellis at the front of the gallery. Oriented to propel the visitor to the left, Smith's story began with collages that featured extracts from *Our Town* and *Main Street*. The trees and houses in this section, positioned on a ground painted to resemble the view from a small town, are seen in silhouette. A pitched roof and some simulated bricks bring this section to a close. The wooden stepladder in front of it is a direct reference to Wilder's notes for the scenery and props of his play; it could be also seen, metaphorically, as another of Smith's "stairways to the stars." At the far end of the room an ocean liner's giant smokestack marks the transition out of small-town America to an international stage—one symbolized by a pair of unfurled beach umbrellas and painted surf, the Riviera of the Lost Generation.

Smith's saga of Isadora Duncan, taken from Dos Passos and also a central motif in the performance *Stardust*, portrays the dancer's loss of innocence and dramatic death by strangulation when her scarf caught in the wheel of a friend's Bugatti.

The American saga of *U.S.A.* continues with a row of sequentially taller telephone poles and the bale of hay from *Hello Hollywood*—Smith's revival of a Burma Shave roadside advertisement that announced the accelerating migration of Americans from country to city. As if to epitomize that change, Smith's final collages—printed on aluminum sheets to reiterate their connection to the metal drums of printing presses—are situated on a gray grid that recalls columns of newspaper print. As the tone of Smith's quotations grows more ominous, so does her sited imagery: the leafy precincts of Anytown turn into the gridded anonymity of the tabloids. Her inquisition into prewar American identity reached its apogee in *U.S.A.* Henceforth, Smith dealt repeatedly with the loss of innocence, her own and society's—the myth of America that had suffused her youth.

U.S.A., 1981
Installation, Holly Solomon Gallery, New York

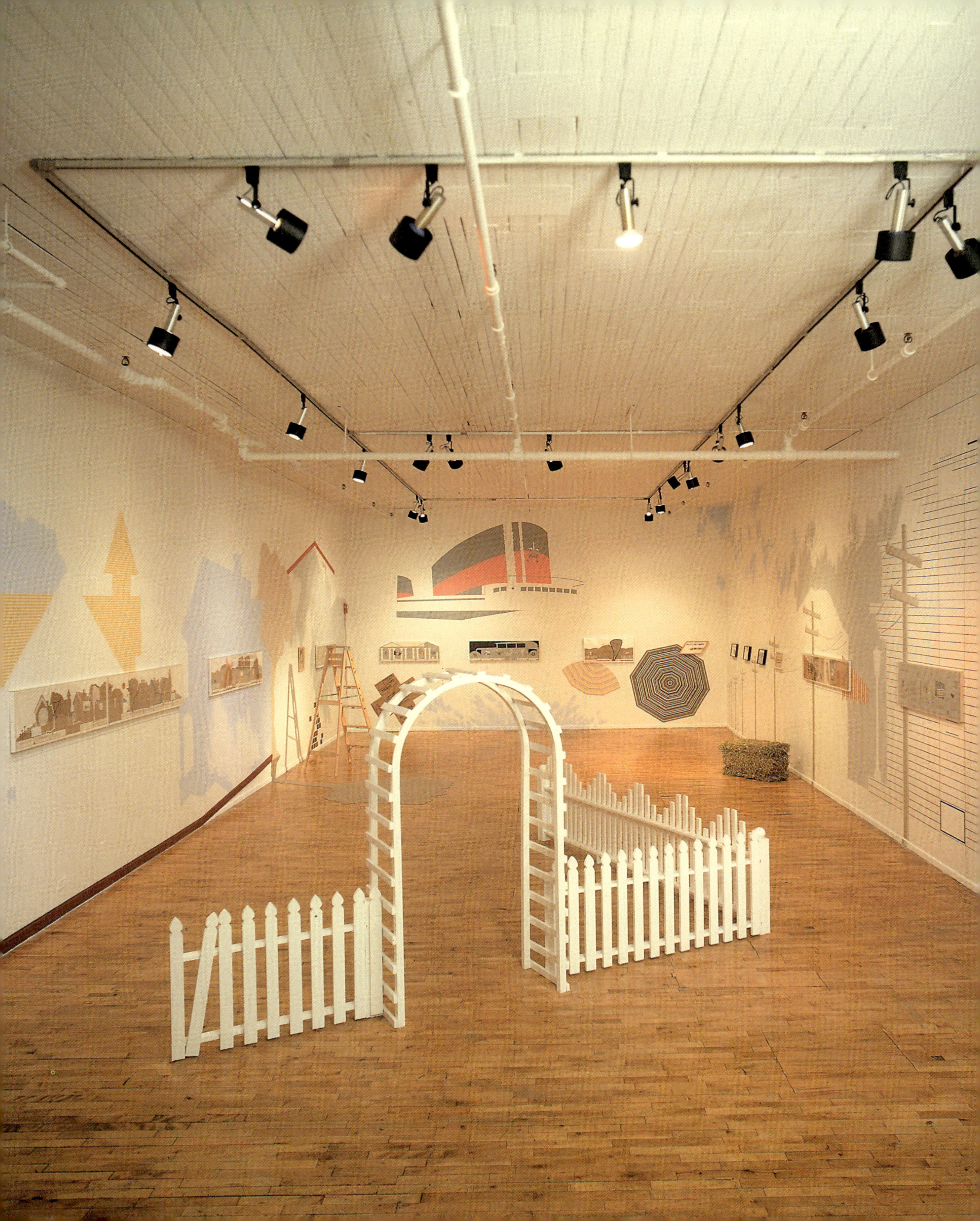

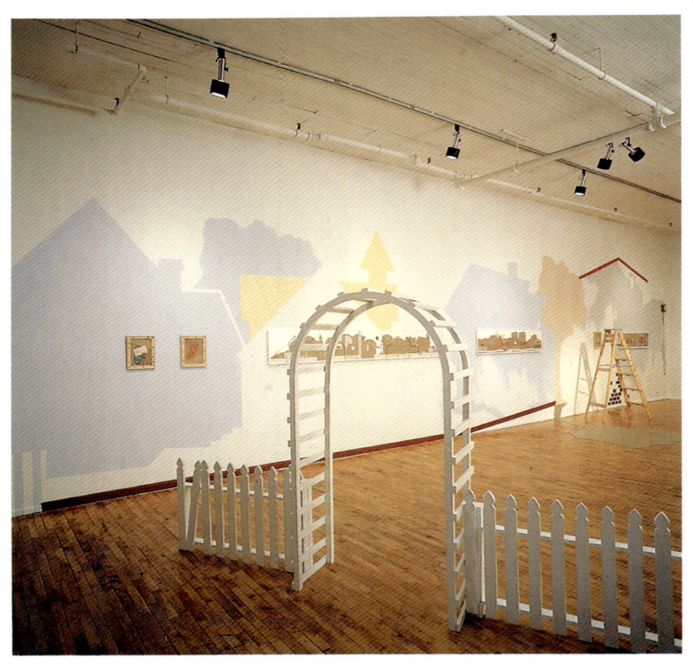

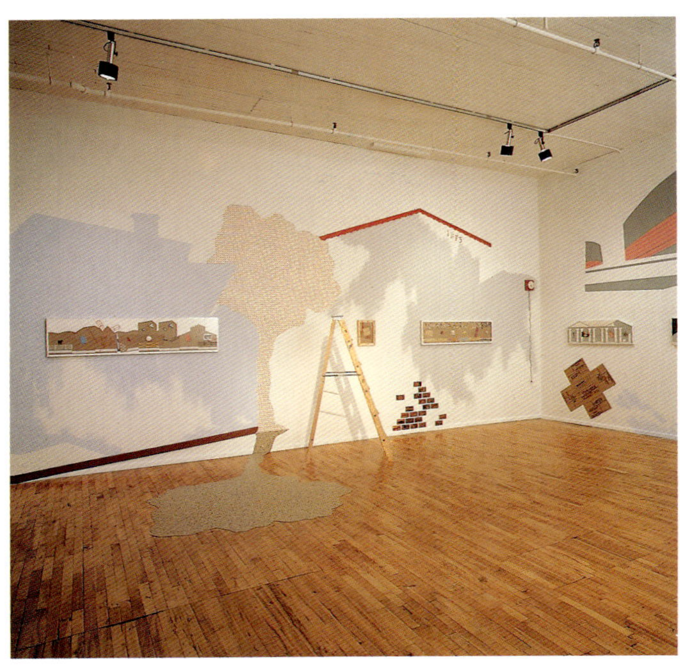

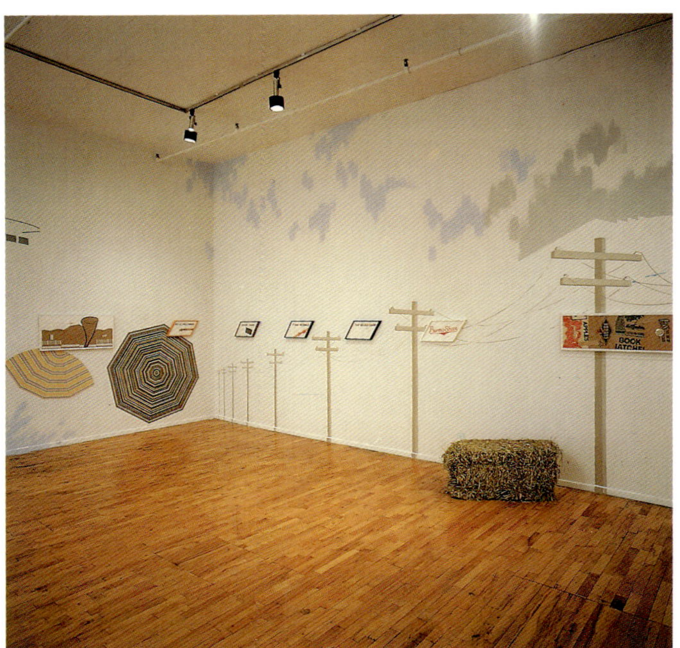

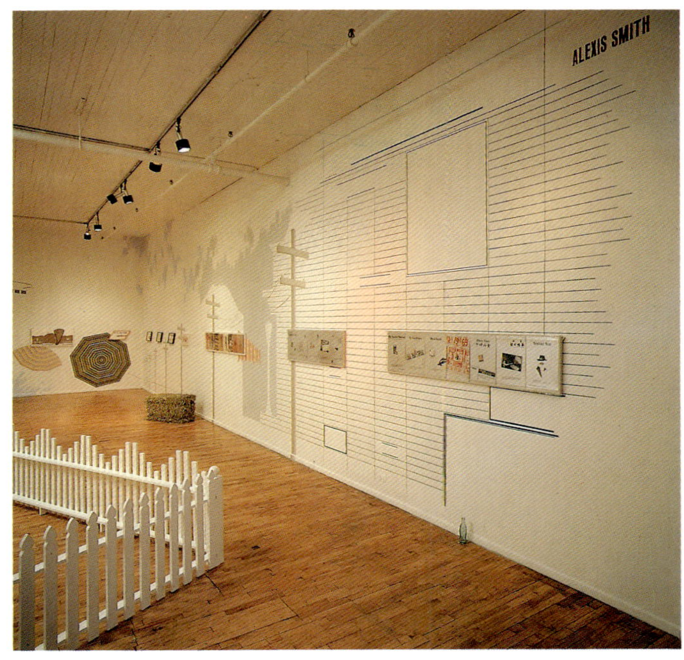
ALEXIS SMITH

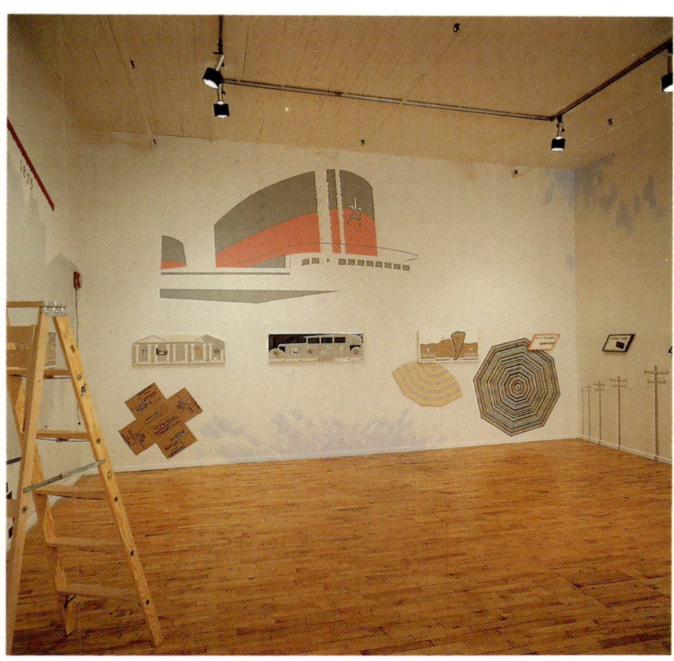

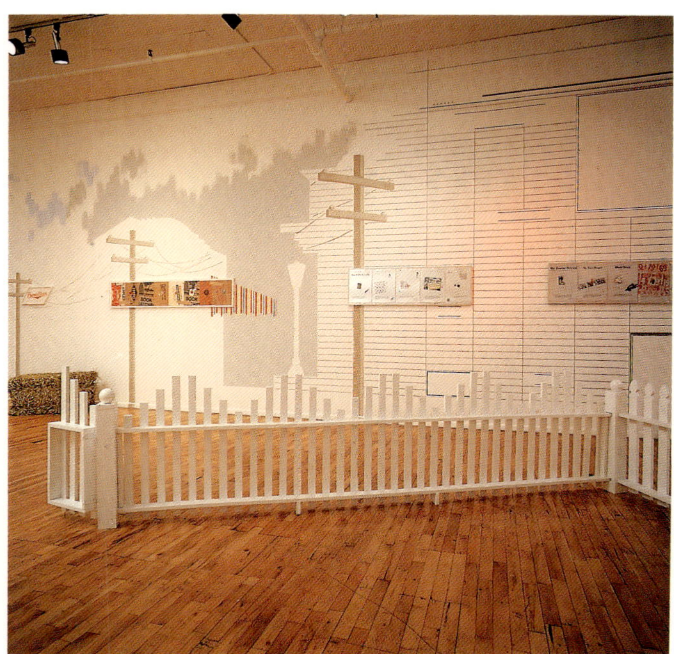

U.S.A., 1981

Composed of thirteen distinct collages, *U.S.A.* summarized Smith's search for an American voice through the writings of several early twentieth-century authors. Architecturally scaled wall paintings enhanced the mood of each of the smaller works, which grew progressively less optimistic from the left side of the room to the right. The picket fence and arch augmented the small-town aura of the first of the collages, "How Ya Gonna Keep 'Em Down on the Farm?," with its plaintively titled song lyrics. Other pieces quote from Thornton Wilder's *Our Town*. The far wall, dominated by an ocean liner's smokestack, tells of Isadora Duncan's rise and fall as described by John Dos Passos in *The Big Money*. A Burma Shave advertisement superimposed on telephone poles leads the viewer from the small town and Isadora to a city life of "mean streets." Hung above a tabloidlike grid, "The American Way" features aluminum plate pages topped by various newspaper mastheads. They serve as background for the dispirited monologue of a walker in the city.

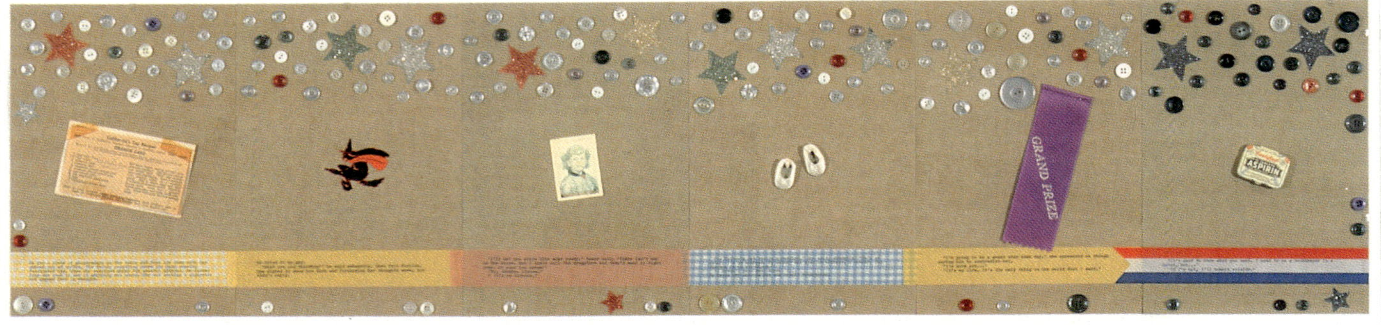

He put a plate of gingersnaps on the table and she ate them with her second cup of coffee. The dainty crunching sound she made chewing fascinated him.

When she remained quiet for several minutes, he turned from the sink to see if anything was wrong. She was smoking a cigarette and seemed lost in thought.

He tried to be gay.

"What are you thinking?" he said awkwardly, then felt foolish.

She sighed to show how dark and foreboding her thoughts were, but didn't reply.

"I'll bet you would like some candy," Homer said. "There isn't any in the house, but I could call the drugstore and they'd send it right over. Or some ice cream?"

"No thanks, please."

"It's no trouble."

"My father isn't really a peddler," she said, abruptly. "He's an actor. I'm an actress. My mother was also an actress, a dancer. The theatre is in our blood."

"I haven't seen many shows. I . . ."

He broke off because he saw that she wasn't interested.

"I'm going to be a star someday," she announced as though daring him to contradict her.

"I'm sure you . . ."

"It's my life. It's the only thing in the whole world that I want."

"It's good to know what you want. I used to be a bookkeeper in a hotel, but . . ."

"If I'm not, I'll commit suicide."

Stardust, 1980
Mixed-media collage, 12 × 60 inches overall
Collection of Martin Sklar

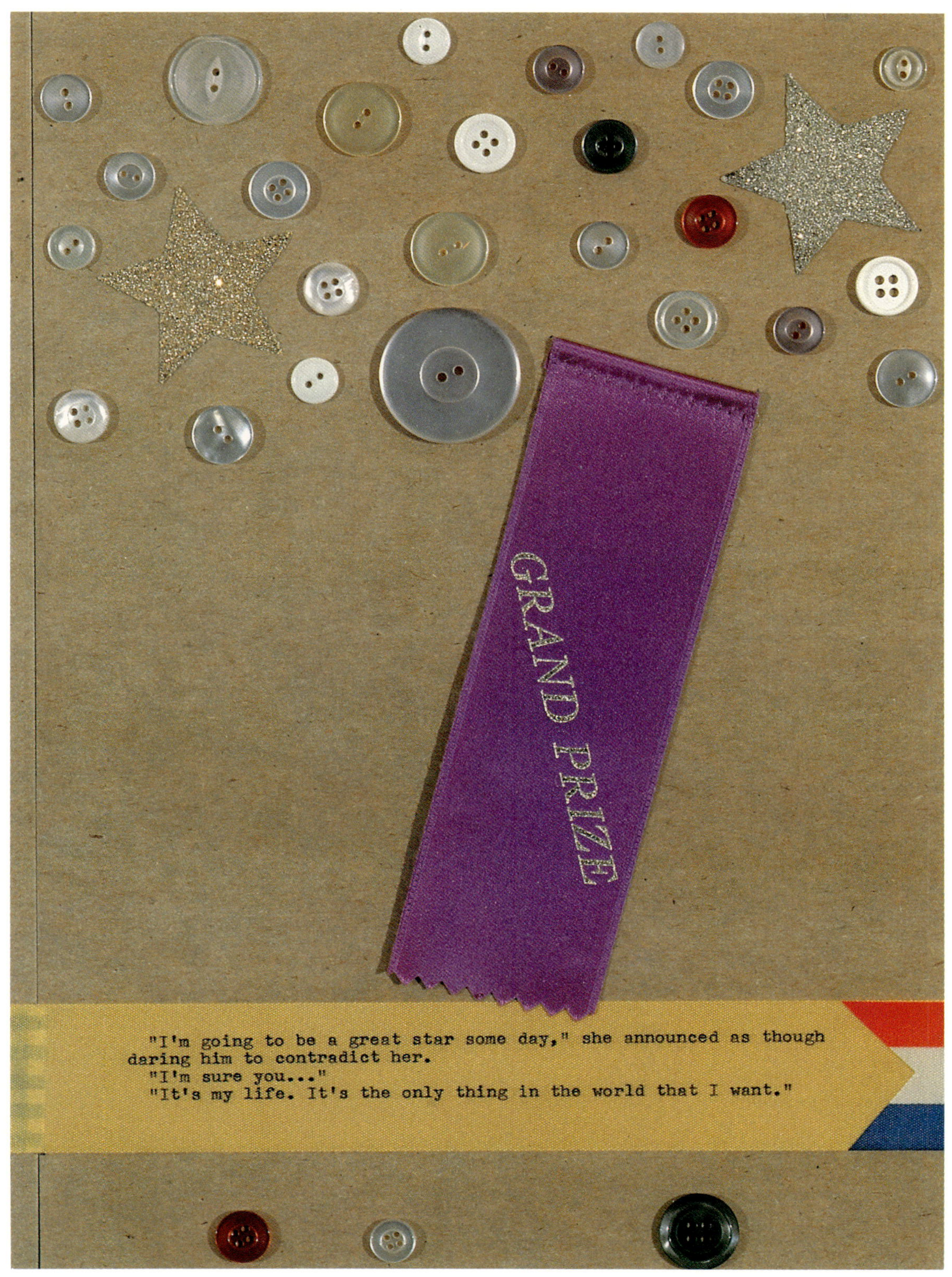
GRAND PRIZE
"I'm going to be a great star some day," she announced as though daring him to contradict her.
"I'm sure you..."
"It's my life. It's the only thing in the world that I want."

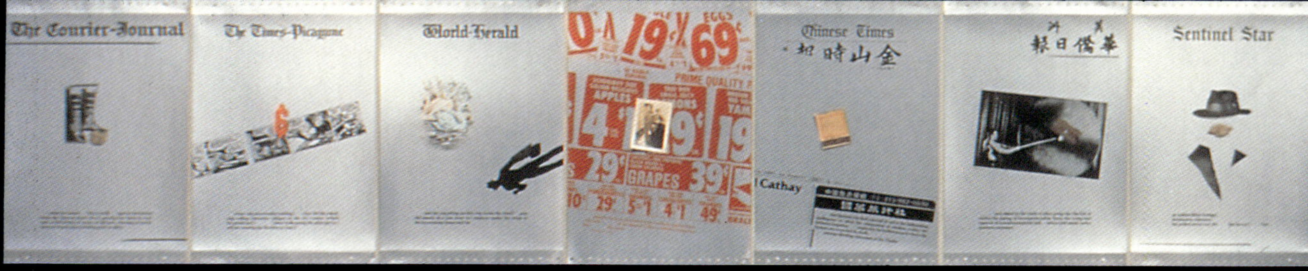

better the streets first a stroll uptown downtown
along the wharves under the el peering into faces in taxicabs
at the drivers of trucks at old men chewing in lunchrooms
at drunk bums drooling puke in alleys

what's the newsvendor reading? what did the elderly
wop selling chestnuts whisper to the fat woman behind the
pickle jars? where is she going the plain girl in a red
hat running up the subway steps?

and the cop joking another cop across the street? and
the smack of a kiss from two shadows under the stoop of the
brownstone house and the

grouchy faces at the streetcorner suddenly gaping black
with yells at the thud of a blow a whistle scampering
feet the event?
tonight now

but instead you find yourself (if self is the bellyaching
malingerer so often the companion of aimless walks) the
job hunt forgotten neglected the bulletinboard where the
futures are scrawled in chalk
among nibbling chinamen at the Thalia

ears dazed by the crash of alien gongs the chuckle of
rattles the piping of incomprehensible flutes the swing and
squawk of ununderstandable talk otherworld music antics
postures costumes

an unidentified stranger
destination unknown
hat pulled down over the has he any? face

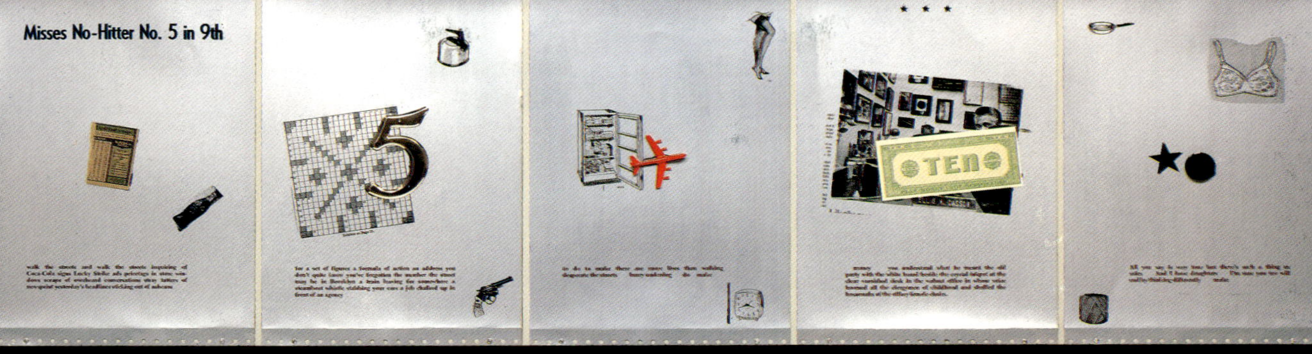

walk the streets and walk the streets inquiring of
Coca-Cola signs Lucky Strike ads pricetags in store windows
scraps of overheard conversations stray tatters of
newsprint yesterday's headlines sticking out of ashcans

for a set of figures a formula of action an address you
don't quite know you've forgotten the number the street
may be in Brooklyn a train leaving for somewhere a
steamboat whistle stabbing your ears a job chalked up in
front of an agency

to do to make there are more lives than walking
desperate the streets hurry underdog do make

money you understand what he meant the old
party with the white beard beside the crystal inkpot at the
clear varnished desk in the walnut office in whose voice
boomed all the clergymen of childhood and shrilled the
hosannahs of the offkey female choirs.

All you say is very true but there's such a thing as
sales And I have daughters I'm sure you too will
end by thinking differently make

The American Way, 1980
Mixed-media collage on aluminum printing plates, 16 × 52 inches
Margo Leavin Gallery, Los Angeles

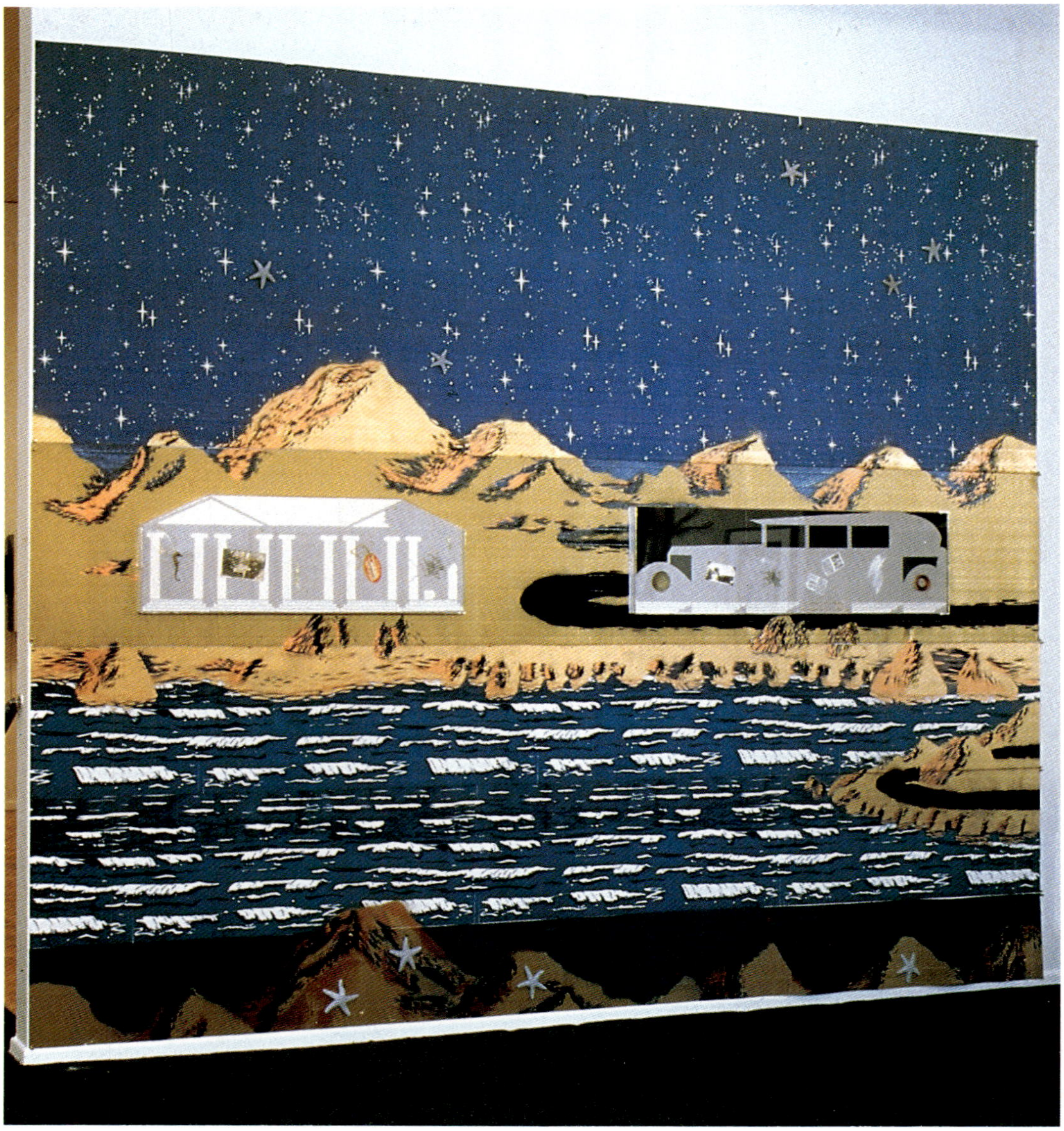

Portable backdrop for **Isadora**, 1981, painted corrugated paper, 10 × 12 feet

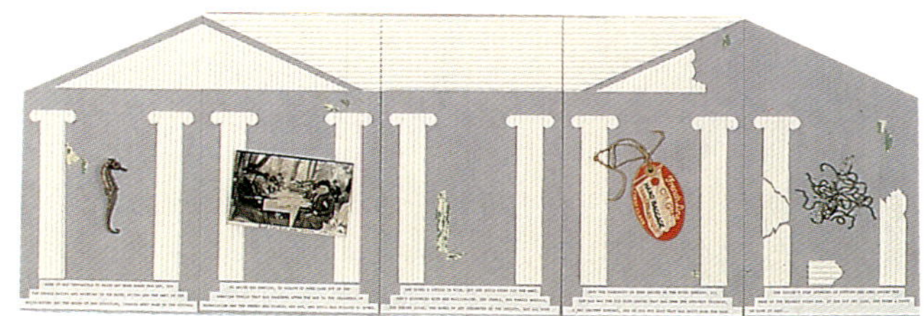

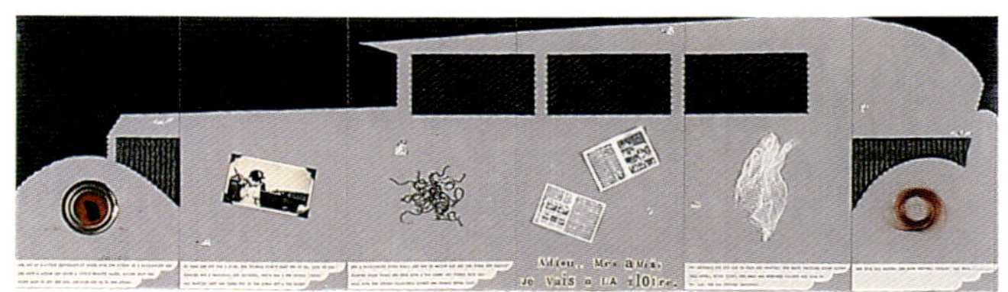

Isadora, Part 1 and Part 2, 1980
Mixed-media collage, two panels,
14¼ × 41½; 14⅛ × 48¾ inches
Collection of Holly Solomon

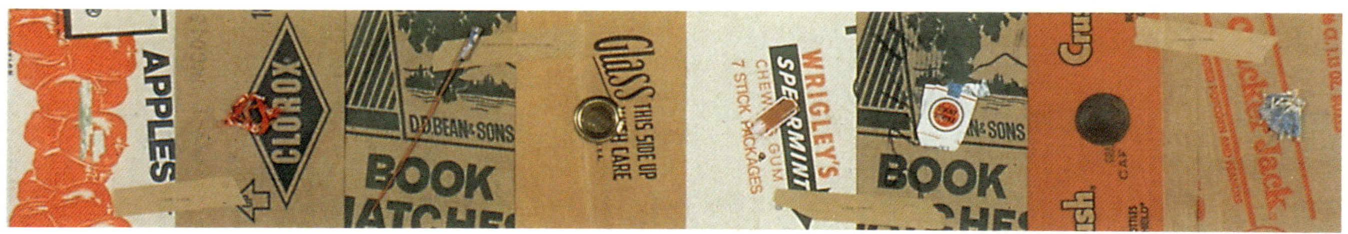

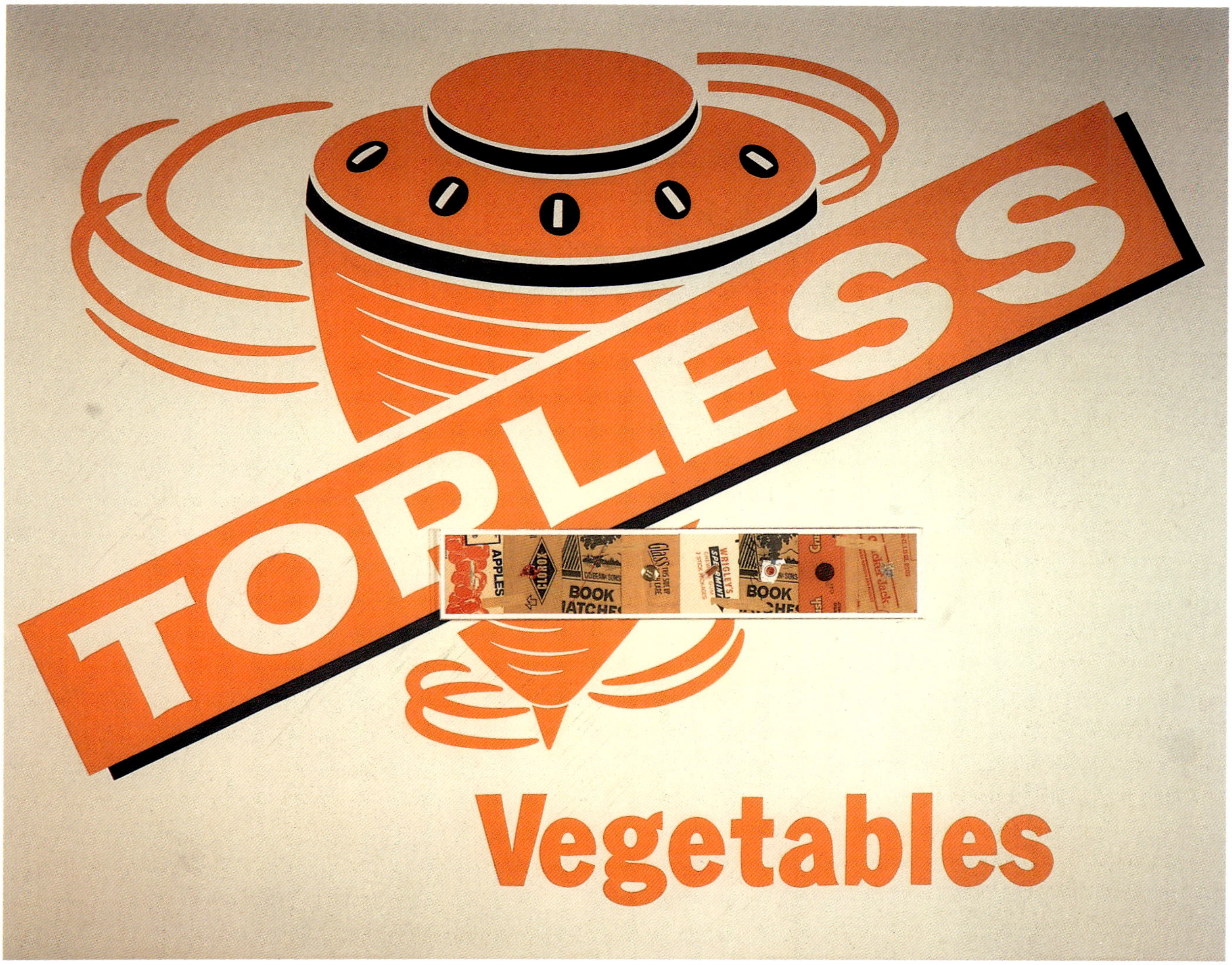

Cannery Row, 1980
Mixed-media collage, 13½ × 70 × 1½ inches
Collection of Anne and William J. Hokin

Installation view, 1986, The Museum of Contemporary Art, Los Angeles

Although now known as *Porgy and Bess*, Smith's original title for this work was *The Promised Land (Porgy and Bess)*—a title that makes evident her caustic analysis of the plight of blacks in America. Smith produced a collaged narrative, using stage directions from the play *Porgy and Bess* as well as actual quotes from the eponymous opera. The result is an enormous dialogue that runs across the piece and serves as a backdrop for the objects. Four panels, each thirteen pages wide, tell the tale of life on Catfish Row in Charleston, South Carolina. Gambling, cheating, and killing among the blacks mirror their oppression at the hands of whites. Bess' only comfort is her love for Porgy. When he is unjustly charged with murder and taken away by the police for trial, Bess succumbs to the entreaties of the local drug dealer, who offers her "happy dust" and lures her to New York. Away from Porgy and loved ones, her life is doomed. The two long panels that tell the tale were hung on opposing walls in this installation, the first over an illusionistically rendered 50-foot-long piano keyboard. A few stray courses of fake bricks anchor the image to the floor, as does a terra-cotta pot of plastic greenery. The calico paper used in some panels of the collage decorates a few feet of the juncture of the opposing wall, punctuated by a framed panel declaring "Intermission" and a painted anchor resting on the floor. The second long panel was hung over another painted version of the ocean liner smokestack from the Isadora Duncan passage of *U.S.A.* of the same year. Musical notes cut out of linoleum affixed to the floor complete the operatic *mise-en-scène* Smith sought.

Though the material circumstances were very different, Bess' plight was no less tragic than Isadora's. With this piece Smith finished her visual cycle of Americana, all of it in a mythic "prehistory" before 1950, and much of it far from Los Angeles.

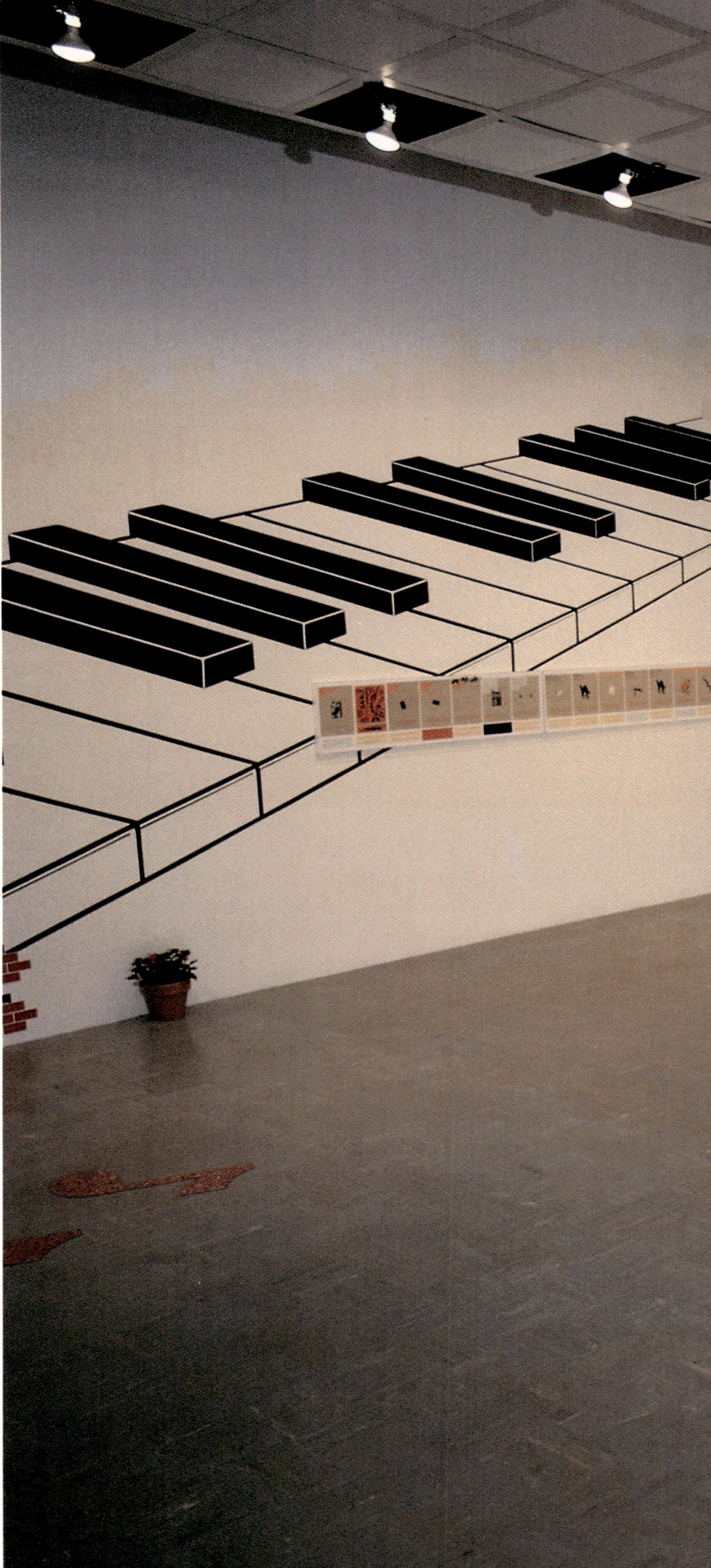

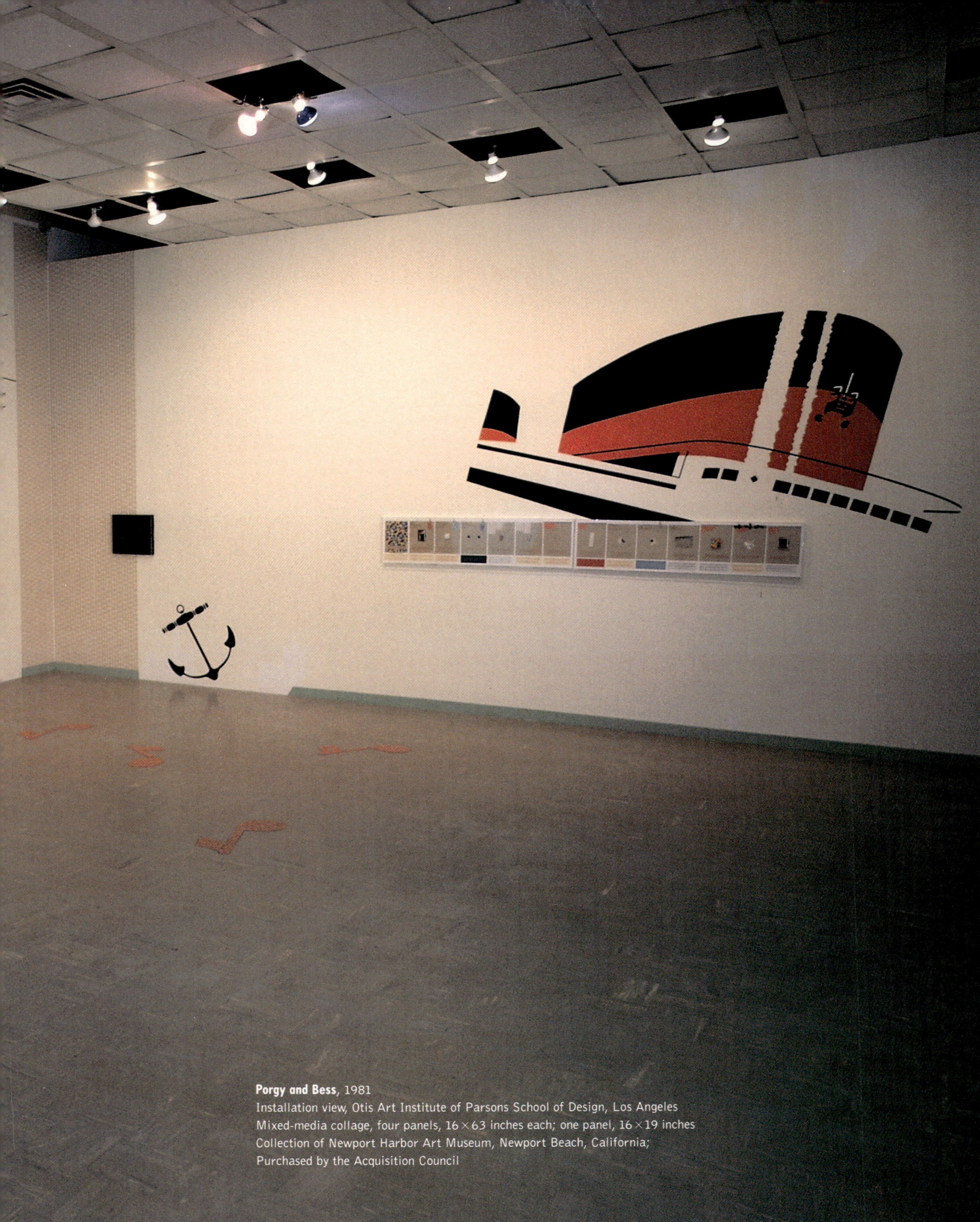

Porgy and Bess, 1981
Installation view, Otis Art Institute of Parsons School of Design, Los Angeles
Mixed-media collage, four panels, 16 × 63 inches each; one panel, 16 × 19 inches
Collection of Newport Harbor Art Museum, Newport Beach, California;
Purchased by the Acquisition Council

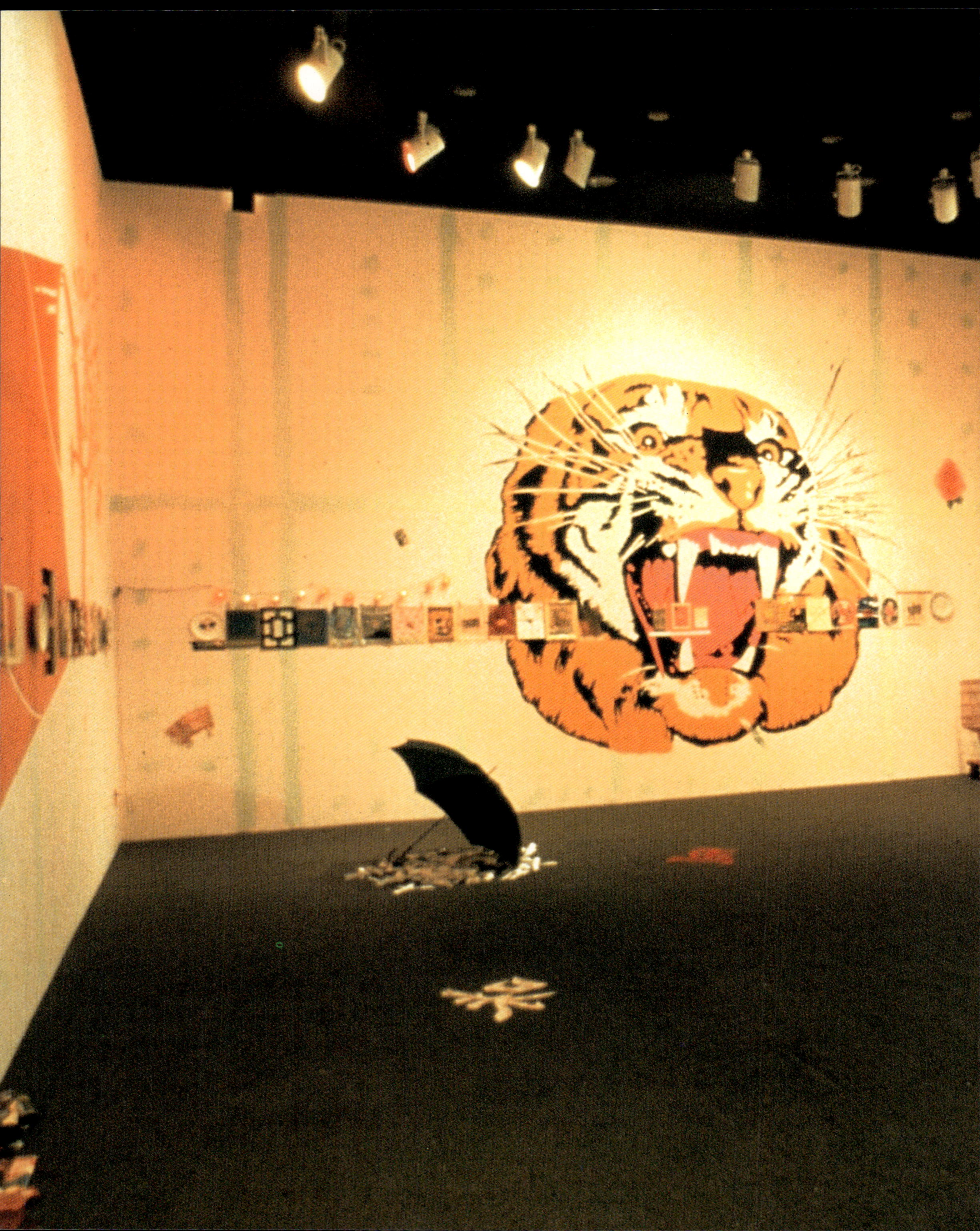

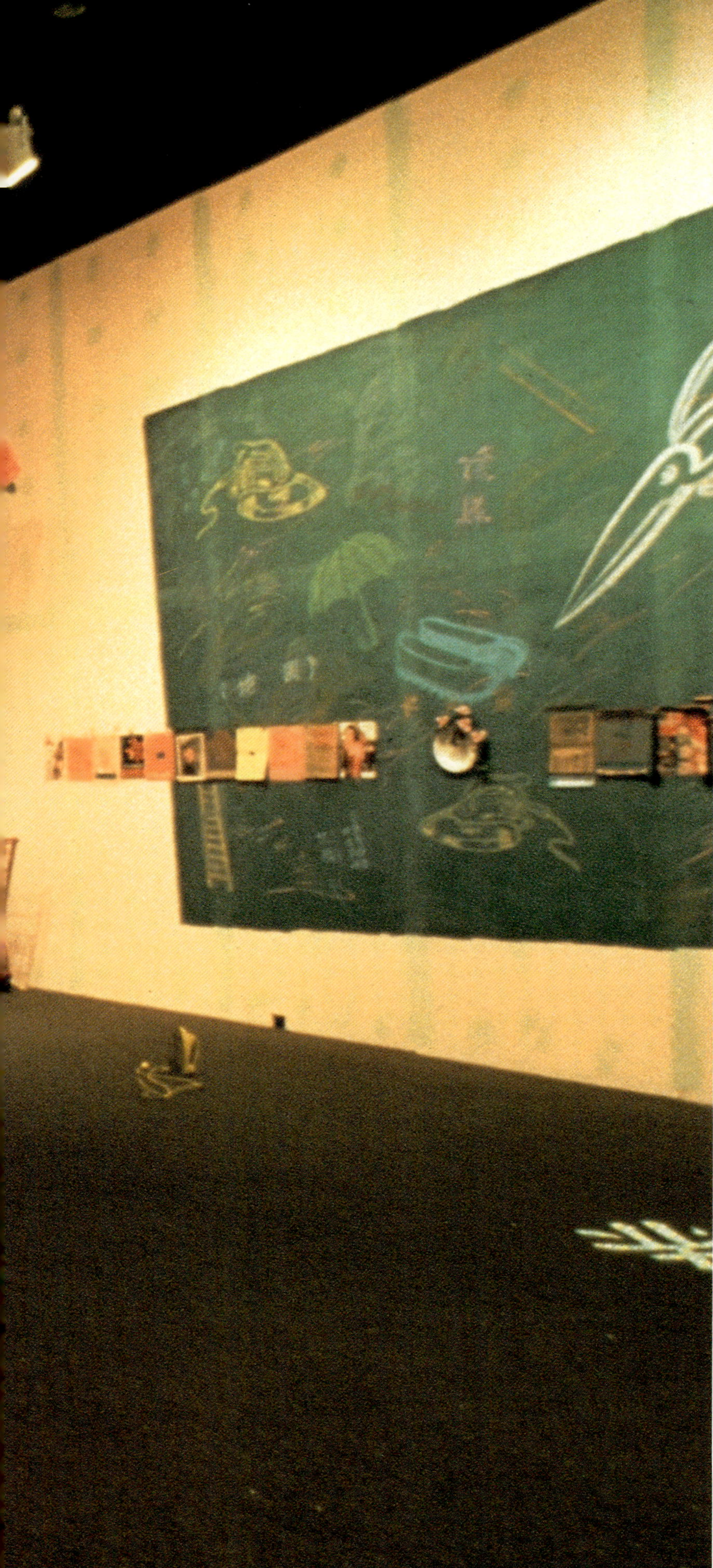

Conceived for the 1981 exhibition "The Museum as Site: Sixteen Projects" at the Los Angeles County Museum of Art, Smith's *Cathay* constituted an exotic and exuberant counterpoint to such contemporaneous installations of American subject matter as *U.S.A.* and *Porgy and Bess*. The largest, most graphically bold, and least literary of her site-specific works, *Cathay* represented another kind of constructed identity—an Occidental one for the Orient. Built to Smith's specifications, the rectangular walls of the space were painted pale pink. Nail heads and taped joints were patched and embellished with green-tinted spackling compound. The result was an overall pattern, something like an abstracted domino, that set up a frenzied visual atmosphere. Looking through the circular entry, itself framed in open red lattice, one saw a giant tiger's head, with fangs bared. On opposing side walls, Smith painted a huge red lighted firecracker and an enormous green chalkboard crowded with sketches of such items as a teapot, an umbrella, a pair of shears, a ladder, and an iron. Chinese-looking ideograms floated among the domestic subjects, inferring a narrative. Hanging at mid-level across these three walls were long stretches of collages, all roughly 12×10 inches. Not framed, and hanging loosely on the wall from their tops only, they were unusually ephemeral collages, even for Smith. Using an array of sources—ads, newspaper pages, and bits of printed fabric—she reinforced the Oriental flavor of the larger imagery. Single mounted ceramic plates, a pun on "china," punctuated the lateral strings of collages. Each of the collages contained Smith's quoted narrations, usually as a strip of paper affixed at the bottom. In

Cathay, 1981
Installation, Los Angeles County Museum of Art

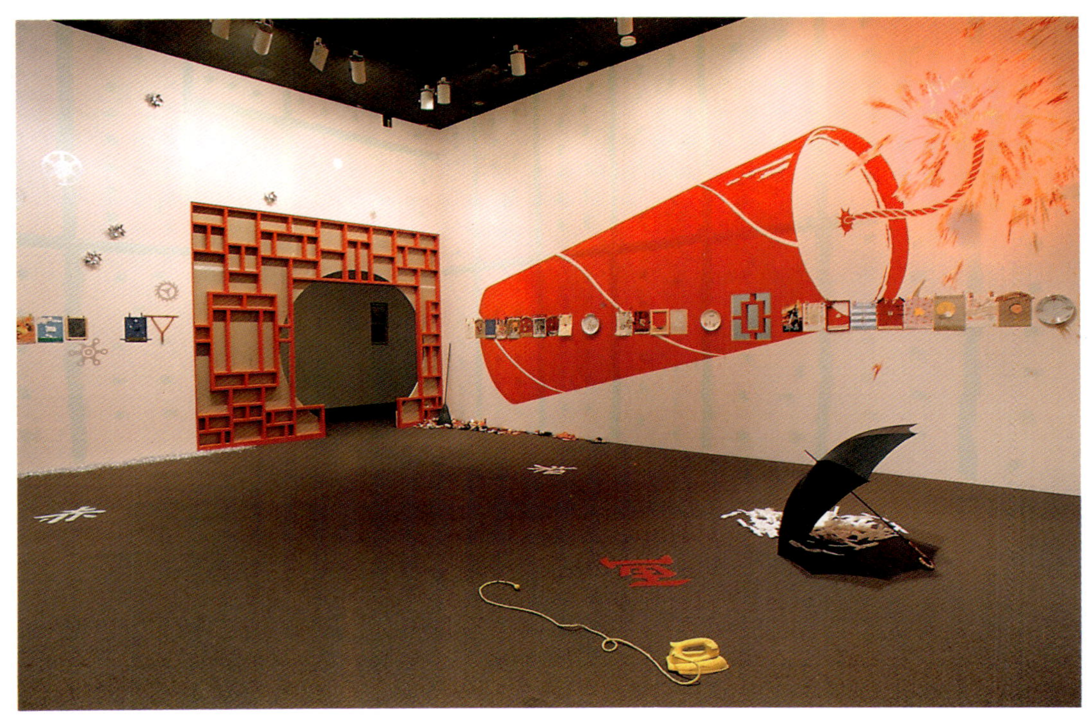

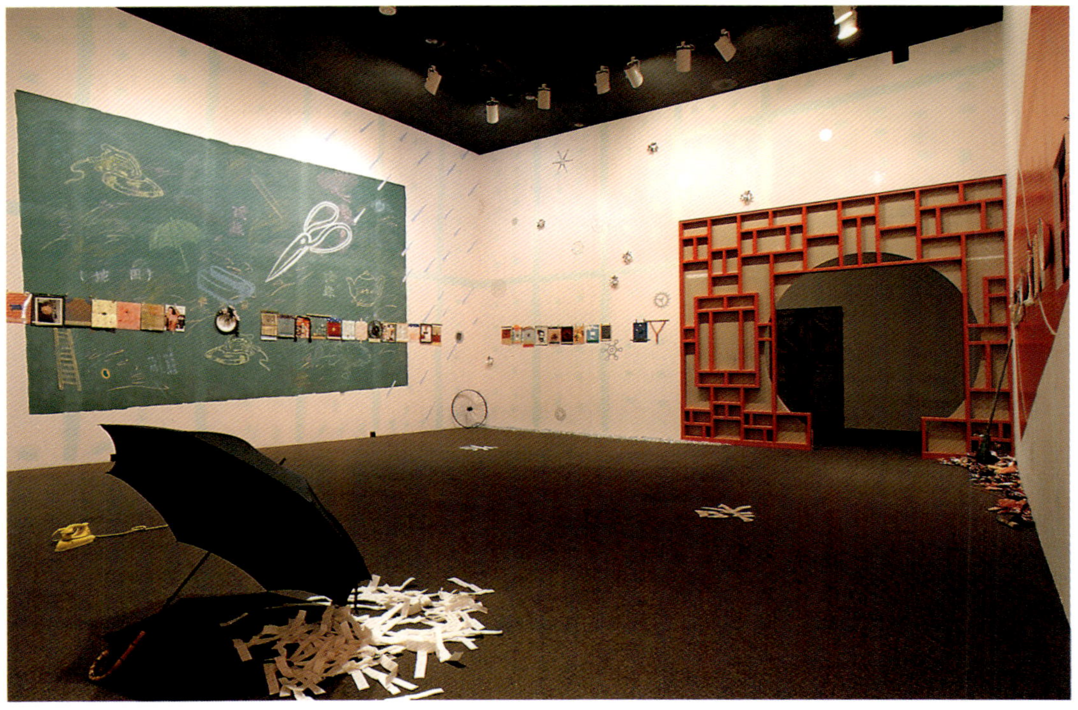

Cathay, 1981

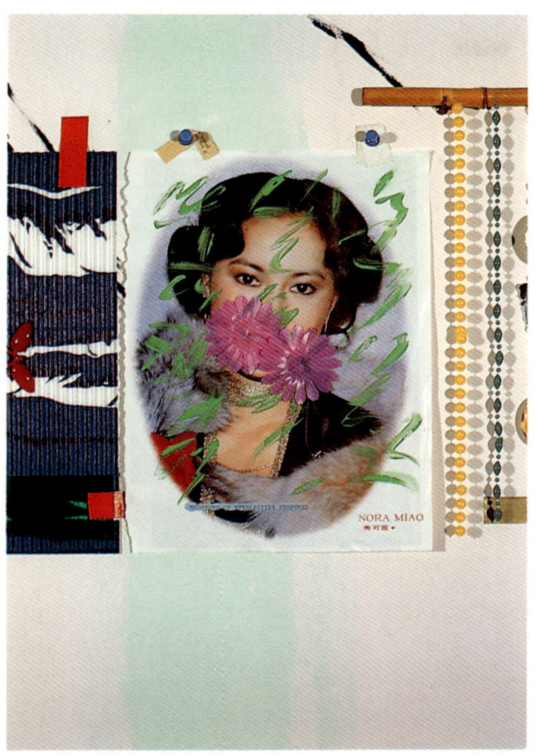

Cathay, 1981
Mixed-media collage, 1 of 72, 12 × 10 inches

this case, she chose passages from *The Good Earth*, *La Chinoise*, Charlie Chan novels, *Shanghai Express*, various how-to-read Chinese manuals, propaganda from contemporary China, and fortune cookie sayings. The juxtaposition of these various voices yielded a gently cacophonous poem, nonsensical in its narrative elisions, that recalled the performance *Stardust*. As in *Stardust*, narrations were repeated, echoing themselves. The disjunctiveness of the words and their small physical presence as strips of paper ultimately negated their significance in the word-image symbiosis previously so important to Smith's work. As if to underscore this demotion, the text in one collage advises, "Once you've caught the meaning, you can forget the words."

In an unusual move into the gallery space, Smith placed a shopping cart, an open umbrella atop a heap of printed fortunes, an iron, a pile of spent fireworks, an iron wheel, and plastic Chinese characters on the floor of the gallery to physically amplify references in the collages and the underlying murals. These three categories of imagery—murals, collages, and junk—so overwhelmed the space that the installation essentially became an extra-literary experience. Smith's appetite for allusion had compelled her to employ painting, collage, and, for the first time, assemblage.

The sayings from fortune cookies or the odd line from a Chinese propaganda booklet signaled Smith's new interest in cliché, while the eclectic range of sources pointed to her new tolerance (previously confined to song lyrics) for non-literary writing. The central paradox of *Cathay* was that from title to contents it concerned a place that exists only in the imagination of the West. In synthesizing a spectrum of cultural clichés, Smith had built a shrine to longing.

Parts of Cathay were reassembled for an installation at The Clocktower, New York, in early 1982, under the title *Chinese Junk*. The piece saluted Cathay's East Coast counterparts a few blocks away in Chinatown. An extract from *Shanghai Express*—"I can't replace our ideals, but I'll buy you a new watch when we get to Shanghai"—was written on the wall and served as a leitmotif for this smaller installation. It spoke for Smith's new attitude toward disillusionment and became a pithy phrase she has often employed since, always with the inference that patience and its handmaiden, time (repeatedly symbolized in her work by watches) are, in the end, the only replacements for innocence.

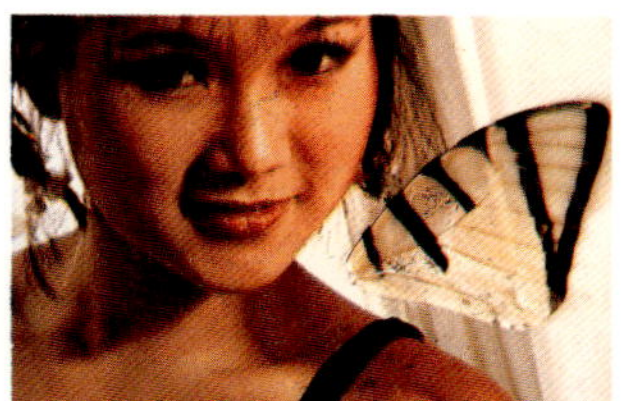

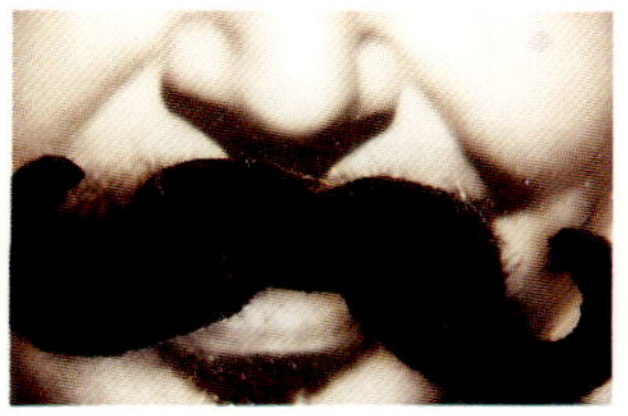

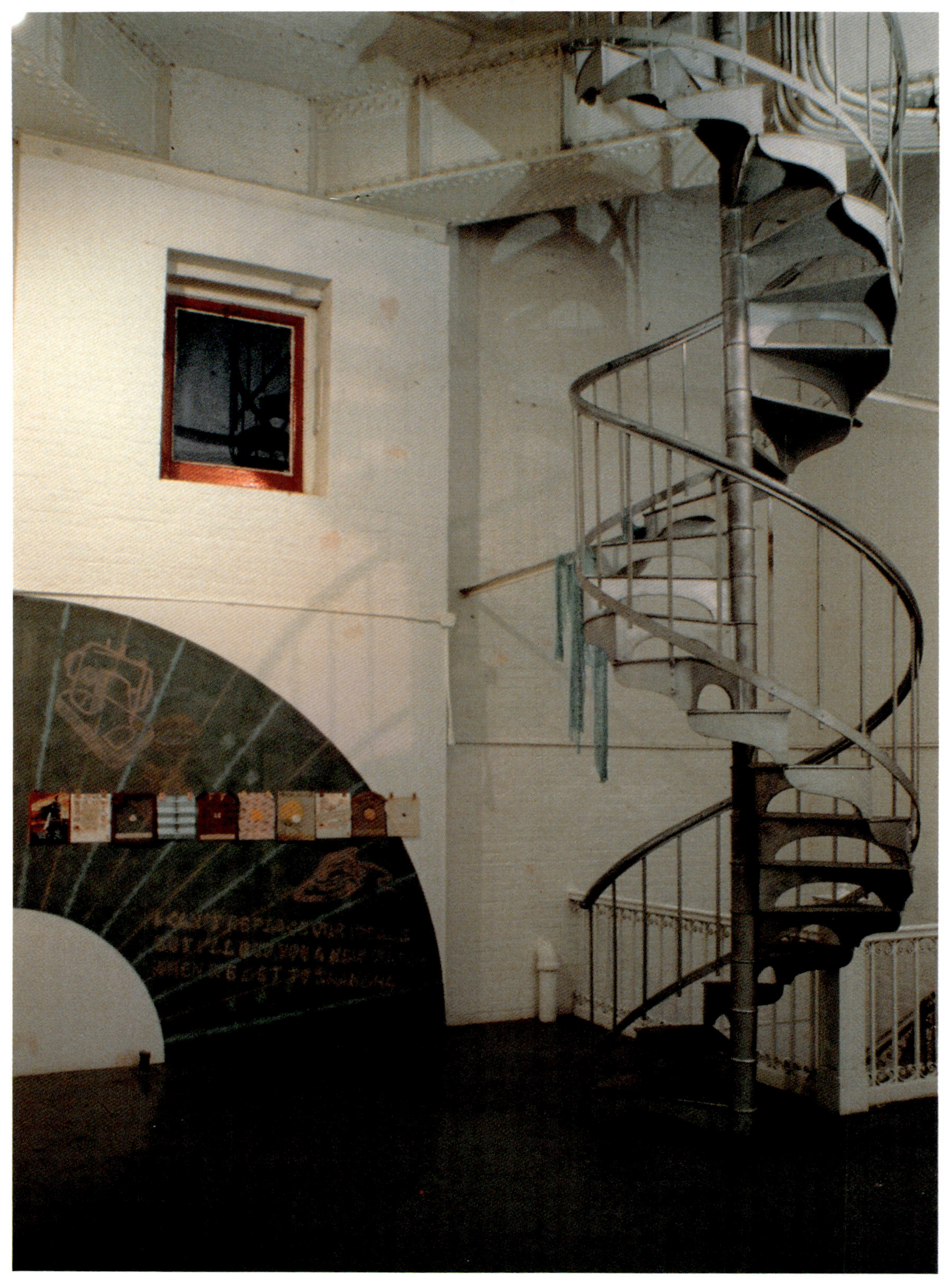

Chinese Junk, 1982
Installation, The Clocktower, New York

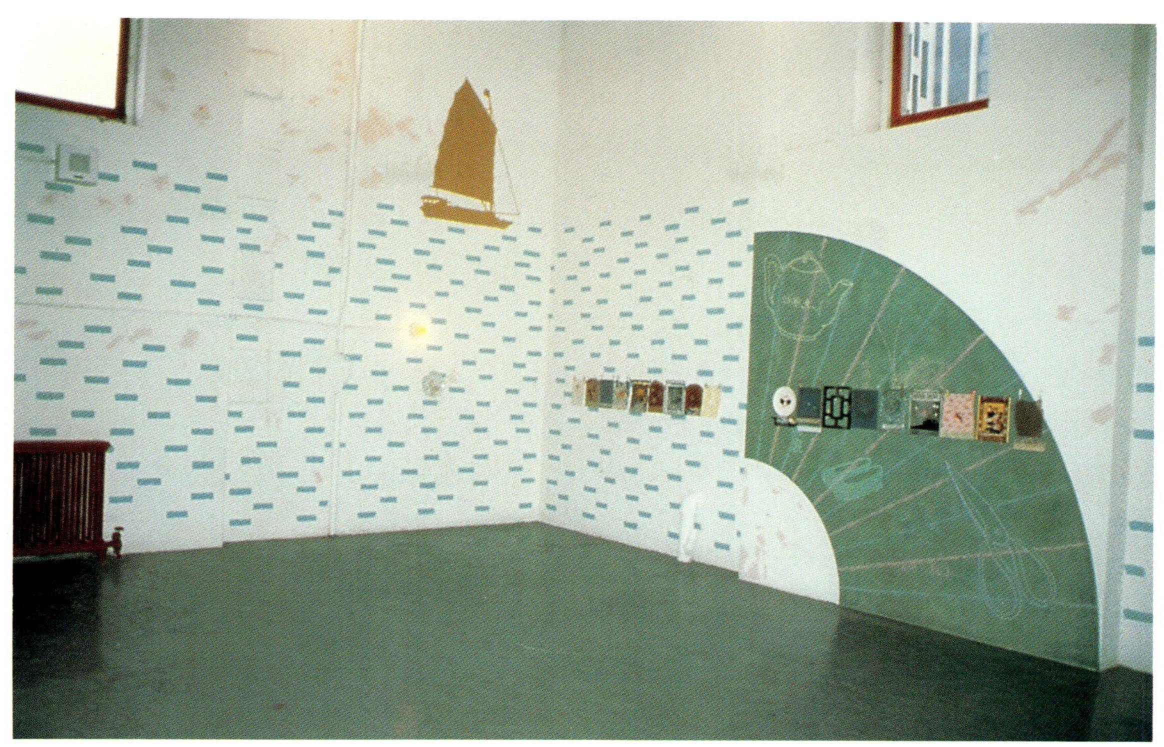

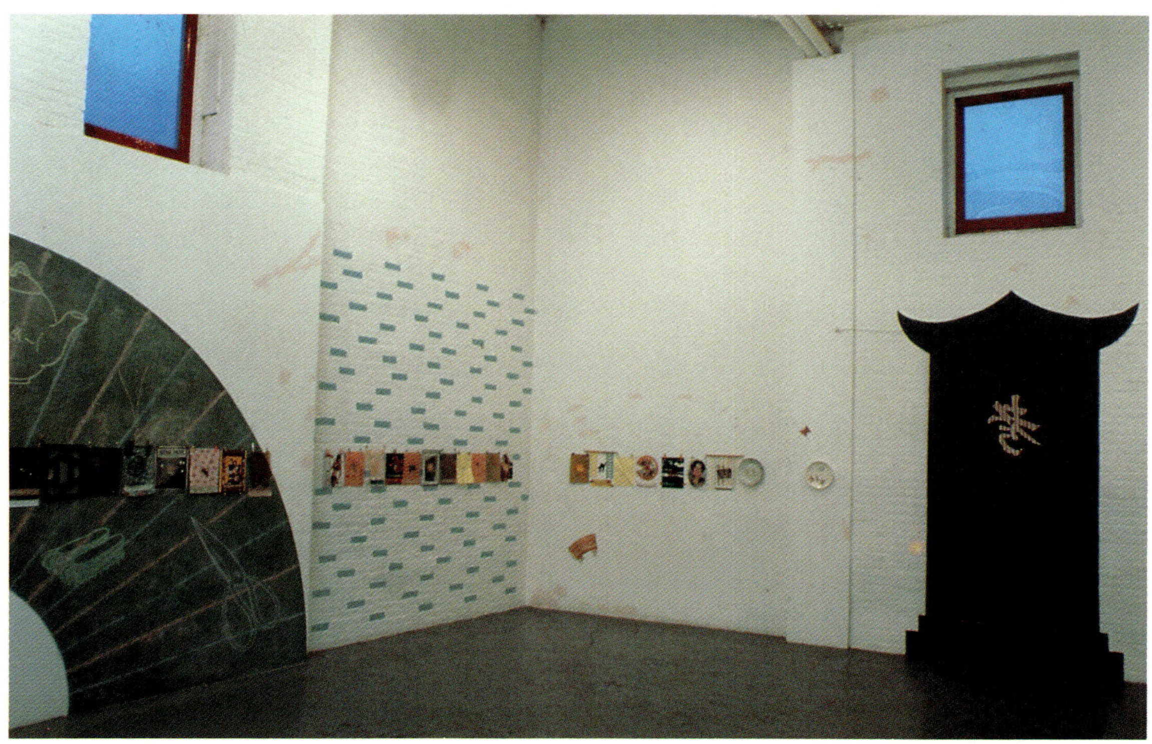

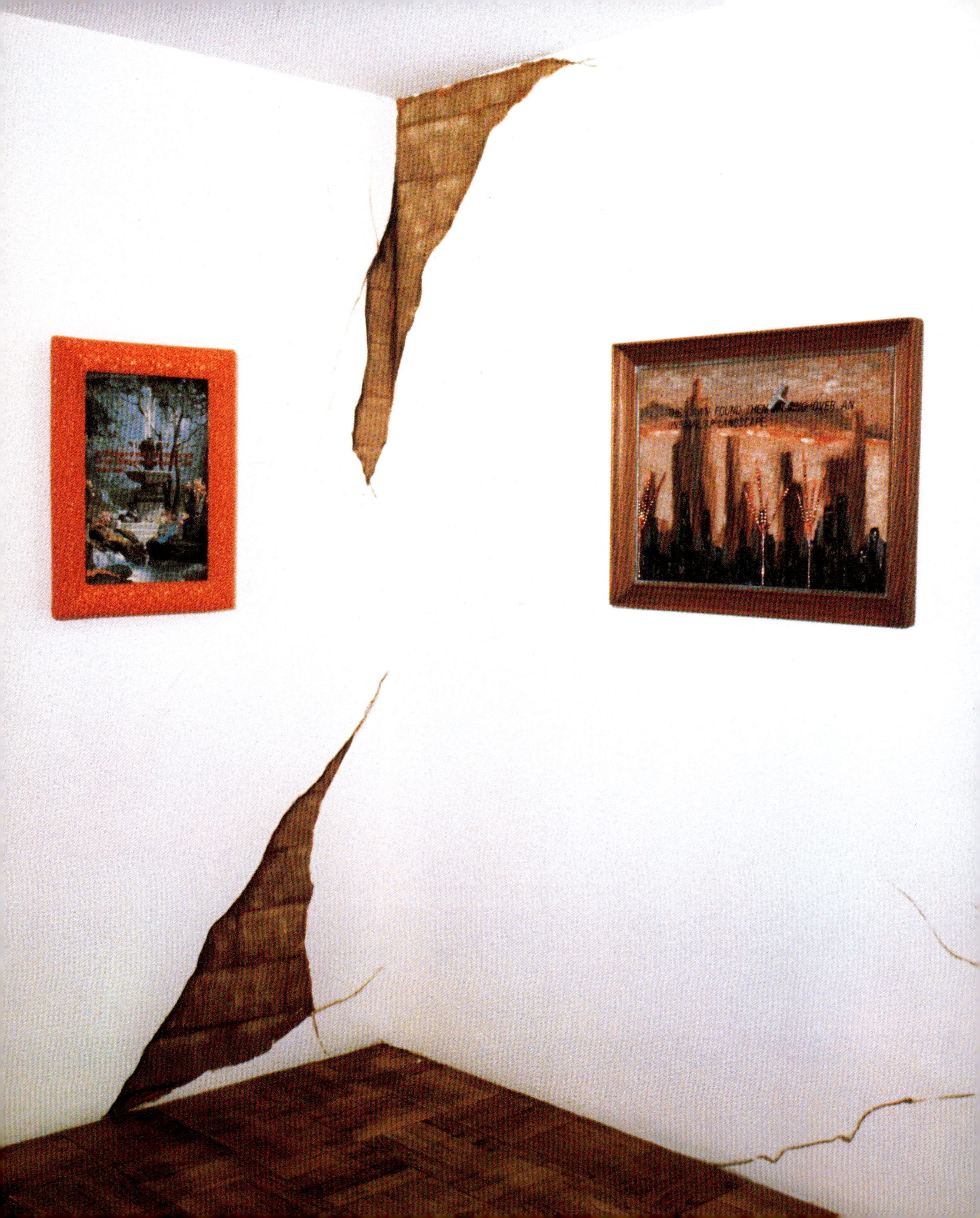
THE DAWN FOUND THEM
OVER AN
LANDSCAPE

By 1982 Smith's new fascination with cliché had supplanted her previous literary appropriations. *Cathay*'s exotic narration was especially eclectic, drawn as it was from a variety of Orientalist sources. By turning to fragments of popular texts, Smith had located a written counterpart to the physical detritus that constituted her visual vocabulary. She became intrigued by popular fiction—especially the interchangeable, standardized plots of pulp novels, most of them blatantly escapist and written for the female reader. In 1982, texts from this genre of exploitative trash generated an installation collectively titled *Satan's Satellites* for the Rosamund Felsen Gallery, Los Angeles. Large murals were painted on the walls with objects attached directly to them—an extension of Smith's use of freestanding assemblages in *Cathay*. One wall showed a typical sci-fi comic-book view of outer space with the inscription "the dawn found them moving over an unfamiliar landscape." Two hubcaps affixed to this mural read as space stations gliding into unknown galaxies. It was a particularly gripping exposition of Smith's ability to recontextualize the microcosmic, making it seem macrocosmic. A second wall featured *Ring of Fire*, a conflagration of red and yellow flames reaching up to a basketball hoop, above which a sign painter had lettered " . . . a hellhole if ever there was one." In *Fool's Gold*, a desert scene of cacti, a broiling sun, and buzzards, an old prospector and his burro sit inside a painted frame, itself inscribed "Sometimes men went crazy from the heat." Both phrases are typical of romantic boilerplate.

An adjoining, smaller room had been painted to mimic the fallen plaster ambience of a cheap Mexican restaurant, replete with velvet paintings. Inside this familiar stage set, decorated to read "south of border," Smith hung twelve collages.

More biting than anything she had previously produced, these collages joined clichéd found imagery with shopworn phrases. Thus, in *Tokyo Rose*, a pinup Latin dancer, her torso in the form of a banana and her hat a bowl of fruit, sports the same words as *Fool's Gold*—"Sometimes men went crazy from the heat." Smith endows the same words with very different inferences—here erotic rather than meteorologic despair—but both messages are delivered with billboard impact. The subordination of text to image that had made *Cathay* a turning point in Smith's art extended into the composition and presentation of the works that made up *Satan's Satellites*. By abandoning literature in favor of pulp, she could more fully exploit the iconic effect of her imagery. Henceforth Smith's art would be unabashedly pop in its sources and realization.

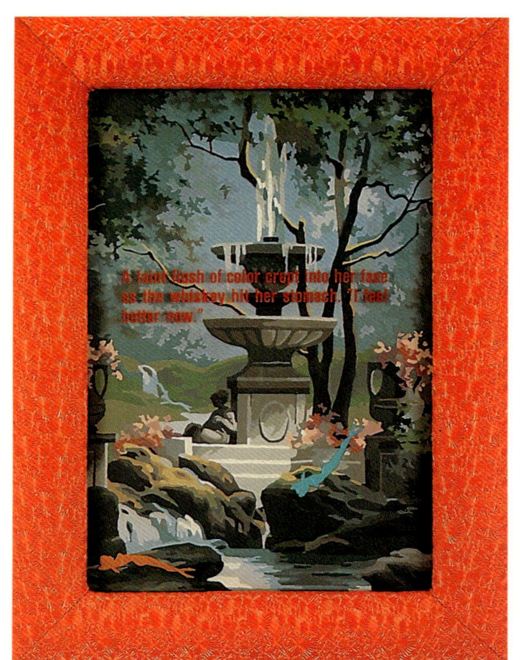

Satan's Satellites, 1982
Installation view, Rosamund Felsen Gallery, Los Angeles

The Pause that Refreshes, 1982
Mixed-media collage, 23¼ × 17½ inches
Collection of Ellen and Jim Isenson

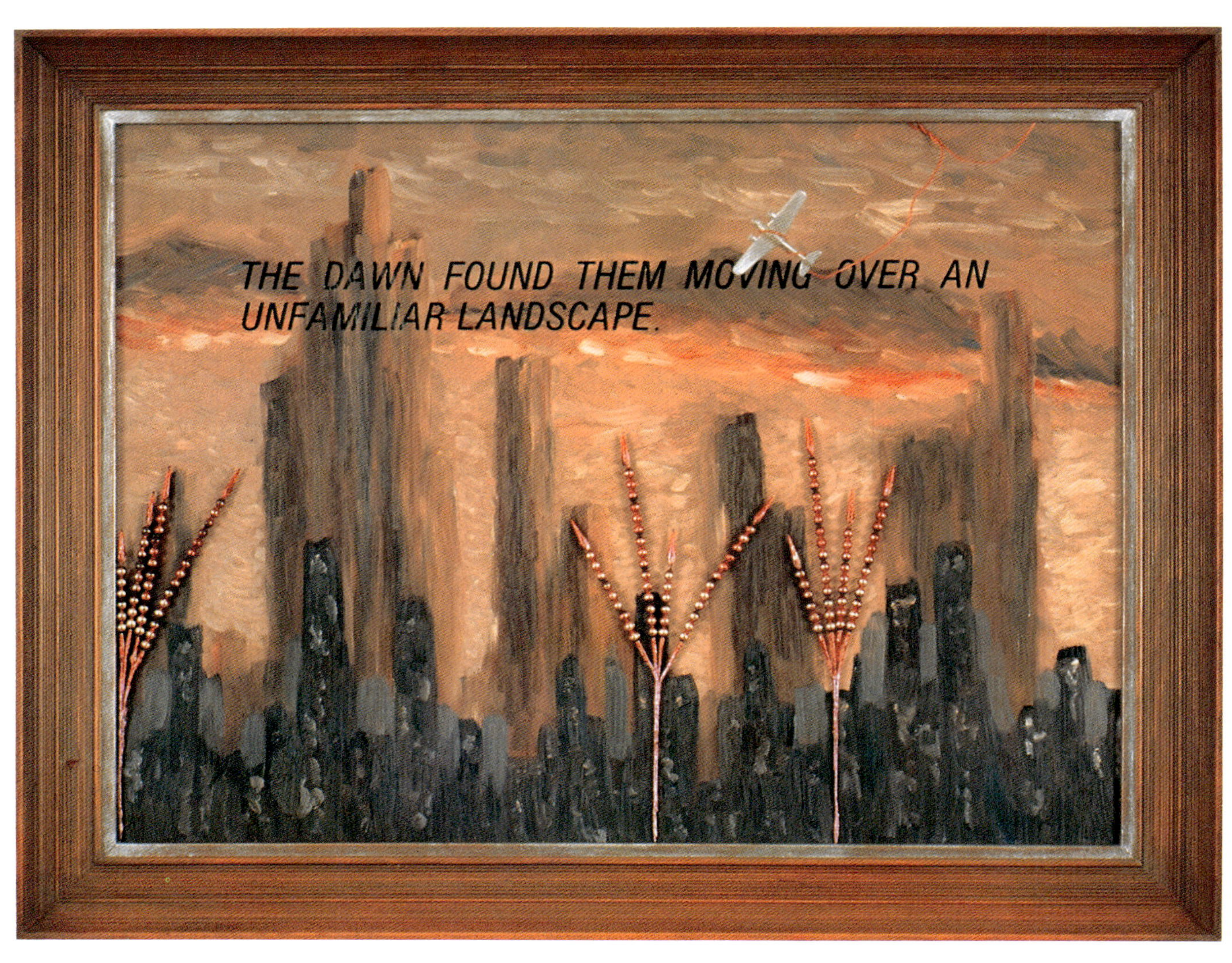

Lost Horizon, 1982
Mixed-media collage, 22 × 28 inches
Collection of the artist

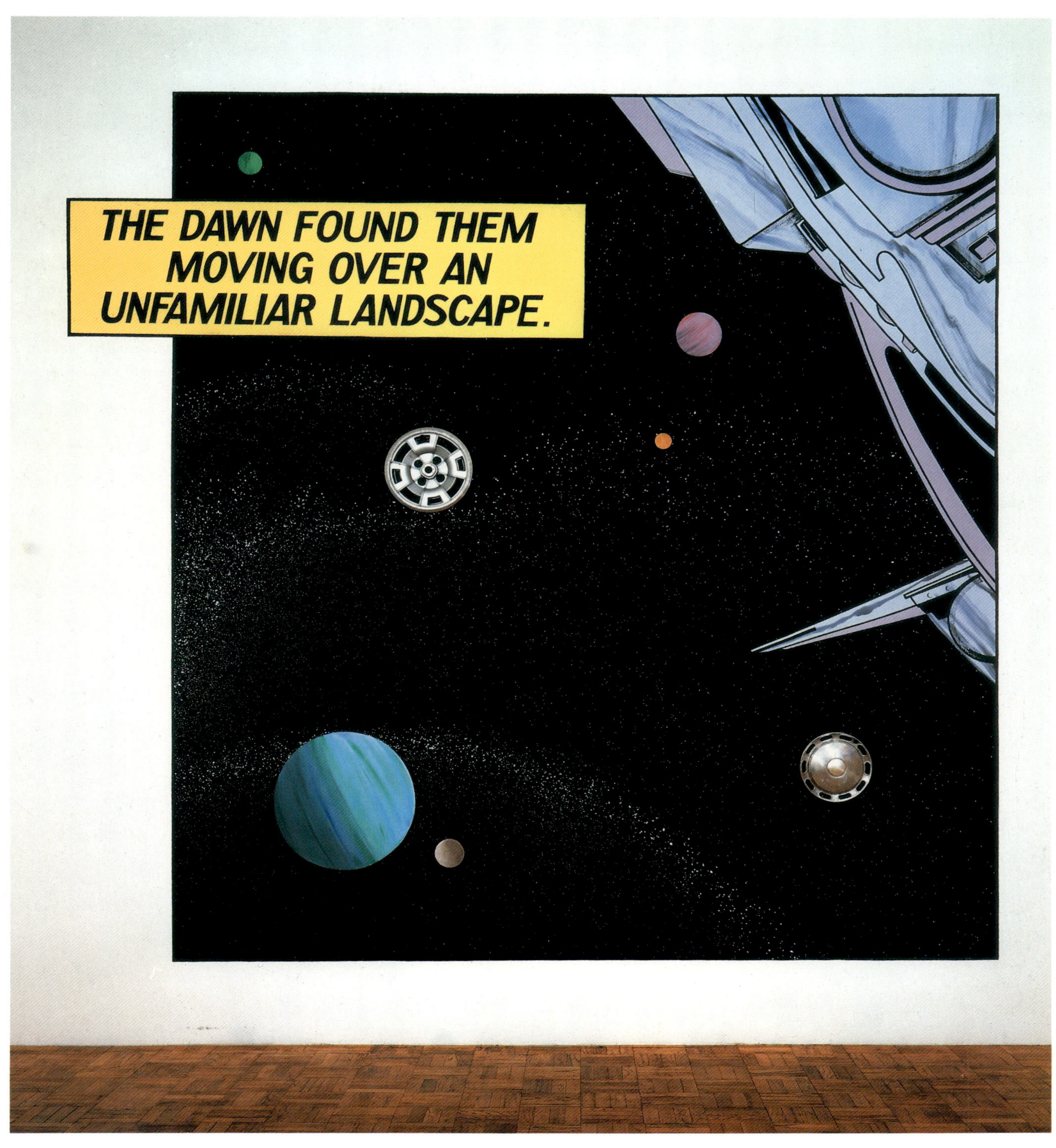

Satan's Satellites, 1982
Painted wall with hubcaps, 13 × 13 feet
Collection of the artist

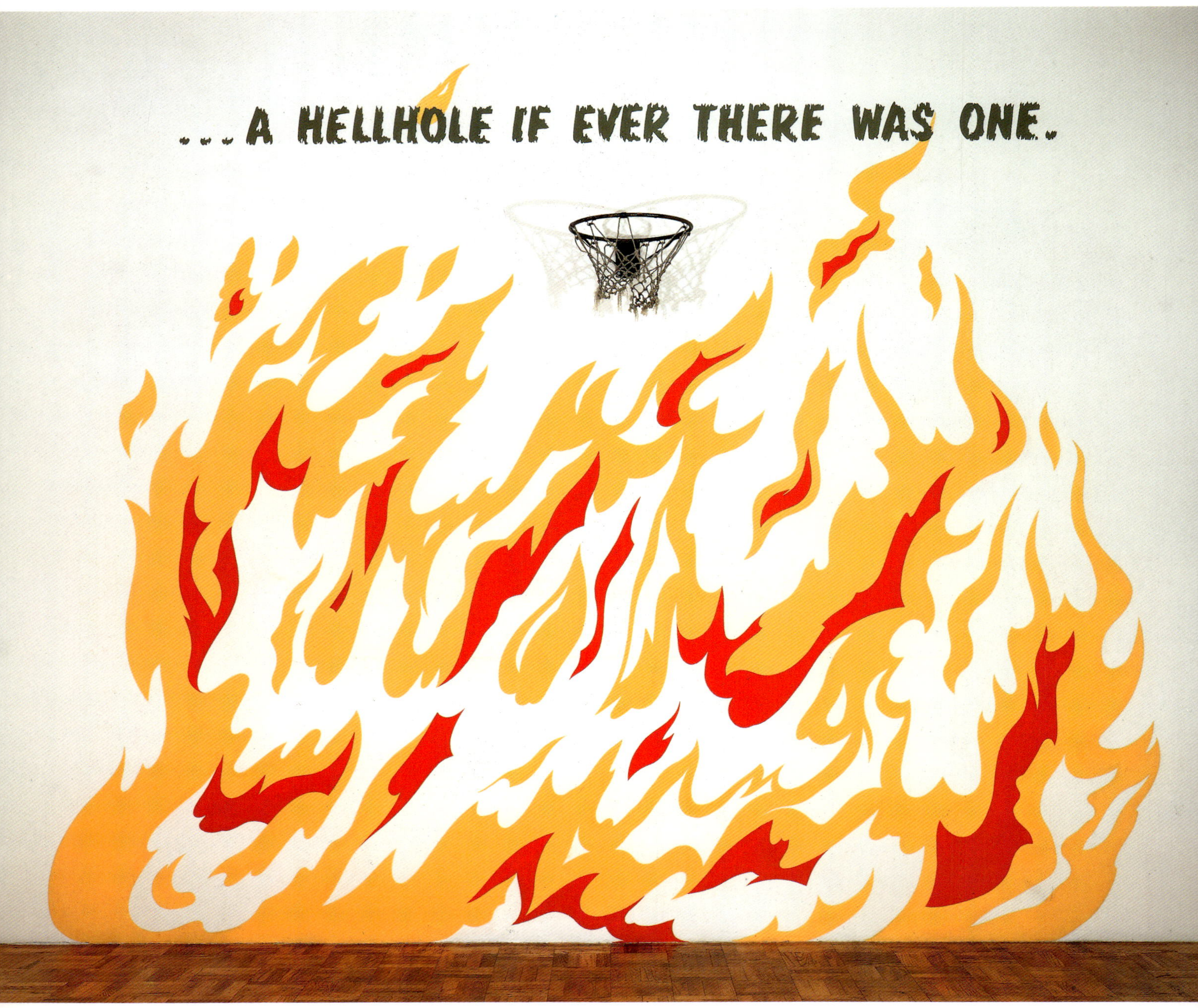

Ring of Fire, 1982
Painted wall with basketball hoop, 11 × 16 feet
Collection of the artist

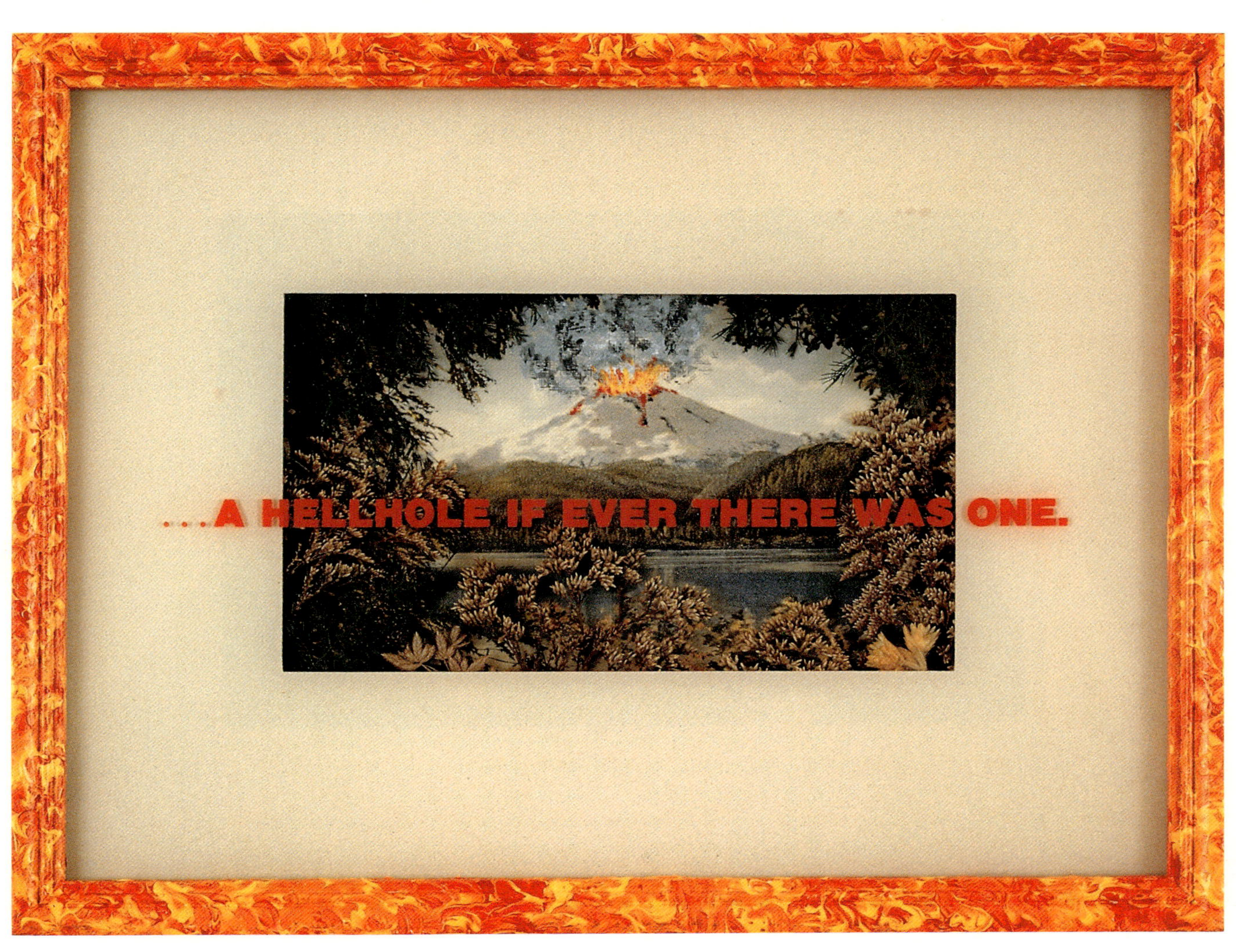

Hot Spot, 1982
Mixed-media collage, 6½ × 8½ inches
Collection of Jeff and Candy Wasserman

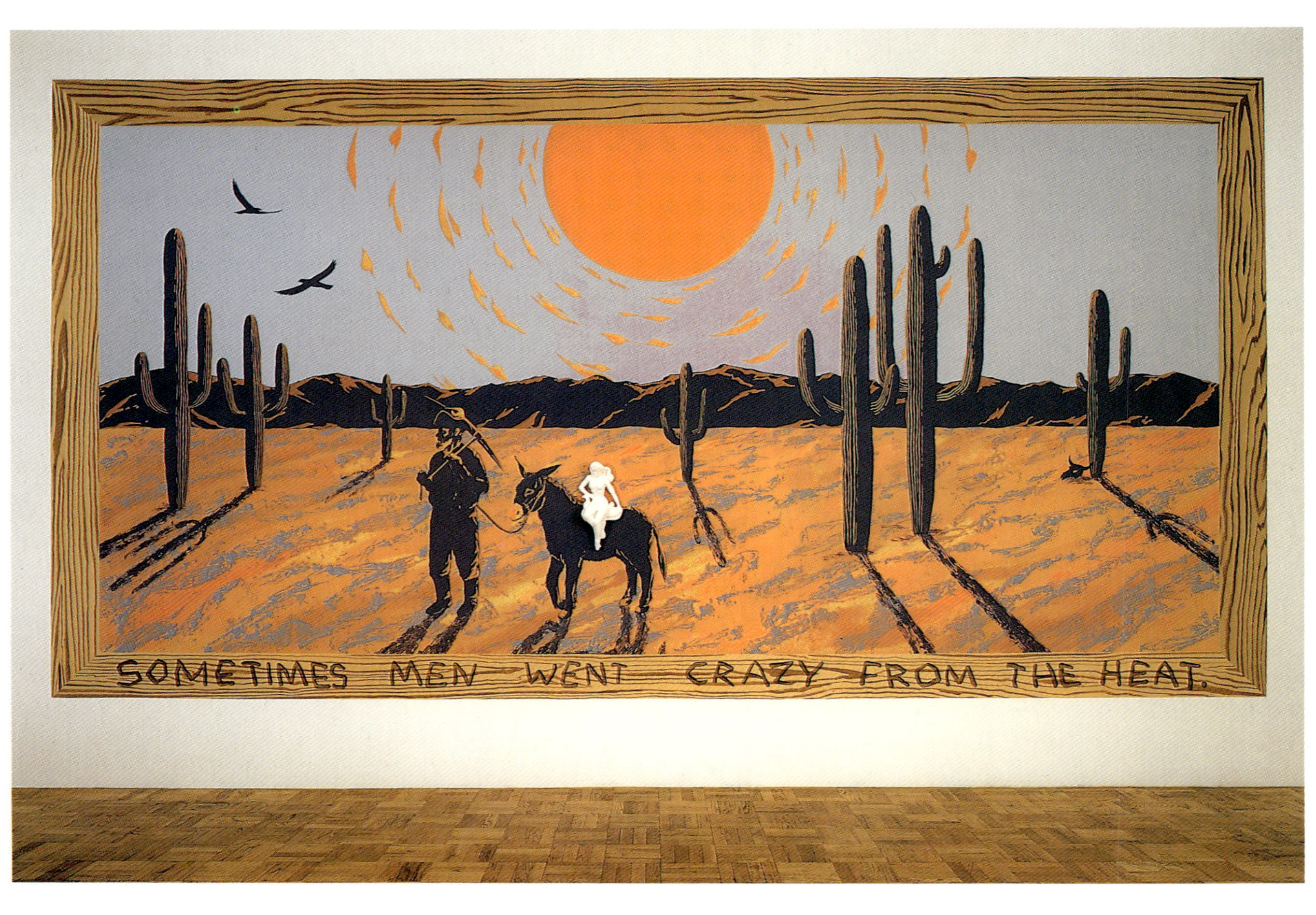

Fool's Gold, 1982
Painted wall with plaster cowgirl, 11 × 22 feet
Collection of the artist

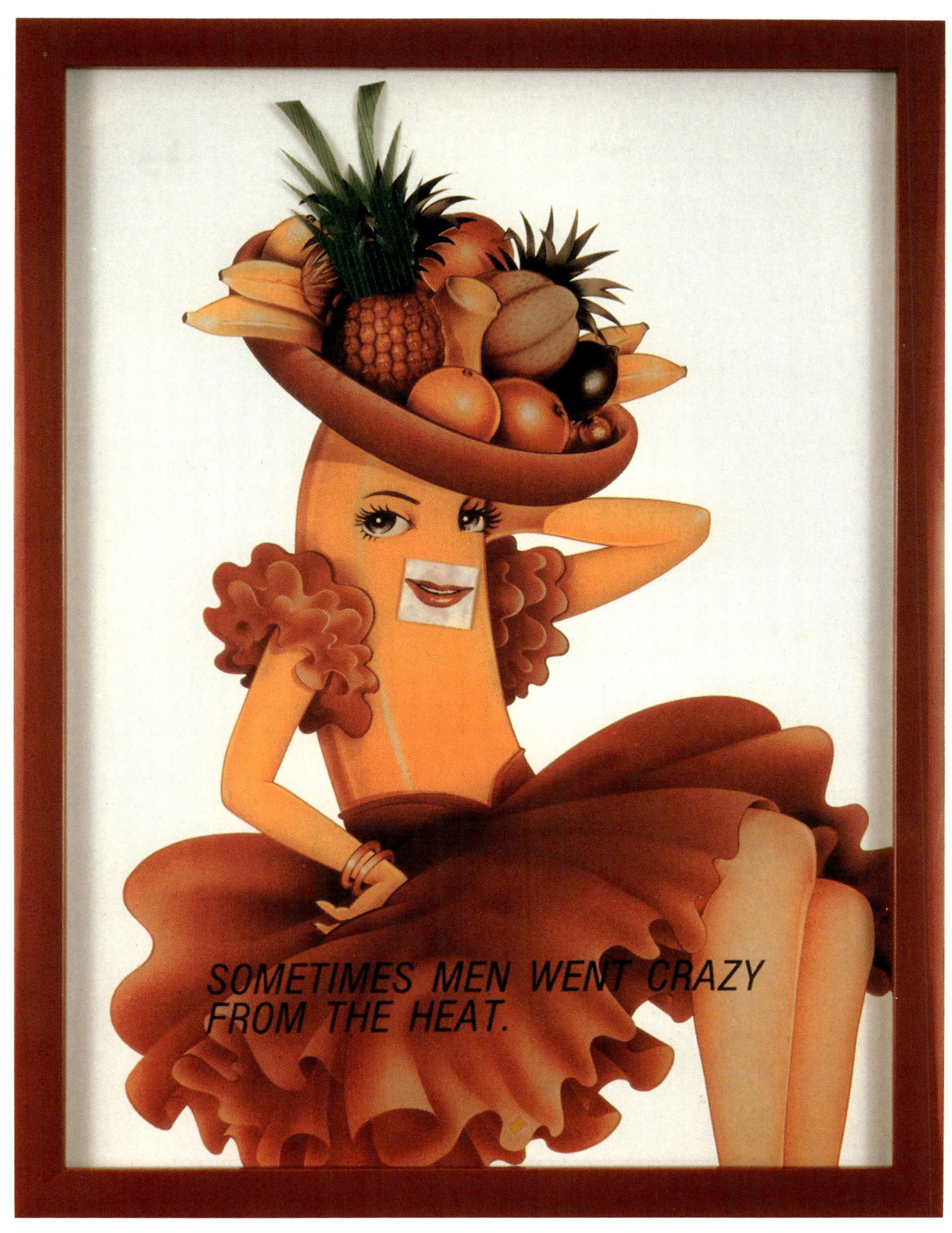

Tokyo Rose, 1982
Mixed-media collage, 21¼ × 16 inches
Collection of Lawrence M. Kauvar

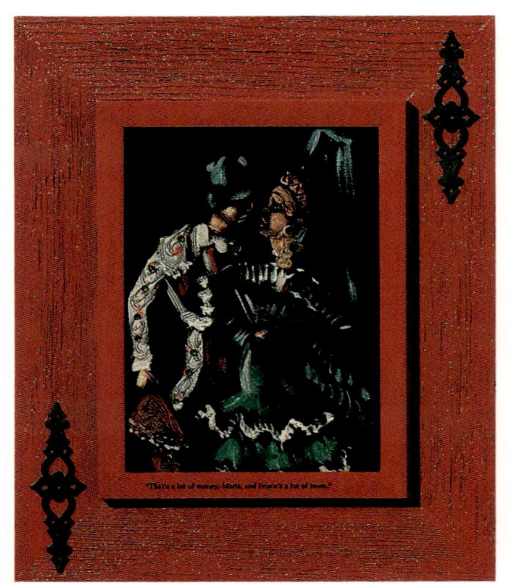

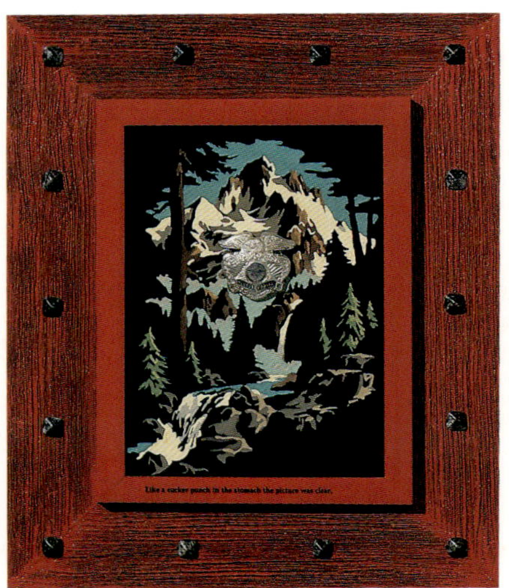

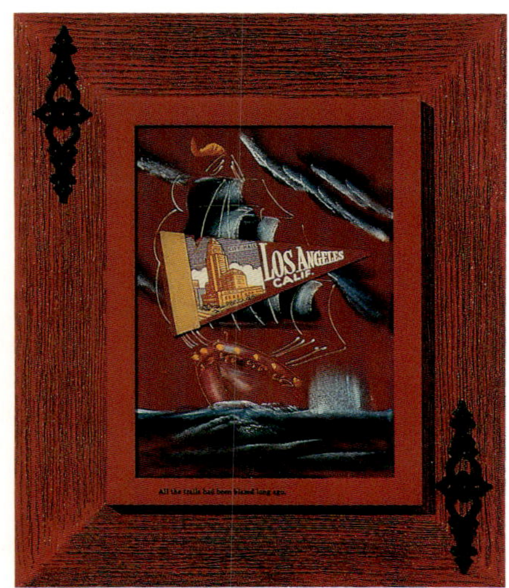

"That's a lot of money, Maria, and Frisco's a lot of town."

Like a sucker punch in the stomach the picture was clear.

All the trails had been blazed long ago.

El Cartero Siempre Llama Dos Veces, 1982
Mixed-media collage, three panels, $21\frac{5}{8} \times 13\frac{3}{4}$ inches each
Margo Leavin Gallery, Los Angeles

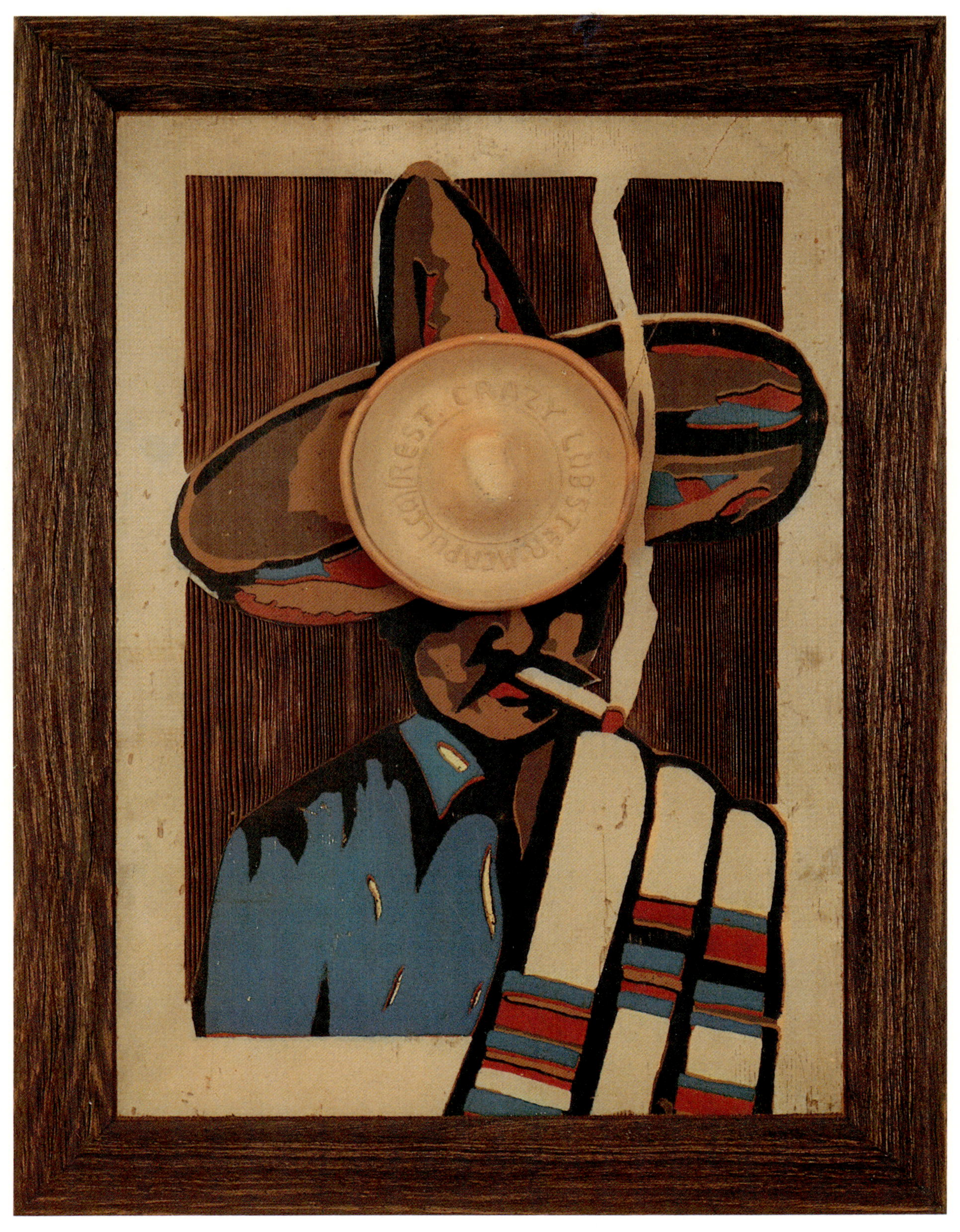

No Way, Jose, 1982
Mixed-media collage, 18¼ × 14 inches
Margo Leavin Gallery, Los Angeles

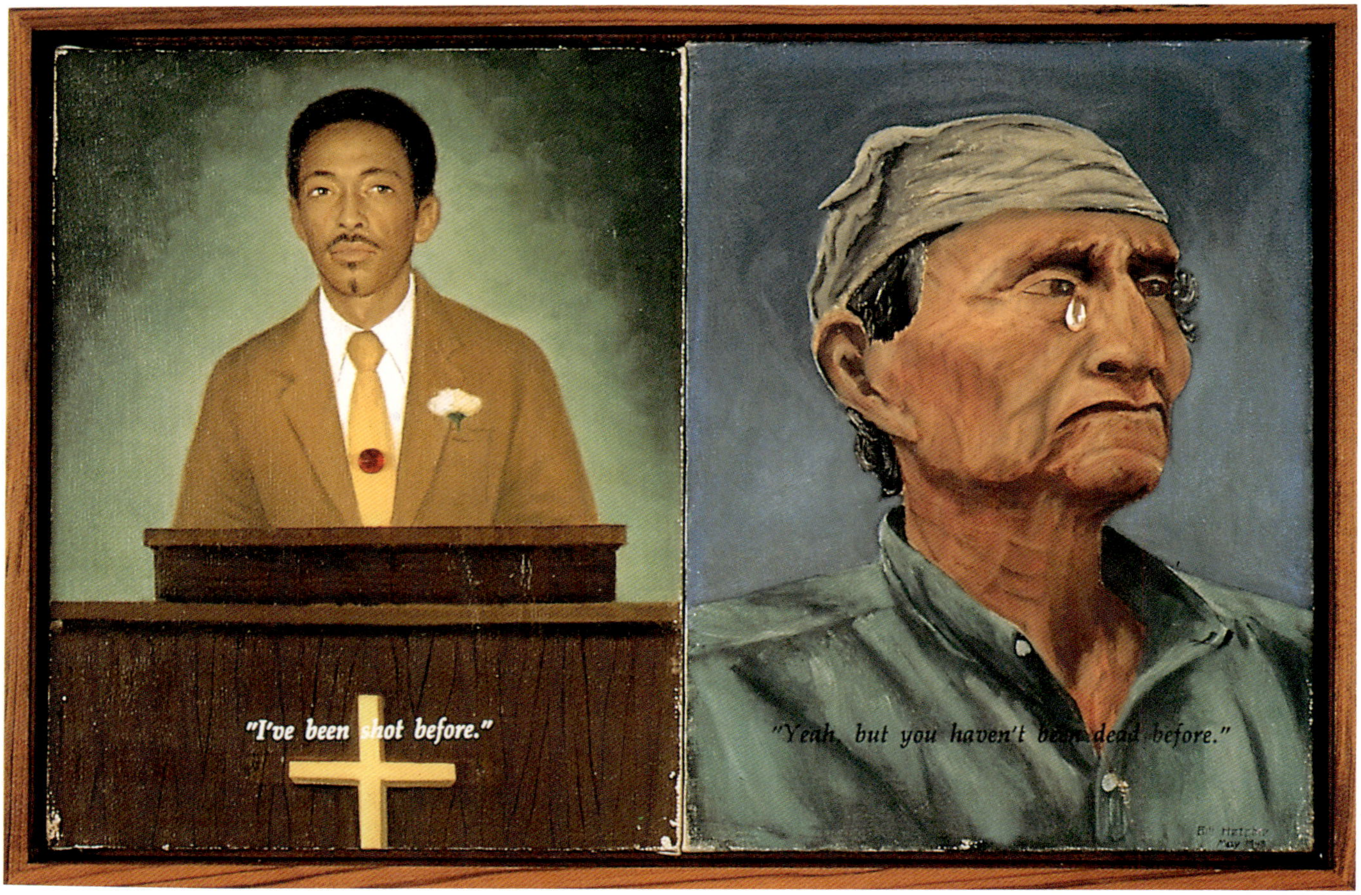

Happy Hunting Ground, 1982
Mixed-media collage, 17½ × 25¾ inches
Collection of the artist

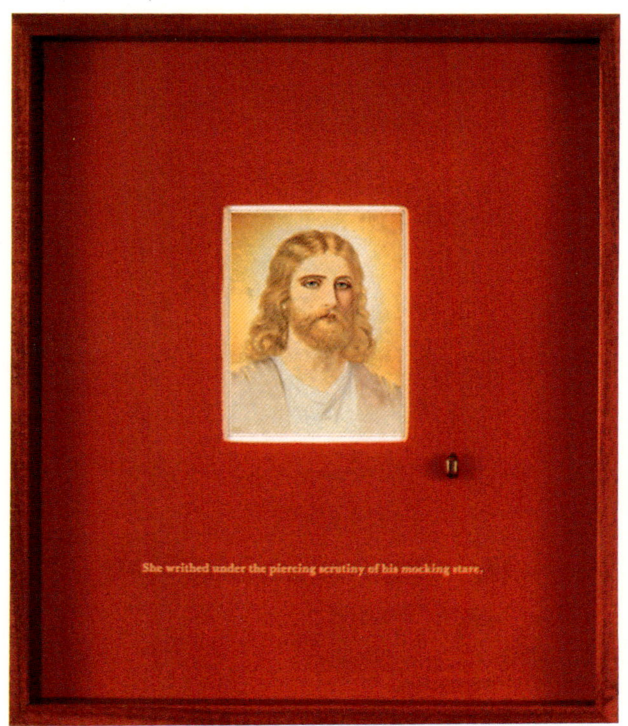

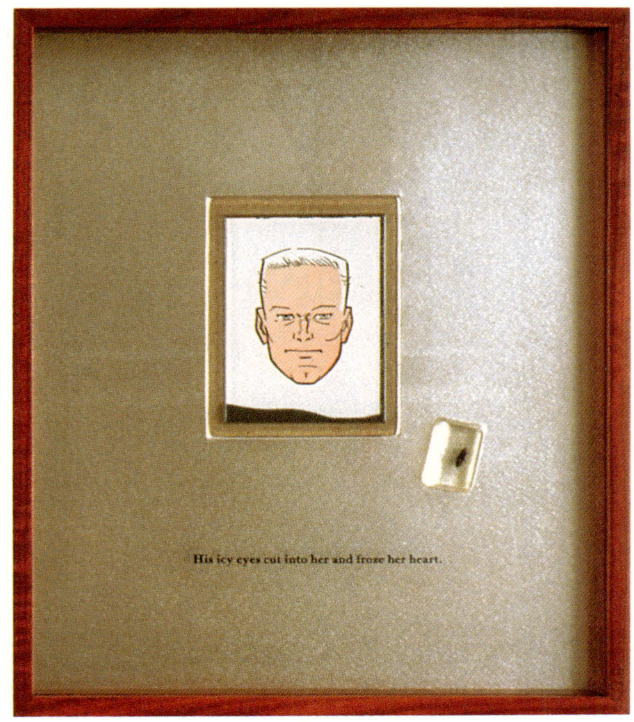

If Looks Could Kill, 1982
Mixed-media collage, two panels, 15¼ × 12¾ inches each
Collection of Jonathan C. Ahearn

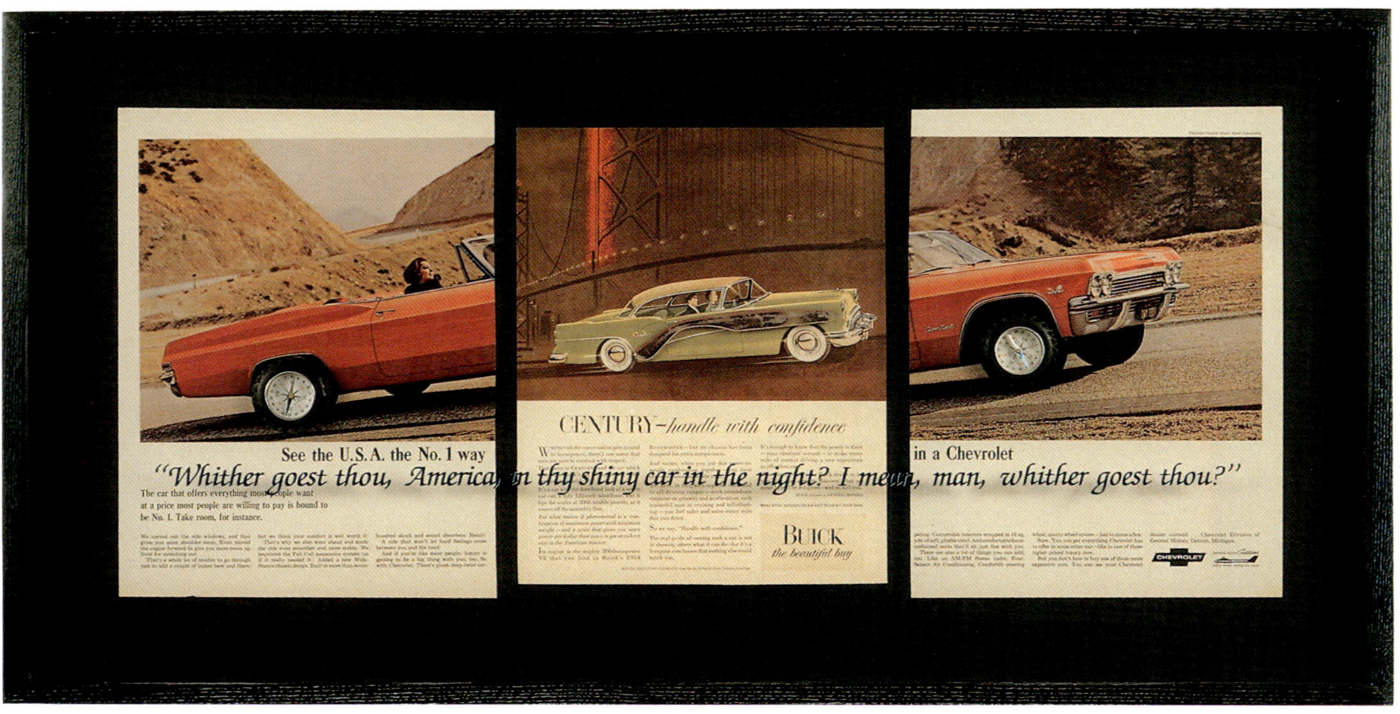

The collages of *Satan's Satellites* featured especially acerbic images and texts, in contrast to the smart-aleck tone of Smith's earlier appropriations of such authors as Raymond Chandler. Some of the pieces also featured cars, which had become a recurrent motif for Smith, symbolizing both freedom and death. *Mustang Sally* (1982) portrays the presence of a car: the Indian figurehead below the word "Pontiac" represents both the General Motors car and the eponymous Indian chief. The image provides a heraldic setting for two conjoined phrases, "The rest of the day went by like a motion picture running wild, sometimes too fast, and again too slow. *There was a traffic jam inside my skull, horns blowing, brakes squealing, head-on collisions.*" Smith here combines one of her frequent references to the movies as a surrogate for life with a metaphorical comparison of driving to consciousness.

A translucent clip earring decorates the Indian's ear and holds a feather in place, while the cheeks and forehead have been marked in red war paint. The gold vinyl and rubber frame offer tactile and olfactory allusions to the car's interior, which the war paint suggests is a battleground. The title, which feminizes the erstwhile warrior and the car he adorned, is borrowed from a pop song about a wild girl. It implies that the battle may be between sexual identities.

Whither Goest Thou, America?, 1988
Mixed-media collage, 19¼ × 37¼ inches
Collection of Kim and Michael McCarty

Concurrent with the 1982 *Satan's Satellites* installation at the Rosamund Felsen Gallery in Los Angeles, Smith presented *Christmas Eve, 1943* at the Margo Leavin Gallery in the same city. If the former addressed itself to a variety of locales—the desert, outer space, cheap Mexican restaurants—the two large galleries filled with the collages of *Christmas Eve* reeked of wartime Los Angeles. Newspaper headlines told of war maneuvers, men were in a variety of uniforms, a collaged poster hectored "Buy War Bonds"; Smith's titles, such as *Bombshell*, reinforced the frenzied mobilization of the early 1940s. The disjointed but continuous narrative that ran across these pieces, almost all comprising two or three panels, concluded in the first room with "Westerns bore me," she said./I was angry; my voice went icy cold. What was it with dames anyway?/The hint of compassion she had seen before seems to have vanished. His icy eyes cut into her and froze her heart./She shivered in his grasp. The air was suddenly frosty./A chill wind blew from the north. High up stars twinkled dimly as the sky filled with scores of white parachutes./ "Looks like a snowstorm," he muttered to himself. It was Christmas Eve, 1943.

Smith enhanced the setting for the show by stenciling candles on the gallery's windows and filling its entryway with an ornament-laden tree. More salient was a new approach to frames, each tailored to enrich its contents. By now, Smith's plexiglass boxes had evolved into all manner of elaborate devices—some found, some fabricated—which for the first time encased the collage assemblages behind glass. Her conjoined texts were silkscreened at the bottom of each piece of glass, effecting an overlay of word on image. Once again she fabricated a narration from a medley of sources—all the sort of popular fiction that characterized *Satan's Satellites*. Like *Satan's Satellites*, *Christmas Eve, 1943* represented a union of verbal and physical detritus.

The title dates the piece to a time Smith knows best through the scavenged memorabilia she hoarded. Pages of newspapers, old photographs, movie posters, the faddish flotsam and jetsam of the moment were abundantly available to her in the thrift

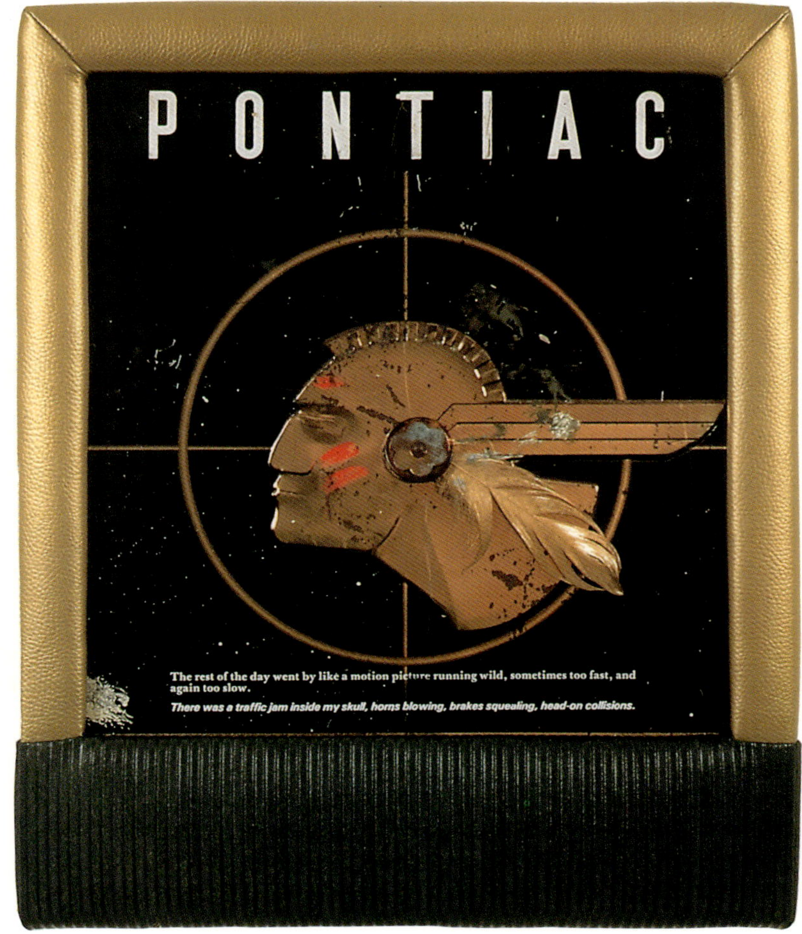

Mustang Sally, 1982
Mixed-media collage, 20⅝ × 16¾ inches
Collection of Alan Shayne

shops and swap meets that serve as her supply sources. During the 1940s, the decade in which she was born, the war effort had brought thousands of new people to Southern California, hastening its fall from sunny Eden to smoggy metropolis. In this sense, the 1940s may be considered L.A.'s last moment of innocence.

Christmas Eve, 1943 was also populated with all kinds of "dames." The female counterpart to a wise guy, a dame only exists in relation to men; it is not a term one woman bestows on another. Smith's dames range from the pathetic shrinking violet of the first panel in *Danger, Curves Ahead* to the veiled and flower-bedecked rococo framed head of its third panel. An abstracted dame is the pun behind *Bombshell*. A rectangular metal tray frames a figure-eight torso, the breasts represented by two plastic fried eggs, the crotch covered by a doily. The female plight is alluded to by titles such as *I Married a Monster from Outer Space* and *Fools Rush In*. It animates the texts in *Winter Wonderland*: "I couldn't eat; I couldn't even get drunk. I knew what that meant./There are times when love takes over; when the darkest corner is touched by light; when the coldest heart feels the glow of warmth." A begowned queen—tomorrow's dame—stands beside her king as she receives a crown from another man in *White Christmas*. Smith embellished an enormous bouquet with a dime-store cupid from Valentine's Day. Across the bottom are the words, "when the trumpet call of good will and good cheer drowns out all the mean little noise. He raised his glass./We clinked. 'To all the dumb dreams that never happen,' she said." Although aware of the fate of most of her females, Smith nevertheless avoids editorializing in favor of a nuance-laden recapitulation of human foibles.

As always with Smith, Hollywood mediates all information—both in tone and in collaged presentation. Perhaps more than ever before in her work, the variously framed units of *Christmas Eve, 1943* function as pages from a script superimposed over stills of its movie.

A series of prints made about this time, *The Twentieth Century* (1983), reiterated Smith's profound connection to the mores of the movies. Employing posters of mostly lurid B-grade films as grounds, she silkscreened two sets of phrases diagonally across the corners. The first reads, "I've died so often/Made love so much/I've lost track of what's real." Its rejoinder, silkscreened diagonally and upside down in the opposing corner, proclaims, "I don't live/I act."

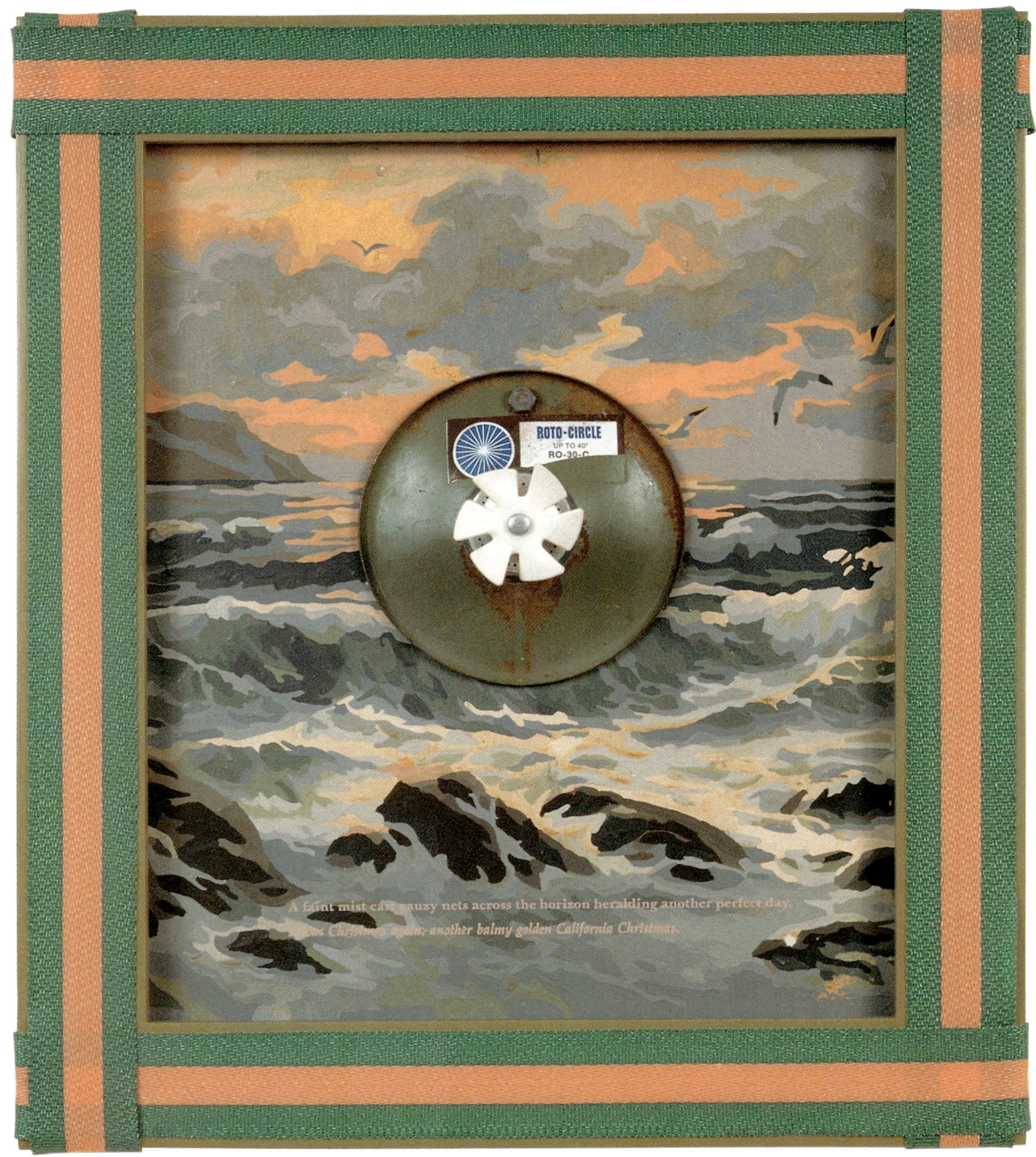

A faint mist cast gauzy nets across the horizon heralding another perfect day.
It was Christmas again, another balmy golden California Christmas.

Sea of Tranquility, 1982
Mixed-media collage, 20⅜ × 17⅝ inches
Collection of the artist

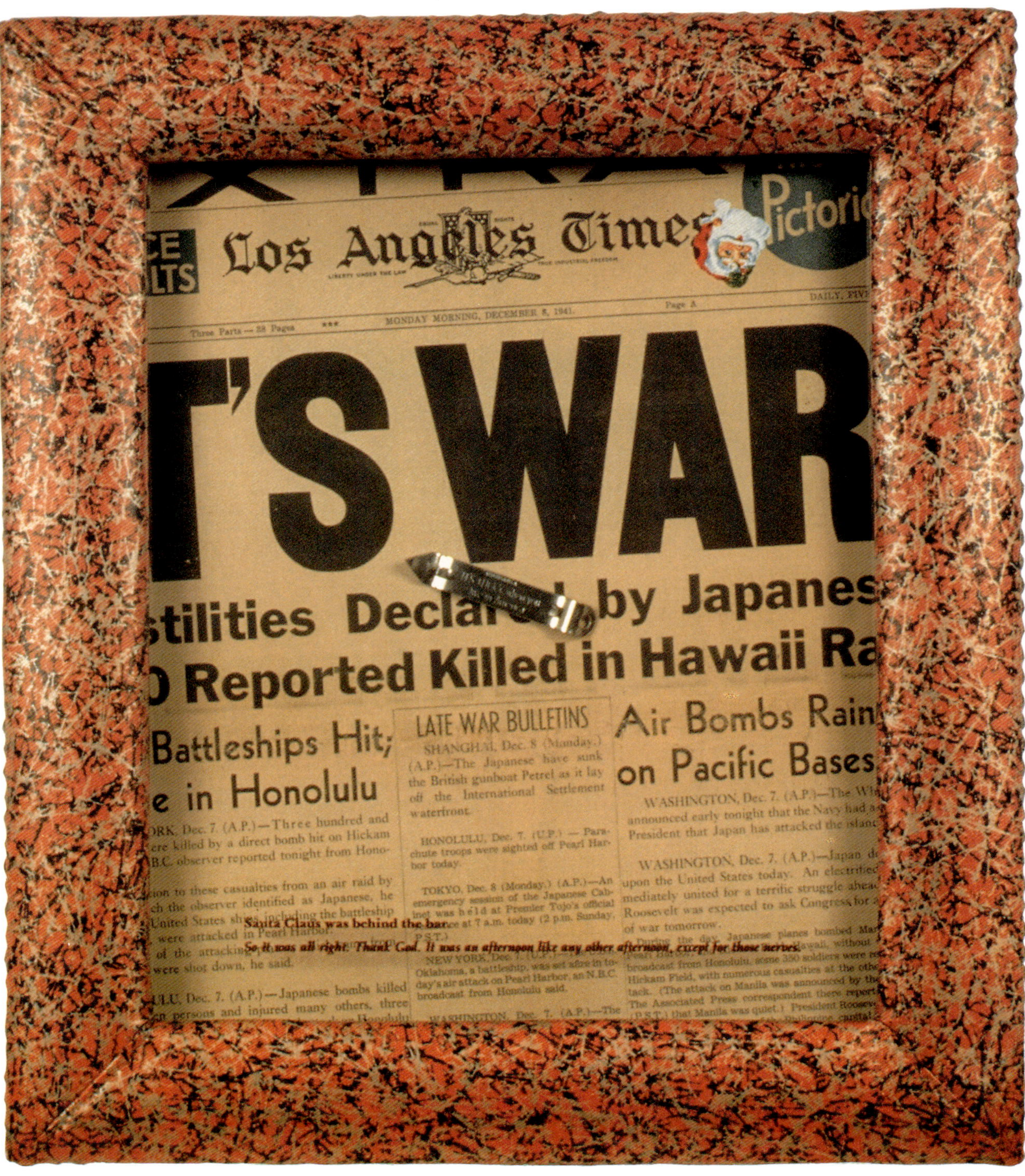

Santa Claus was behind the bar.
So it was all right. Thank God. It was an afternoon like any other afternoon, except for those nerves.

It's Lucky When You Live in America, 1982
Mixed-media collage, 21⅜ × 18½ inches
Collection of Lenore and Bernard Greenberg

I had myself another Manhattan from a passing tray.
Everything was all right. I hadn't done anything. Everything was the same as it had been.

Coconut Grove, 1982
Mixed-media collage, 21½ × 18½ inches
The Capital Group, Inc., Los Angeles

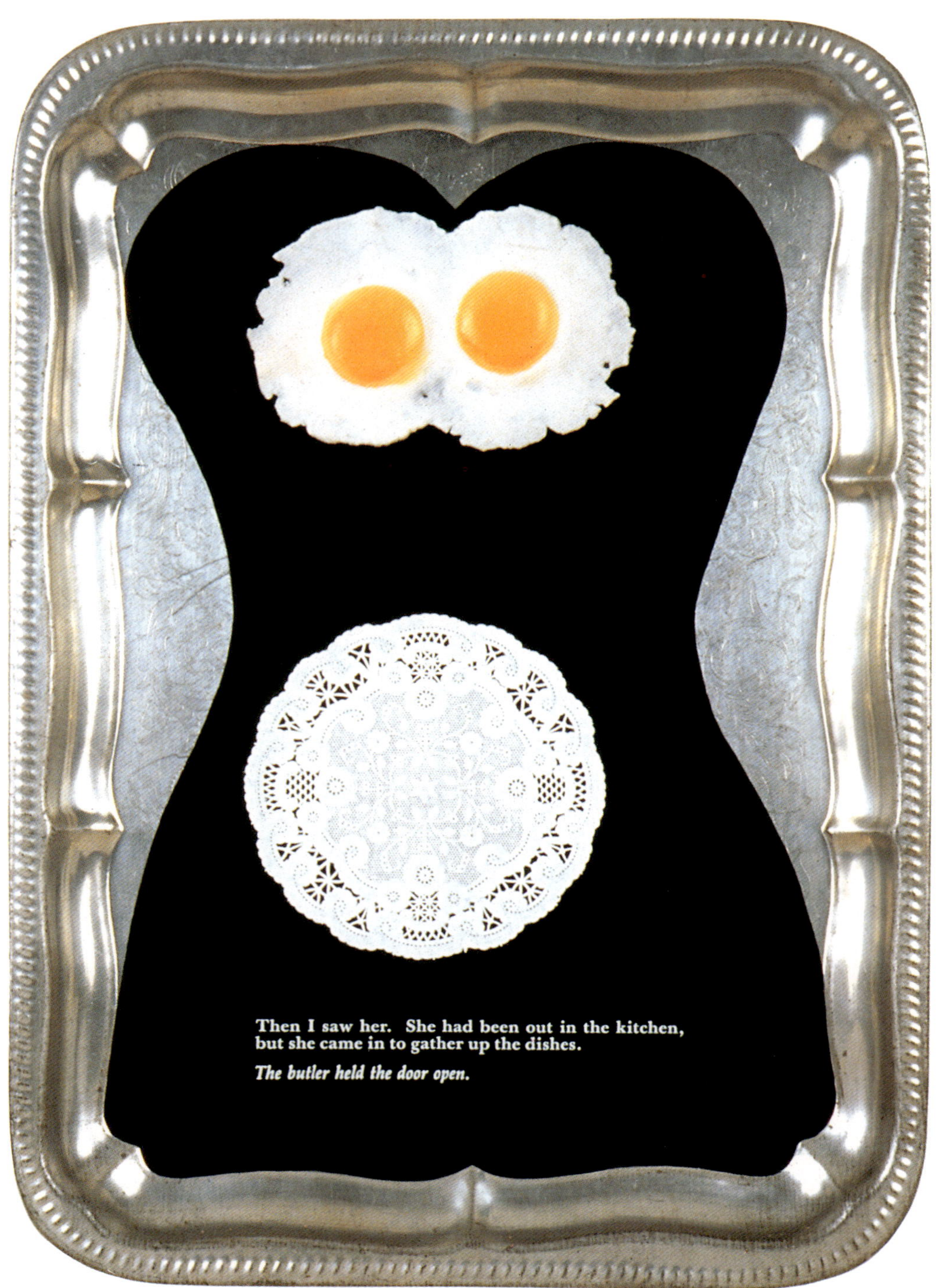

Then I saw her. She had been out in the kitchen, but she came in to gather up the dishes.

The butler held the door open.

Bombshell, 1982
Mixed-media collage, 17⅞ × 12⅝ inches
Collection of Merry Norris

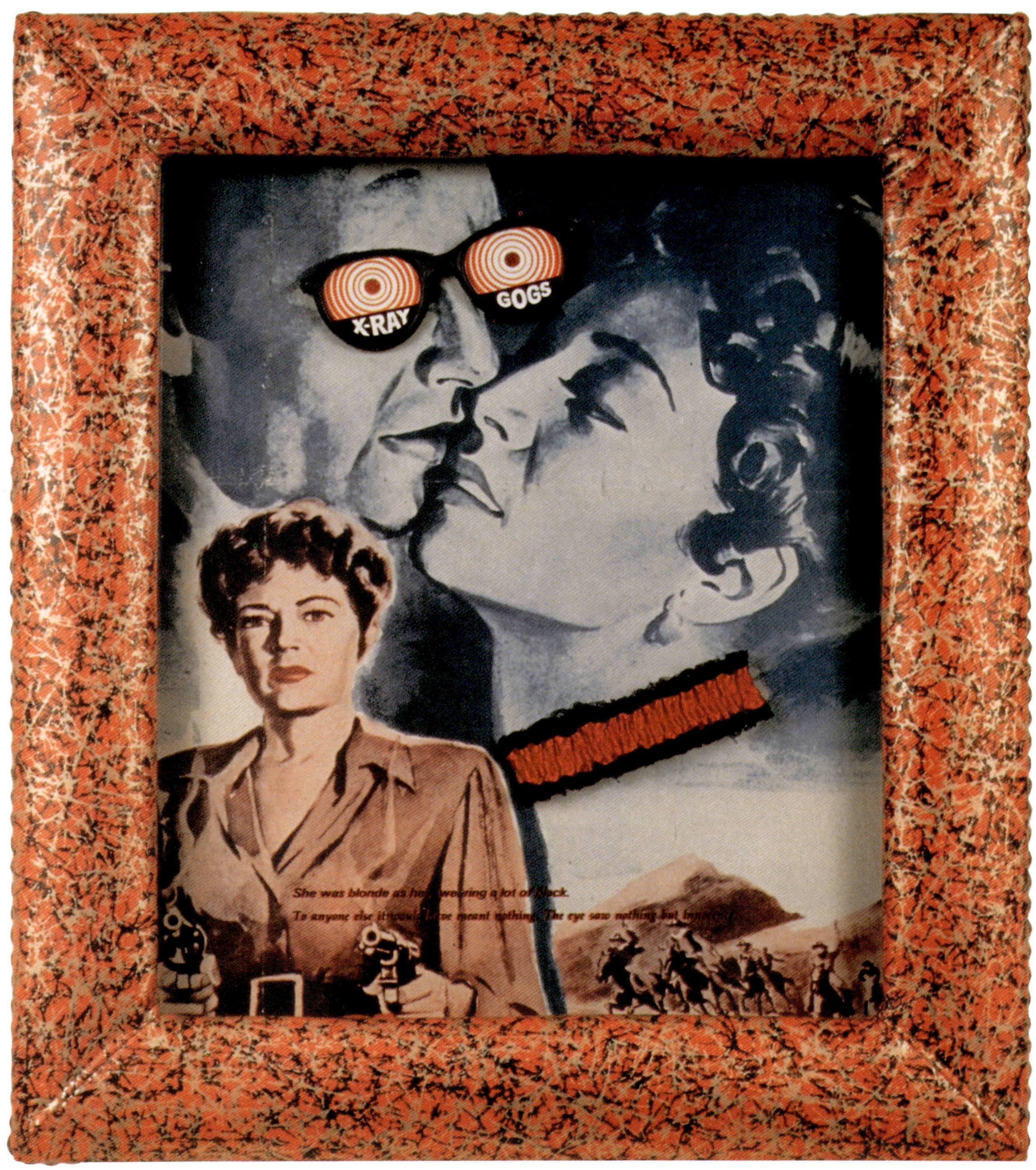

She was blonde as hell, wearing a lot of black.
To anyone else it would have meant nothing. The eye saw nothing but innocence.

Madame X, 1982
Mixed-media collage, $21\frac{3}{8} \times 18\frac{1}{2}$ inches
Collection of Richard Rosenzweig and Judy Henning

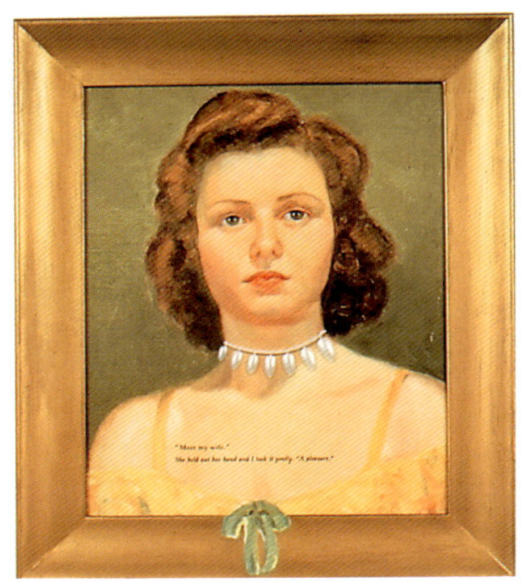

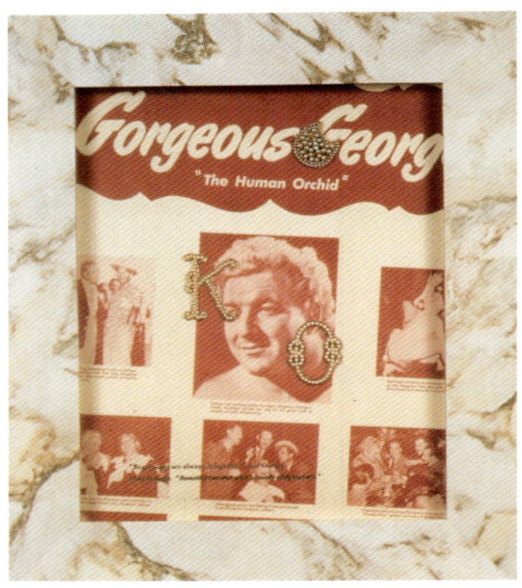

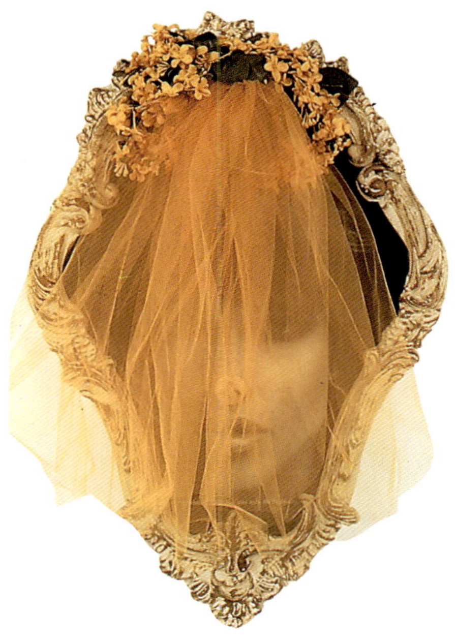

"Meet my wife."
She held out her hand and I took it gently. "A pleasure."

"Beginnings are always delightful," said Goethe.
I had to laugh. "Beautiful blondes aren't usually philosophers."

But somehow I knew this was only the beginning.

Danger, Curves Ahead, 1982
Mixed-media collage, three panels, $20\frac{7}{8} \times 17\frac{7}{8}$;
$21\frac{1}{8} \times 18\frac{1}{8}$; 24×16 inches
Margo Leavin Gallery, Los Angeles

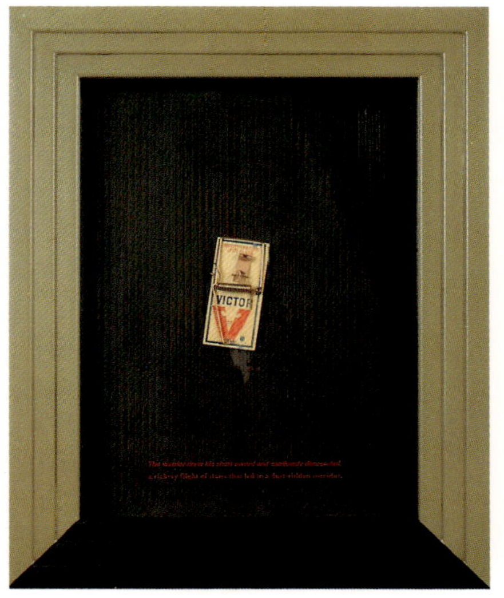

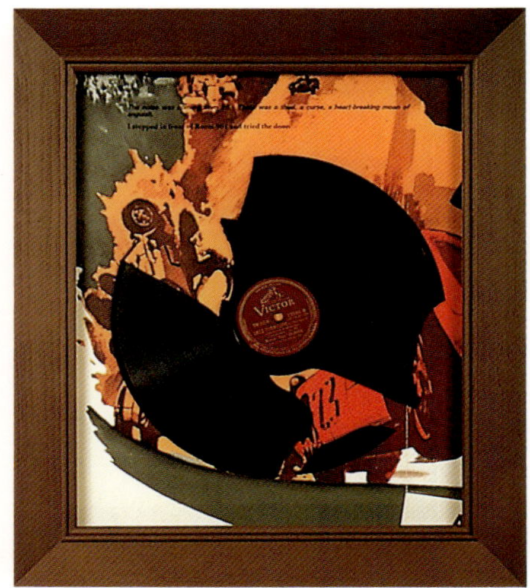

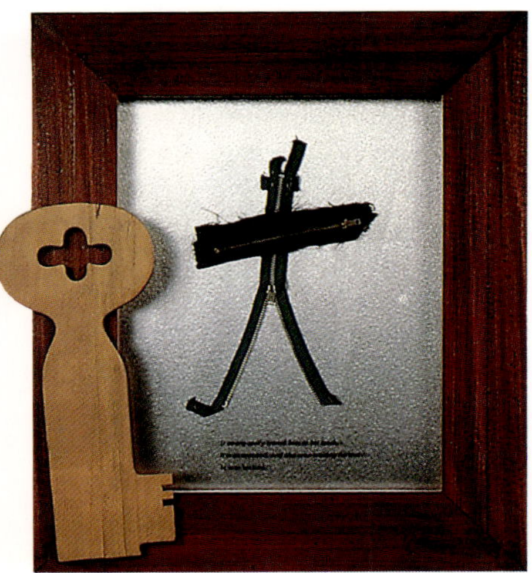

The warrior drew his short sword and cautiously descended.

a rickety flight of stairs that led to a dust-ridden corridor.

The noise was coming from 25. There was a thud, a curse, a heart-breaking moan of anguish.

I stopped in front of Room 901 and tried the door.

It swung easily toward him at his touch.
It was cracked, and she was waiting for me.
It was locked.

Forbidden Cargo, Forbidden Fruit, Forbidden Planet, 1982
Mixed-media collage, three panels, $20\frac{7}{16} \times 16\frac{7}{16}$;
$20\frac{7}{8} \times 17\frac{7}{8}$; $20 \times 18\frac{1}{8}$ inches
Collection of Peg and Chuck Rosenquist

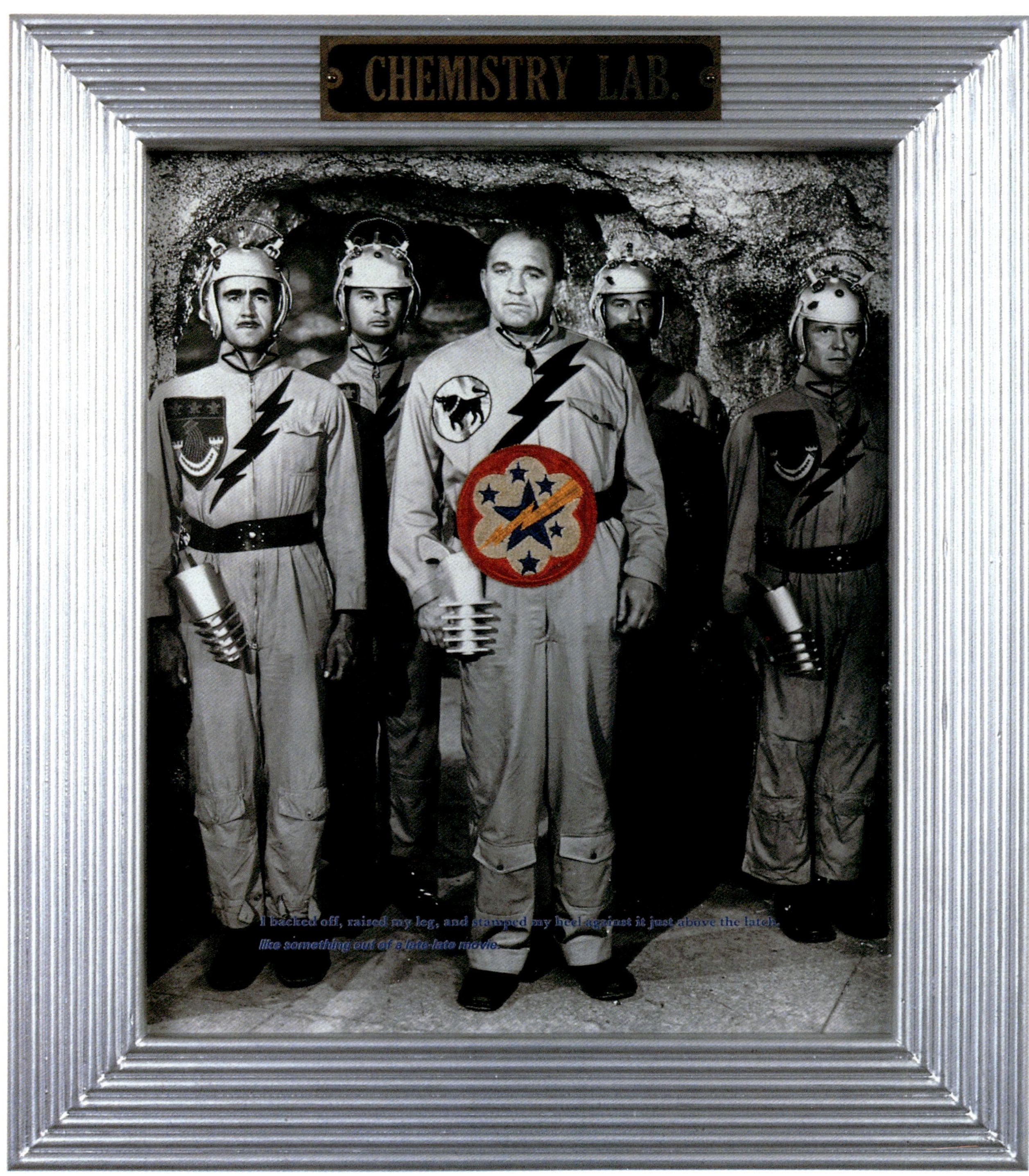

I backed off, raised my leg, and stamped my heel against it just above the latch.
like something out of a late-late movie.

Robot, 1982
Mixed-media collage, 20¾ × 17¾ inches
Collection of the artist

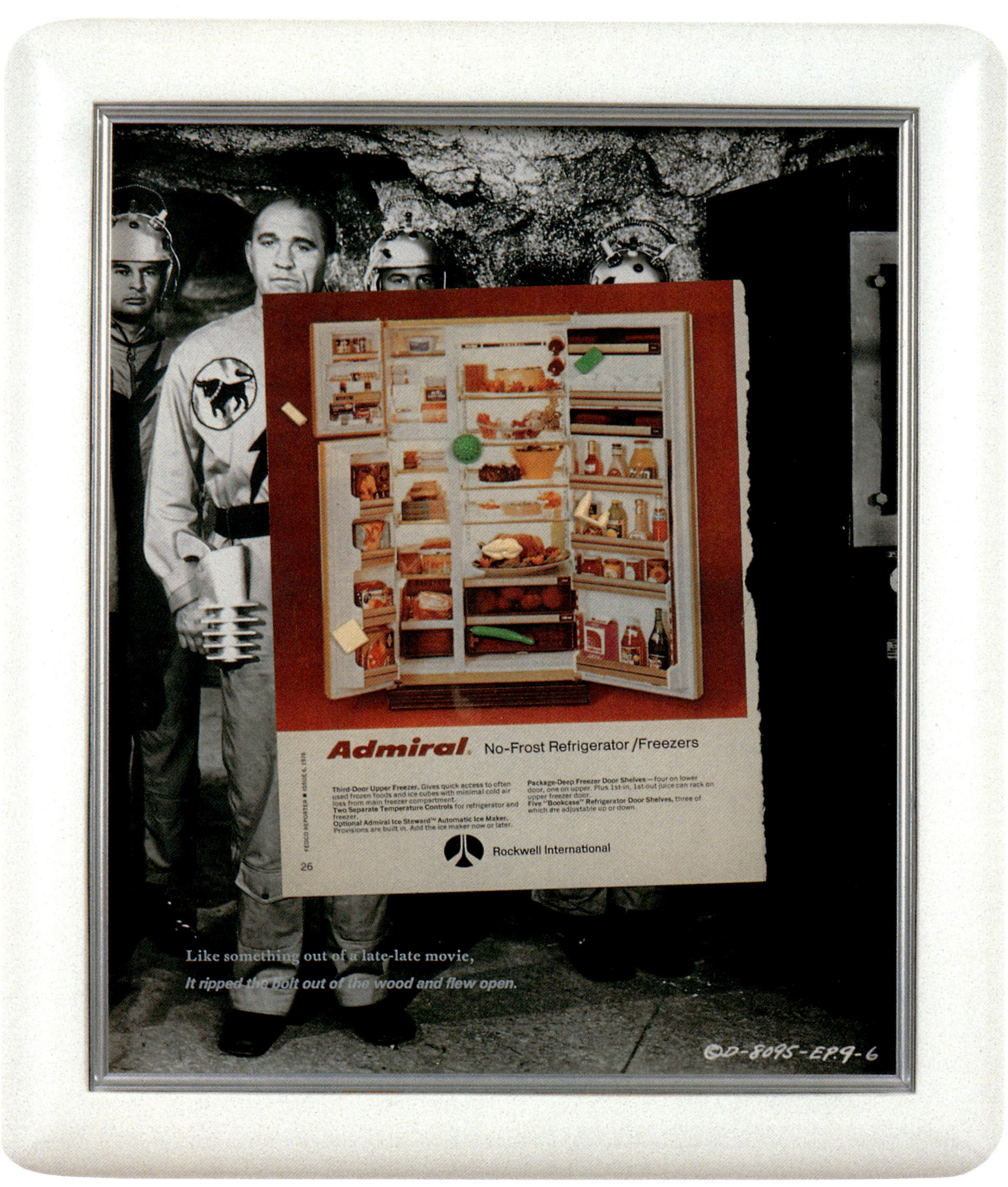

like something out of a late-late movie.

It ripped the bolt out of the wood and flew open.

I Married a Monster from Outer Space, 1982
Mixed-media collage, 19½ × 16½ inches
Collection of the artist

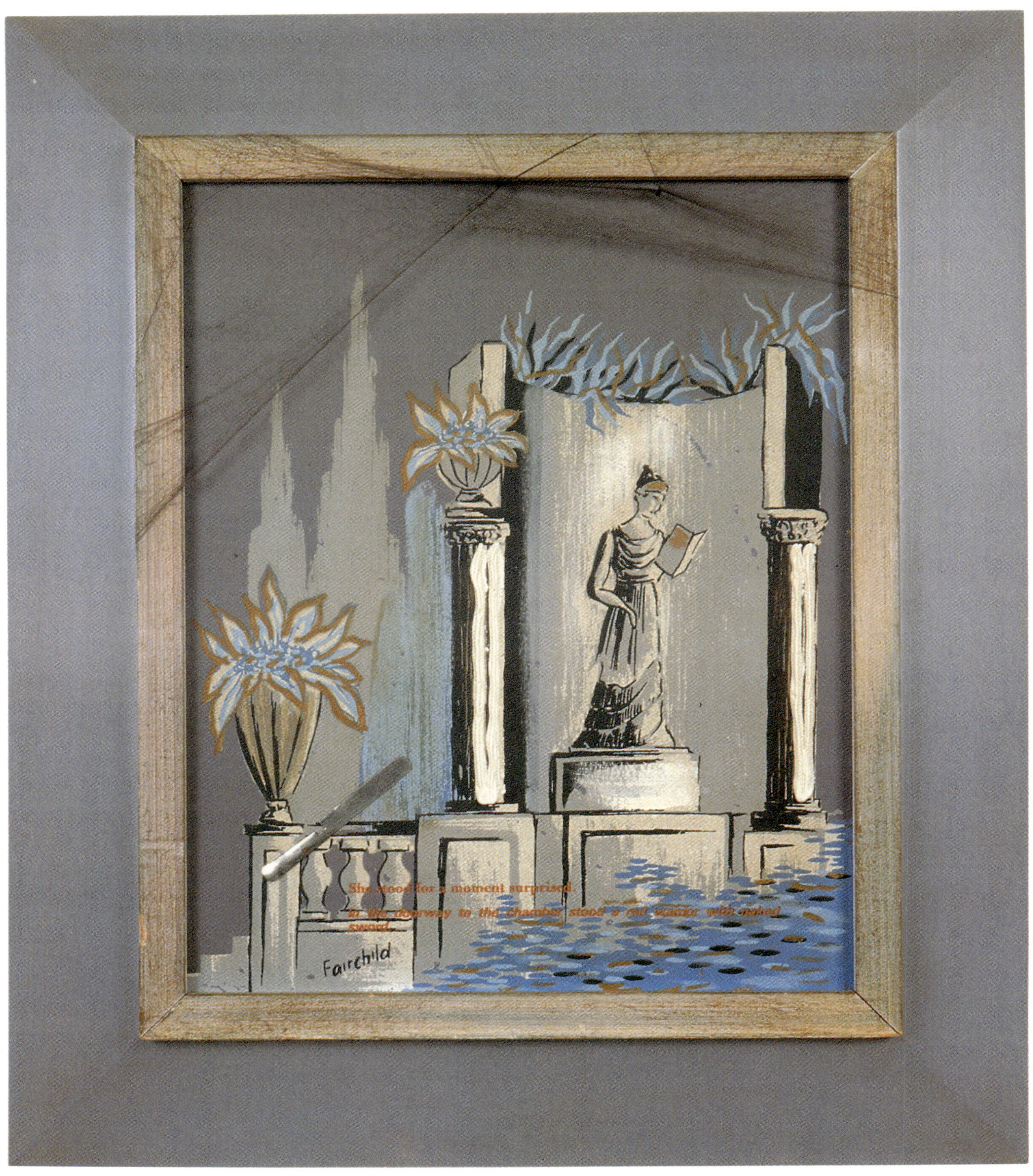

She stood for a moment surprised.

In the doorway to the chamber stood a red warrior with naked sword.

Fools Rush In, 1982
Mixed-media collage, 21 × 18⅛ inches
Collection of the artist

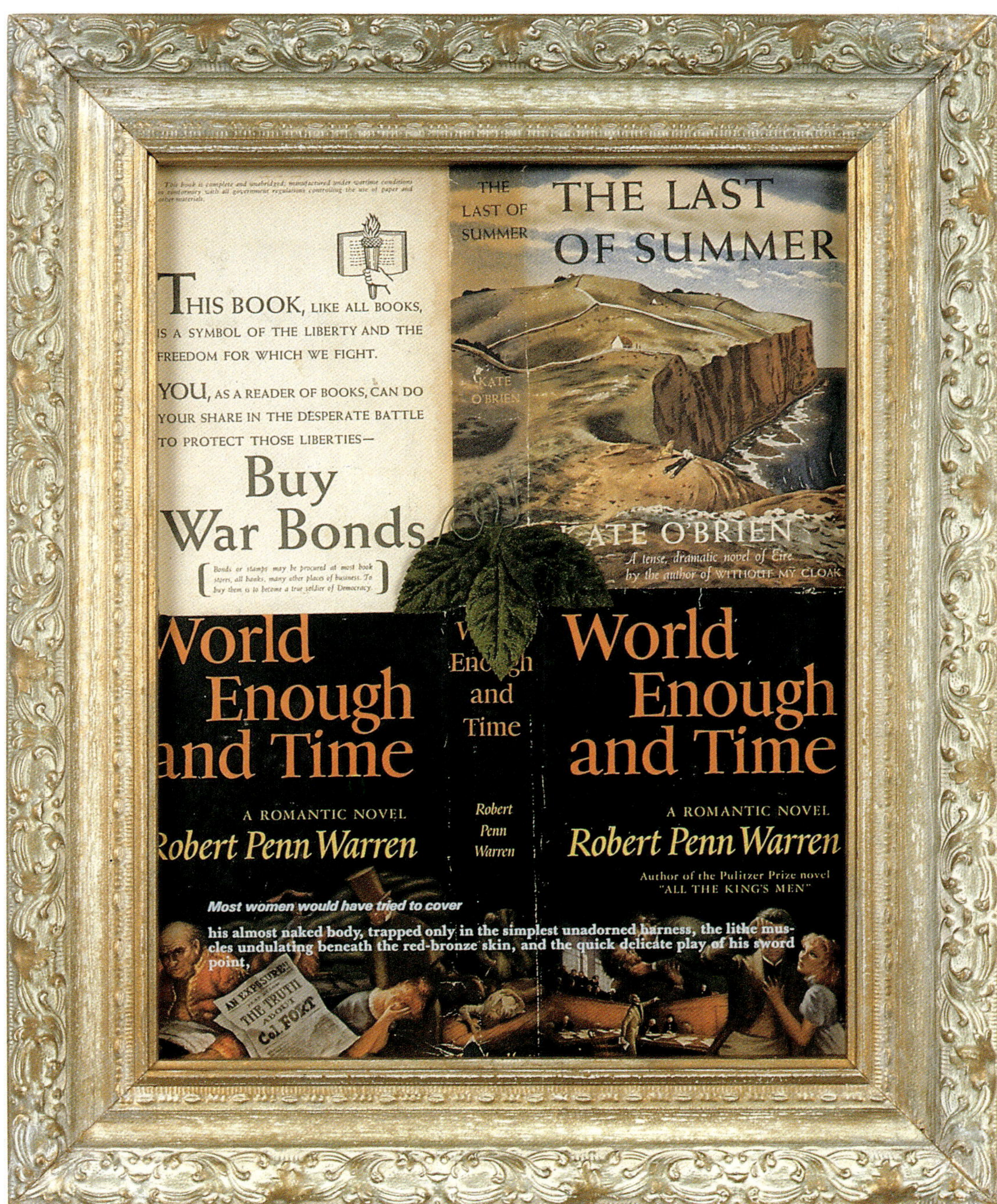

Most women would have tried to cover

his almost naked body, trapped only in the simplest unadorned harness, the lithe muscles undulating beneath the red-bronze skin, and the quick delicate play of his sword point,

Dust Jacket, 1982
Mixed-media collage, 20⅜ × 16⅜ inches
Lannan Foundation, Los Angeles

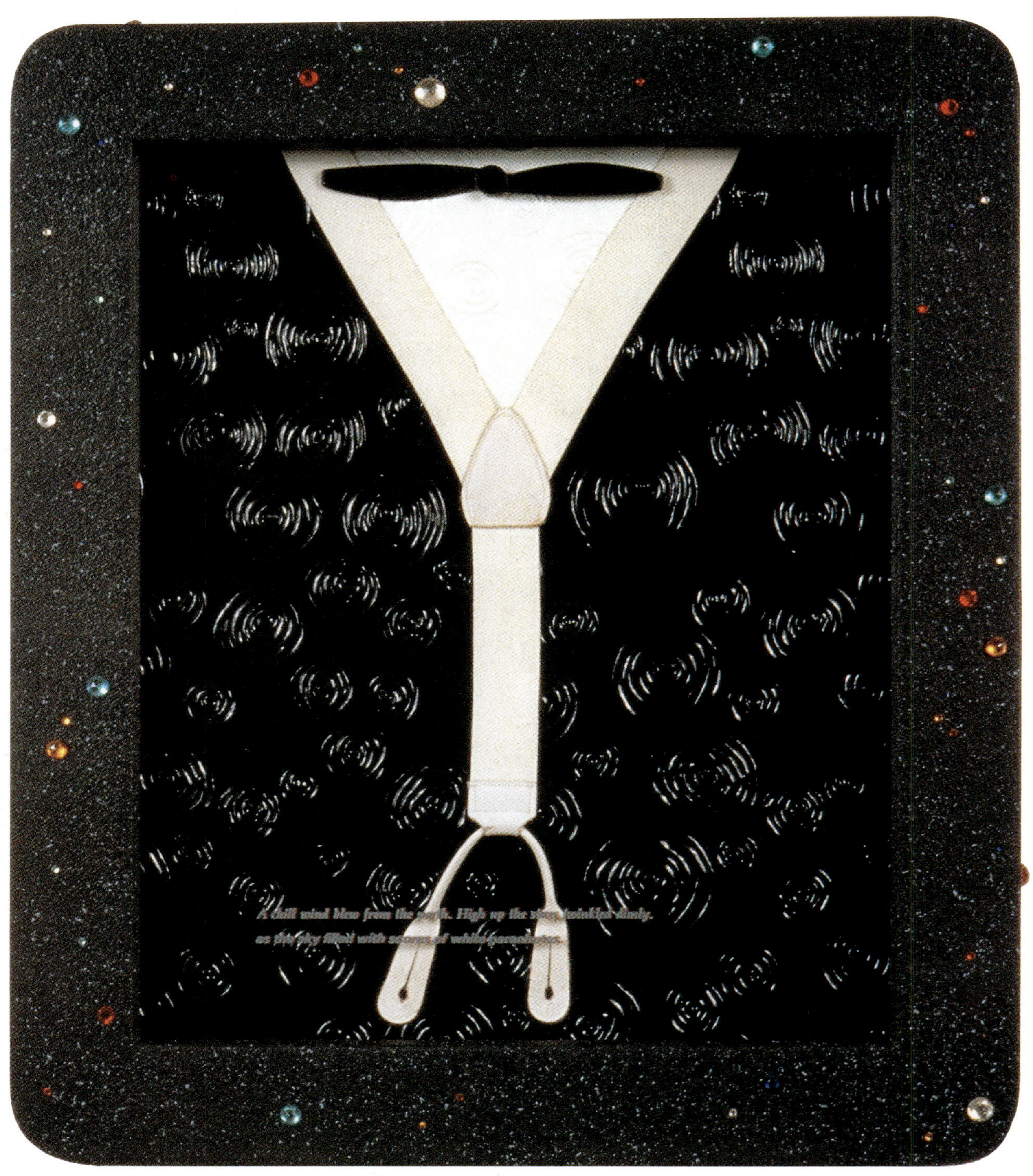

A chill wind blew from the north. High up the stars twinkled dimly.
as the sky filled with scores of white parachutes.

Christmas Eve, 1943, 1982
Mixed-media collage, two panels, 20½ × 17½;
20½ × 17 inches
San Diego Museum of Art; Gift of the Frederick R. Weisman Foundation

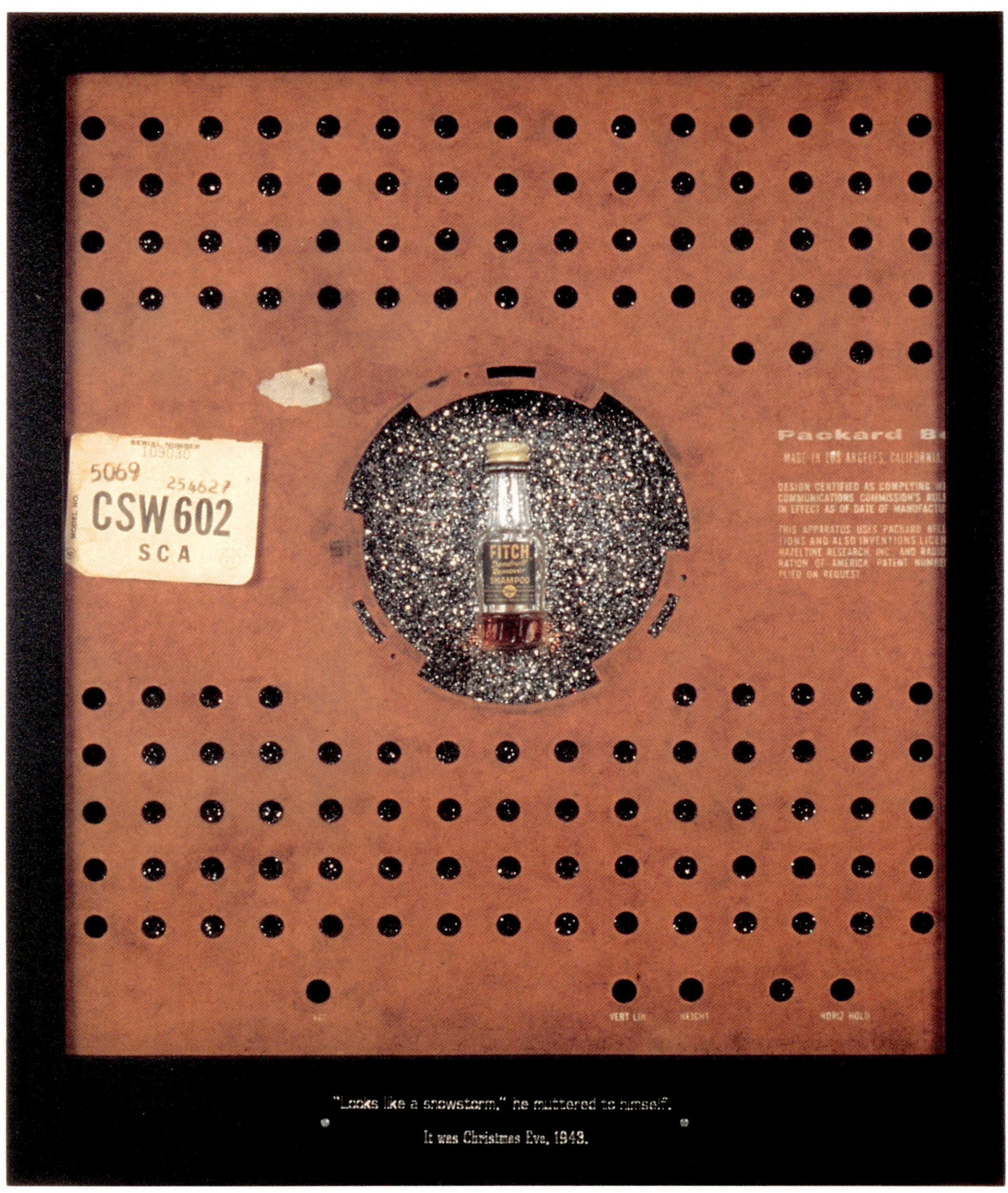

"Looks like a snowstorm," he muttered to himself.
It was Christmas Eve, 1943.

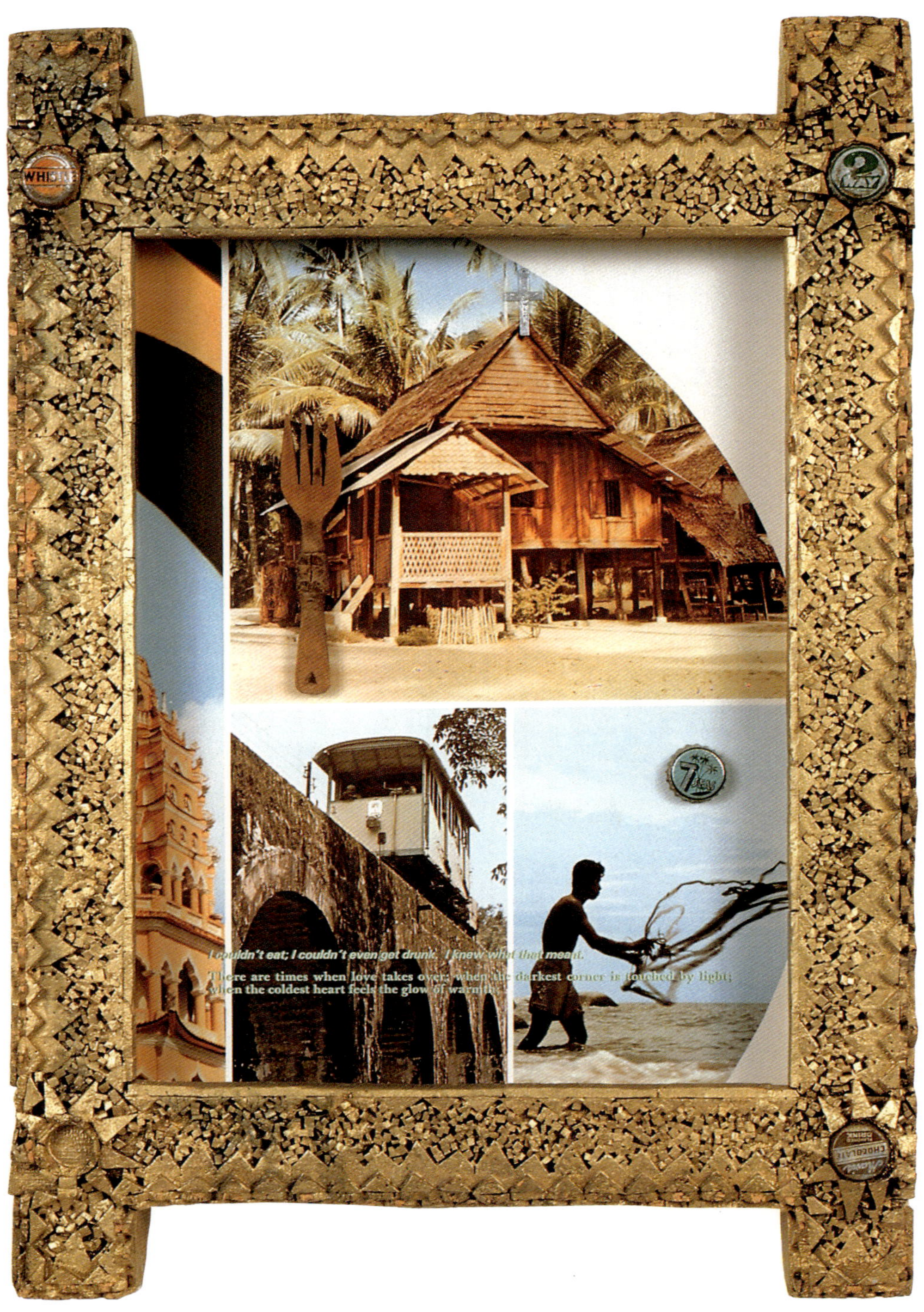

I couldn't eat; I couldn't even get drunk. I knew what that mean't.

There are times when love takes over; when the darkest corner is touched by light; when the coldest heart feels the glow of warmth;

Winter Wonderland, 1982
Mixed-media collage, 24½ × 16¾ inches
Collection of Richard Rosenzweig and Judy Henning

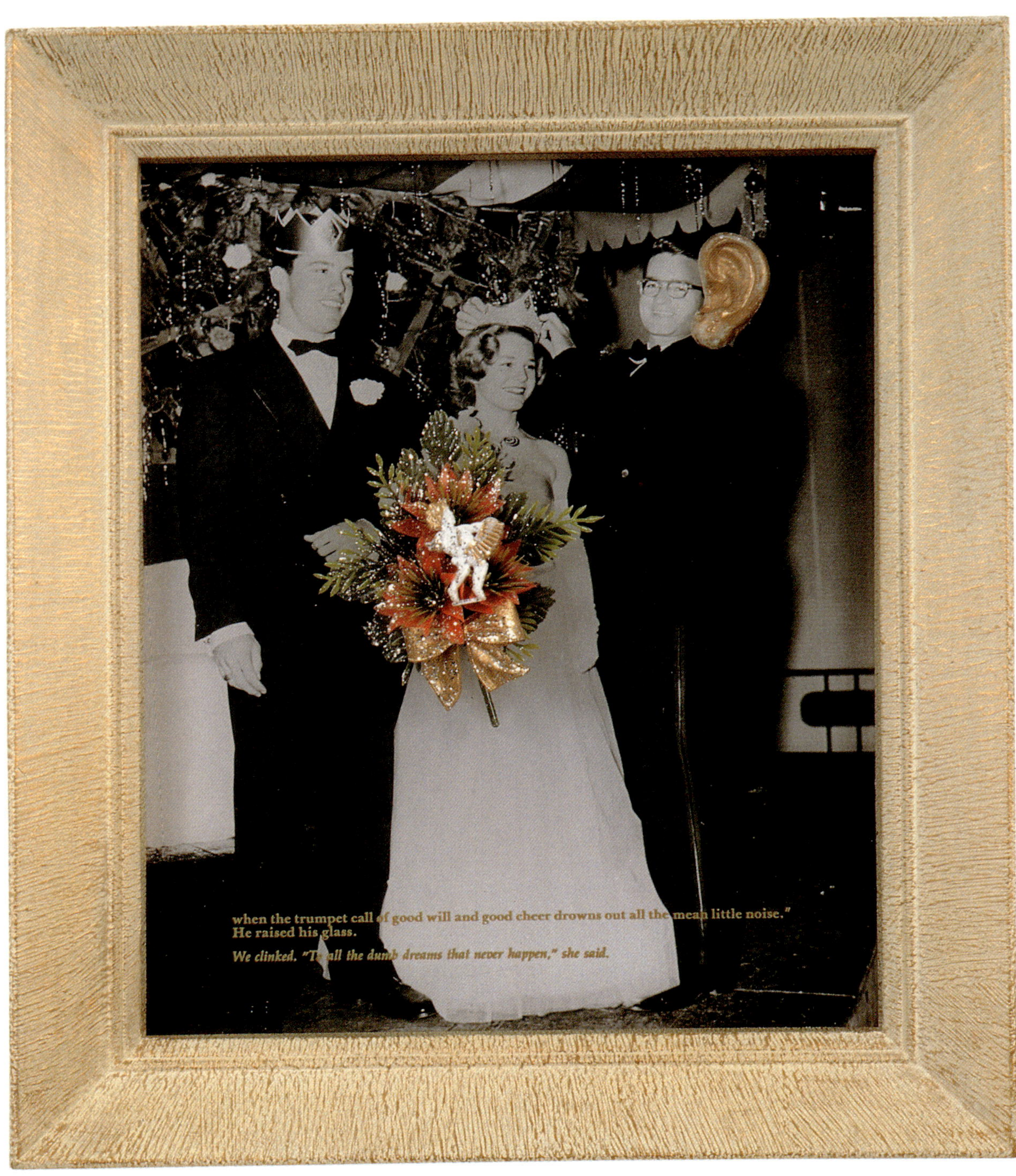

when the trumpet call of good will and good cheer drowns out all the mean little noise."
He raised his glass.

We clinked. "To all the dumb dreams that never happen," she said.

White Christmas, 1982
Mixed-media collage, 20¼ × 17¼ inches
Collection of James and Linda Burrows

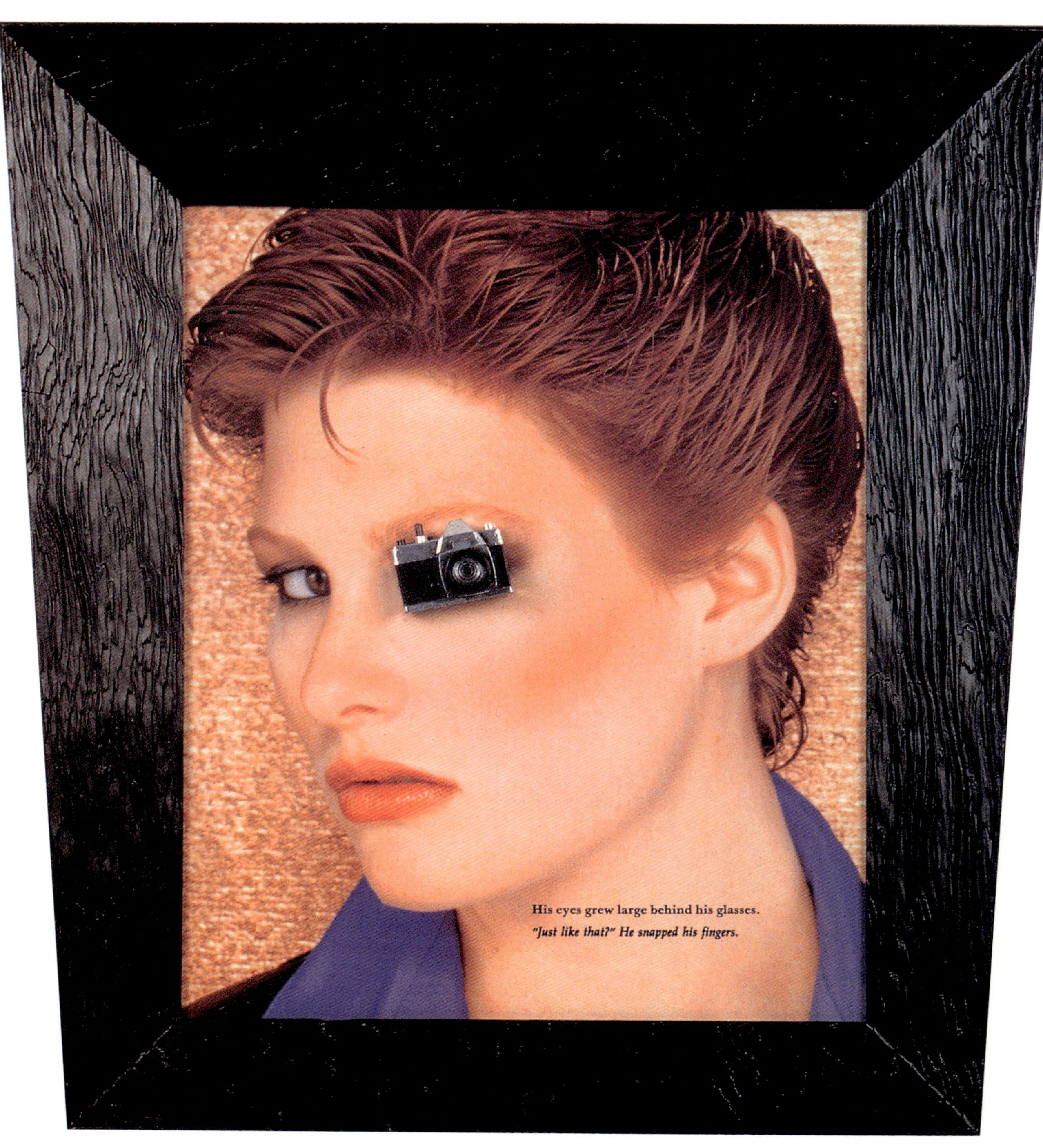

His eyes grew large behind his glasses.
"Just like that?" He snapped his fingers.

Snapshot, 1982
Mixed-media collage, 21¾ × 20 inches
Collection of Harold I. Huttas

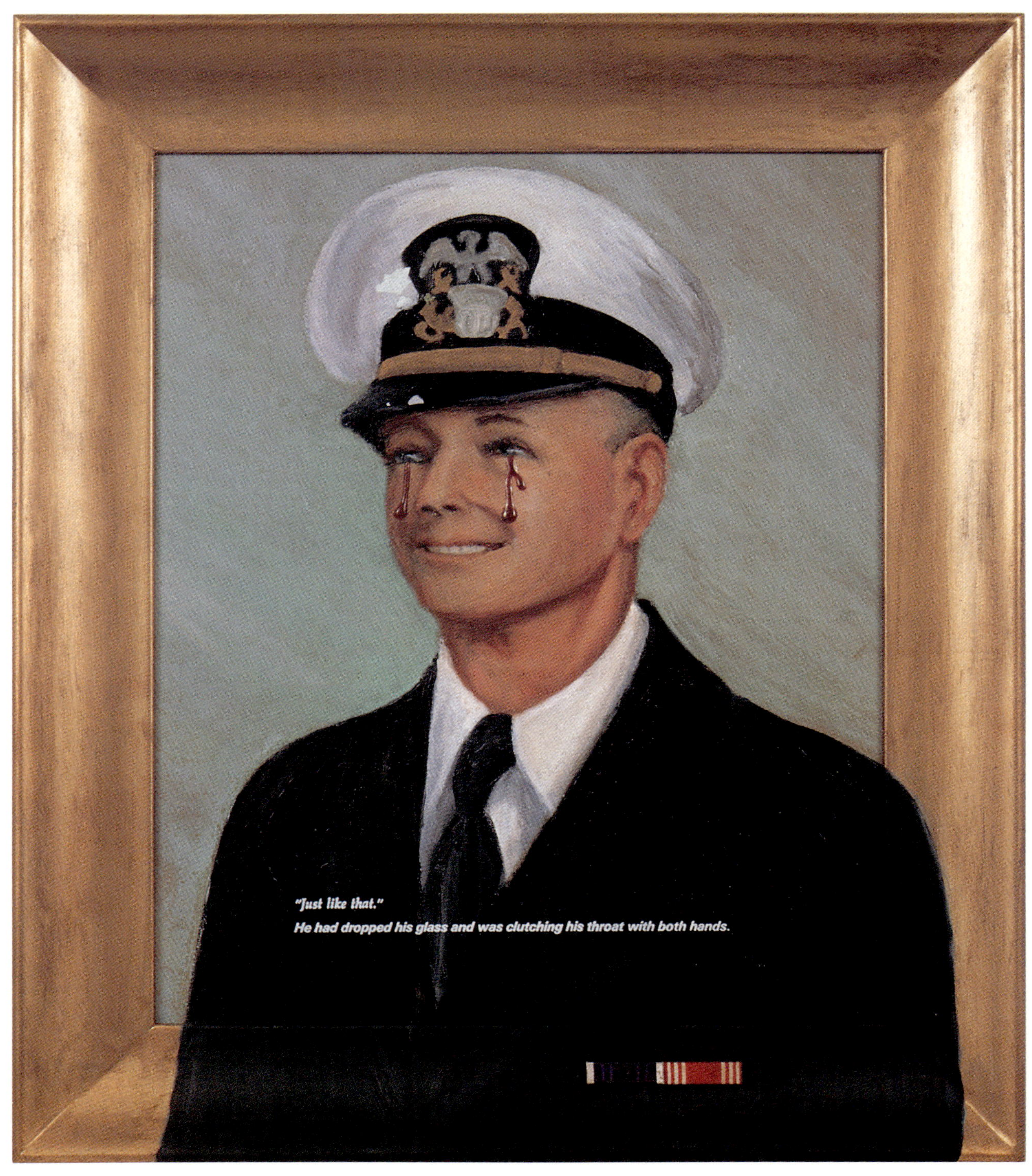

"Just like that."

He had dropped his glass and was clutching his throat with both hands.

Bloody Mary, 1982
Mixed-media collage, 20⅞ × 17⅞ inches
Margo Leavin Gallery, Los Angeles

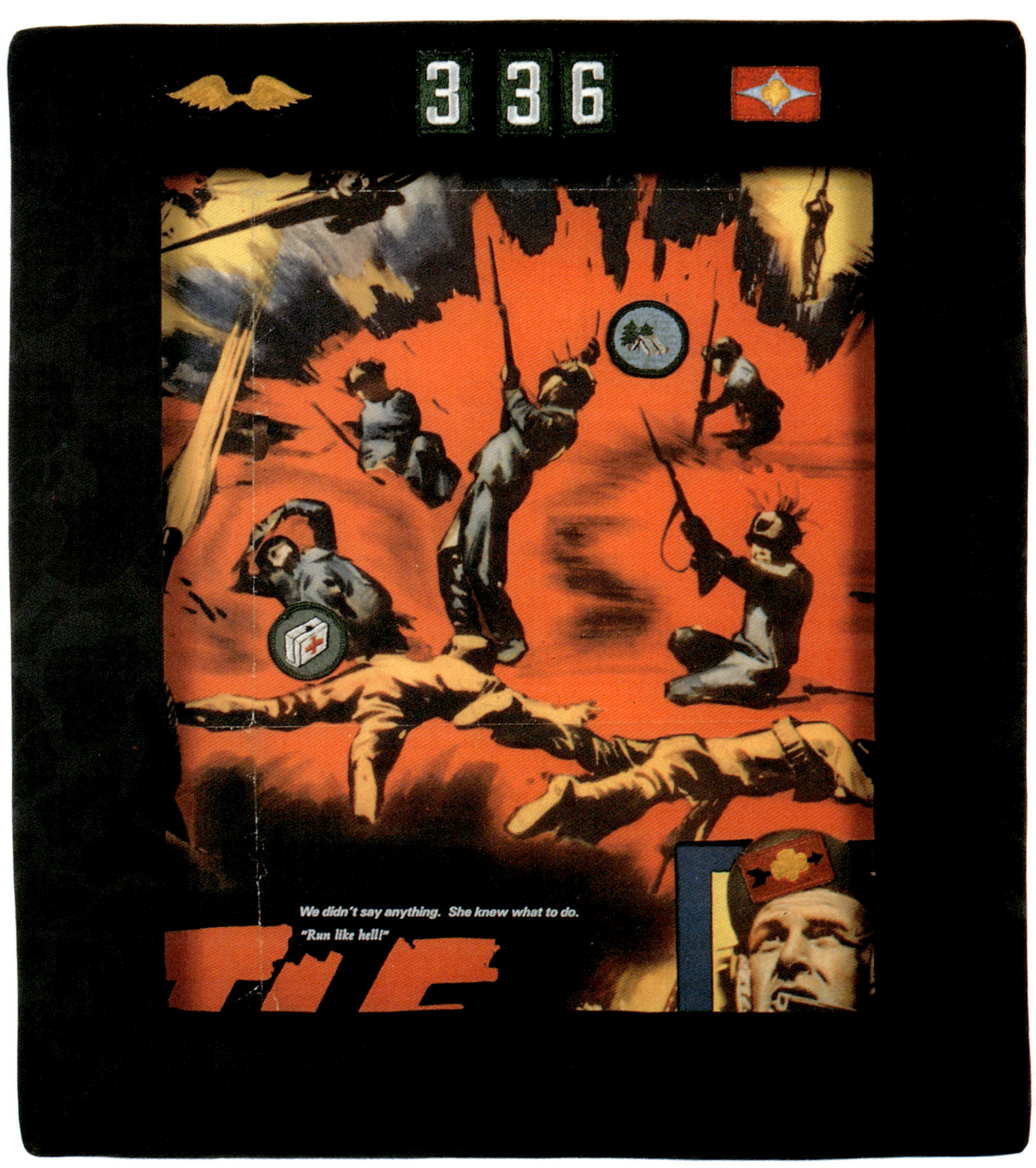

We didn't say anything. She knew what to do.

"Run like hell!"

Hell's Angels, 1982
Mixed-media collage, 21⅜ × 18⅝ inches
The Capital Group, Inc., Los Angeles

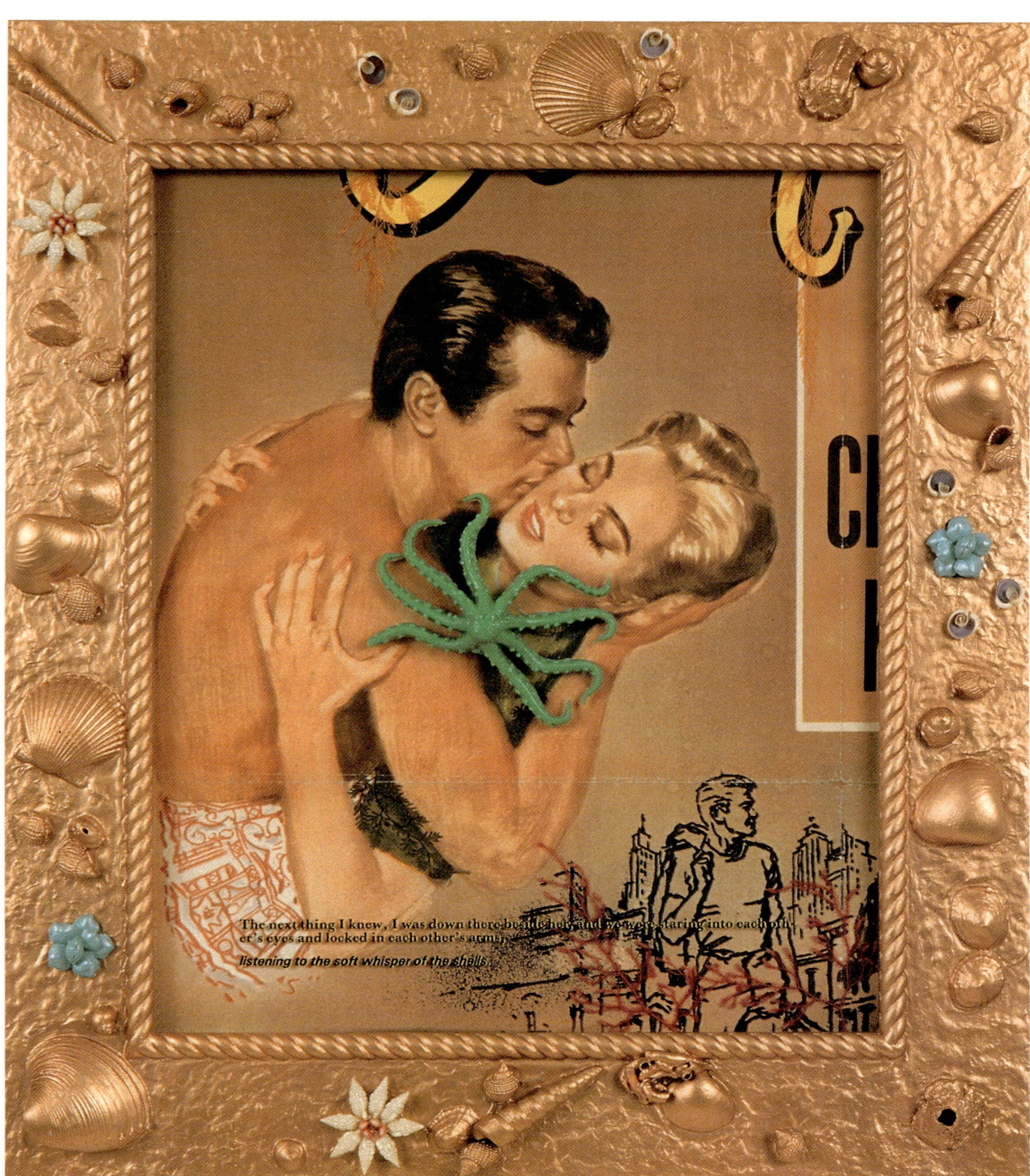

The next thing I knew, I was down there beside her, and we were staring into each other's eyes and locked in each other's arms,

listening to the soft whisper of the shells.

From Here to Eternity, 1982
Mixed-media collage, 21½ × 18½ inches
Collection of Max Palevsky

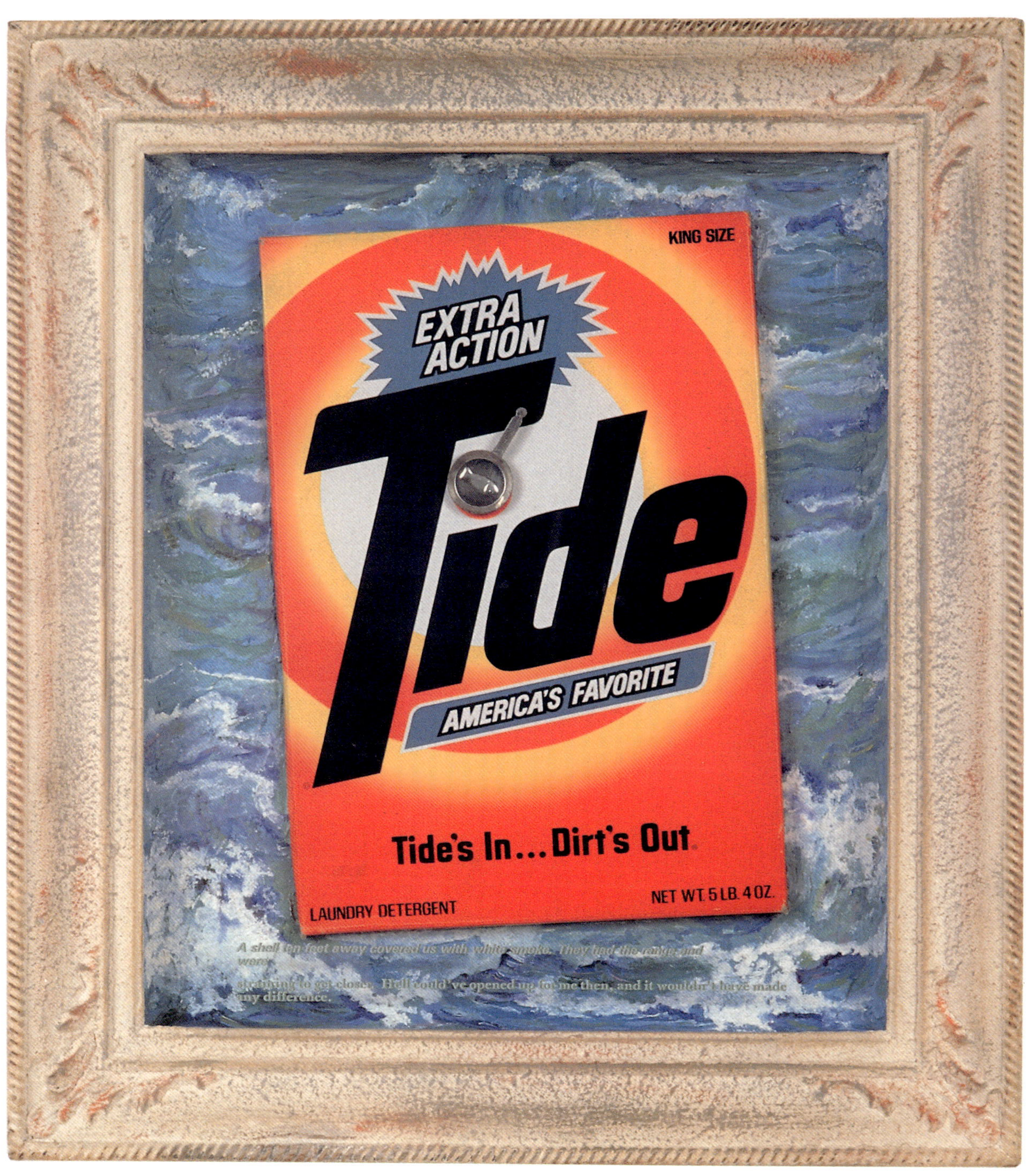

A shell ten feet away covered us with white smoke. They had the range and were

straining to get closer. Hell could've opened up for me then, and it wouldn't have made any difference.

Ebb Tide, 1982
Mixed-media collage, 21 × 18¹⁄₁₆ inches
The Walt Disney Company, Los Angeles

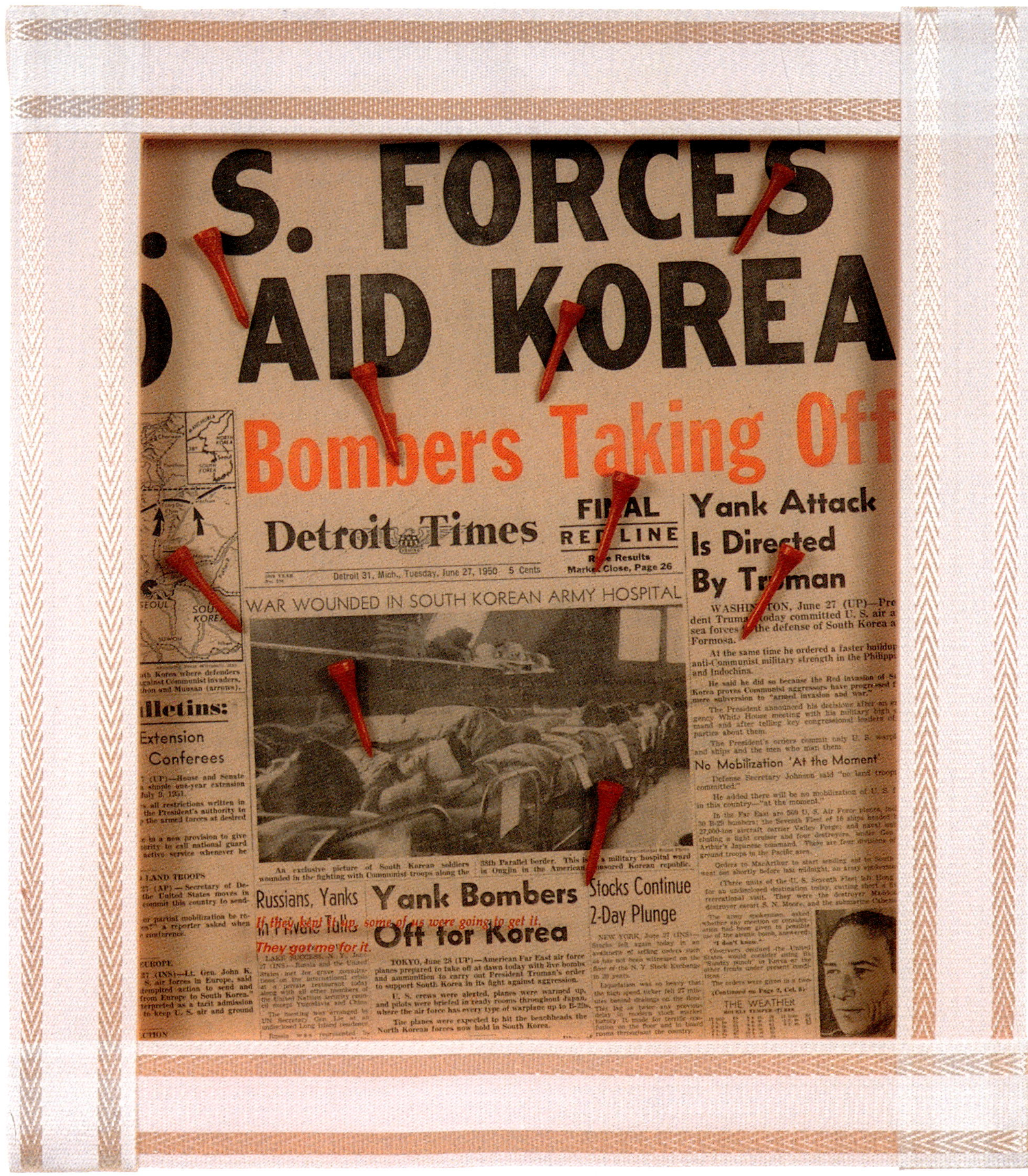

If they kept it up, some of us were going to get it.
They got me for it.

Nine Holes, 1982
Mixed-media collage, 20⅝ × 17¾ inches
Collection of James and Linda Burrows

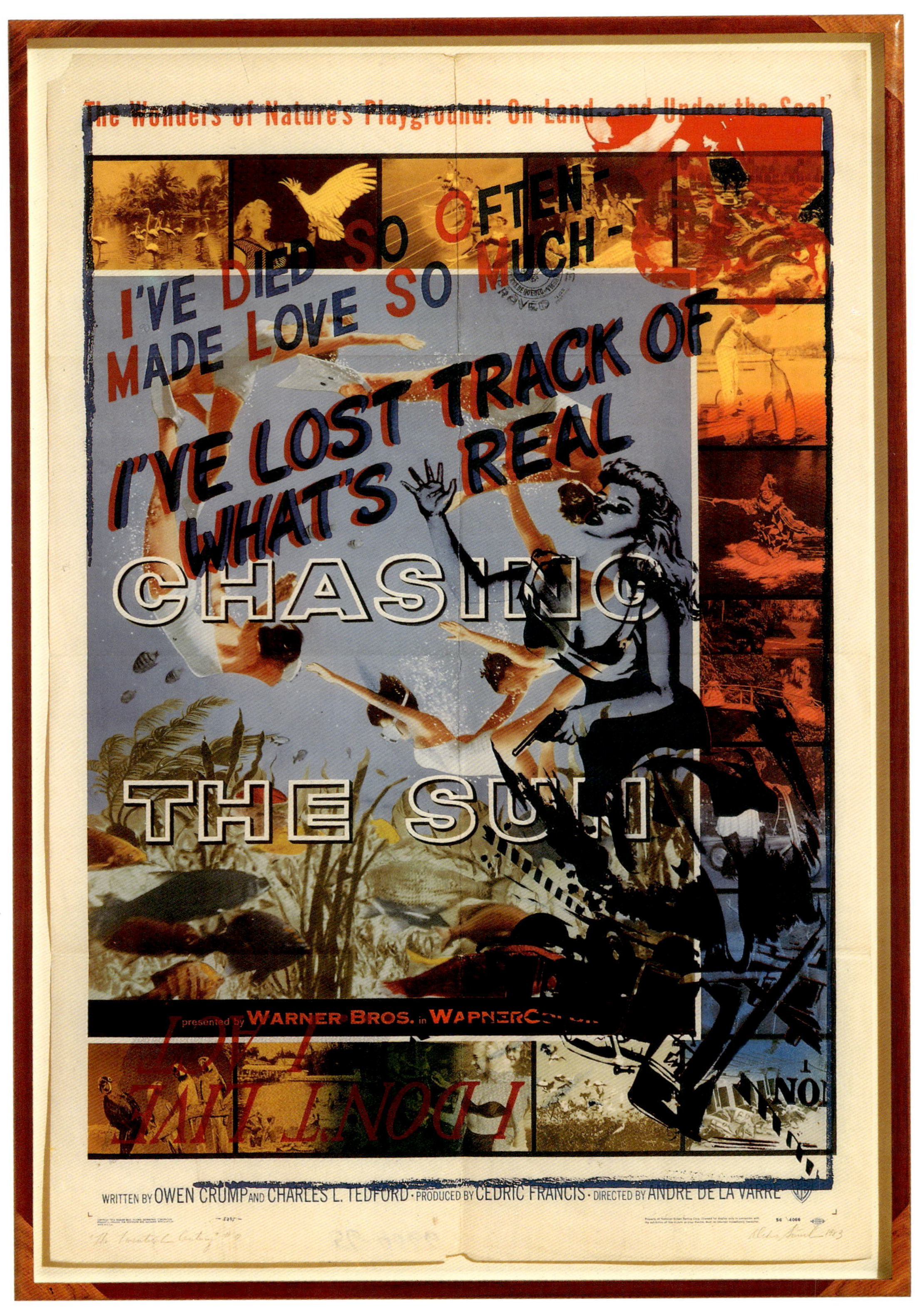

The Twentieth Century #19, 1983
Silkscreen on movie poster, 42 × 27½ inches
Collection of Linda Kent

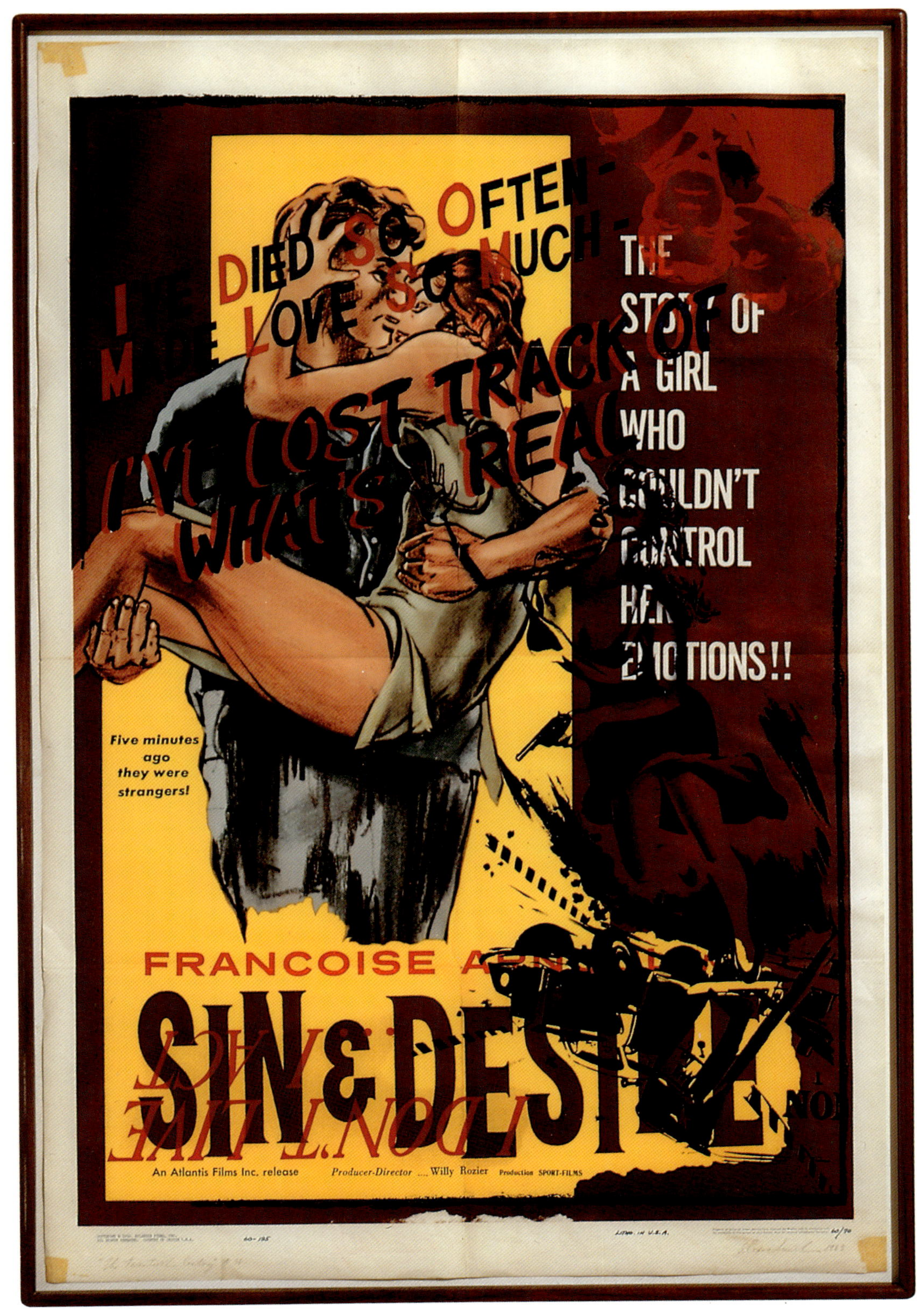

The Twentieth Century #31, 1983
Silkscreen on movie poster, 42 × 27½ inches
Margo Leavin Gallery, Los Angeles

For an exhibition at the Margo Leavin Gallery in Los Angeles in 1985, Smith produced a series of independent collages, the *Jane* series. She used a common name to bind a body of mostly easel-size works that both demonstrate and question the fate of a variety of women. The cumulative impact depended on the especially rich word-image conjunction. In some ways, the show looked as demure as its title. Its component collages are physically smaller and more introspective than their immediate predecessors.

The *Jane* series was an outgrowth of Smith's earliest interest in heroines, personified by Isadora Duncan. As she recalled, "I started with Jane Doe, then I made the comparison between Tarzan and Jane and Jayne Mansfield and Mickey Hargitay being parallels, then I thought of other Jane couples: Dick and Jane, Jane Russell and Howard Hughes, Paul and Jane Bowles. Then I thought of the English Janes: Jane Eyre, Jane Austen, then Calamity Jane." Exhausted from a year spent working on *The Grand*, a theater remodeling in Grand Rapids, Michigan, Smith wanted to return to her studio and to engage a subject that had at least some autobiographical overtones.

In the fictional and factual Janes, Smith perceived a metaphorical power. Slang for everywoman, Jane could speak to universal situations. "I started collecting these things and drawing parallels between the lives of these women who had a tough time. I was at a point in my life when you wake up one morning and realize that your life isn't going to work out quite the way you imagined." The connections between the Calamity Janes and Smith's life were obvious: just turned

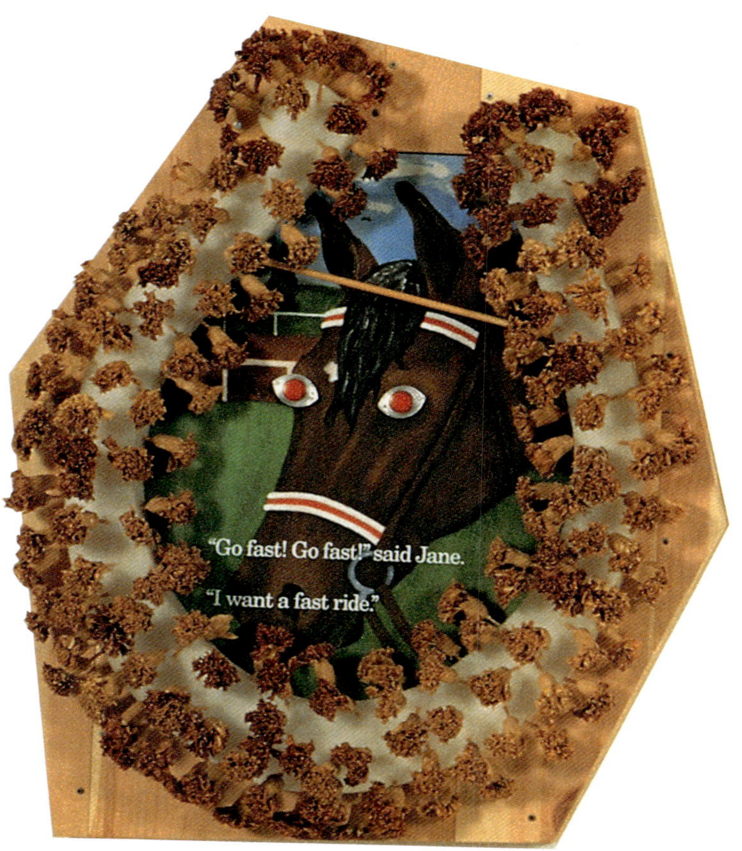

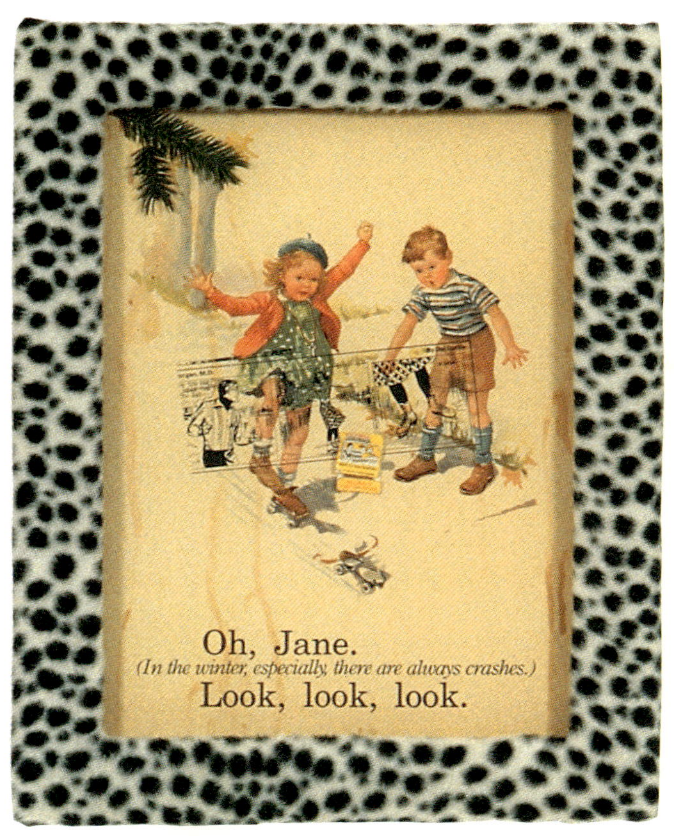

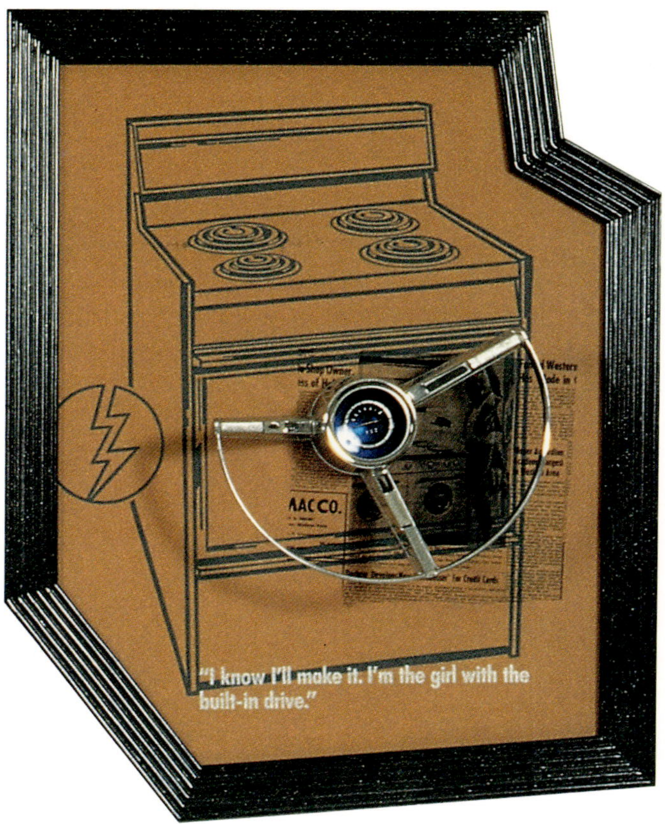

Jane Doe, 1985
Mixed-media collage, three panels, 29⅜ × 24¾; 29 × 22½; 29⅜ × 23 inches
Refco Group, Ltd., Chicago

thirty-five, she had severed ties with her New York dealer, and her father had recently died, leaving her essentially without family. The early 1980s were also the heyday of Neo-Expressionism, a painting style that fostered enormous, disjunctive pictures—many of them incorporating appropriated material and all by men who achieved a fame and commercial success unknown to contemporary artists since the rapid rise of Pop art in the early 1960s. Smith's concerns, however, were not bombastic. Moreover, though she intended her gender to be self-evident in the work, she has repeatedly cautioned in interviews against reading the *Janes* as a feminist tract. Her intentions remained transformative, even aesthetic, rather than sociopolitical: "what I'm trying to do is generate a mythology out of things we experience everyday to give a kind of meaning to everyday life and show the story and patterns as they exist in the things we gloss over."

The tales of the Janes are far from triumphant. All seek to control their destinies, a wish compromised more often than not by anatomy, biology, and/or chemistry. Frequently paired against a mythic male counterpart—Tarzan, Dick, et al.—Jane is forever a subordinate in love, deluded by it or by other emotions, and constitutionally weaker, somehow disadvantaged.

The single-image Janes—Calamity Jane foremost among them—betray a related victimization. In *Hell on Wheels*, for example, a gun-toting Calamity (played by Frances Farmer looking eerily like Smith herself) cries plaintively, "I just wish they'd leave me alone, and let me go to hell by my own route." Plastered across her torso and lower face are the Salvation Army's so-called "Articles of War" (a temperance statement) and a label torn from a bottle of Thunderbird wine. This Jane is weary from her trials with "them," asking only for tolerance of her independence. It can also be seen as a self-portrait appropriately inscribed.

The Janes are as physically varied as the parts of *Christmas Eve, 1943* and share their 1940s-early 1950s look. Against the flotsam of old Hollywood—photos, magazine and newspaper pages, maps, pieces of fabric—Smith has collaged such items as a key ring, charm bracelet trinkets, business cards, and snapshots. As before, frames serve to enhance her images: the glossy pink and black frames of the two parts of *The Girl Can't Help It* subtly configure two female torsos—one eulogizing Jayne Mansfield's impressive bust, the other, with a camera strung over it, alluding to her grisly death by decapitation. In the *Jane* series, Smith often had her quotations silkscreened directly on the collaged surfaces to form a seamless meta-object.

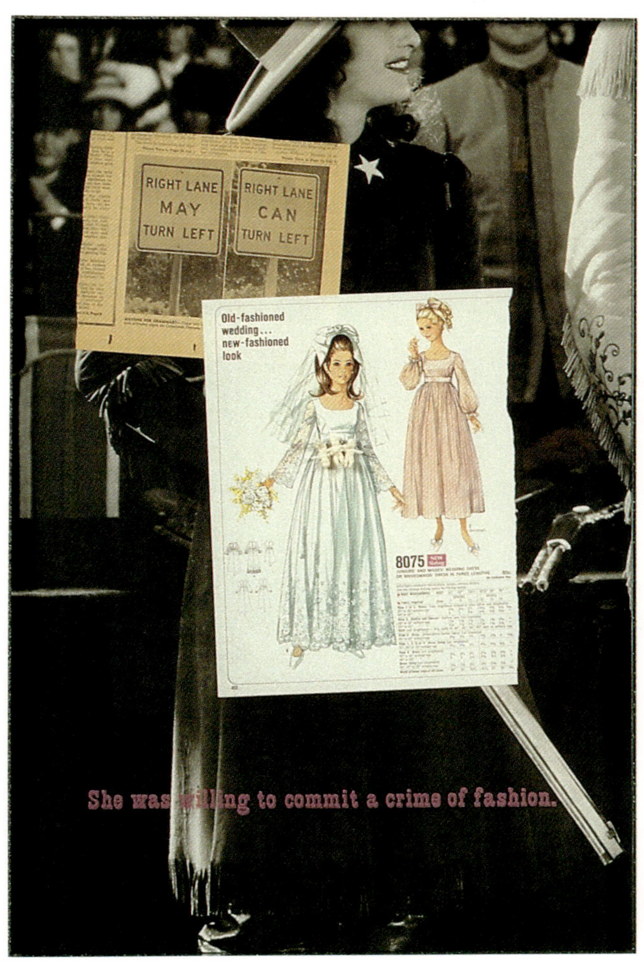

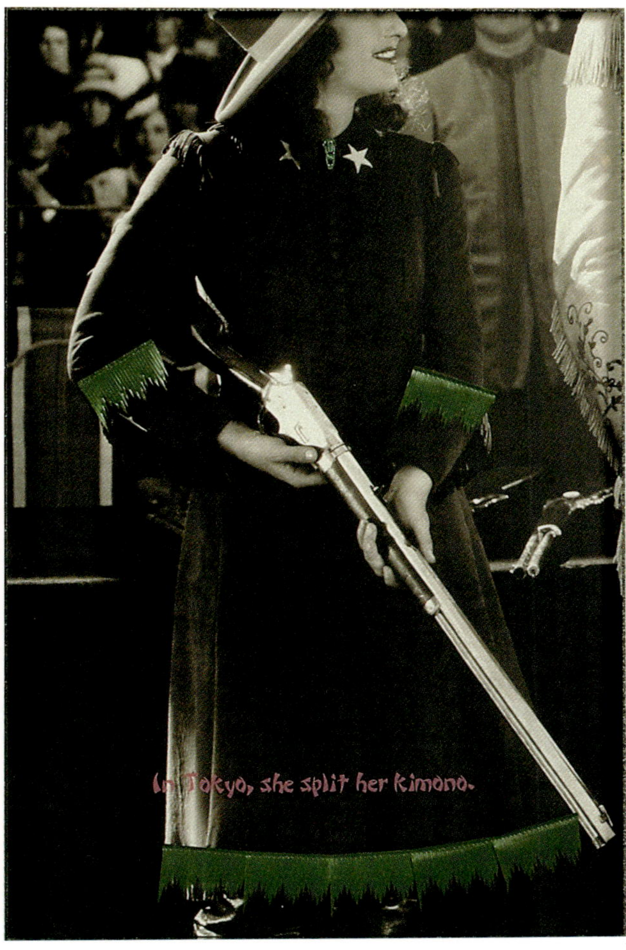

Calamity Jane, 1985
Mixed-media collage, two panels, 32 × 20¾ inches each
Collection of Anne and William J. Hokin

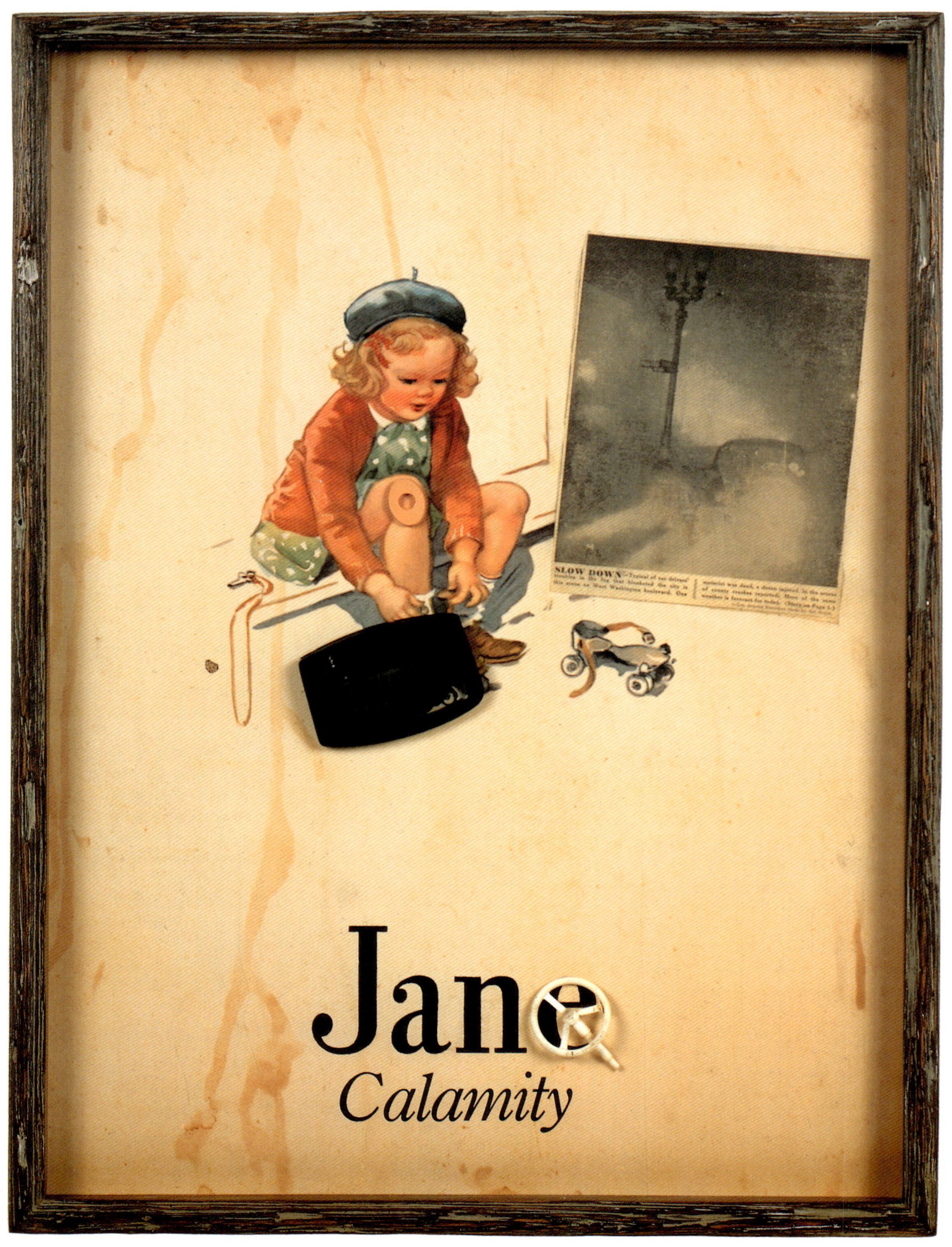

Calamity and Deadwood, 1985
Mixed-media collage, two panels, 24⅝ × 18⅛ inches each
Collection of Andres and Vanessa Moraga

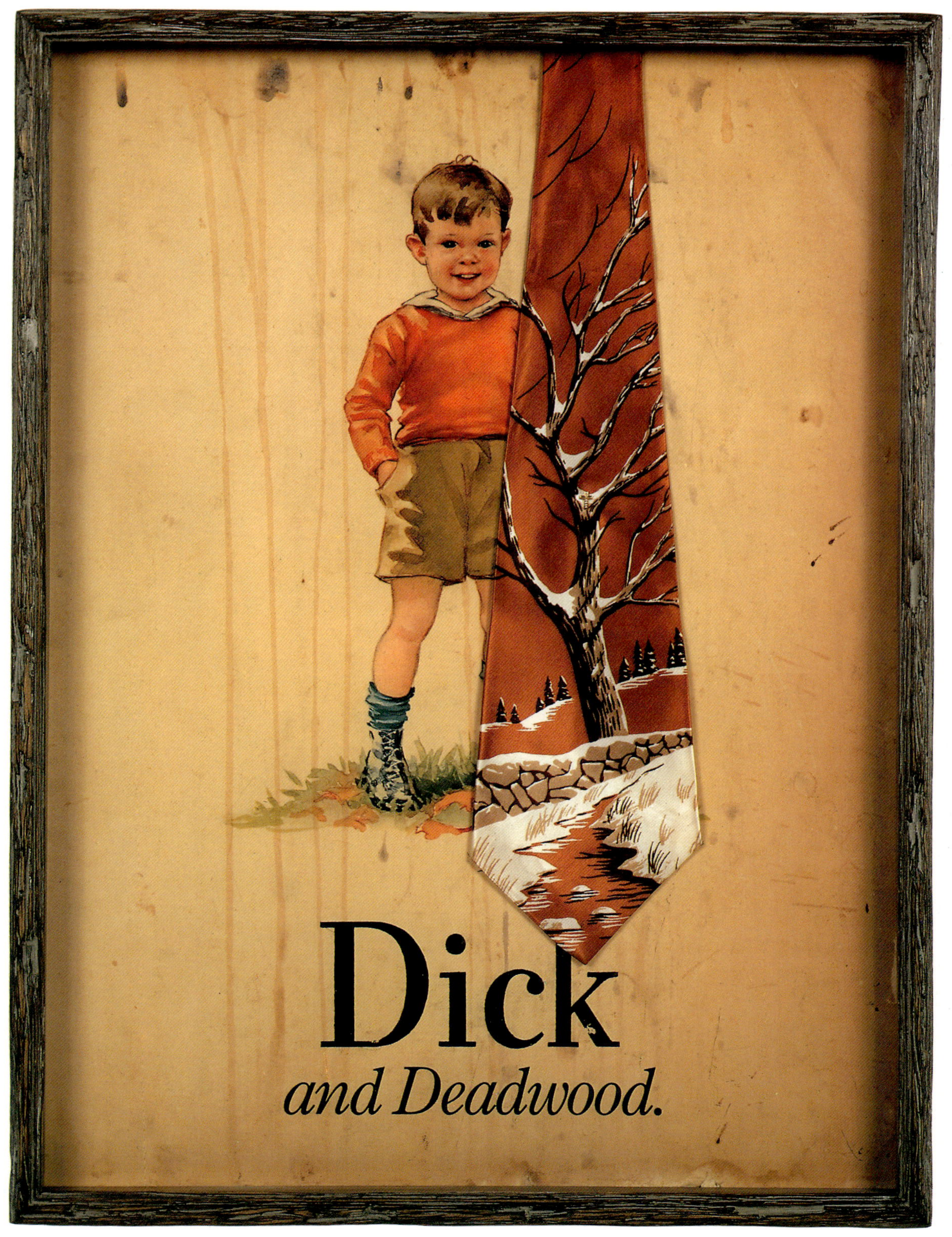
Dick
and Deadwood.

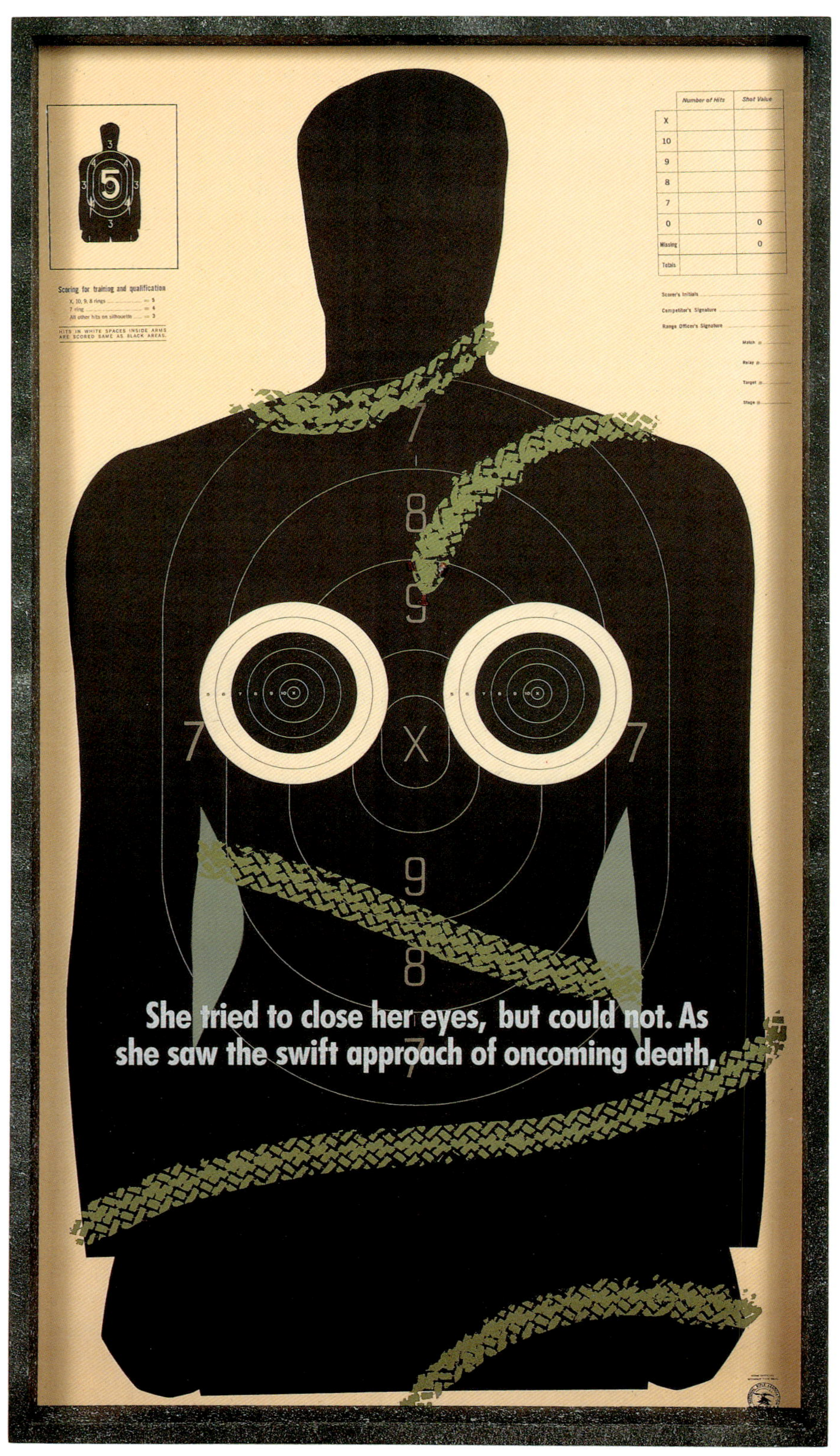

Asphalt Jungle, 1985
Mixed-media collage, two panels, 45⅛ × 25 inches each
The Museum of Contemporary Art, Los Angeles;
The El Paso Natural Gas Company Fund for California Art

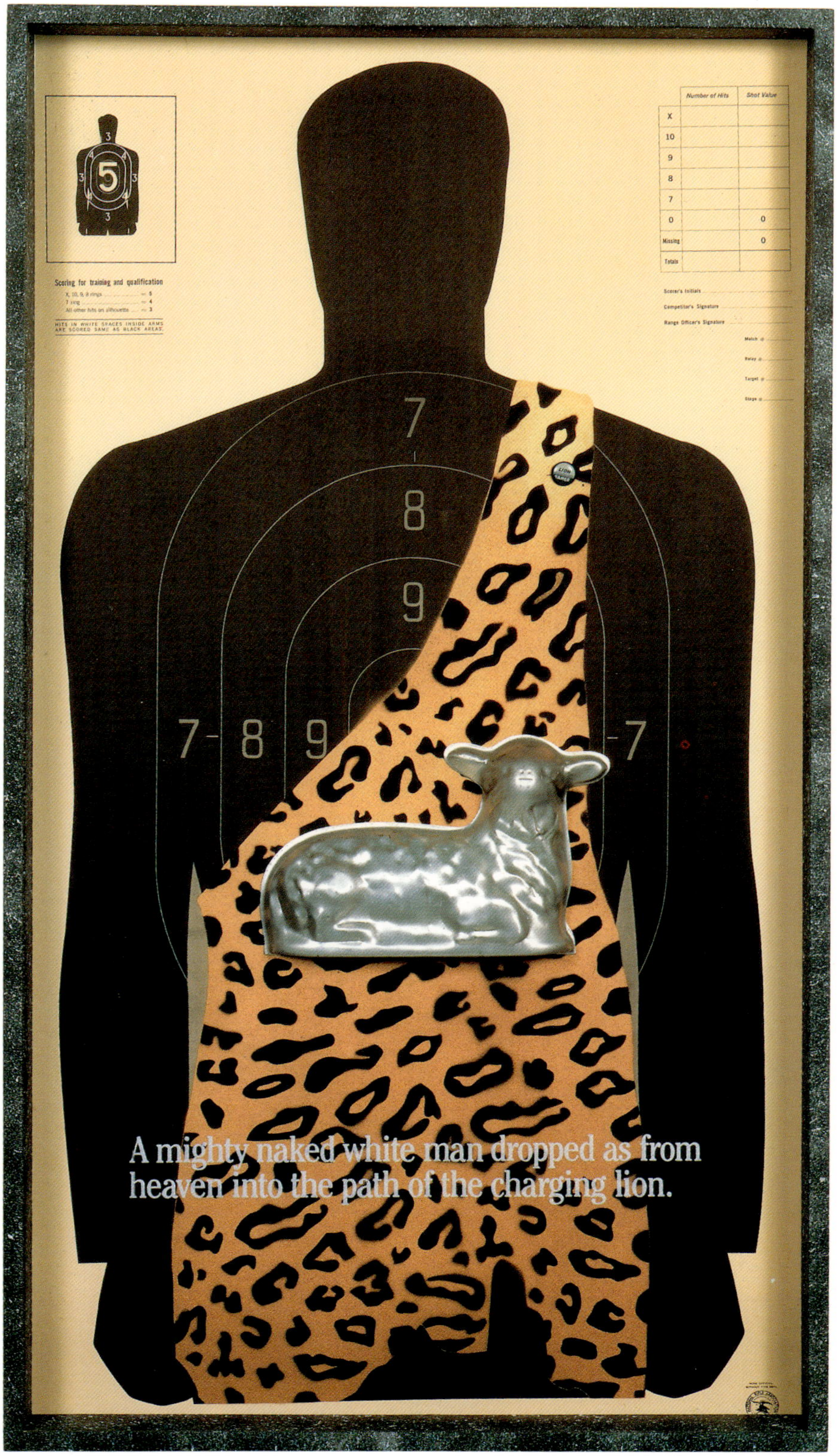

A mighty naked white man dropped as from heaven into the path of the charging lion.

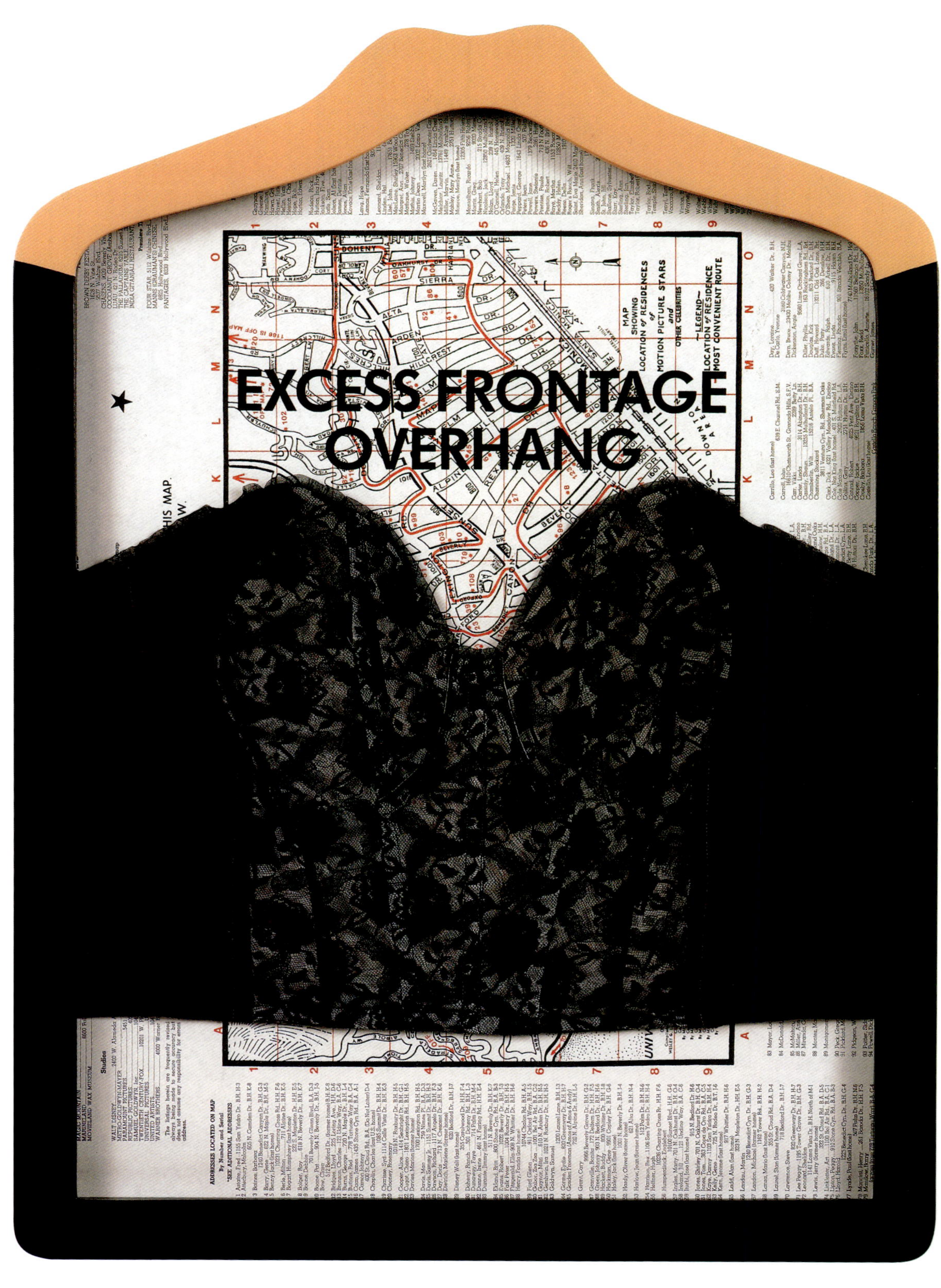

The Girl Can't Help It, 1985
Mixed-media collage, two panels, 26⅛ × 18⅞ inches each
Collection of Merry Norris

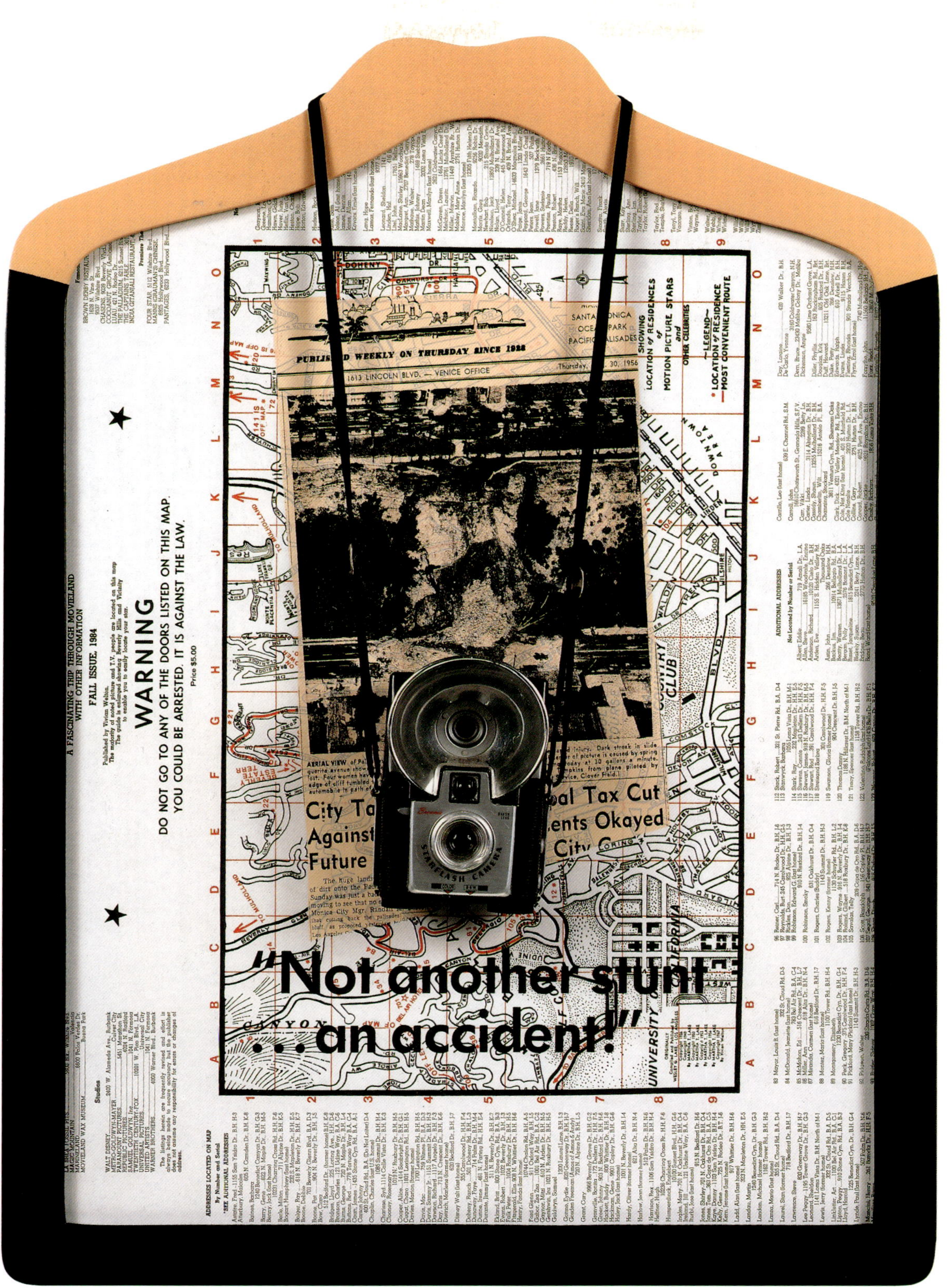
A FASCINATING TRIP THROUGH MOVIELAND WITH OTHER INFORMATION
FALL ISSUE, 1984
WARNING
DO NOT GO TO ANY OF THE DOORS LISTED ON THIS MAP. YOU COULD BE ARRESTED. IT IS AGAINST THE LAW.
Price $5.00
SHOWING LOCATION of RESIDENCES of MOTION PICTURE STARS and OTHER CELEBRITIES
—LEGEND—
• LOCATION of RESIDENCE
—MOST CONVENIENT ROUTE
SANTA MONICA
OCEAN PARK
PACIFIC PALISADES
1613 LINCOLN BLVD. — VENICE OFFICE
STARFLASH CAMERA
COUNTRY CLUB
"Not another stunt
...an accident!"

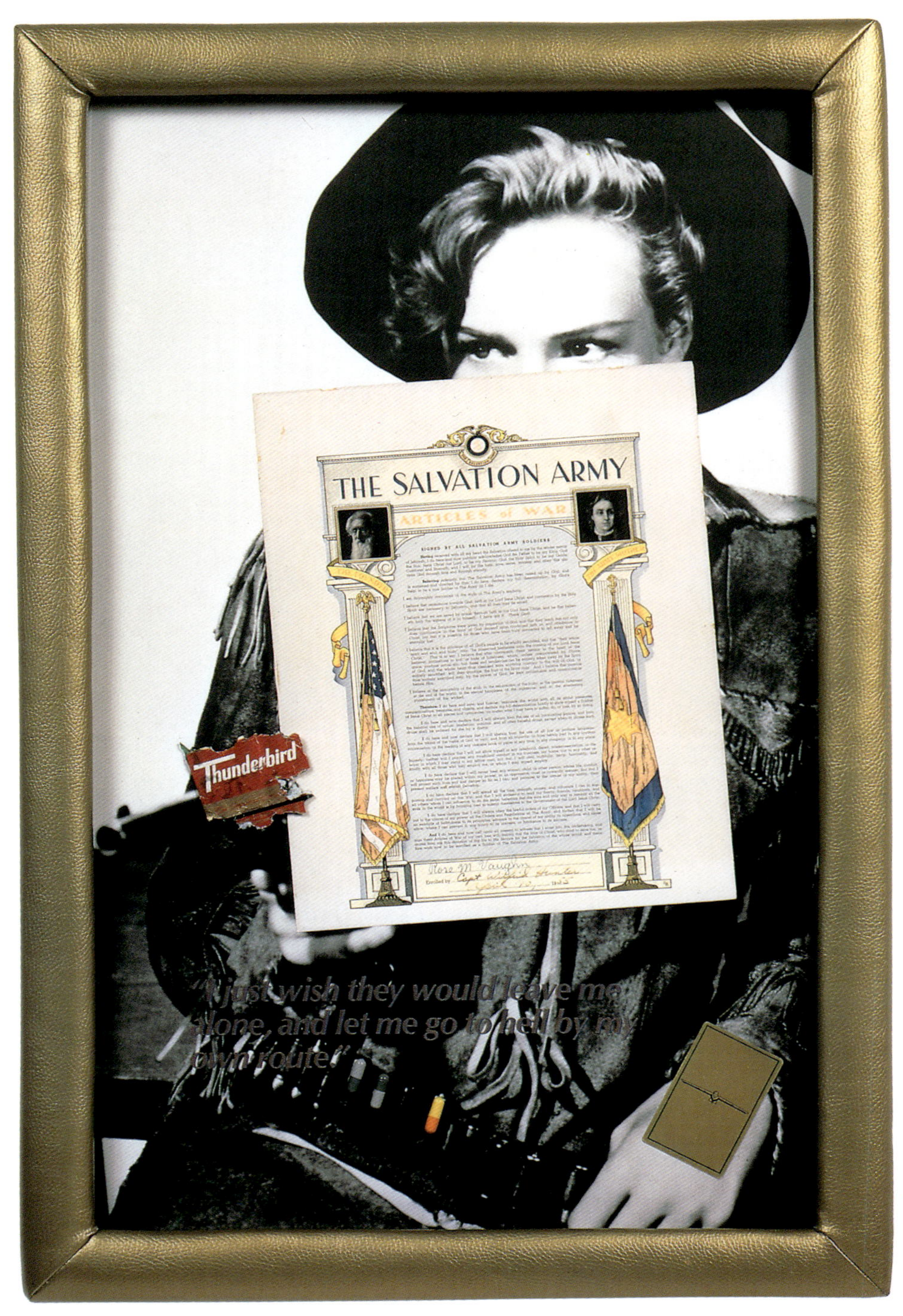

"I just wish they would leave me alone, and let me go to hell by my own route."

Hell on Wheels, 1985
Mixed-media collage, 32¾ × 21½ inches
Collection of Laila and Thurston Twigg-Smith

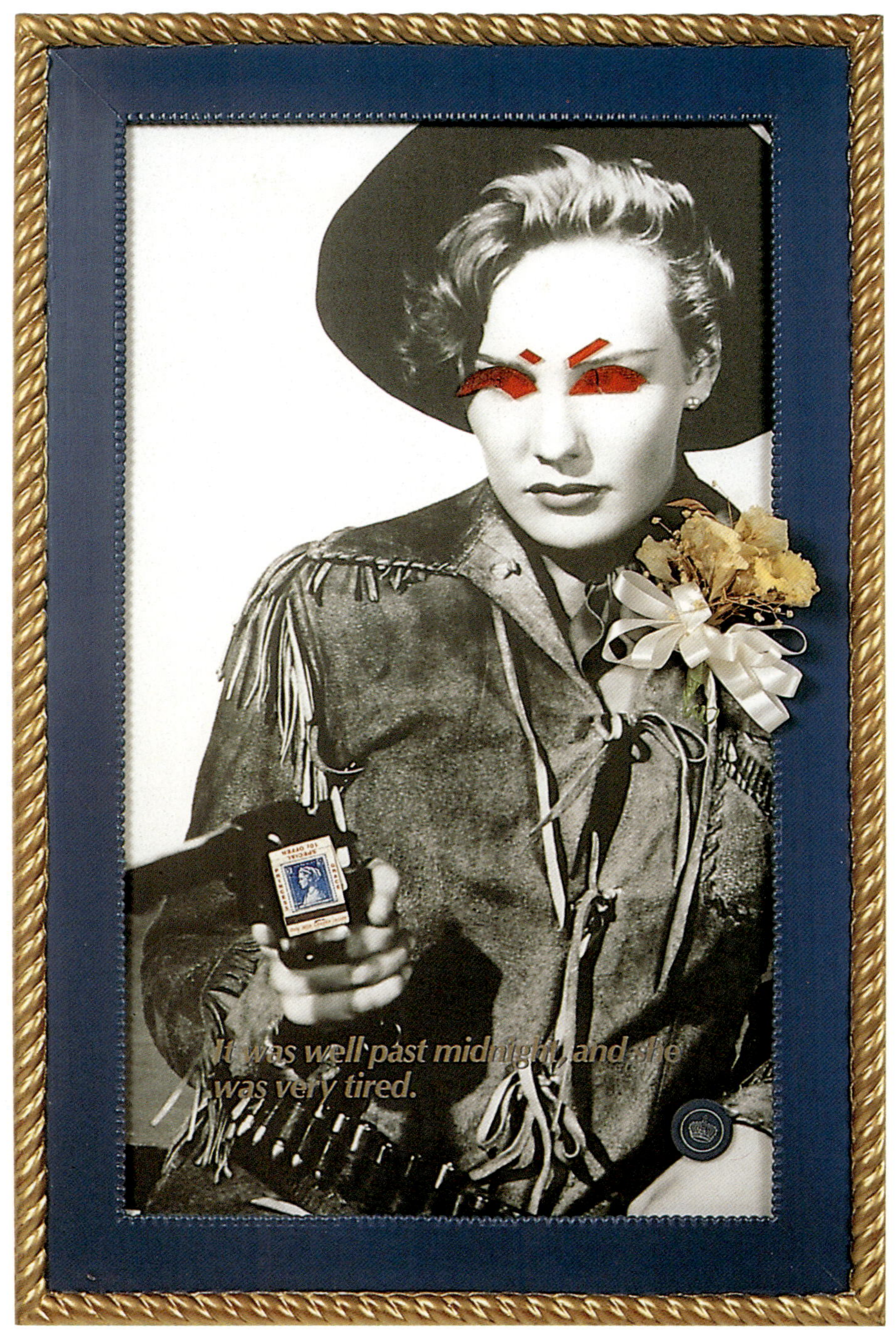

It was well past midnight, and she was very tired.

Cinderella Story, 1985
Mixed-media collage, 32½ × 21 inches
Collection of James and Linda Burrows

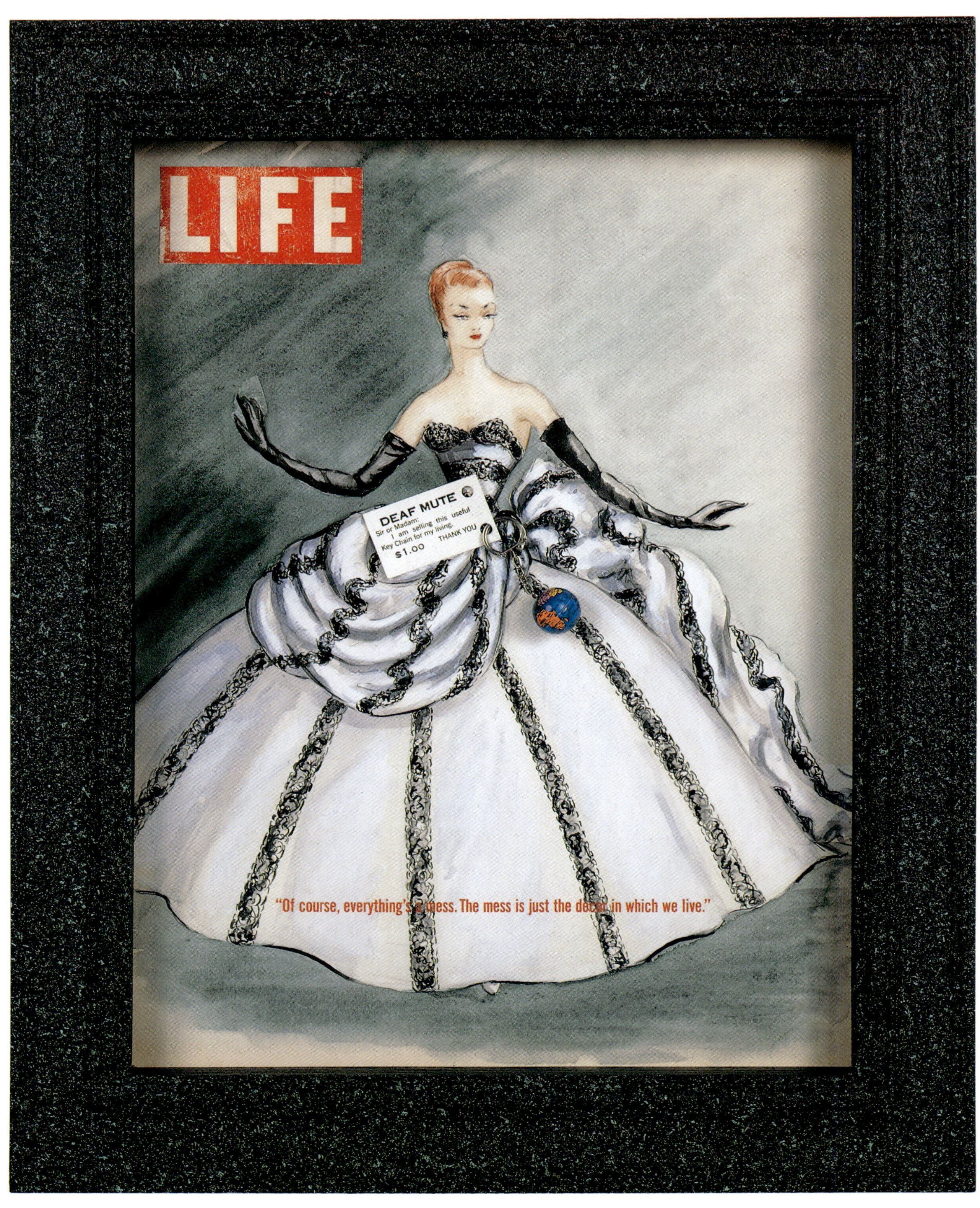

Days of Our Lives, 1985
Mixed-media collage, 24½ × 19½ inches
Collection of John Margulies

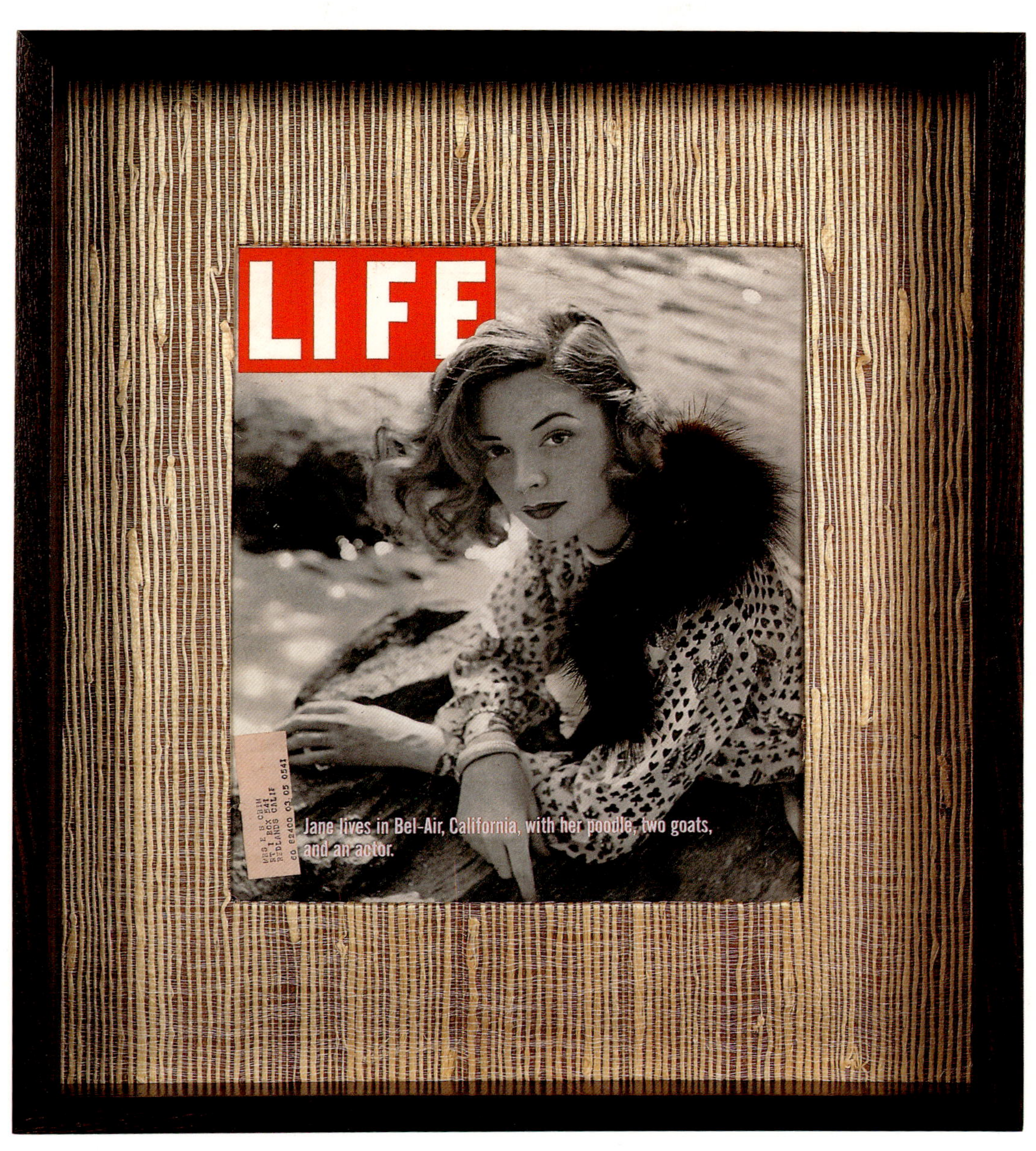

Wild Life, 1985
Mixed-media collage, $18\frac{3}{8} \times 16\frac{3}{8}$ inches
Santa Barbara Museum of Art, California; Gift of Bruce Murkoff

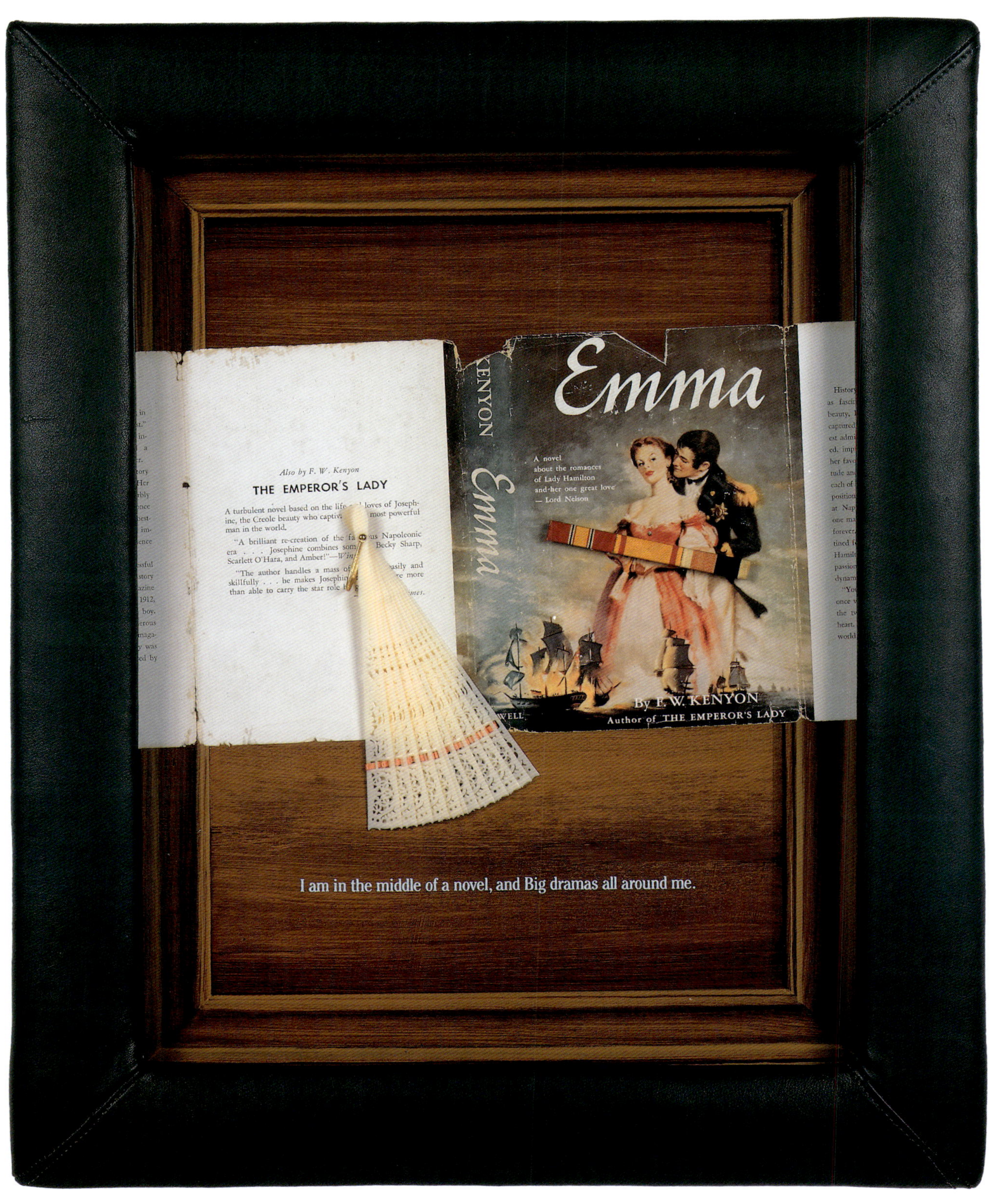

Another World, 1985
Mixed-media collage, 24½ × 19¾ inches
Security Pacific Bank, Los Angeles

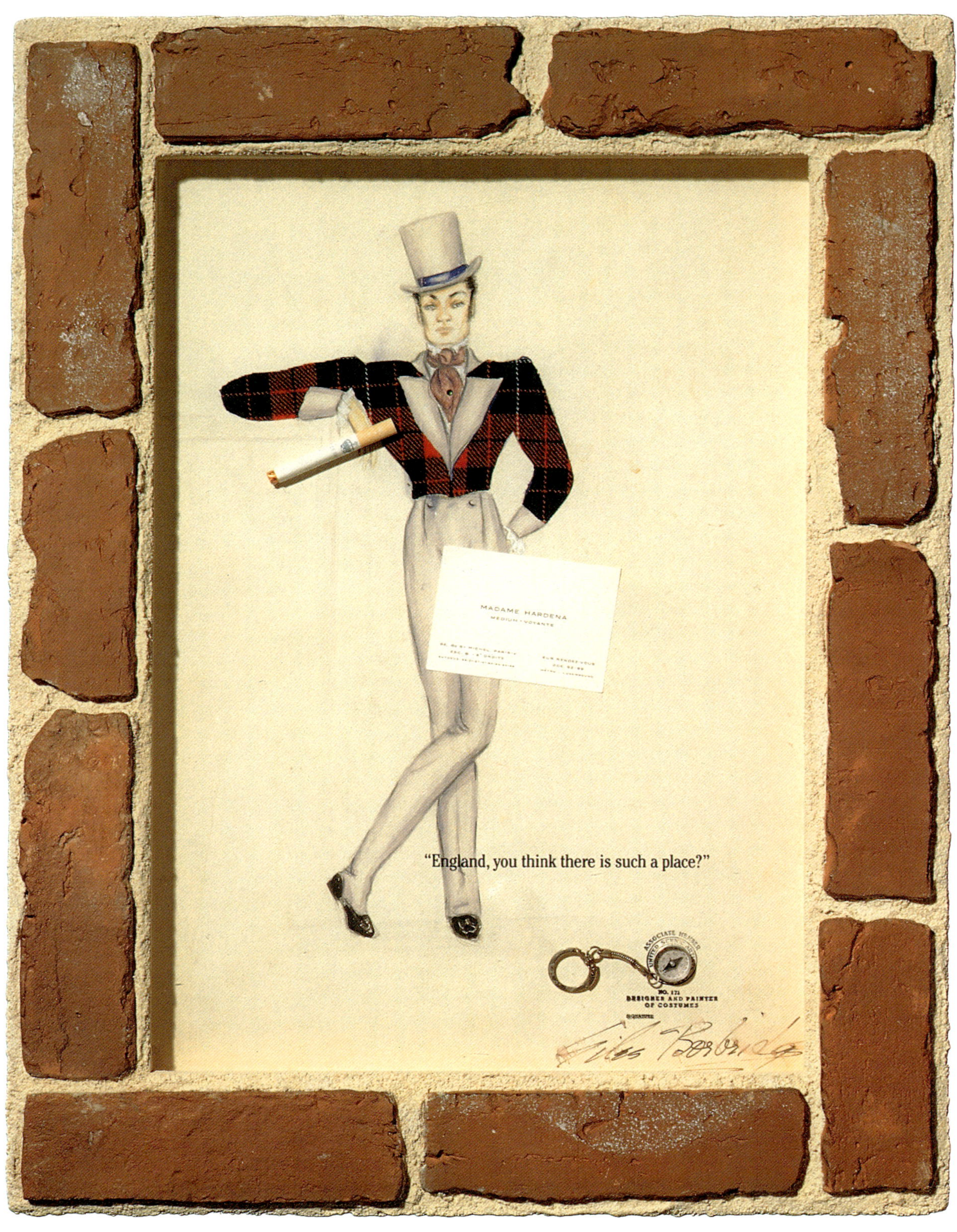

Persuasion, 1985
Mixed-media collage, 24¾ × 19 inches
Private collection

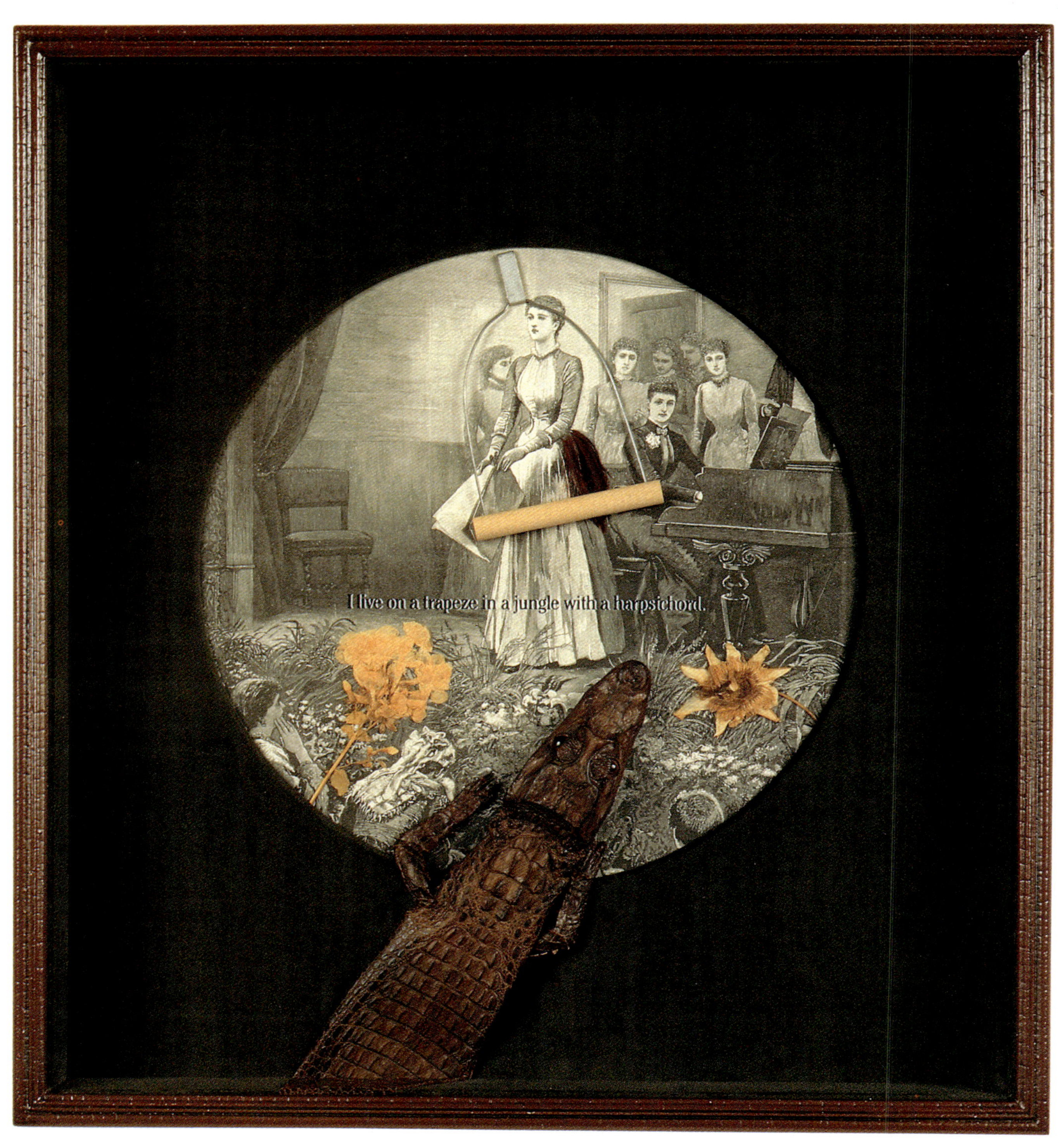

Jane Eyre, 1985
Mixed-media collage, 20¾ × 18⅞ inches
Security Pacific Bank, Los Angeles

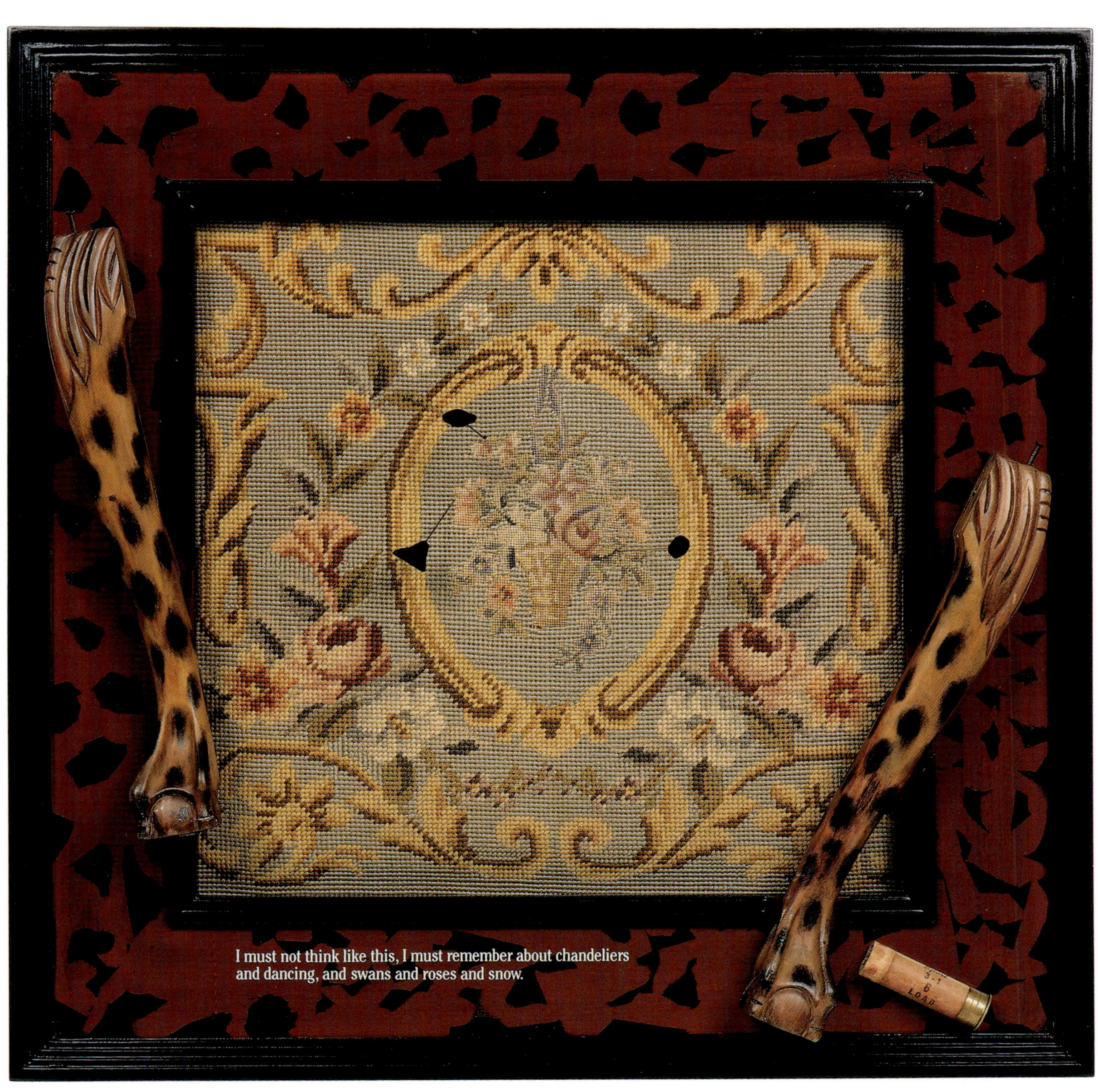

Lady Jane, 1985
Mixed-media collage, 22¾ × 22¾ inches
Collection of Diane Dixon and Lavi Daniel

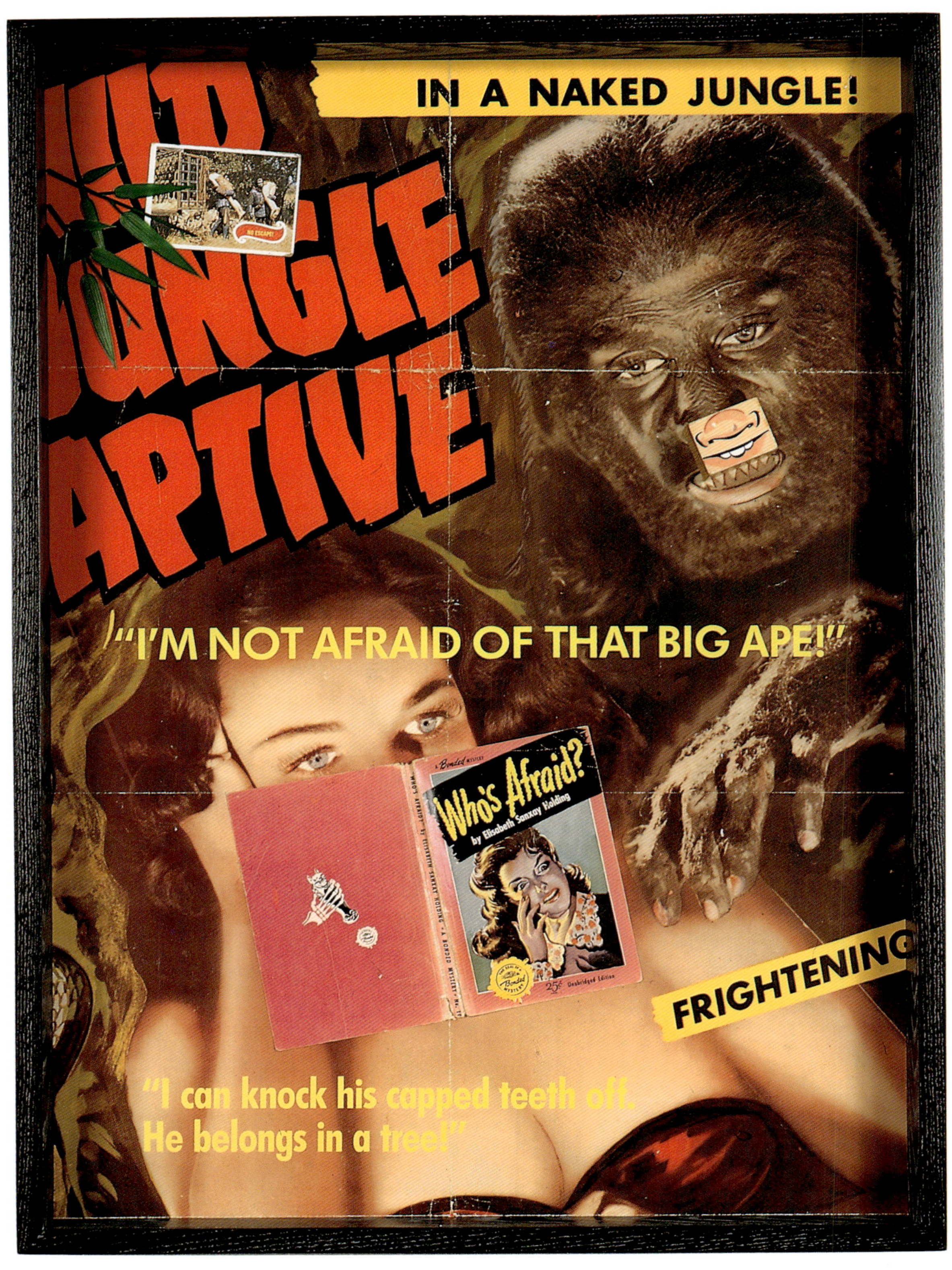

The Ape Man, 1985
Mixed-media collage, 29⅛ × 21¼ inches
Collection of Douglas S. Cramer

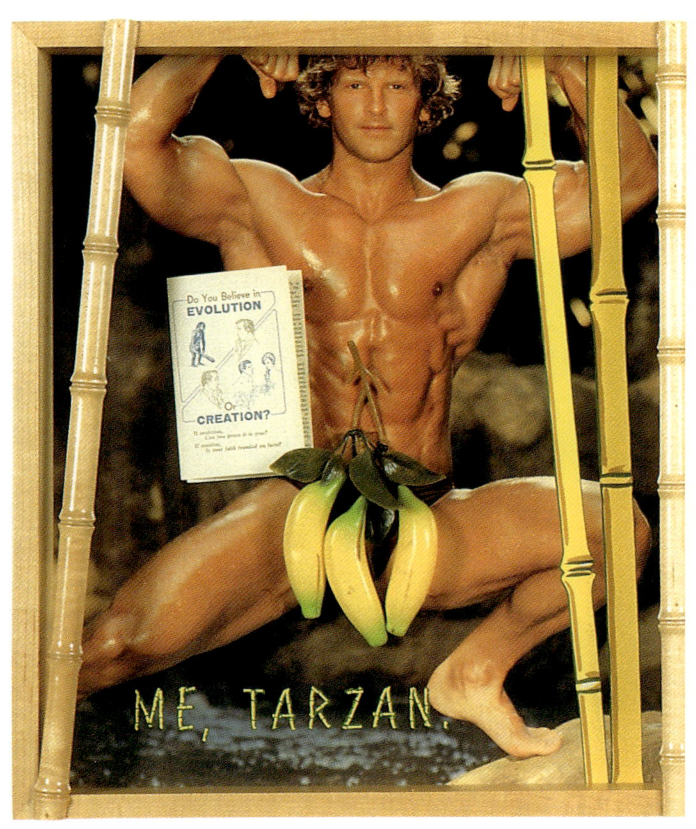

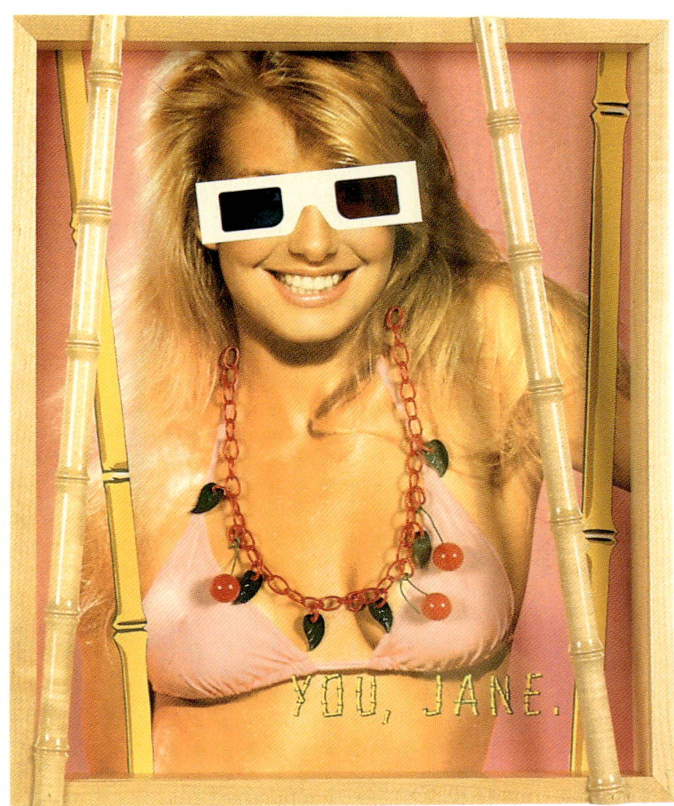

Me Tarzan, You Jane, 1985
Mixed-media collage, two panels, 19 × 15½ inches each
Collection of Peg and Chuck Rosenquist

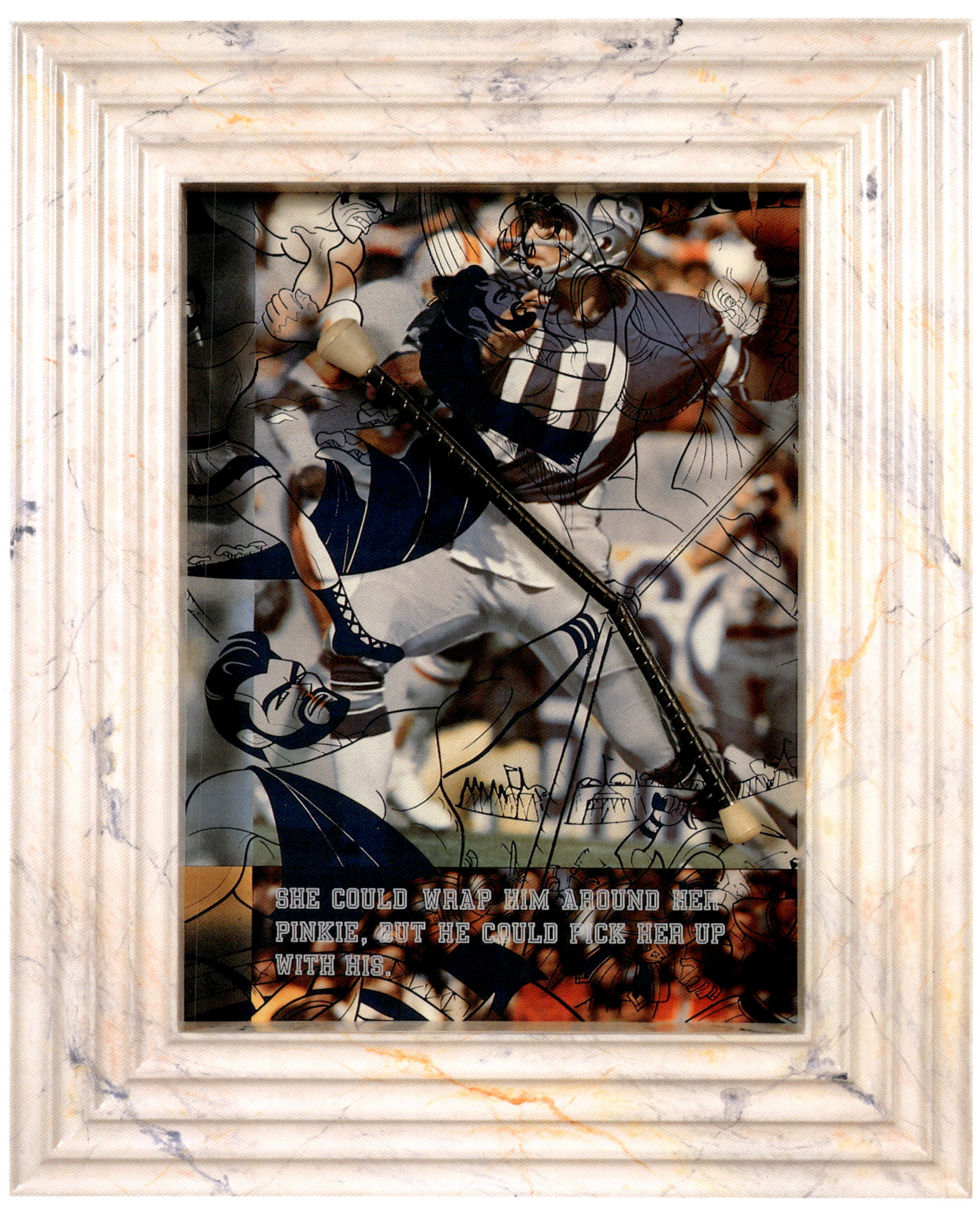

The Perfect Couple, 1985
Mixed-media collage, 38⅜ × 30½ inches
Collection of Mr. and Mrs. Robert J. Woods

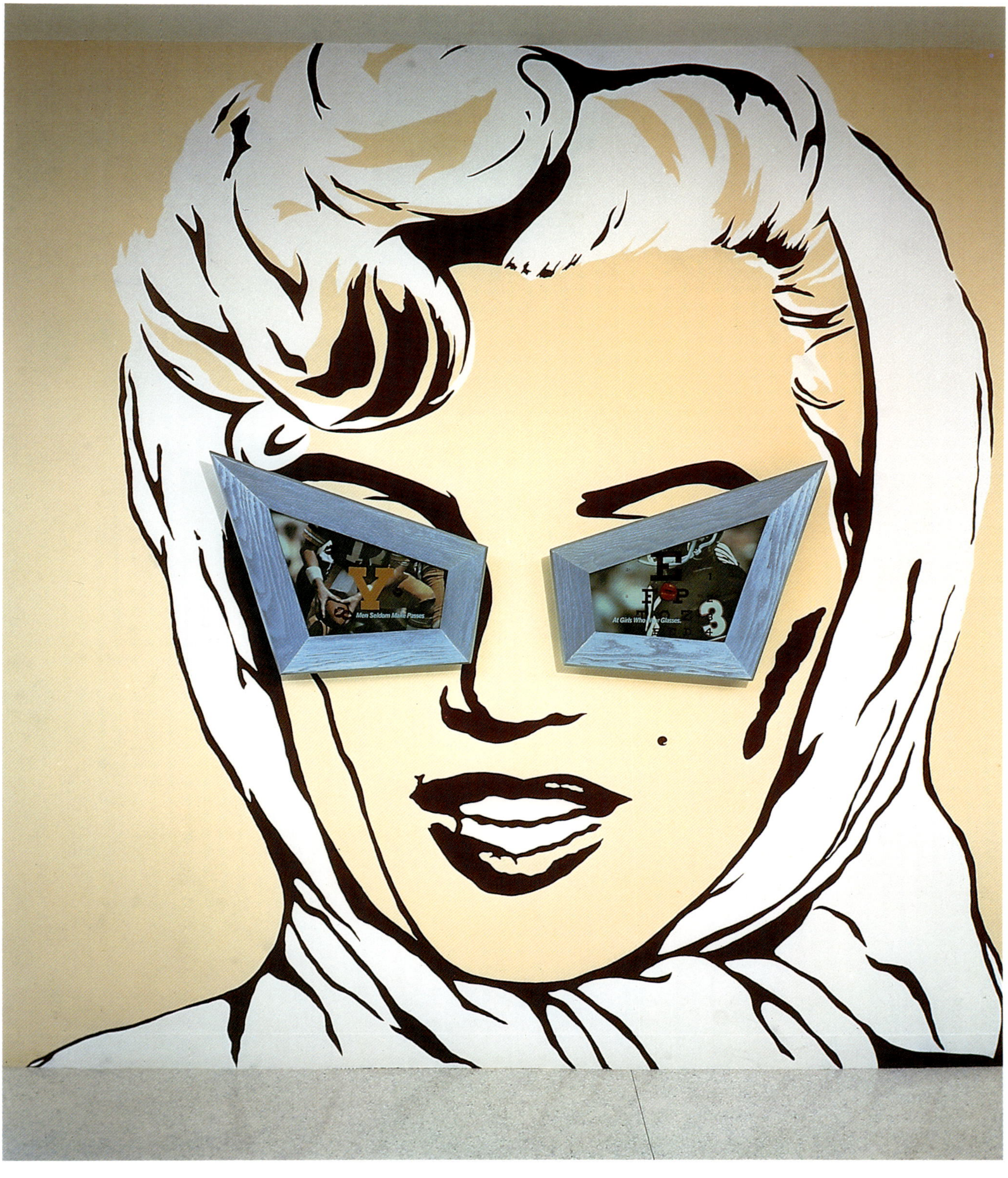

Men Seldom Make Passes at Girls Who Wear Glasses, 1985
Mixed-media collage on painted wall: two panels,
27 × 33 × 5 inches each; 10 × 15 feet × 5 inches overall
Collection of the artist

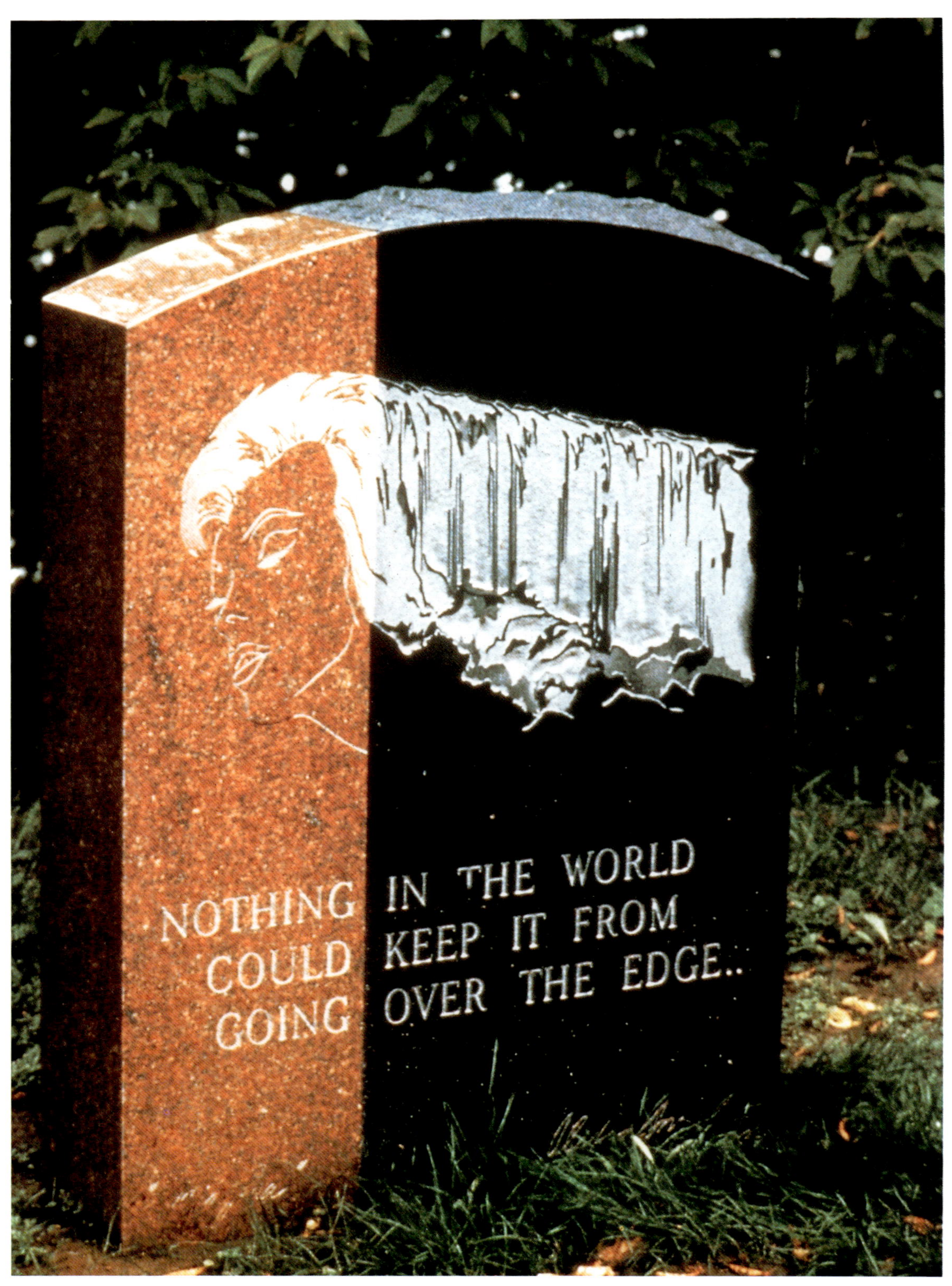

Niagara, 1985
Granite, 44 × 32 × 8 inches
Art Park, Lewiston, New York

Niagara (1985), one of a number of mini-monuments Smith worked on during this period, memorializes an icon of the 1950s, Marilyn Monroe. A granite marker, it was designed for an outdoor sculpture and performance park in upstate New York near Niagara Falls. The lighter, left side of the piece features Monroe's face. The dark right side shows her hair becoming an enormous waterfall. The quotation beneath the images is from the movie screenplay *Niagara:* "Nothing in the world could keep it from going over the edge. . . ." The ambiguous antecedent of "it" is Smith's nod to the chaotic and confused public/private existence of Monroe as a symbol for the women of the era. Their frenzied lives come to a literal conclusion in *Iron Sorrows* (1990), part of the larger installation *On the Road,* where a stop sign is encircled and defaced with mangled pieces of metal—the result of some cosmic collision.

In successive exhibitions at the Margo Leavin Gallery in Los Angeles, Smith presented two interconnected groups of work, *On the Road* (1988) and *Eldorado* (1990). Wall-bound and freestanding constructions, they were elaborations on her traditional collage format. Both the pieces in *On the Road* and those in *Eldorado* were inspired by Jack Kerouac's paean to wanderlust and postwar America, *On the Road*. Published in 1957, Kerouac's book tells of a cross-country drive that is the Beat generation's *Pilgrim's Progress*. In a 1983 interview, Smith, describing how she functioned as an artist in Los Angeles, had praised the automobile as a powerful extension of her artistic need to organize things and as a place of meditative solitude conducive to thinking. As she concluded, "I think cars are really wonderful; they've become the twentieth-century archetype for libido, power, purpose, destiny and control." These two series reasserted more graphically than ever Smith's deep attraction to the signs and symbols of outdoor advertising and to the visual-verbal literacy it spawned. Her search for a common vocabulary had, in fact, led her to two, often intersecting, languages, one represented by the verbal clichés and images of Hollywood, the other by the words and icons of the American automobile culture.

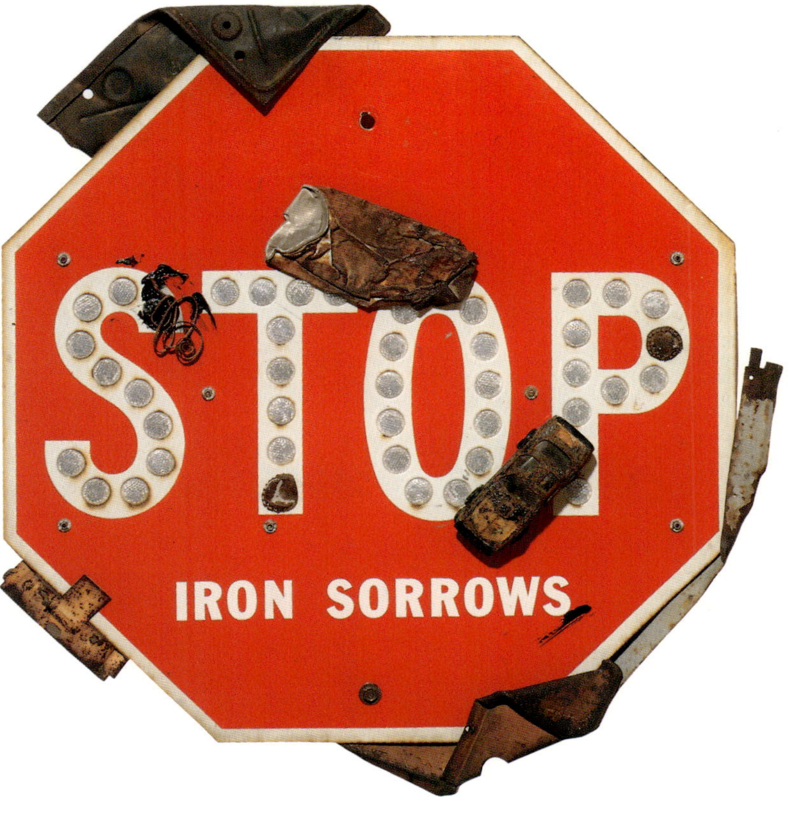

Iron Sorrows, 1990
Mixed-media collage, 27 × 25½ inches
Collection of Max Palevsky

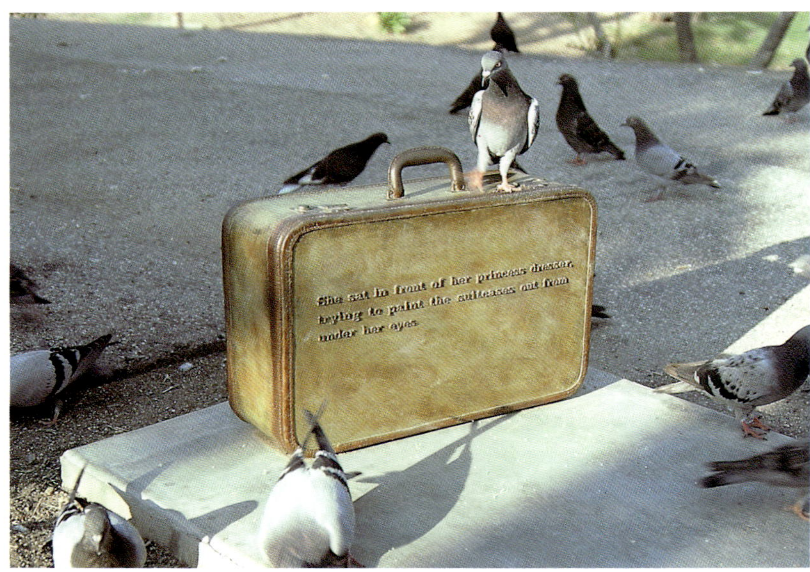

Mini-monument, 1986
Bronze, 17 × 21 × 7 inches
MacArthur Park, Los Angeles

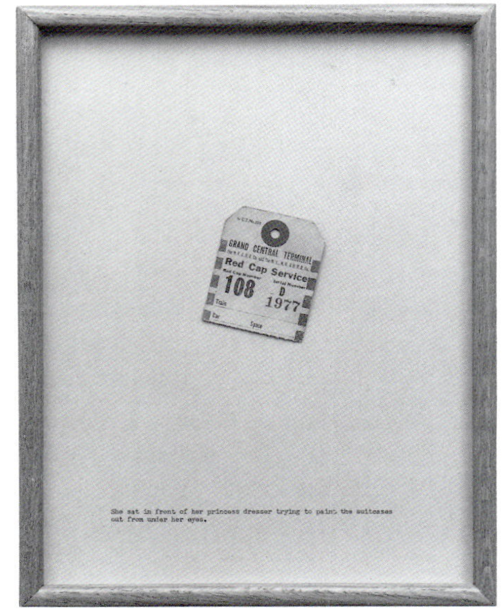

Chandlerism #5, 1978
Mixed-media collage, 12 × 9¼ inches
Collection of Audrey Strohl

Both shows at Margo Leavin projected a sense of travel, each piece—many in two parts—a stop on an extended odyssey across the nation. The ice cream cones of *Rocky Road* (1990), the freestanding sandwich board of *Fruits 'n' Nuts* (1990), and the tire sign of *Eldorado* (1990) had all started life as roadside advertisements. Other reminders of travel are everywhere: the suitcase of *Lonesome Traveler* (1989), the souvenir frame of *Peaches* (1990), the tire tracks across *The Holy Road* (1988); even the panoramic landscapes of *Moonlight Serenade* (1989) and *Viewmaster* (1988) speak of wanderlust. The sense of propulsion reaches an apogee in pieces such as *Running on Empty* (1988), where an enlarged gas gauge verging on E wails out lines from Kerouac—"He drove like a fiend and never rested"—or the related *Eight Ball* (1988), with its lament, "I was rushing through the world without a chance to see it."

The ceaseless movement of people provoked Kerouac's wonderment and concern. His plaintive query, "Whither goest thou, America, in thy shiny car in the night? I mean, man, whither goest thou?," is taken up by Smith as the text for the whirling maelstrom of *Eldorado* as well as for the American map that underlies *Pair o' Dice* (1990). By repeating Kerouac's question in such large and dominant pieces as these, Smith seems to embrace a rare moralizing tone.

Kerouac's saga offered countless vignettes of the life on the road that is the quintessential American experience. Smith's longtime preoccupation with the symbols of time, travel, and romance coalesced perfectly with Kerouac's story. His verbal panorama formed a harmonious counterpoint to the array of images Smith had at hand. Thus, the overall impression of the Margo Leavin exhibitions was of the vastness of the country, its over-

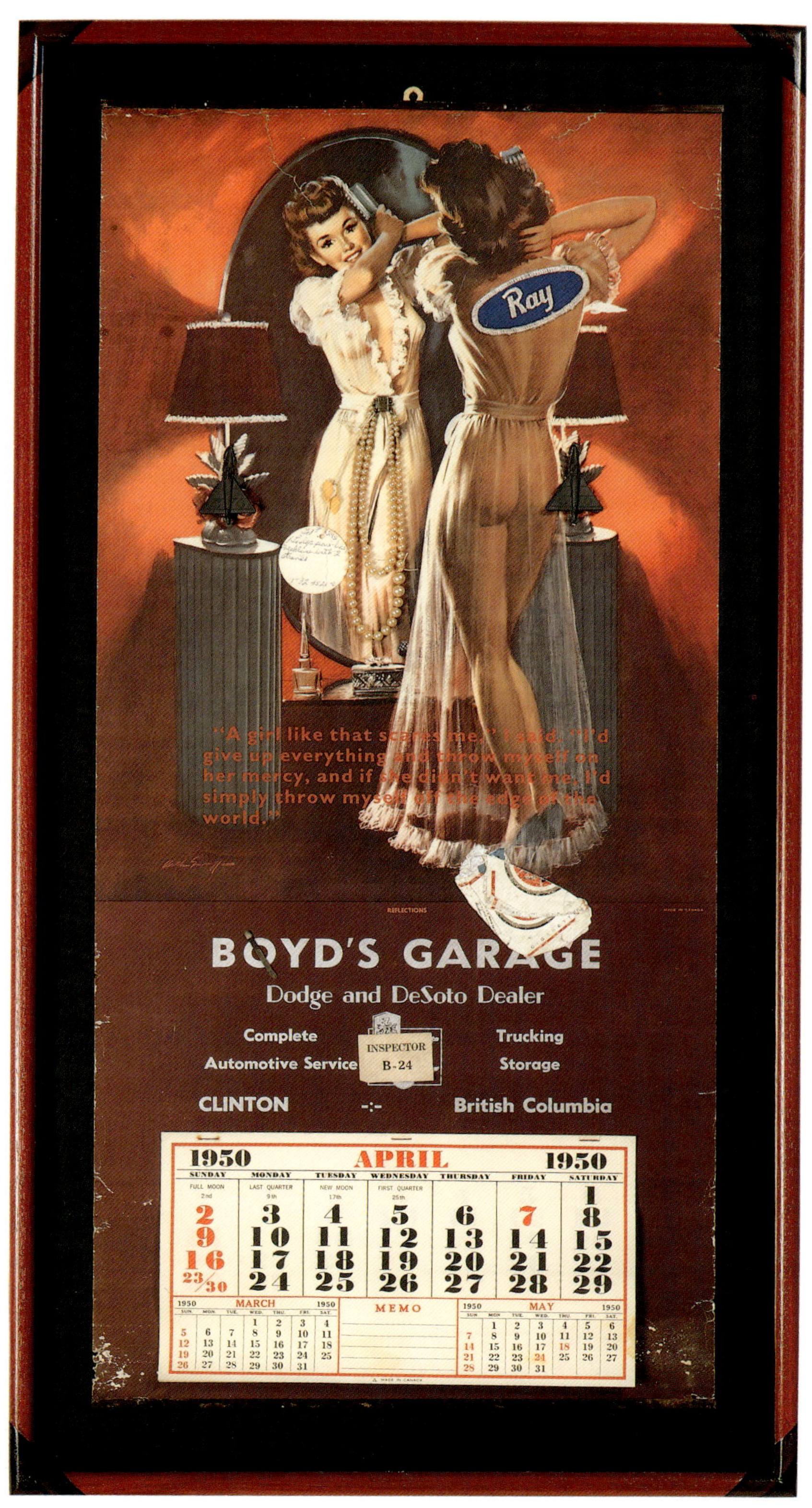

Desolation Angel, 1987
Mixed-media collage, 38⁵⁄₁₆ × 19¹³⁄₁₆ inches
Collection of James and Linda Burrows

whelming geography. The panoramas of *Palm Reader* (1990), *Native American* (1990), and *Rock of Ages* (1988), or the maps of *Route 66* (1988) and *Pair o' Dice* presented spatial data that substantiated the scale of America, a place whose limitless opportunity only mirrored its expansiveness. In her two-part *Mercury* (1988), beneath a photo of James Dean sprawled in a chair, Smith quotes Kerouac: "And only because he had no place he could stay in without getting tired of it and because there was nowhere to go but everywhere." The passage concludes in the next panel, where Dean's head is replaced by a sheet of mug shots of sailors: "And besides he knew the road would get more interesting ahead, always ahead . . ." This imperative to move ahead, whatever the psychic cost, is the focal point of both Kerouac's and Smith's work.

The girls that abound in Kerouac's ode also populate Smith's collages. The good-girl type, as in *Miss America* (1988), a large posterboard advertisement for Golden State milk, is overwritten with the words, "I met her in a soda fountain." Its pictorial elements—from the snapshot of Gail Storm to a varsity letter E turned sideways to form an M—typify the squares. Other good girls brush their hair, as in the garage calendar that makes up *Desolation Angel* (1987), or pose adoringly for their menfolk, as in *Peaches* (1990). The "bad" girl is represented by a poster for a sensationalist teenage movie embellished with entangled jumper cables connecting boys to girls. The words repeat Kerouac's lurid mantra, "Oh, man, she was only 15 and wearing jeans and waiting for someone to pick her up." The underlying film poster screams, "They live only for today!"

With the works in *On the Road* and *Eldorado*, Smith's subjects moved forward in time from pre-World War II America to its more recent past. Her art had evolved in focus from a literary one that largely comprised twentieth-century classics (mostly written before 1940) to such sources as Kerouac and rock-and-roll lyrics of the 1960s. By joining more commonplace, often media-derived messages to her usual, ordinary objects, Smith shed all vestiges of formal reserve and made her work unapologetically public. It had transcended the constraints of its origins in collage.

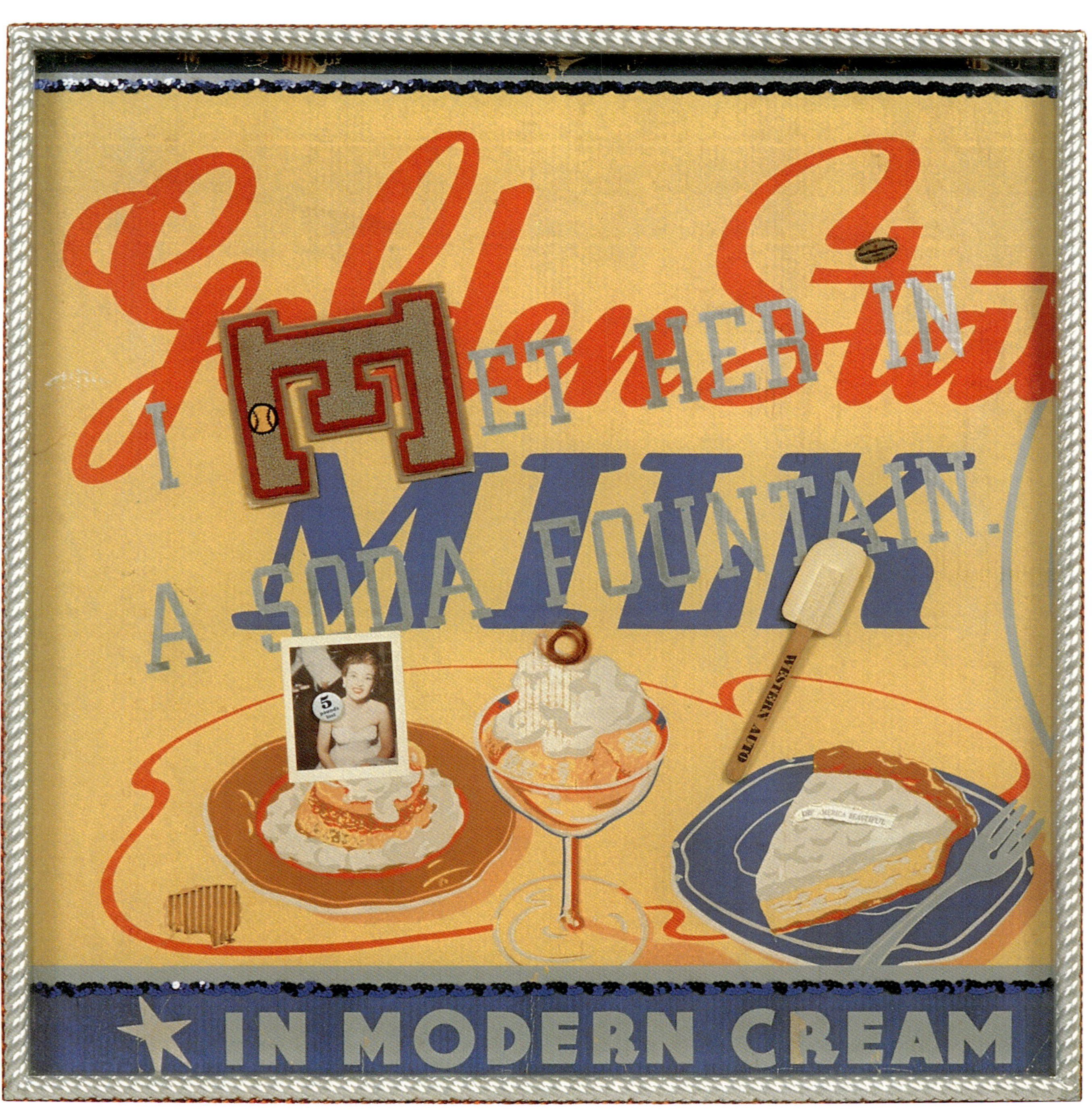

Miss America, 1988
Mixed-media collage, 36⅜ × 35 7/16 inches
Collection of Nina MacConnel

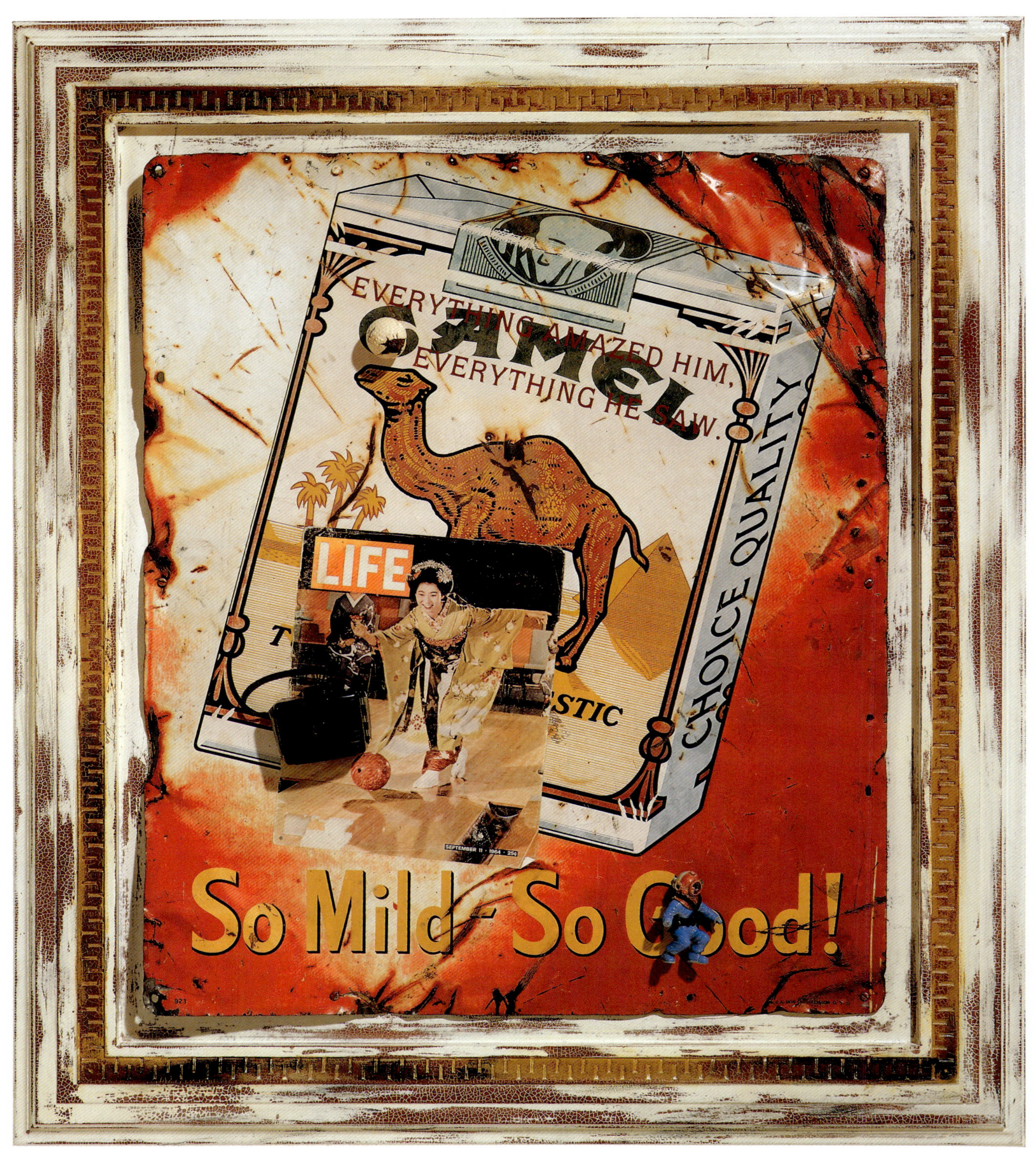

Seven Wonders, 1988
Mixed-media collage, 47¼ × 41 inches
Margo Leavin Gallery, Los Angeles

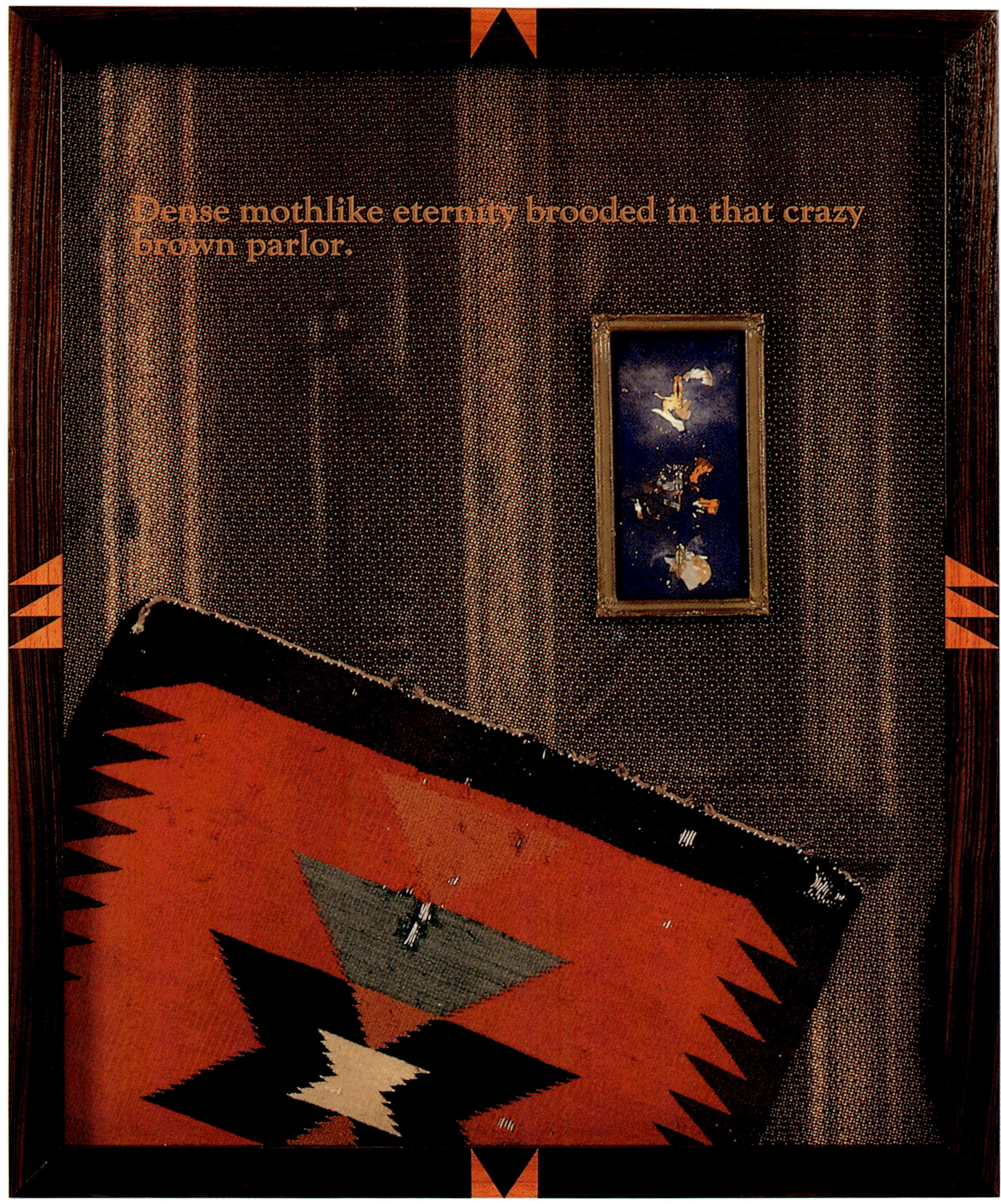

Heirloom, 1988
Mixed-media collage, 34¹⁄₁₆ × 27½ inches
Margo Leavin Gallery, Los Angeles

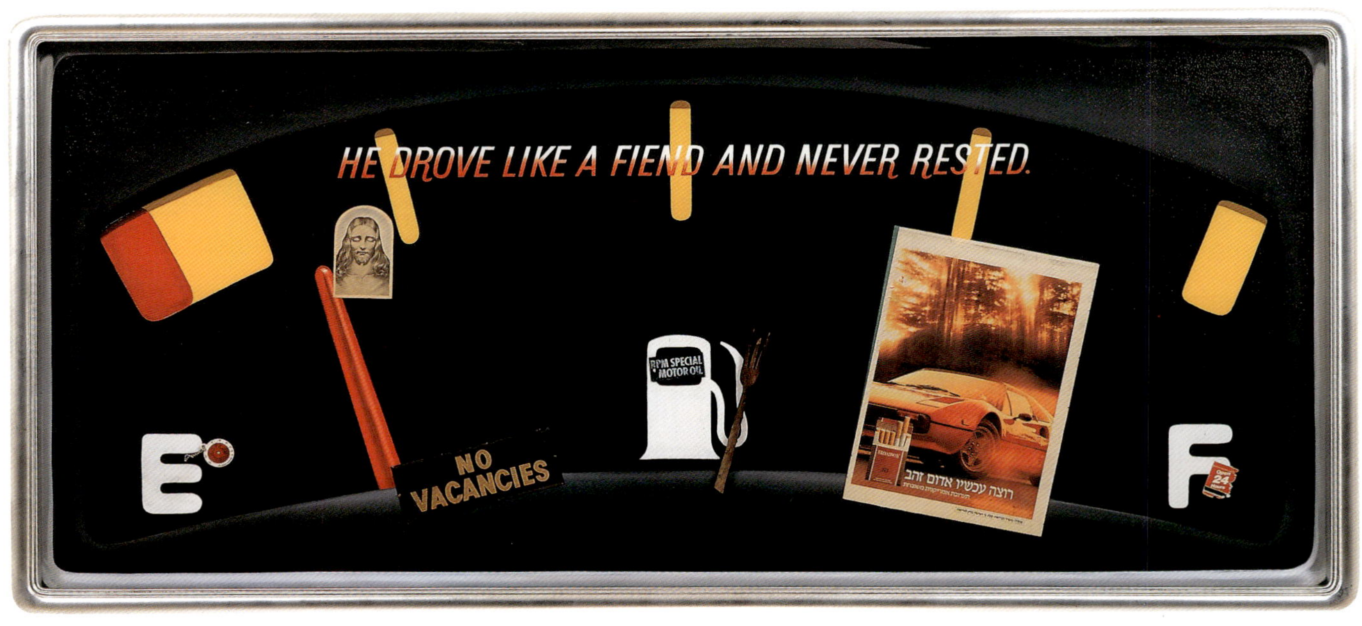

Running on Empty, 1988
Mixed-media collage, $34\frac{1}{2} \times 74\frac{7}{16}$ inches
The High Museum of Art, Atlanta;
Gift of The Eli Broad Family Foundation

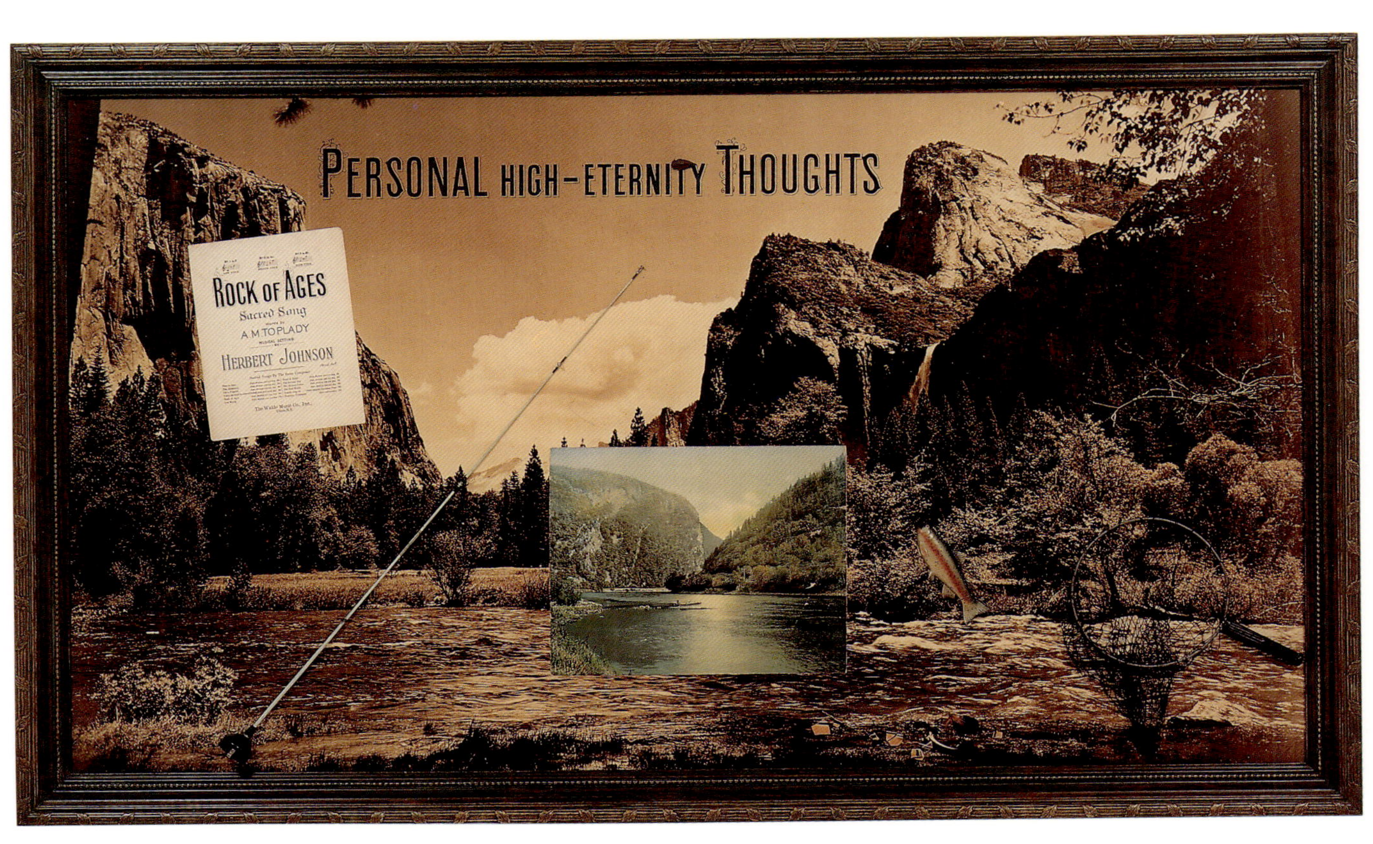

Rock of Ages, 1988
Mixed-media collage, 54¼ × 90⁵⁄₁₆ inches
The Capital Group, Inc., Los Angeles

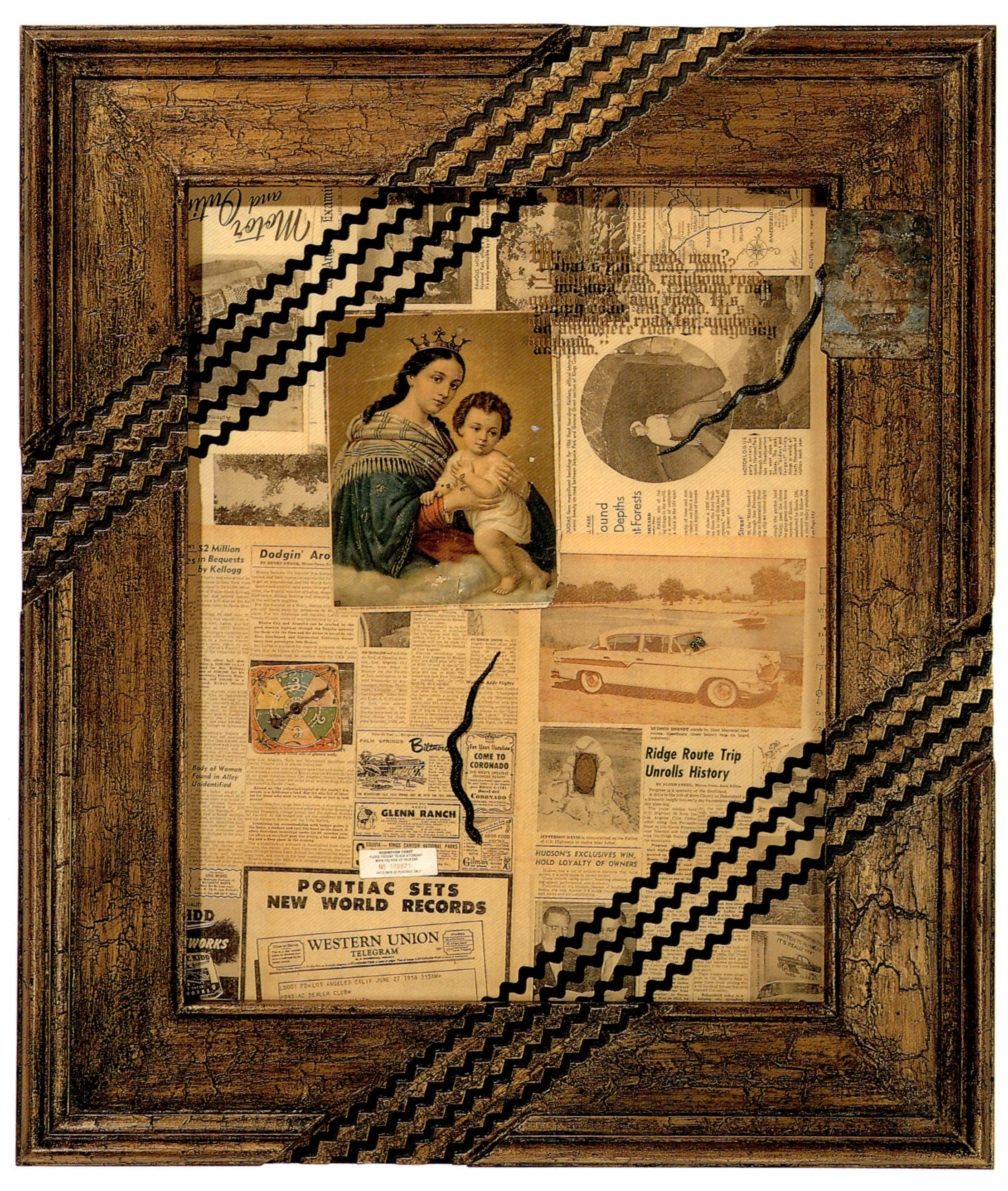

The Holy Road, 1988
Mixed-media collage, 38¾ × 31¾ inches
Collection of Richard Rouillard

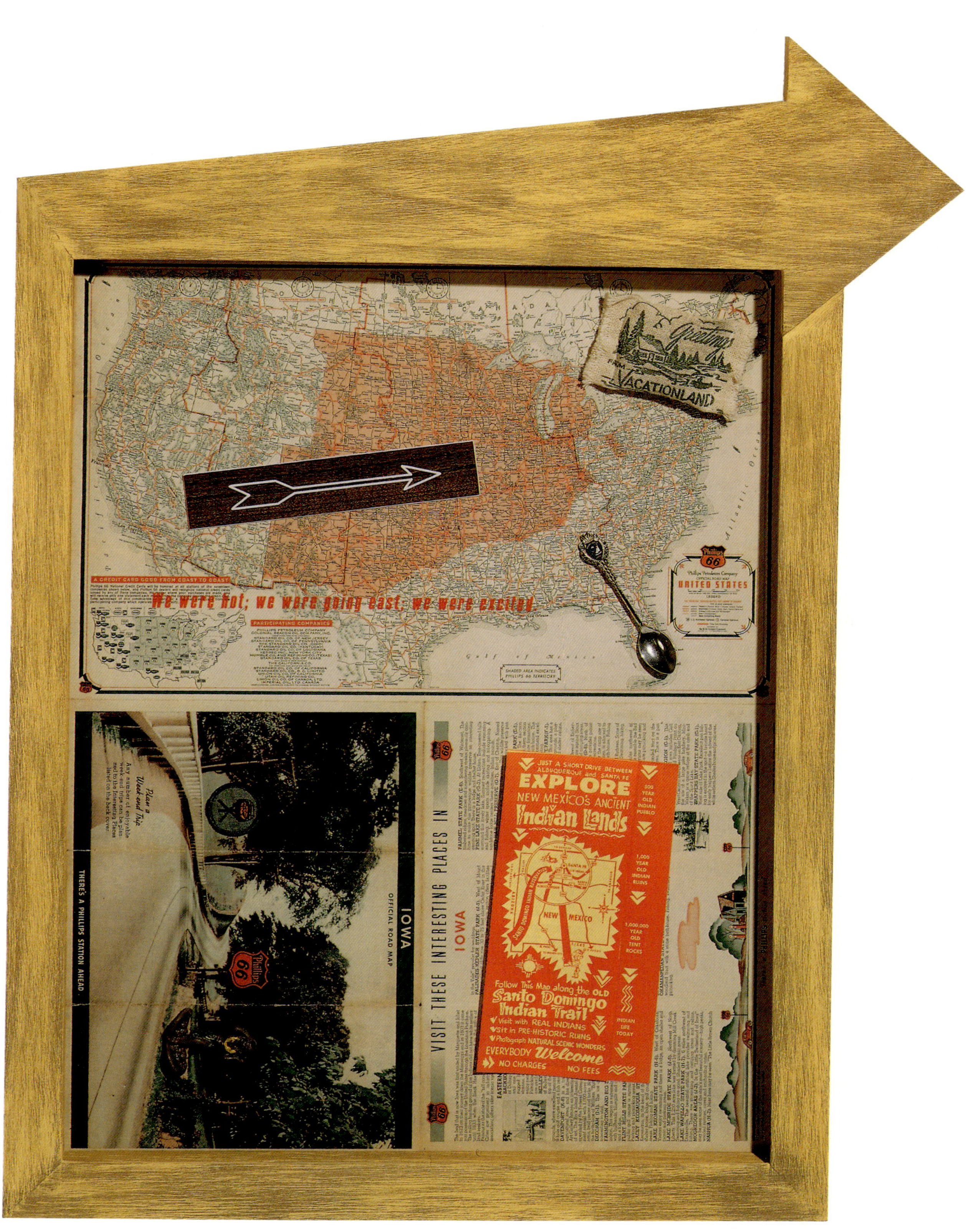

Route 66, 1988
Mixed-media collage, 31¼ × 21 inches
Collection of Bernard and Rosalie Kornblau

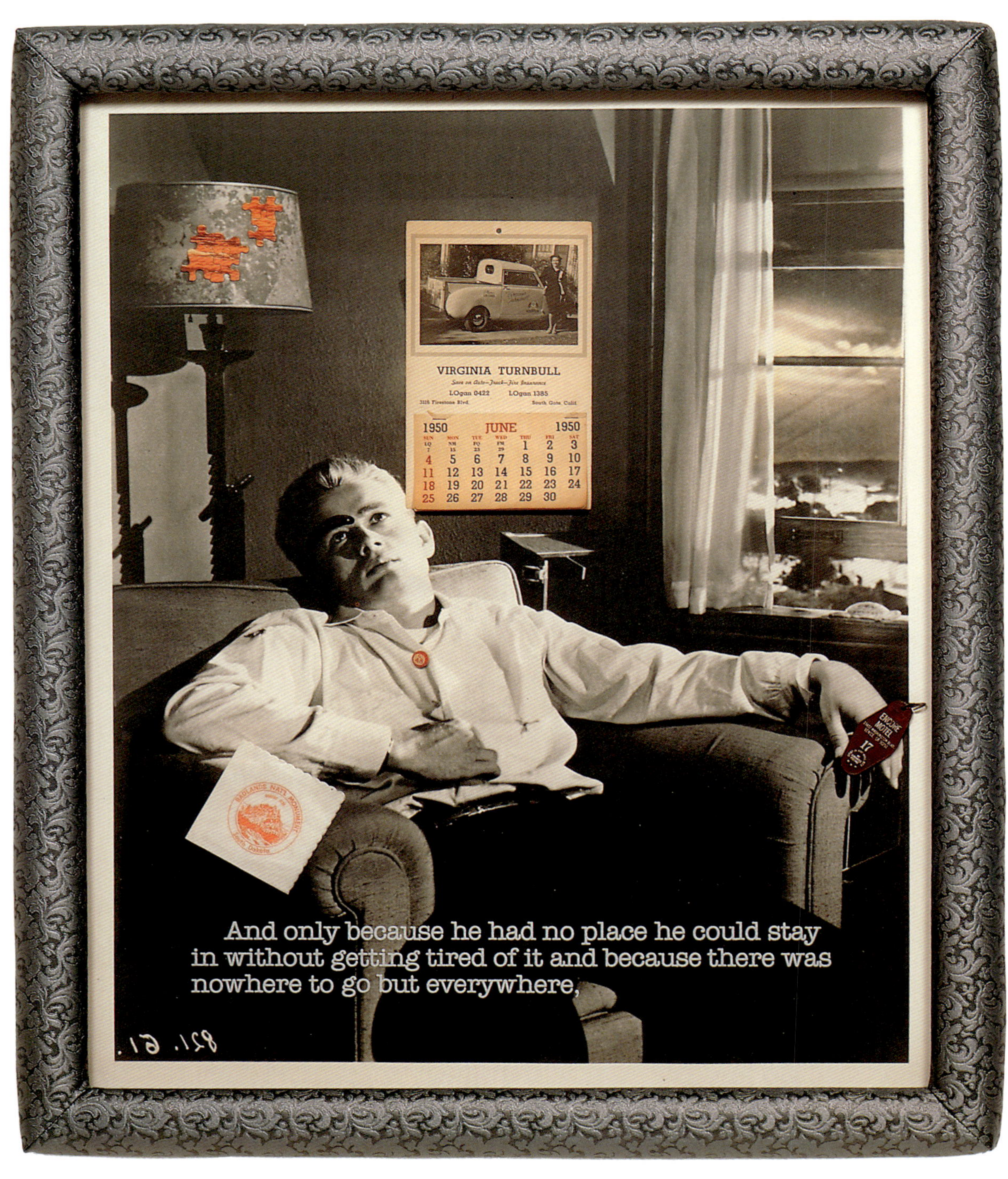

Mercury, 1988
Mixed-media collage, two panels, 43¾ × 36⅝ inches each
Collection of James and Linda Burrows

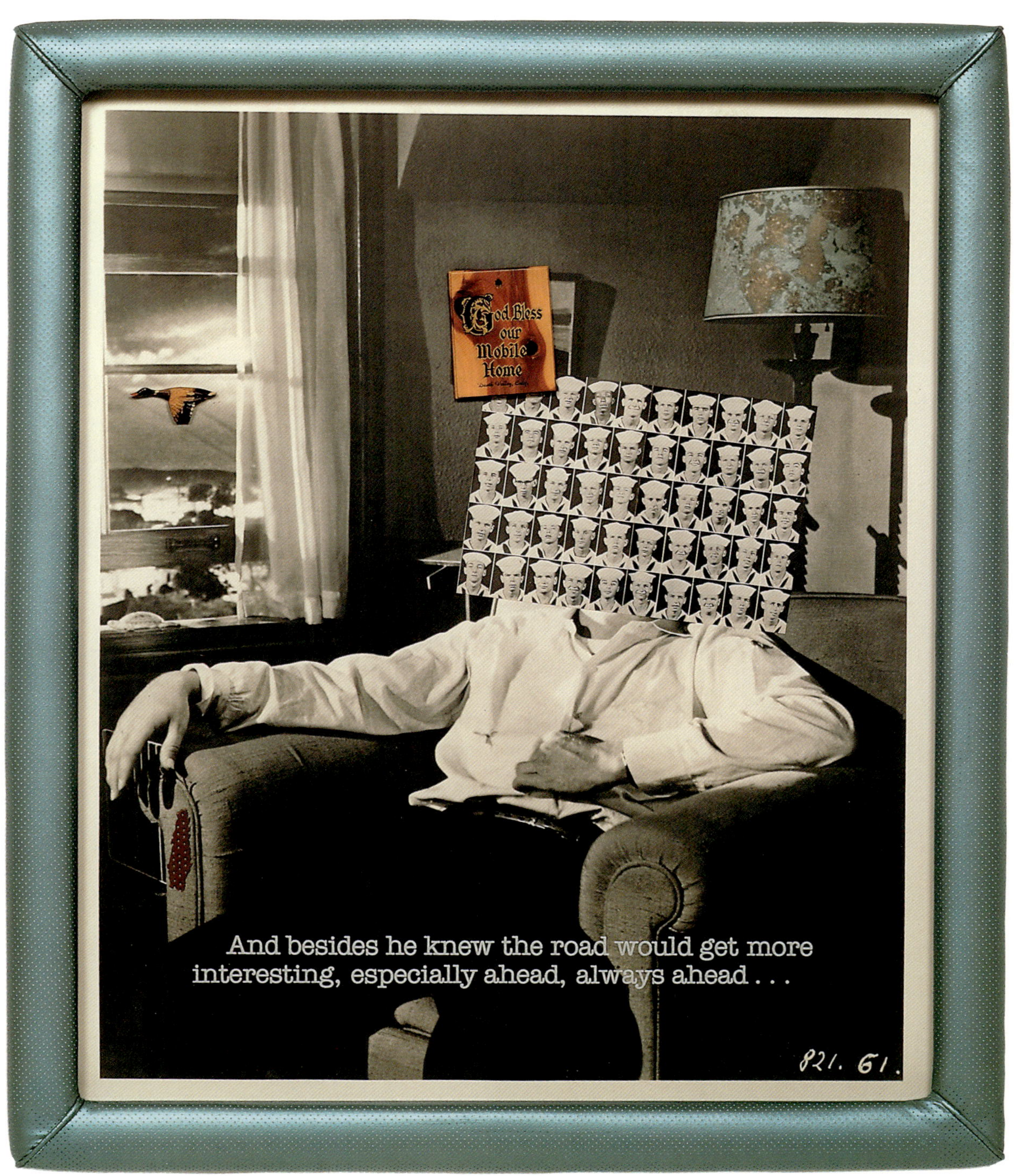
God Bless
our
Mobile
Home
And besides he knew the road would get more
interesting, especially ahead, always ahead . . .
821. 61.

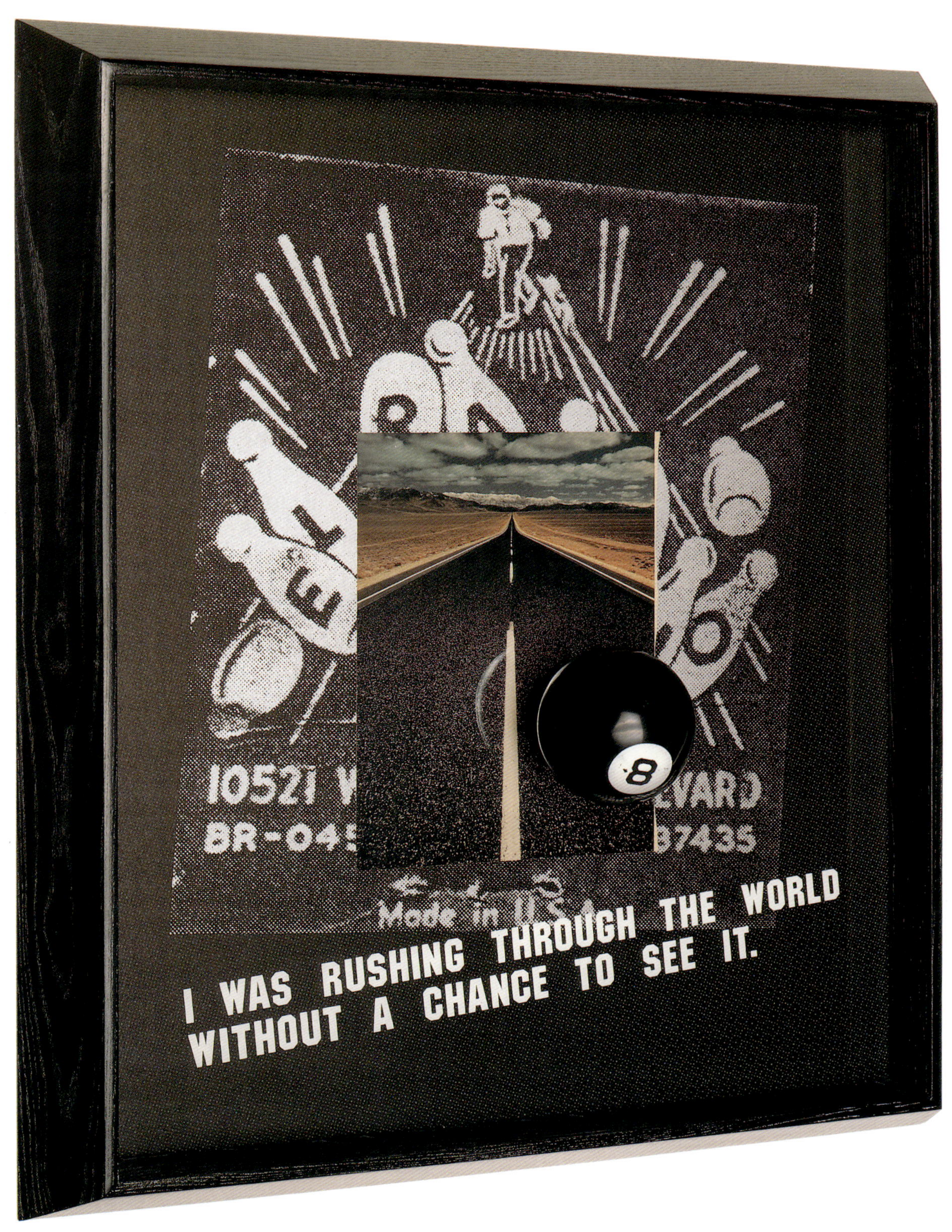

Eight Ball, 1988
Mixed-media collage, 28⁹⁄₁₆ × 24⅛ inches
Collection of Harold I. Huttas

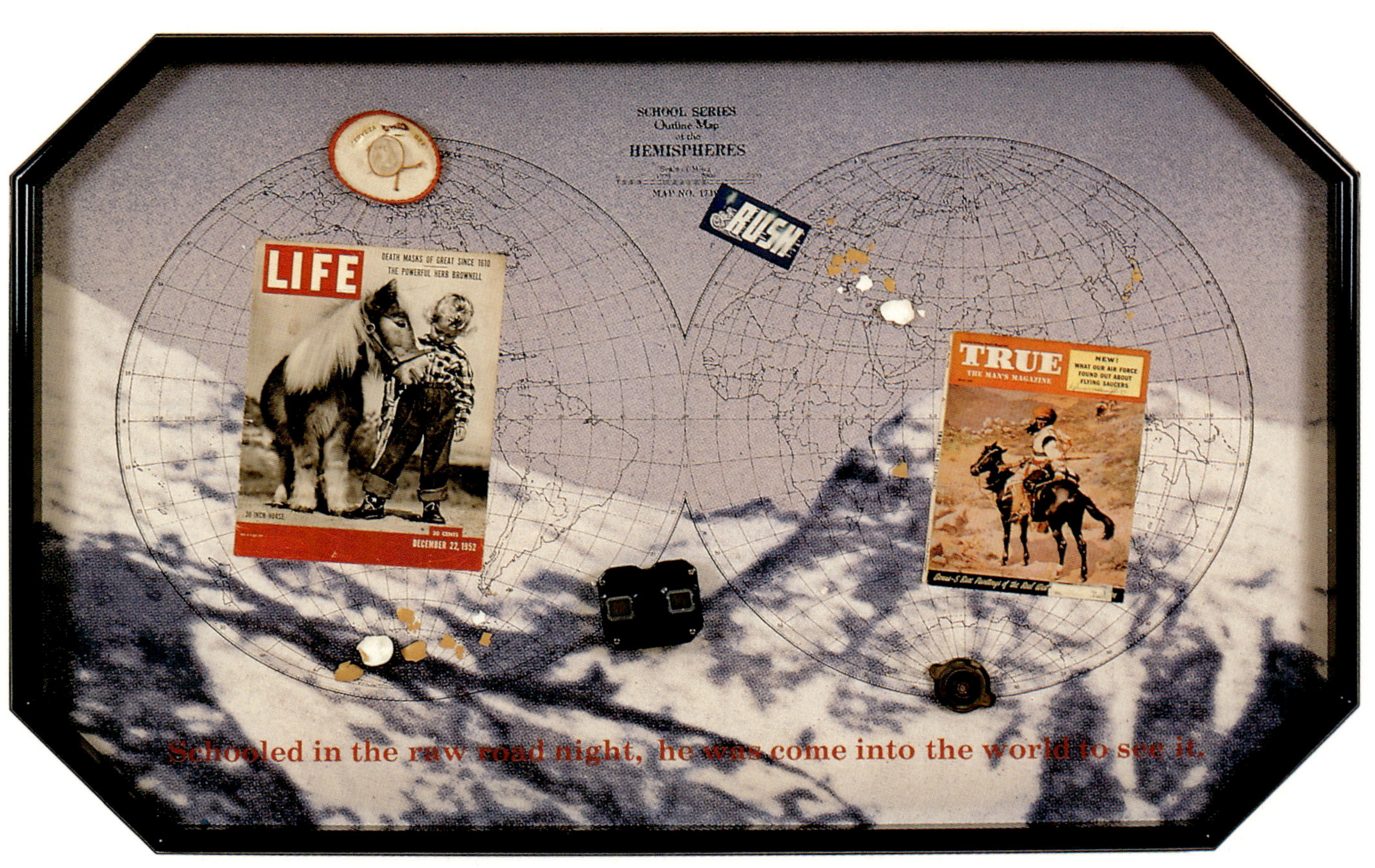

Viewmaster, 1988
Mixed-media collage, $35\frac{5}{16} \times 56\frac{5}{16}$ inches
The Progressive Corporation, Cleveland

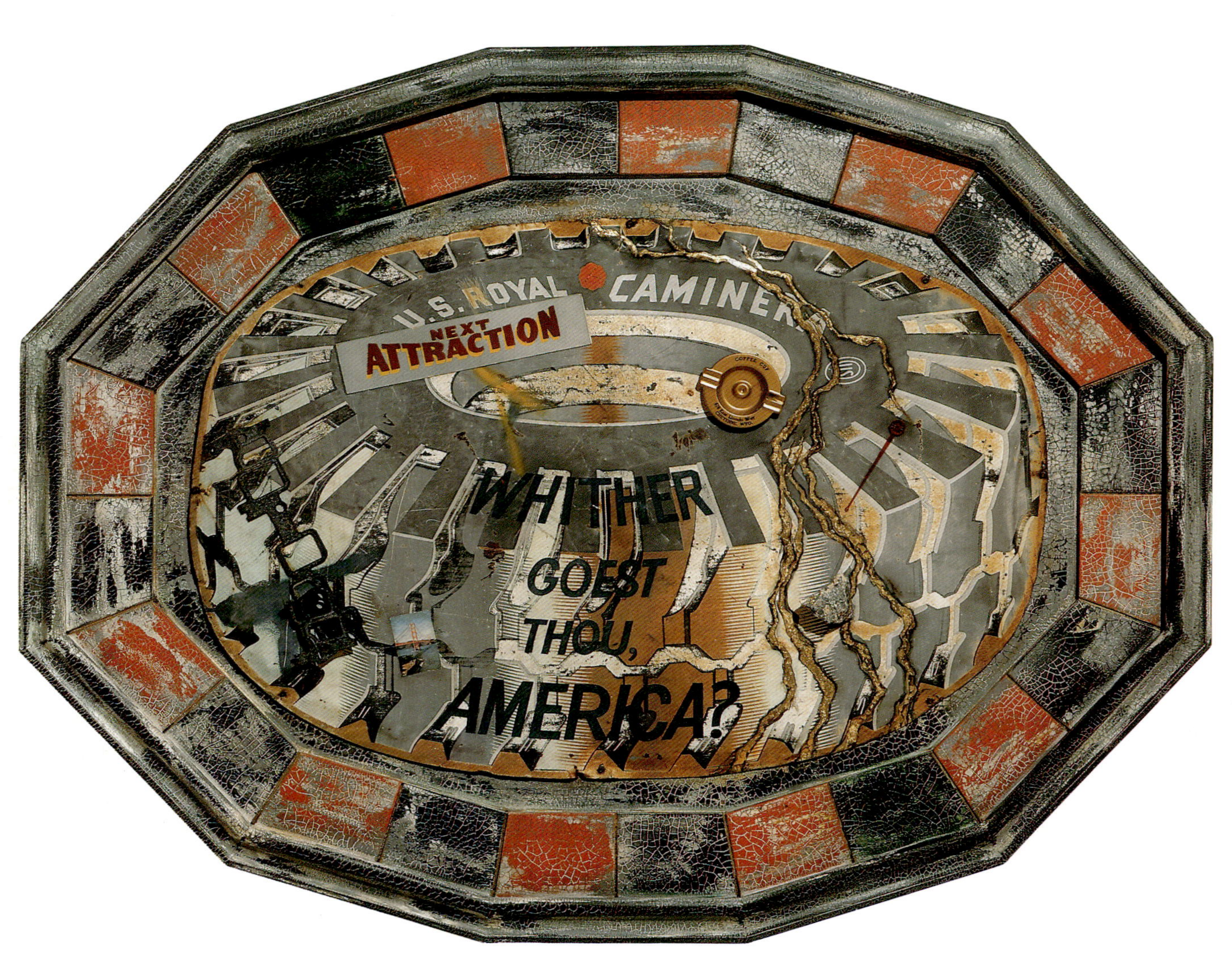

Eldorado, 1990
Mixed-media collage, 51½ × 65¾ inches
Collection of Maurice Marciano

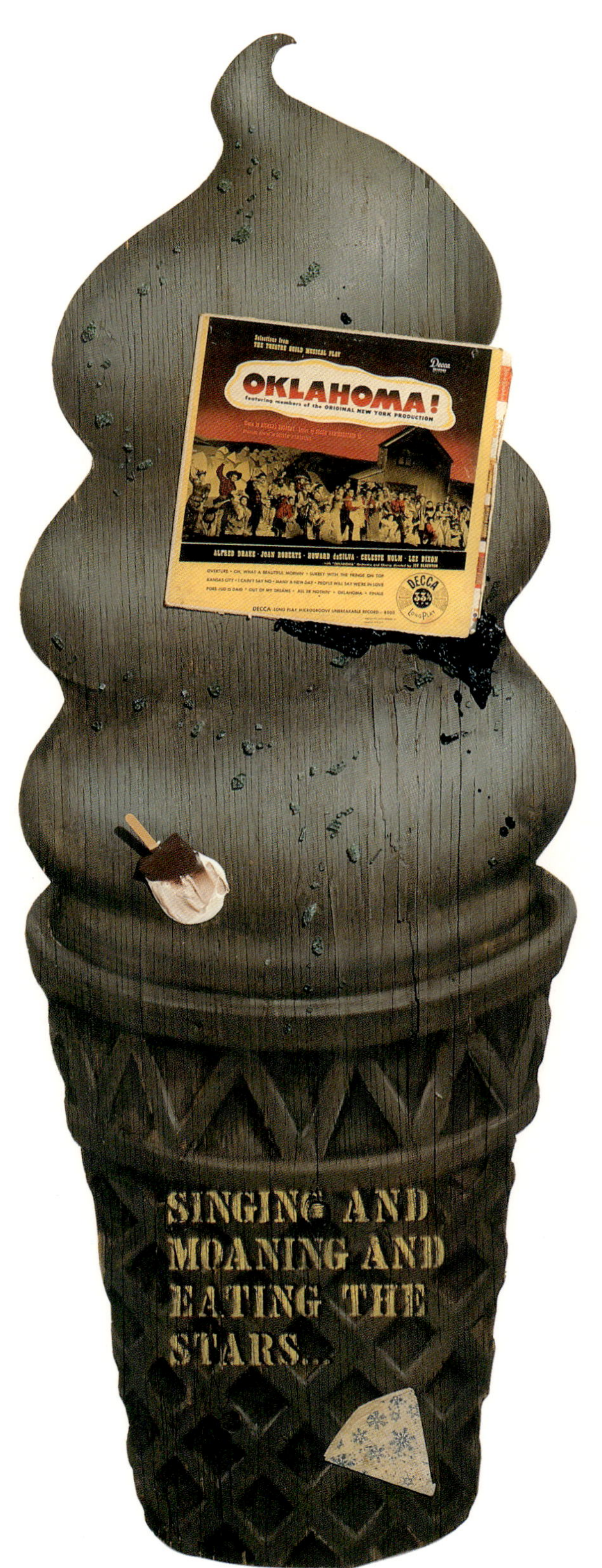

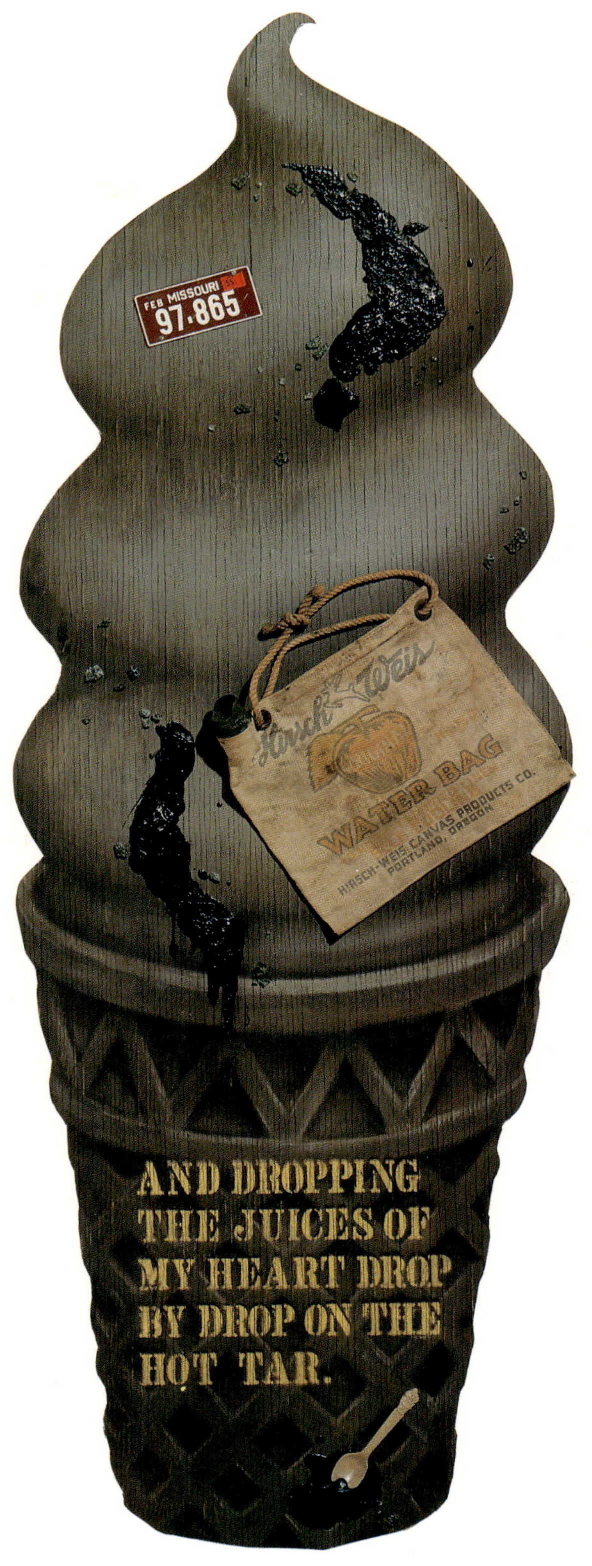

Rocky Road, 1990
Mixed-media collage, two panels, 64 × 23 inches each
Margo Leavin Gallery, Los Angeles

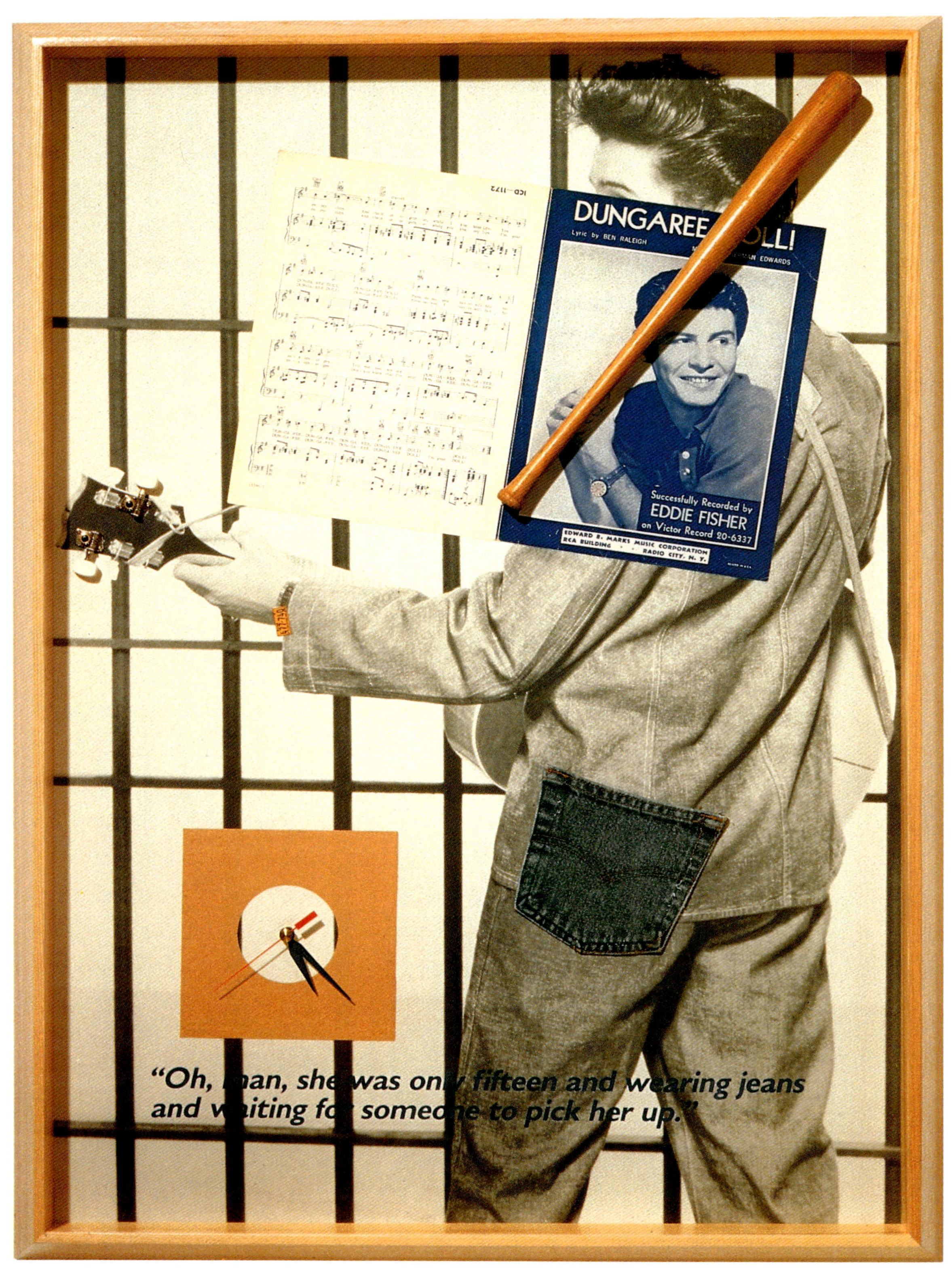

Jailbait, 1988
Mixed-media collage, 42¼ × 30⅝ inches
Collection of Anne and William J. Hokin

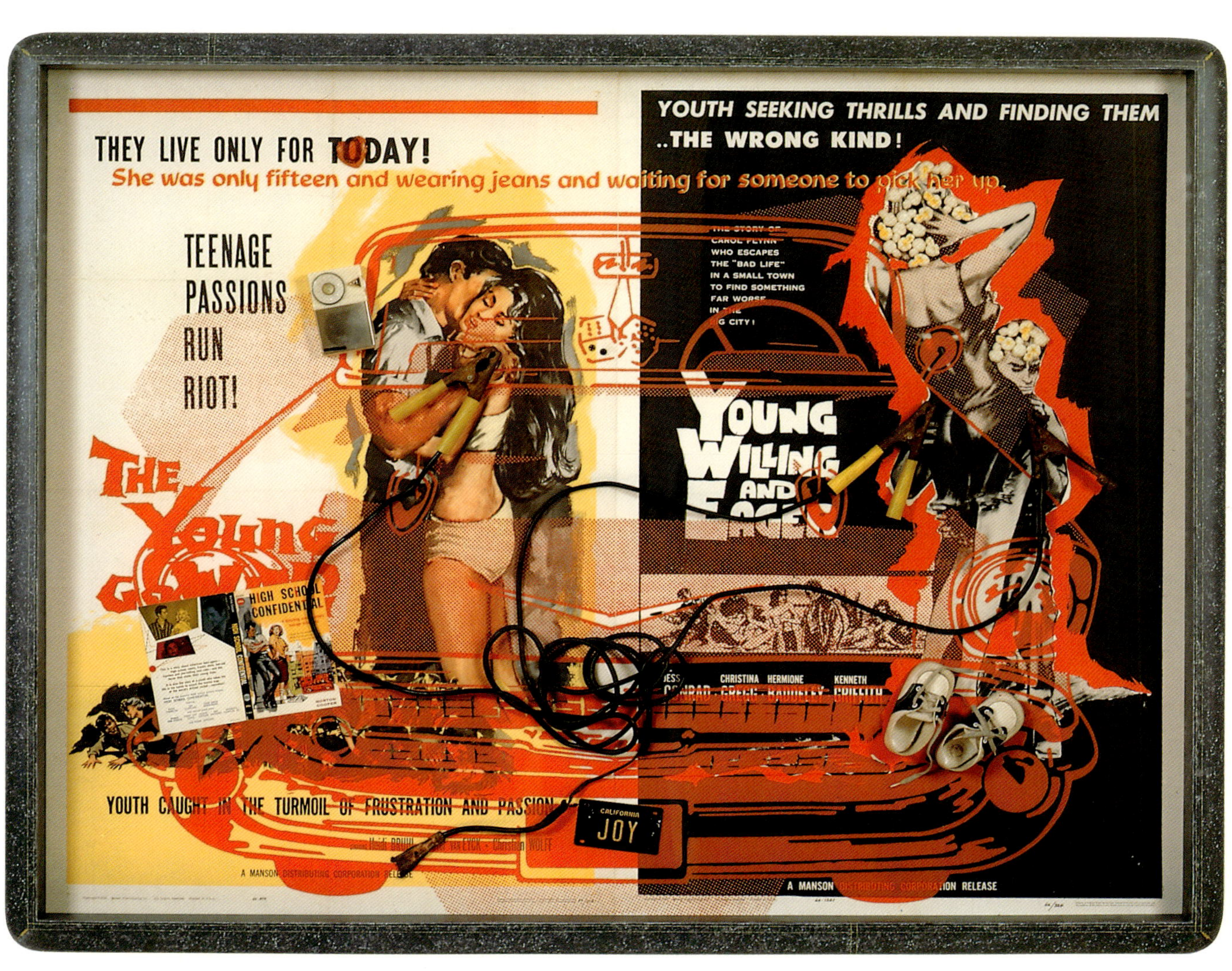

Blue Denim, 1990
Mixed-media collage, 44½ × 57 inches
Collection of Mandy and Cliff Einstein

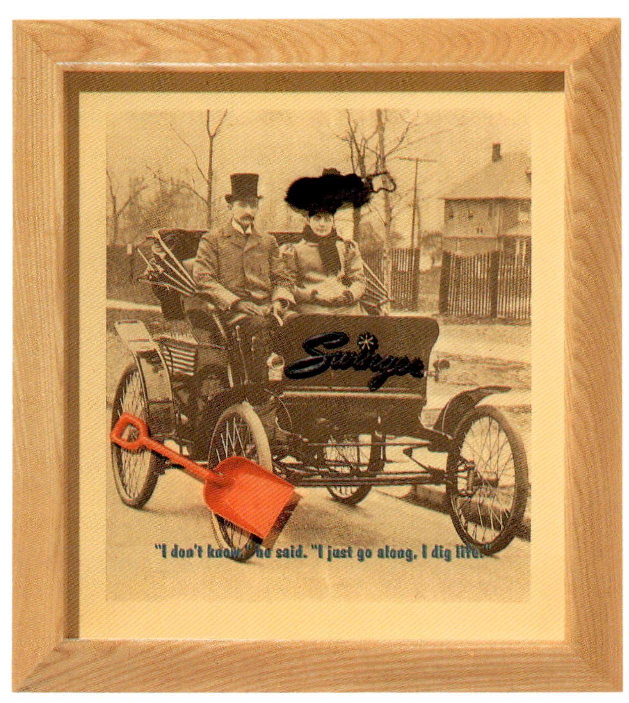

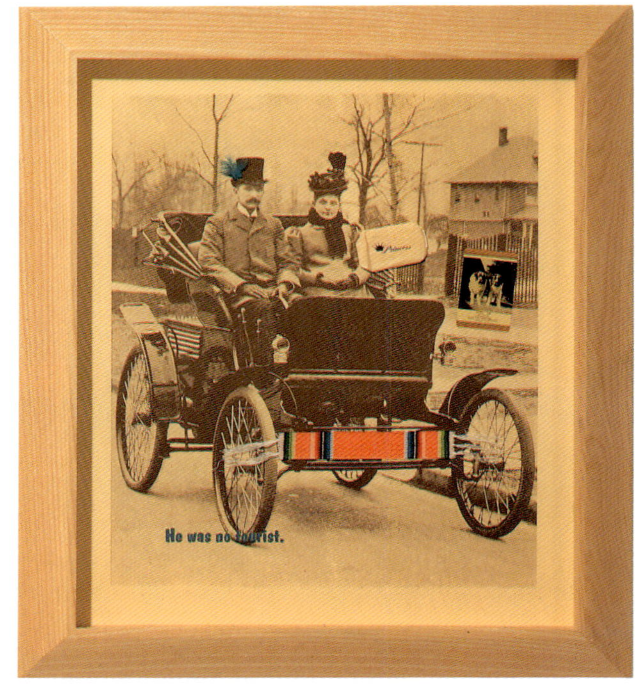

King of the Road, 1988
Mixed-media collage, two panels, 29¾ × 26 inches
Collection of Joy and Jerry Monkarsh

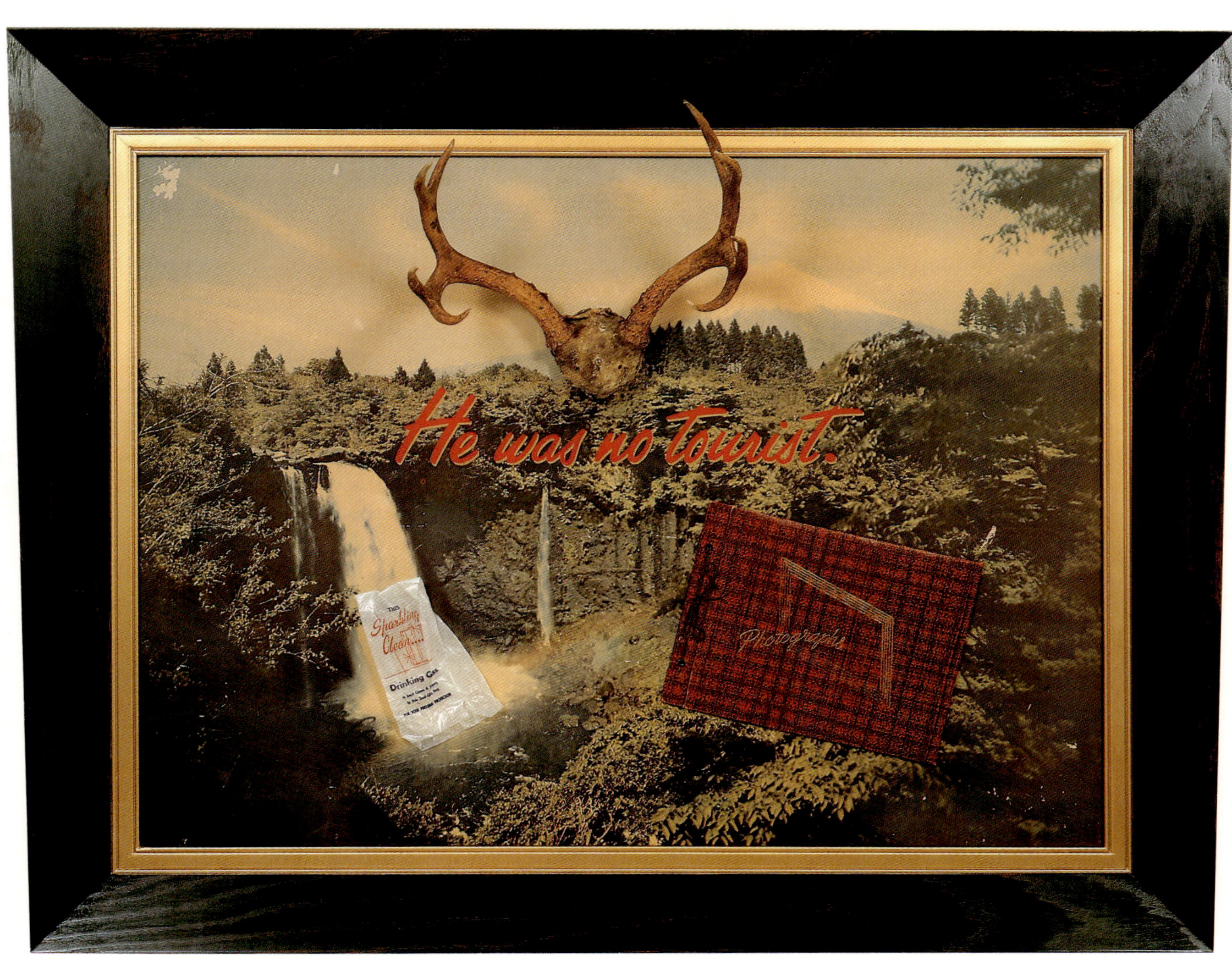

Native American, 1990
Mixed-media collage, 45¼ × 58¼ × 14 inches
Collection of James and Linda Burrows

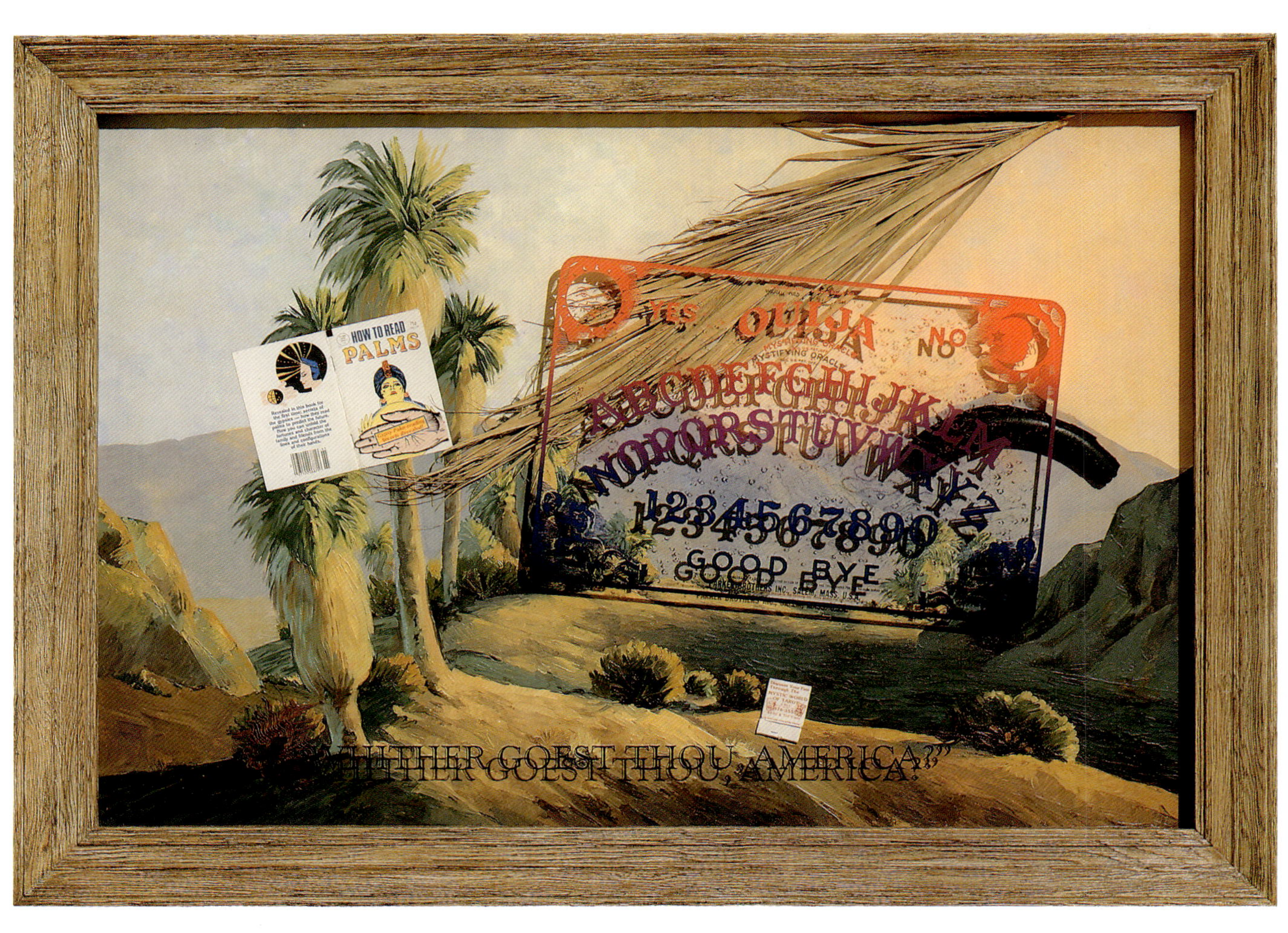

Palm Reader, 1989
Mixed-media collage, 30¾ × 43 inches
The Capital Group, Inc., Los Angeles

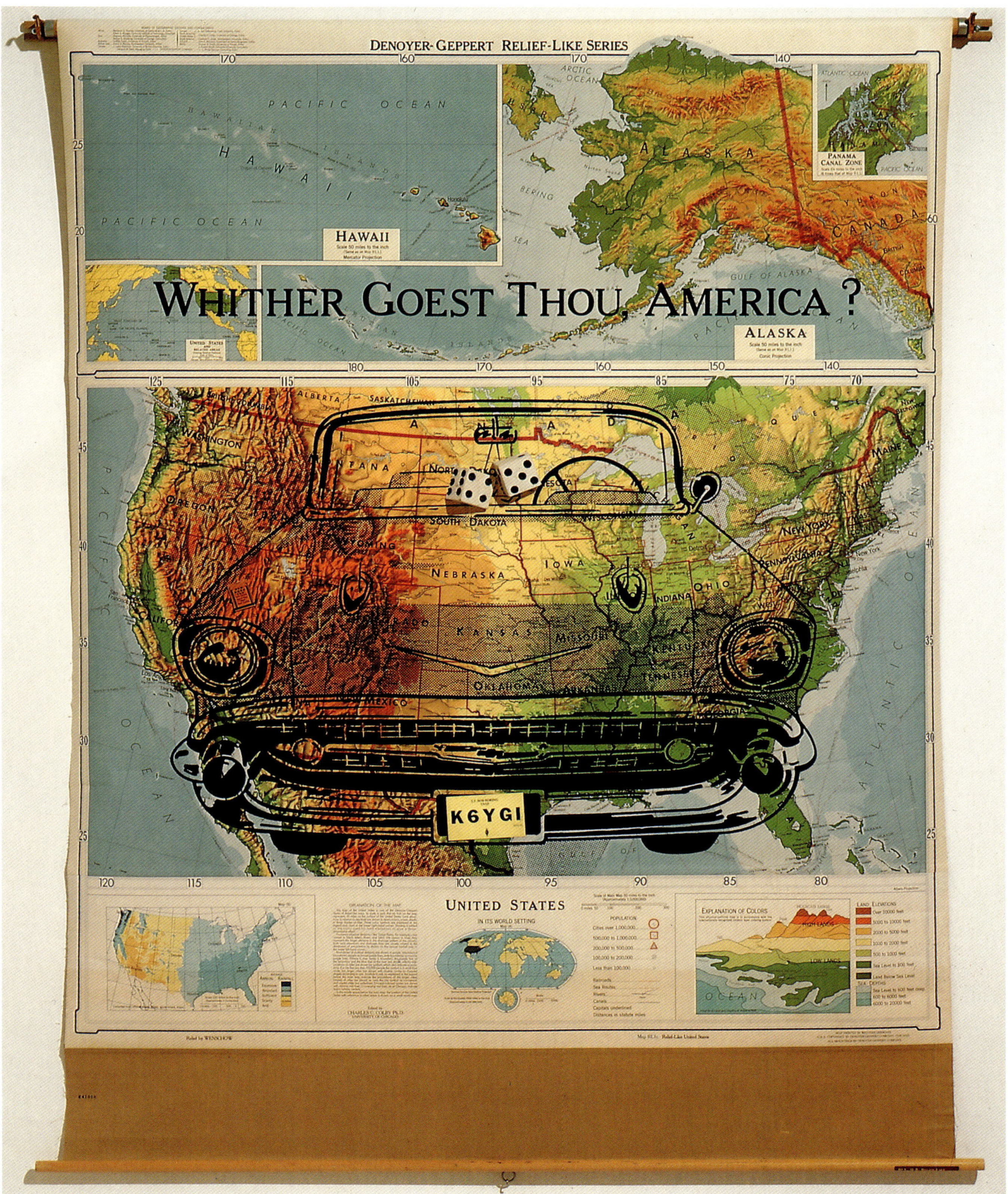

Pair o' Dice, 1990
Mixed-media collage, 85½ × 67 × 3 inches
Morrison & Foerster, Irvine, California

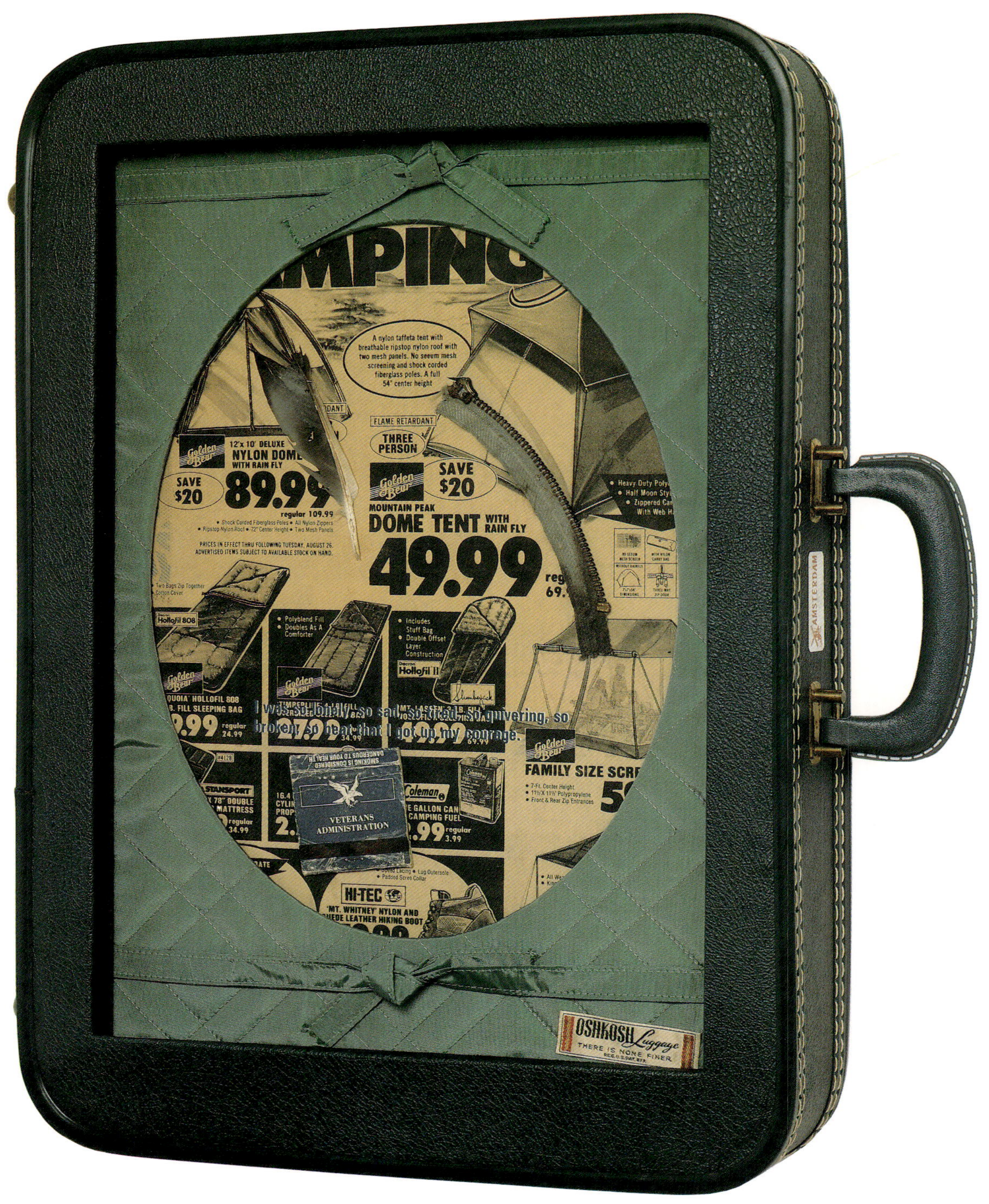

I was so lonely, so sad, so tired, so quivering, so broken, so beat that I got up my courage.

Lonesome Traveler, 1989
Mixed-media collage, 20⅝ × 15¼ × 3⅛ inches
Collection of Rosamund Felsen

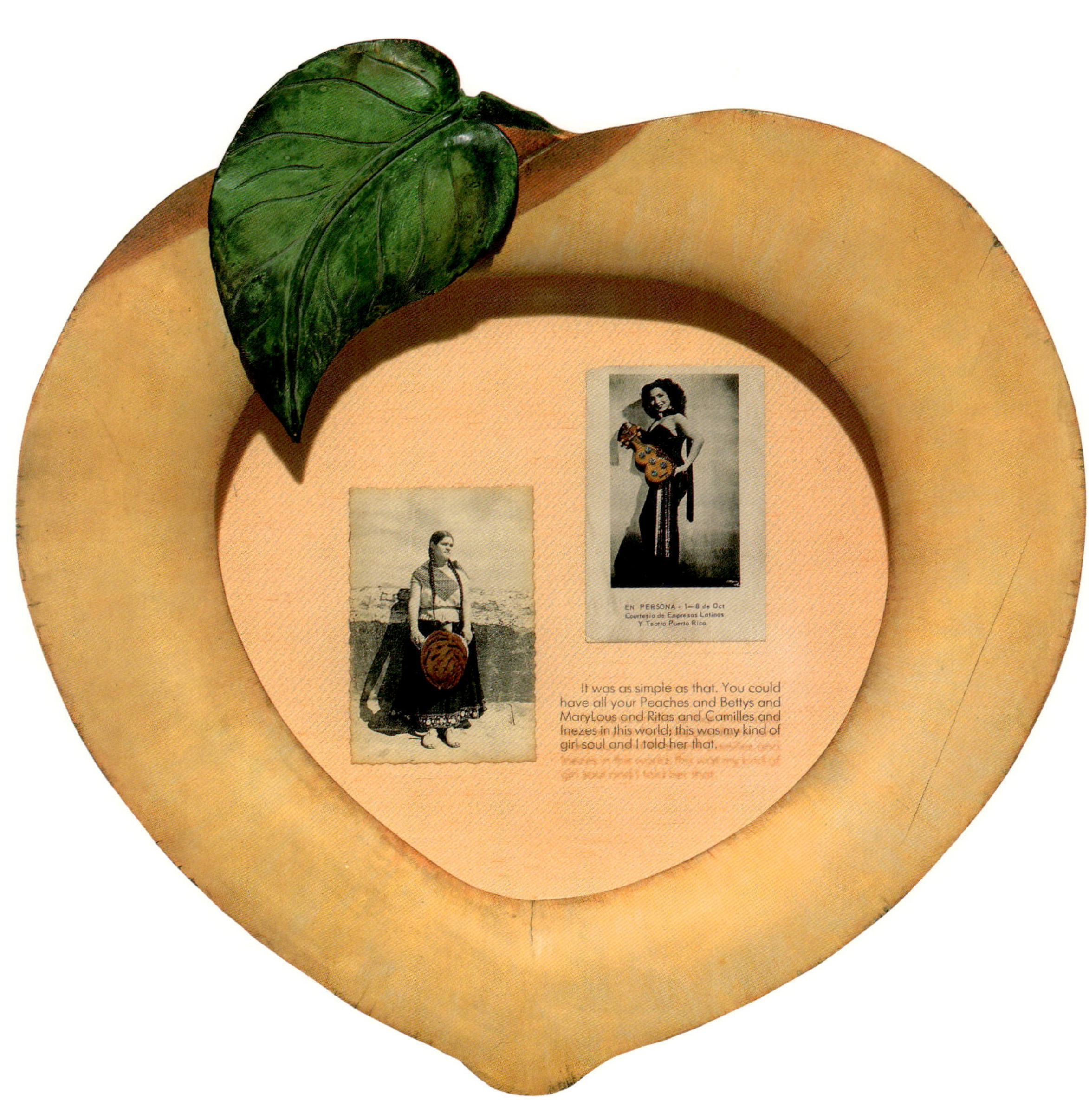

Peaches, 1990
Mixed-media collage, 20½ × 20 × 3 inches
Collection of the artist

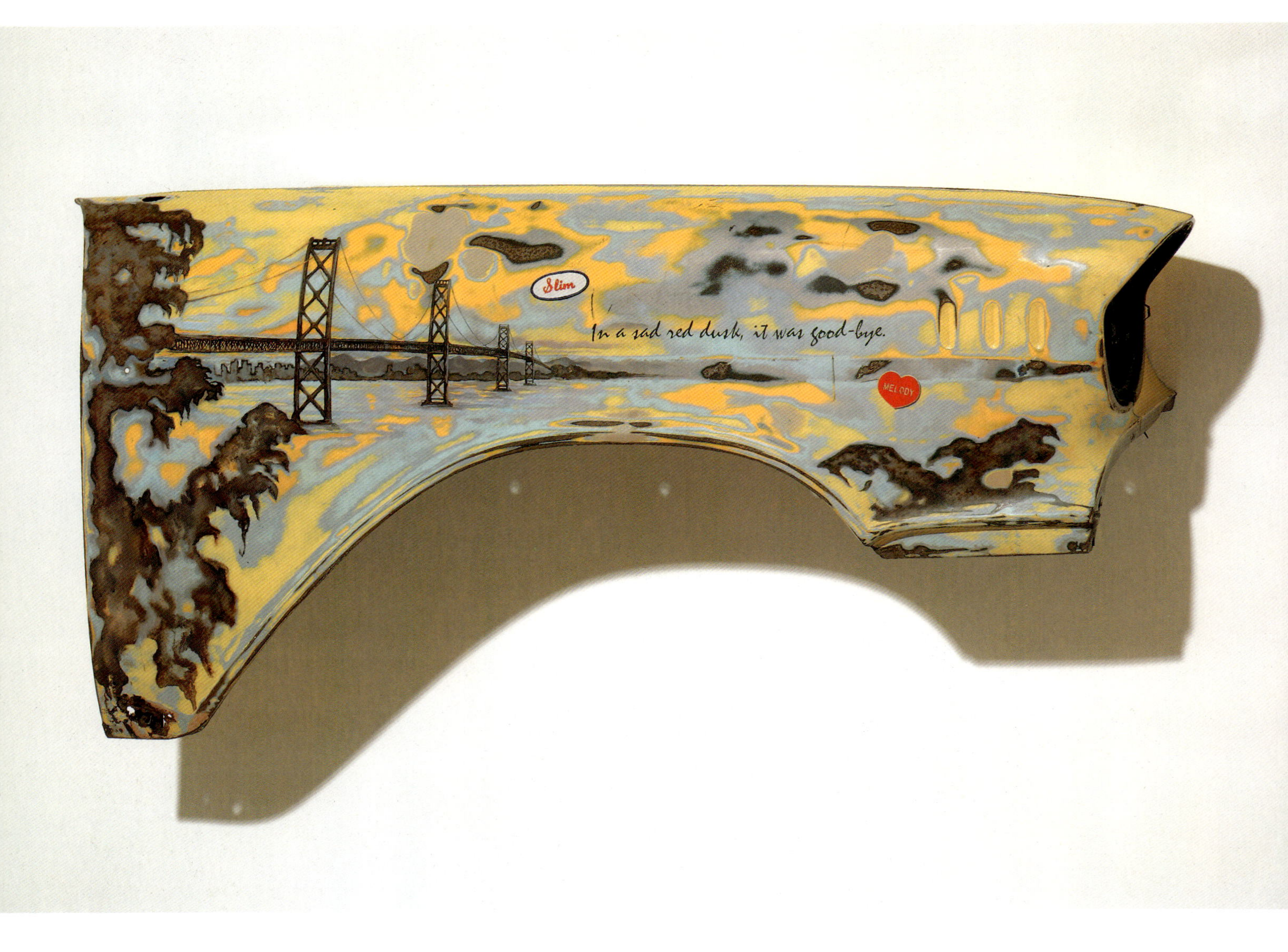

Adios, 1990 (in collaboration with Lucia Vinograd)
Mixed-media collage, 31 × 63½ × 12 inches
Collection of James and Linda Burrows

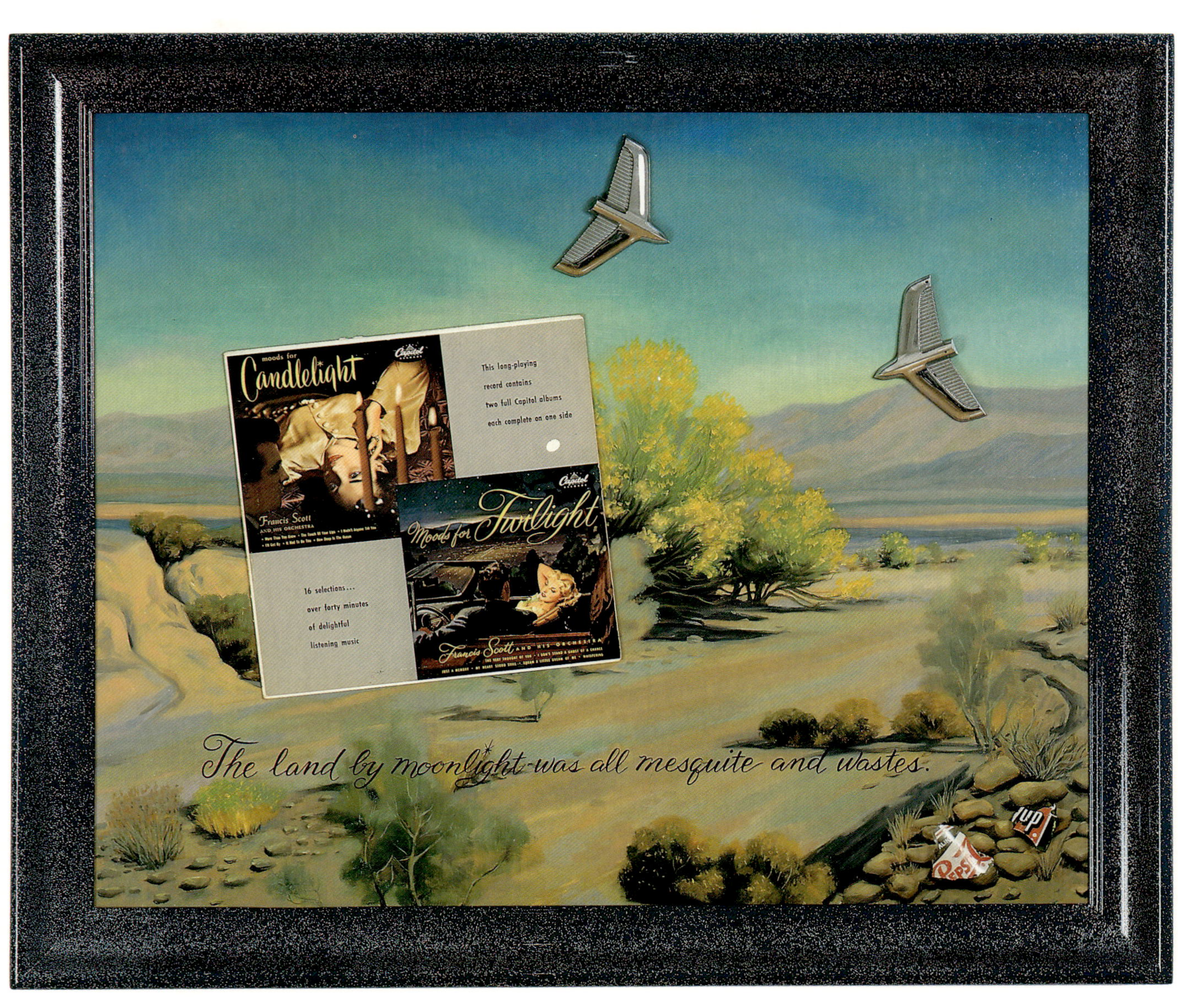

Moonlight Serenade, 1989
Mixed-media collage, 32¾ × 38½ inches
Collection of Anne and William J. Hokin

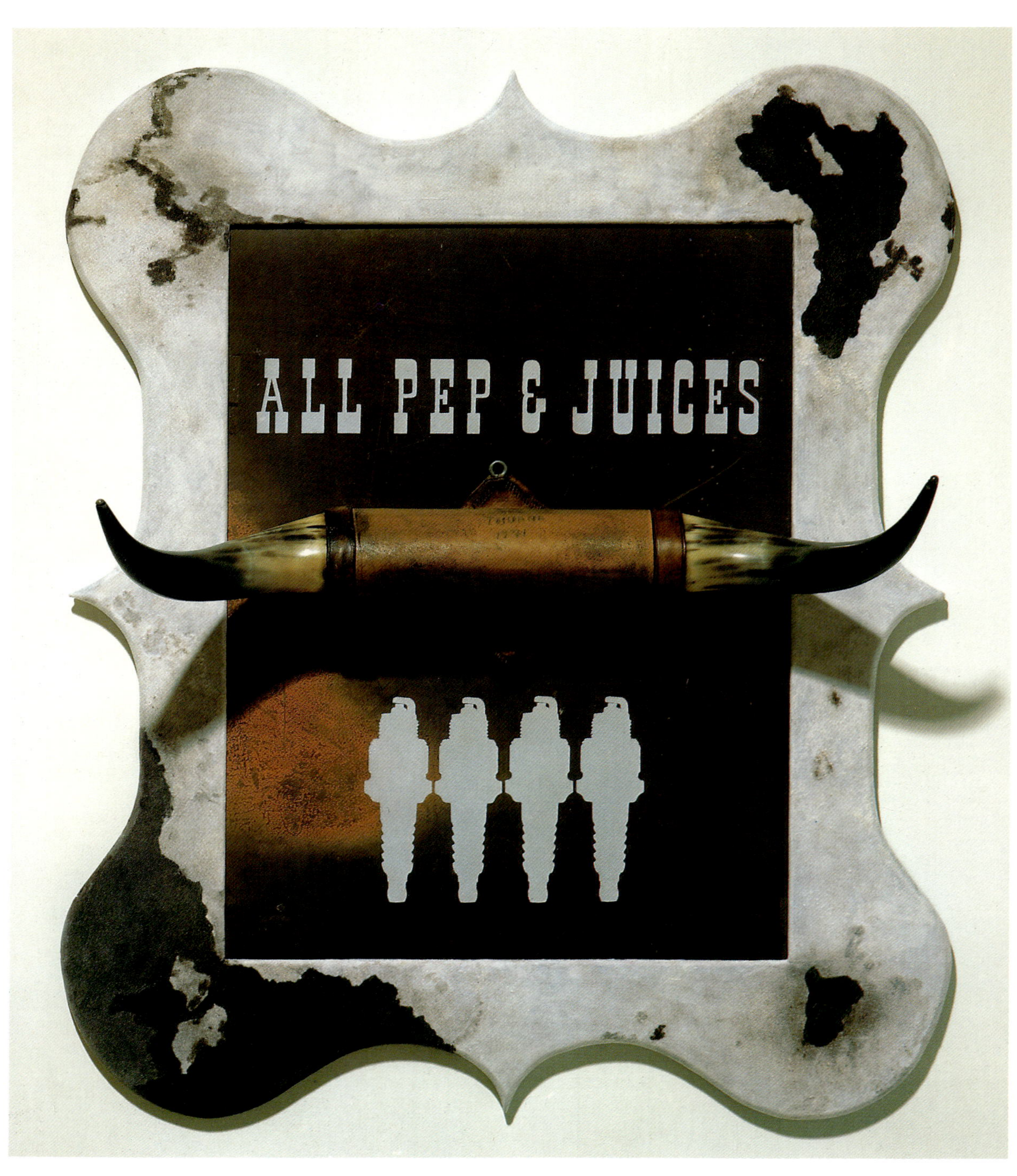

All Pep and Juices, 1990
Mixed-media collage, 39½ × 32 × 11 inches
Margo Leavin Gallery, Los Angeles

Fruits 'n' Nuts, 1990
Mixed-media collage, 35¼ × 24 × 16 inches
Josh Baer Gallery, New York, and Margo Leavin Gallery, Los Angeles

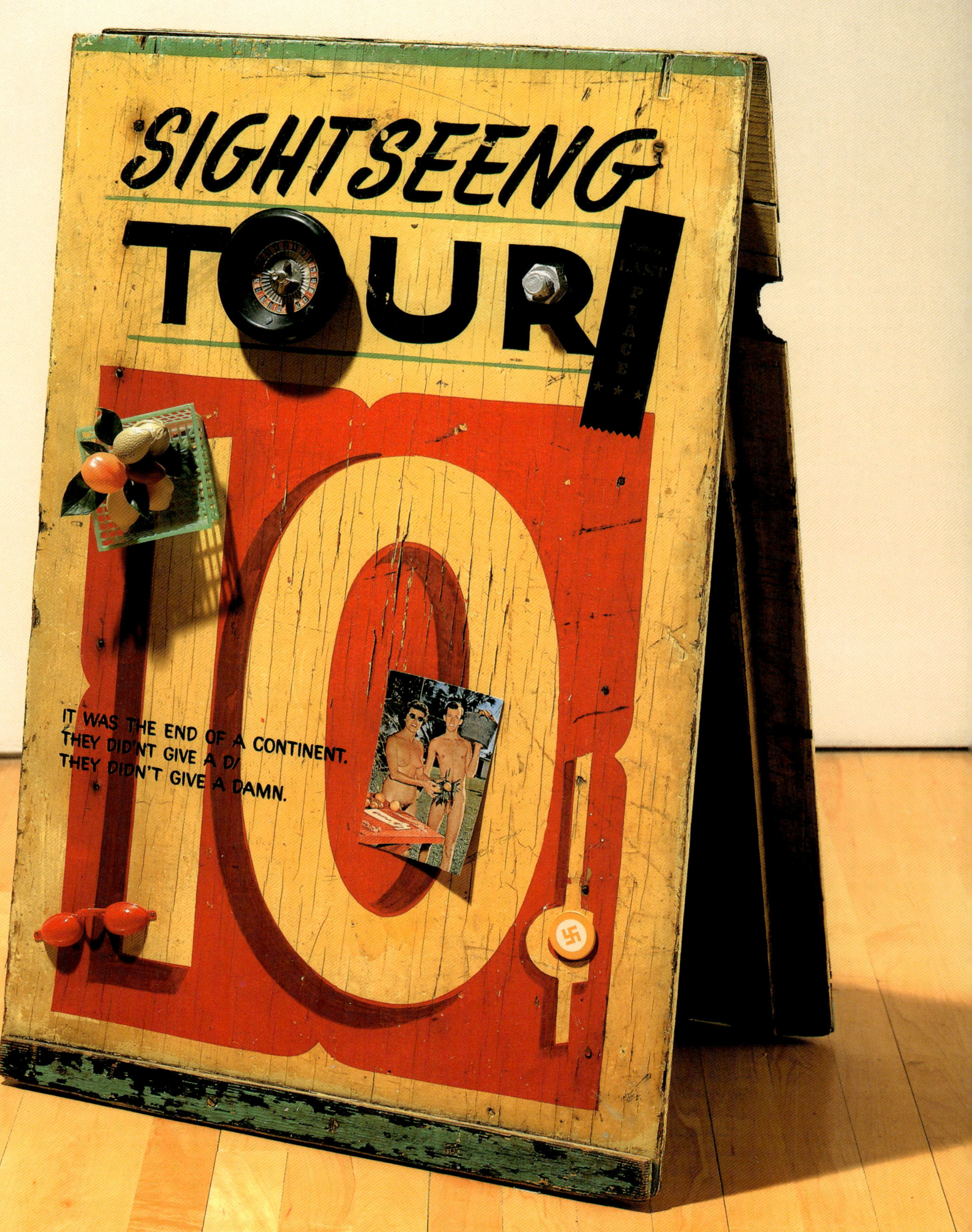
SIGHTSEENG
TOUR
LAST
PEACE
10
IT WAS THE END OF A CONTINENT.
THEY DIDN'T GIVE A D/
THEY DIDN'T GIVE A DAMN.

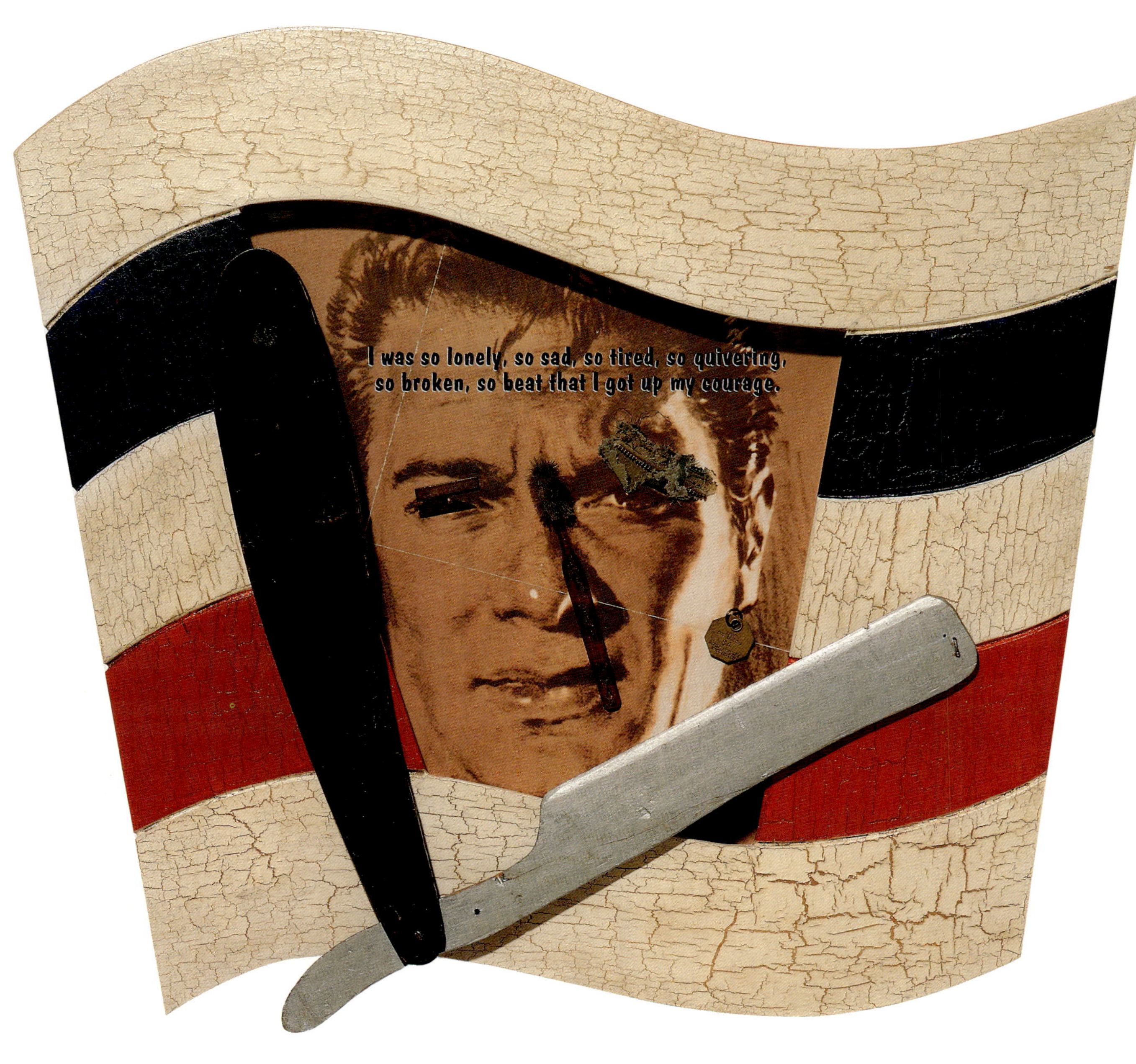

Old Glory, 1989
Mixed-media collage, 25 × 27 inches
Collection of Mr. and Mrs. Les Charles

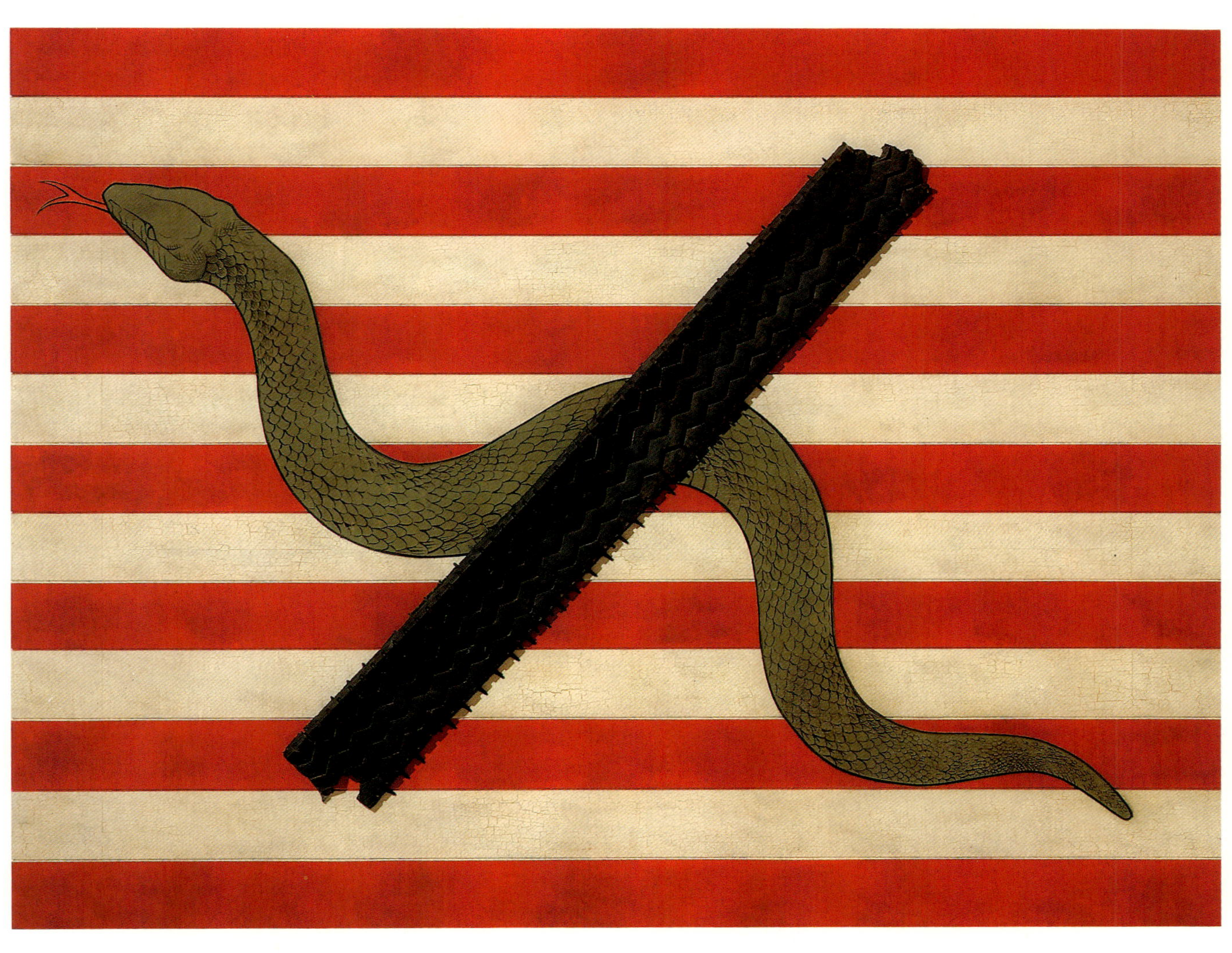

Jack, 1990
Mixed-media collage, 71½ × 93 inches
Collection of Laila and Thurston Twigg-Smith

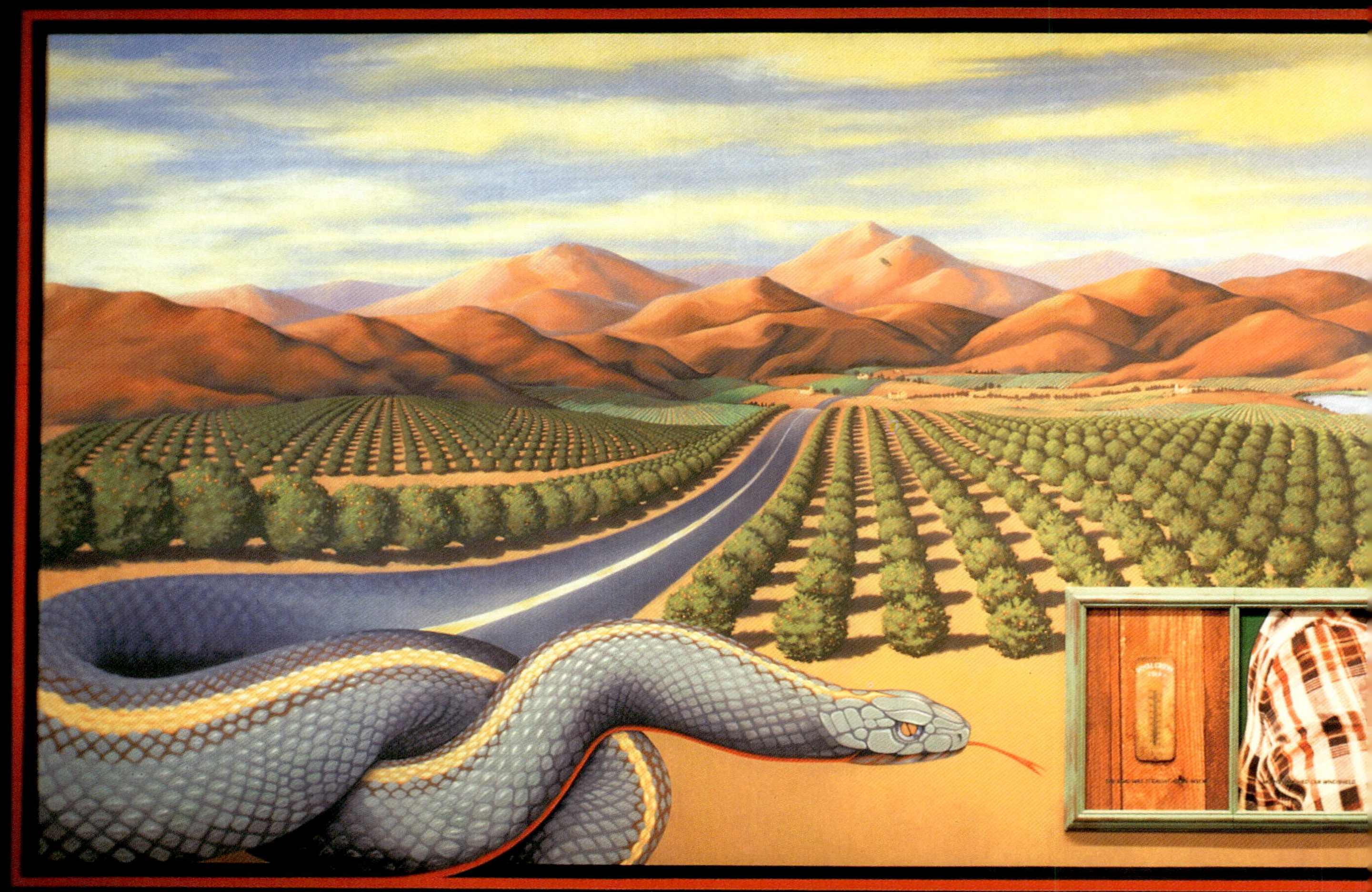

In response to an invitation from The Brooklyn Museum to realize a project in its cavernous Moderne entrance lobby, Smith reverted to an earlier format of wall-bound, collaged objects on a painted ground. Here, however, the ground would be the entire height and width of the 22 x 64-foot wall that stands about 60 feet opposite the museum's front doors. Smith and two assistants used the set design studio of UCLA's theater department to paint this enormous expanse of muslin. Using orange-crate labels as models, she composed an idyllic California landscape—straight rows of orange groves receding into a mountain range topped by a bright sky with streaks of yellow clouds. At right is an enormous bough of fruit and blossoms. At left, Eden's demise is symbolized by a meandering distant highway that becomes a huge coiled snake in the foreground. Hanging in the lower section are eight assemblages, each an overscaled 5×3

Same Old Paradise, 1987
Grand Lobby installation, The Brooklyn Museum, New York
Mixed-media collage on painted canvas backdrop, 22 × 64 feet overall

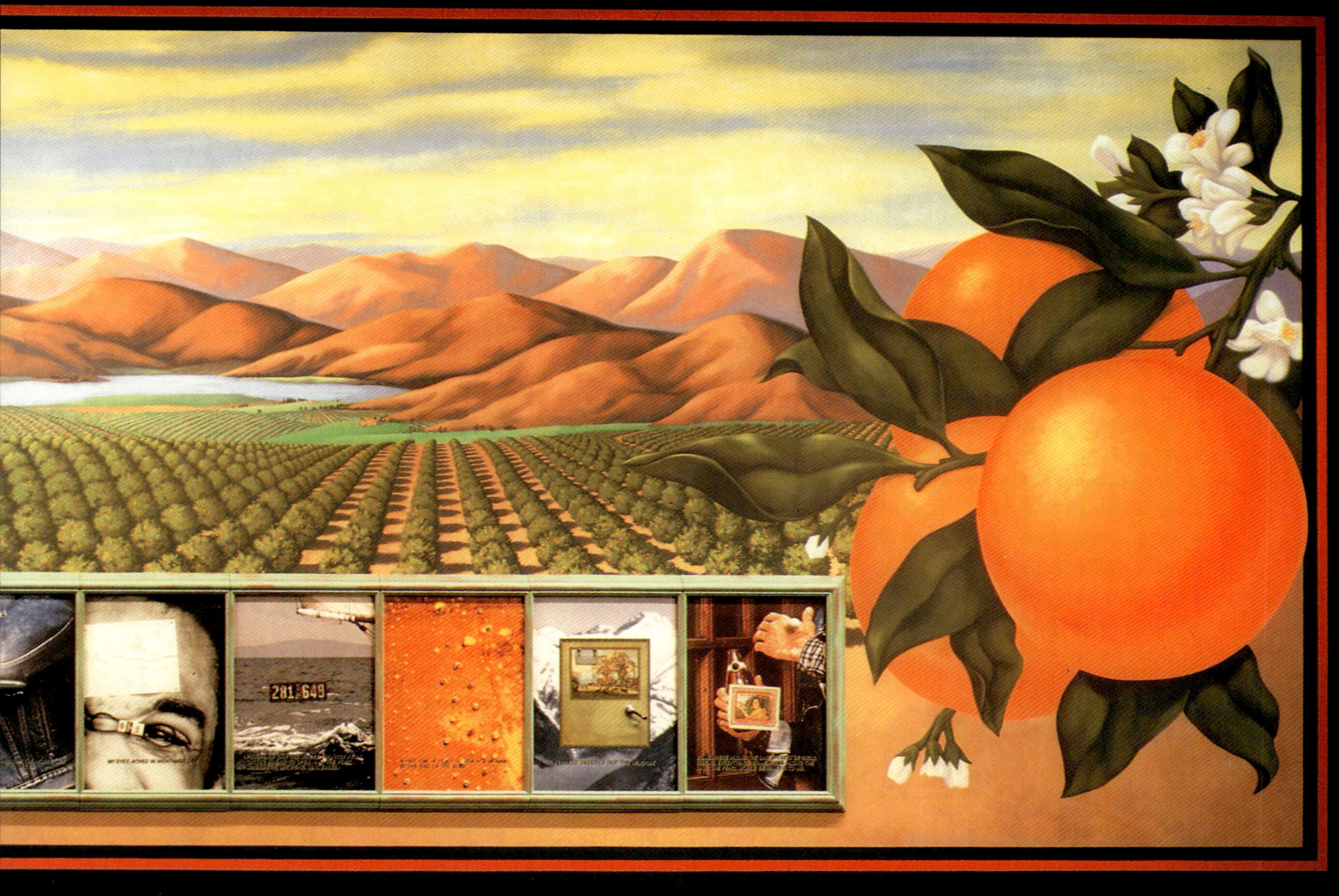

feet, hung in a multipartite frame. Big billboard-derived images of other landscapes, clothed bodies, and a face become grounds for smaller items such as a fan belt, calendar, thermometer, or a rusted license plate. Quotes from Jack Kerouac's *On the Road* define the work as a quest, best exemplified by the exclamatory, "I suddenly saw the whole country as an oyster for us to open, and the pearl was there, the pearl was there."

Kerouac's was a real odyssey; Smith has wandered through America by means of its self-defining literature and physical cast-offs. Whereas Kerouac moved from town to town, ever westward toward the future, Smith considered the myths that have dominated this country, decade by decade, up to about 1970. But each artist seems to have discovered that the ideal exists in what is already around us and is the only means to nurture the ideal within ourselves.

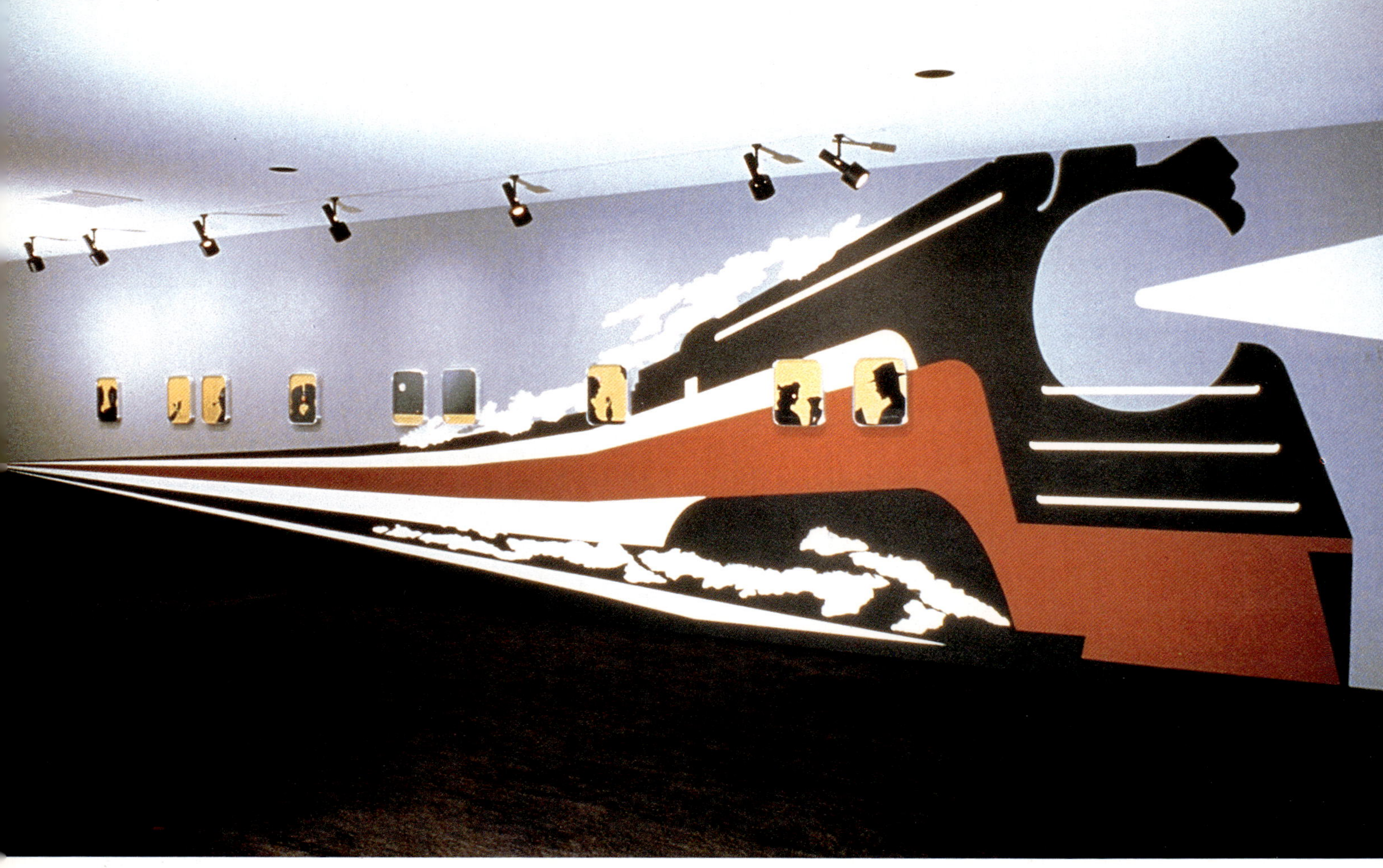

Starlight (1982), Smith's first public project, animates an otherwise undistinguished savings bank. The piece plays to the glamour of the bank's West Hollywood locale and matches the renovation of the bank office in a 1930s streamlined Moderne style. Designed to cover a 9×39-foot wall, the receding perspective of the locomotive's lines camouflages a wheelchair ramp. The title refers to a prewar Southern Pacific luxury train, "The Daylight," which ran between Los Angeles and San Francisco, and pays homage to the stars that frequently used it.

Against a light gray field, Smith painted the black and red forms of a modern locomotive, enveloped in steam, its strong headlight illuminating the oncoming night. The metal framing of the collages approximates the rounded corners of car windows. These individual works contain the silhouettes of many types of people. Their printed dialogue is lifted from classic train movies such as *Shanghai Express*. From this movie, Smith again used a quotation that had appeared in the *Cathay* installation and *Chinese Junk*: "I can't replace our ideals but I'll buy you a new watch when we get to Shanghai." For this phrase, a keystone in Smith's reconciliation with disillusionment, she fashioned the silhouette of a woman's gloved hand, adorned with a toy watch and holding a cigarette, its trailing smoke cut from gold netting.

Starlight, 1982
Mixed-media collages on painted wall, 9×39 feet overall
Unity Savings and Loan, West Hollywood

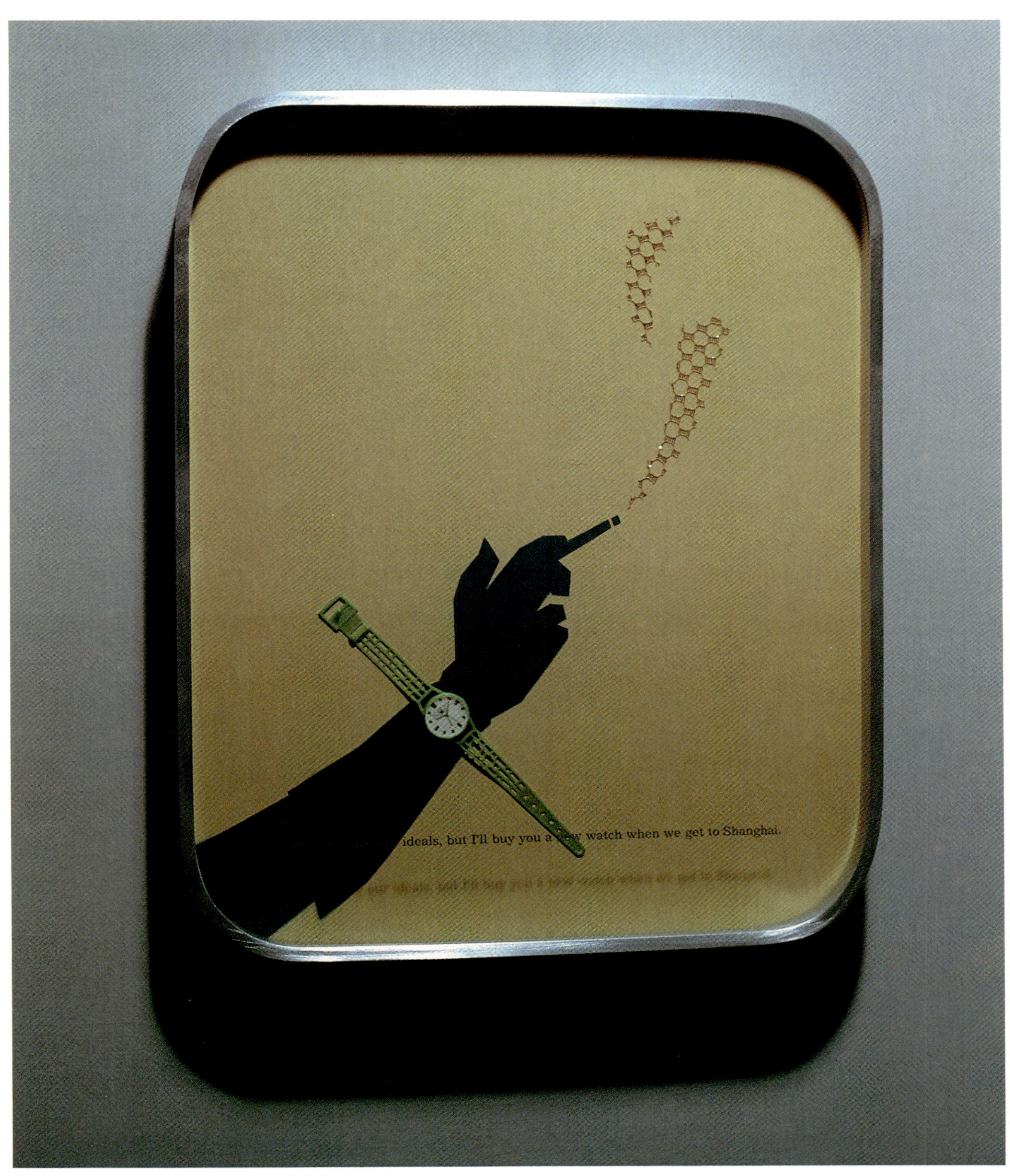

Shanghai Express, 1982
Mixed-media collage from **Starlight**, 15 × 12 × 1¼ inches
Unity Savings and Loan, West Hollywood

In 1982 Smith was asked by the city of Grand Rapids, Michigan, to propose a renovation of the three-story entryway to an existing performing arts center, De Vos Hall. Part of a typically bleak 1980s municipal structure, the Keeler Grand Foyer (as Smith's designated area is known) presented her with an unusually formidable task. Poorly organized and illuminated, the space was further marred by a rust-orange carpet that, for budgetary reasons, could not be replaced. A massive two-story staircase is the foyer's most prominent architectural feature, and Smith took her cues from it. The unifying motif became cascading water in homage to the city's geographical location on the banks of the Grand River. From within a jagged, stylized riverbed on the top level, the painted water pours down to a high point on the middle level, then rushes down the walls of the ground floor. A fascia and soffit between the top and middle levels have an eddy of patterns. The overall impression is of traversing a rapids. Beneath the stairwell, Smith painted a grotto with a shade tree and added two cast-iron park benches.

Large, schematized faces of a man and woman decorate the top level. On the second level, Smith used a smaller version of the piano keyboard first seen in *Porgy and Bess*, decorated with Art Deco patterns reminiscent of American Indian designs. Atop the keyboard are twenty copper-framed collages, composed in a geometric style that echoes the grid of the keyboard. Their quotations are vintage Smith—mostly 1930s and 1940s phrases taken from the lyrics of popular songs, such novels as *Gentlemen Prefer Blondes*, plays of the era, or various sayings of stage characters like Will Rogers.

In an effort to evoke the glamour of the glorious prewar years of Hollywood, Smith in effect collages the language of that moment onto contemporaneous decorative motifs, executed in such techniques as glazing, combing, rag rolling, and Spanish tile. To locate the work in Grand Rapids, Smith combined landscape and ideogrammatic features of the site and culture. The grotto on the first level is part of this naturalist ambience, and the waterfalls at either side of the stairs are hung with large beaded collages derived from drawings by Native Americans of the region. On the opposite side of the lobby, a projection booth has been crowned with a giant simulated "Grand" theater marquee, its face lettered "The Keeler Grand Foyer," yet another reference to the heyday of the movies.

Smith's attempt to infuse local themes with her brand of collective cinematic memory is deliberate and marks all her public commissions. "My personal theory is that the imagery of something should be appropriate to the content of the place. It should be built into the concept in such a way that it's the most fundamental thing. That's the key to all my pieces. In the studio, you can make any content you want. In public art, the content is based on who is going to look at the piece, how they will experience it physically as well as visually."

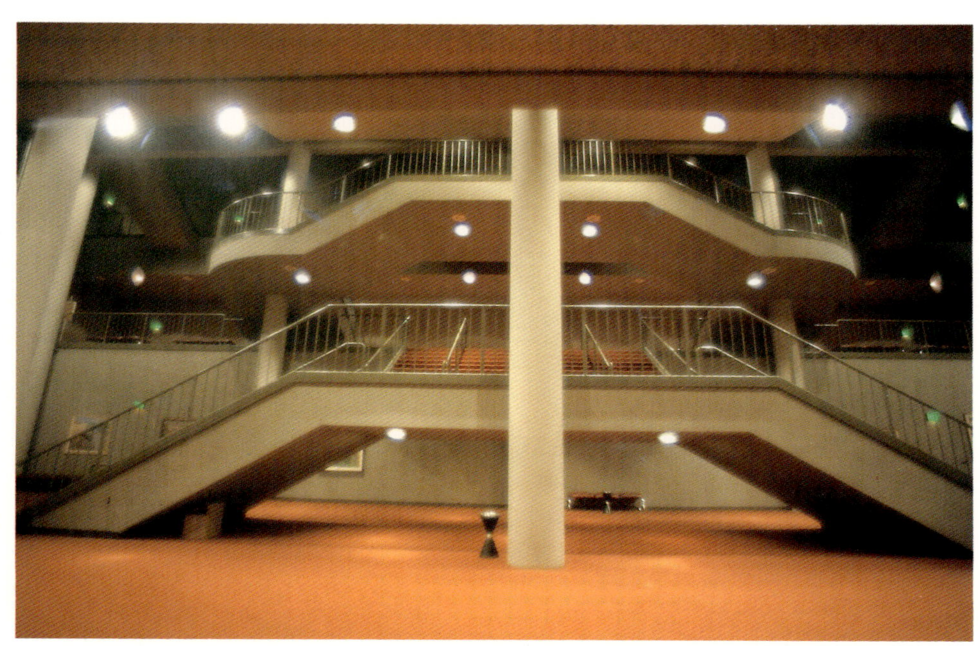

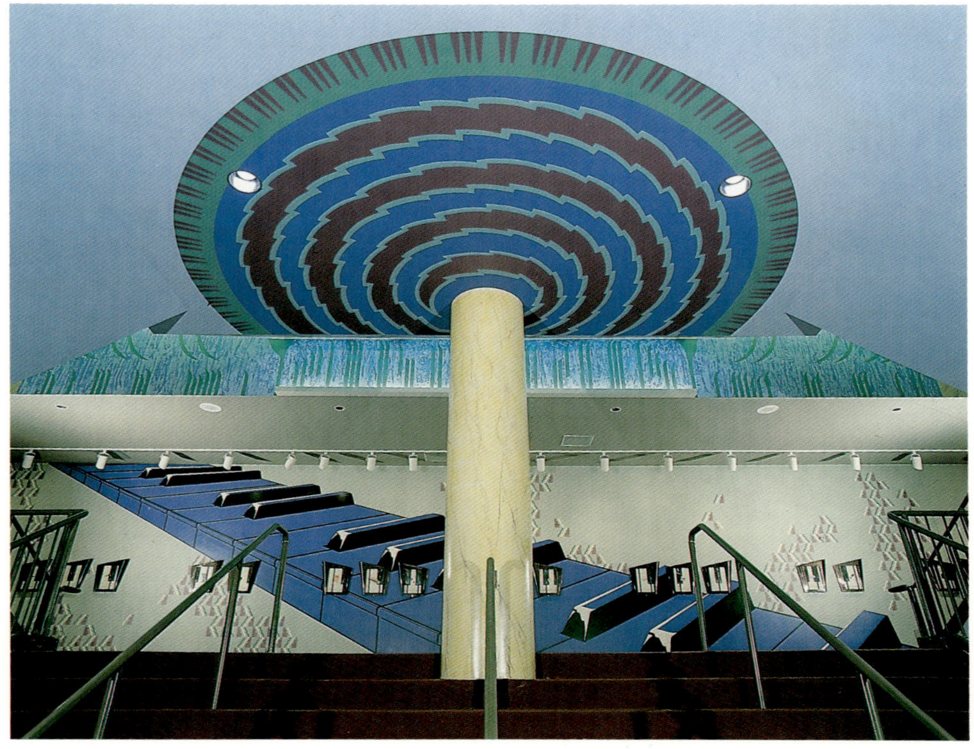

Keeler Grand Foyer, De Vos Hall,
Grand Rapids, Michigan.
As built, 1980.

The Grand, 1983
Mixed-media collage installation, second level
Keeler Grand Foyer

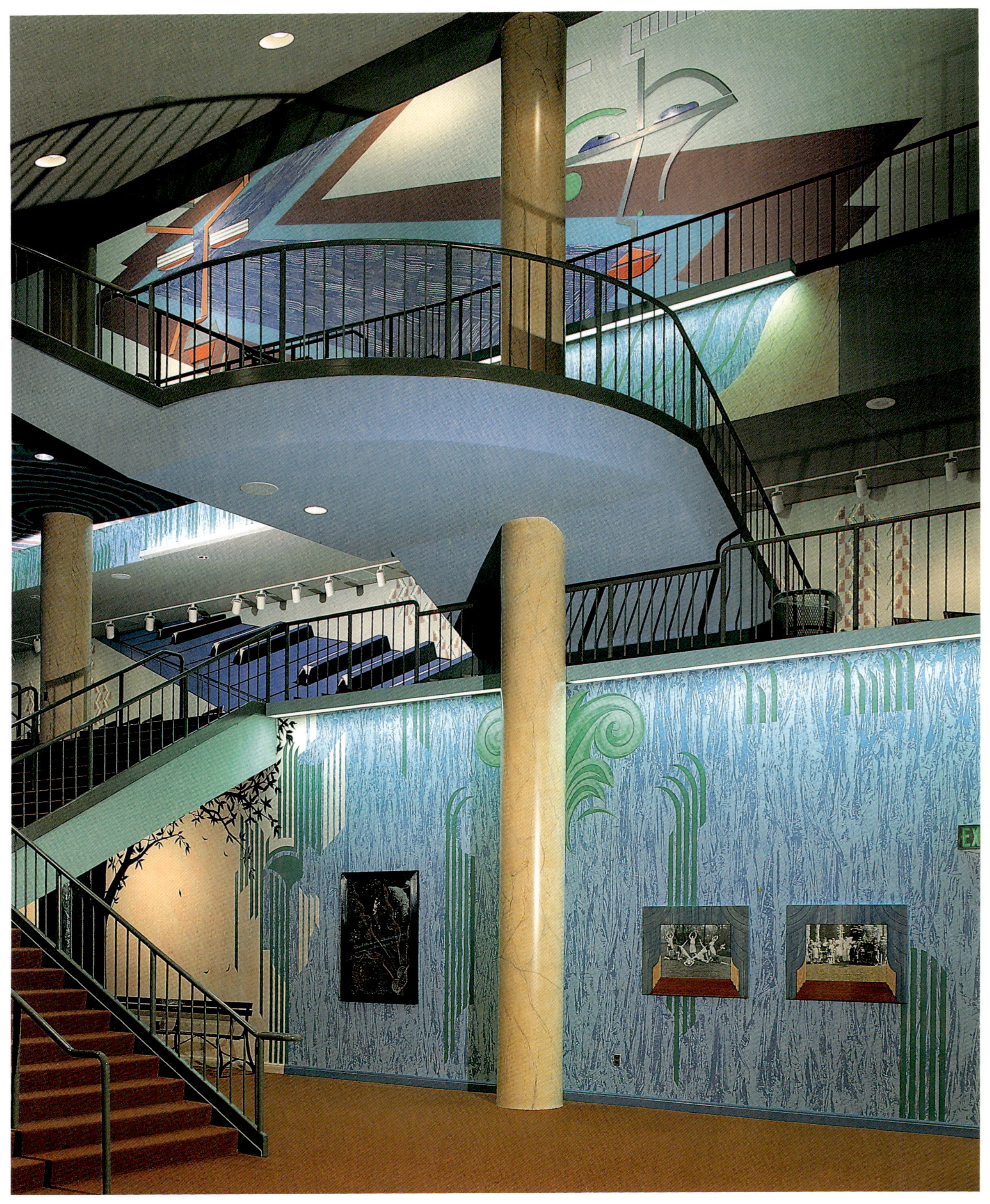

The Grand, 1983
Mixed-media installation, 6,000 square feet on three levels
Keeler Grand Foyer, De Vos Hall, Grand Rapids, Michigan

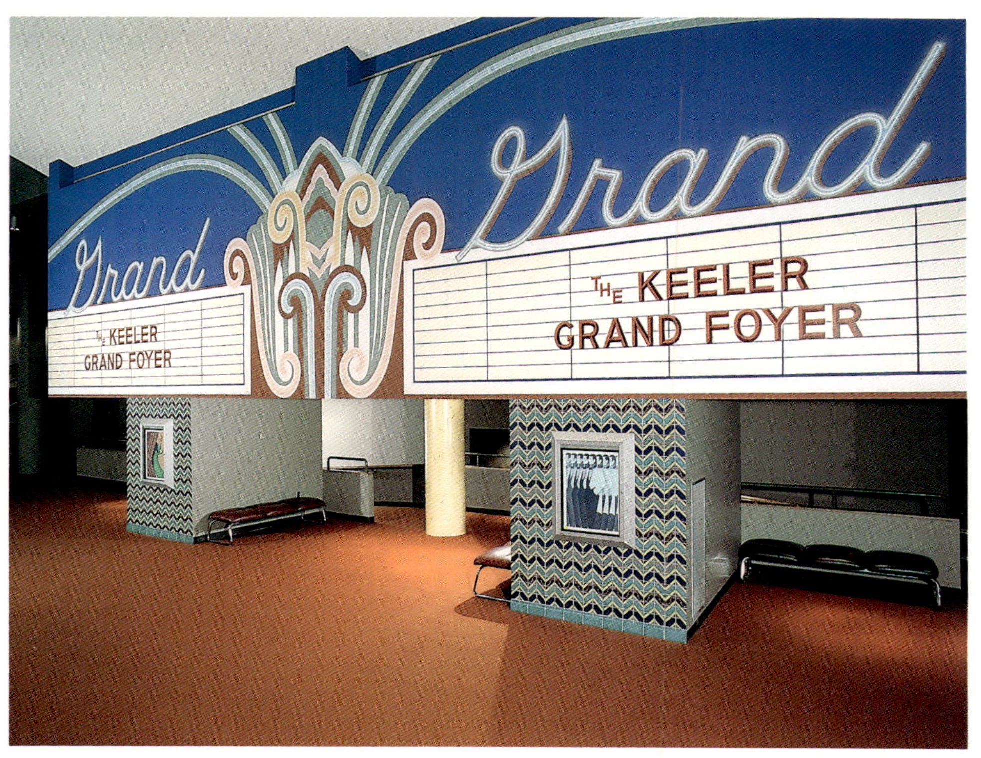

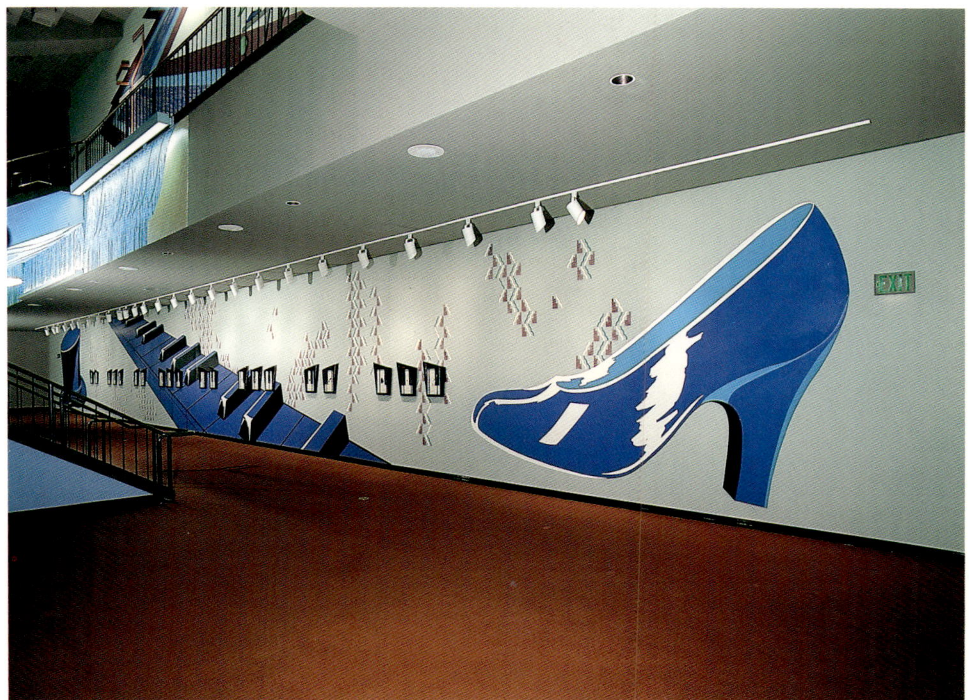

The Grand, 1983
Views of lower level marquee and second level

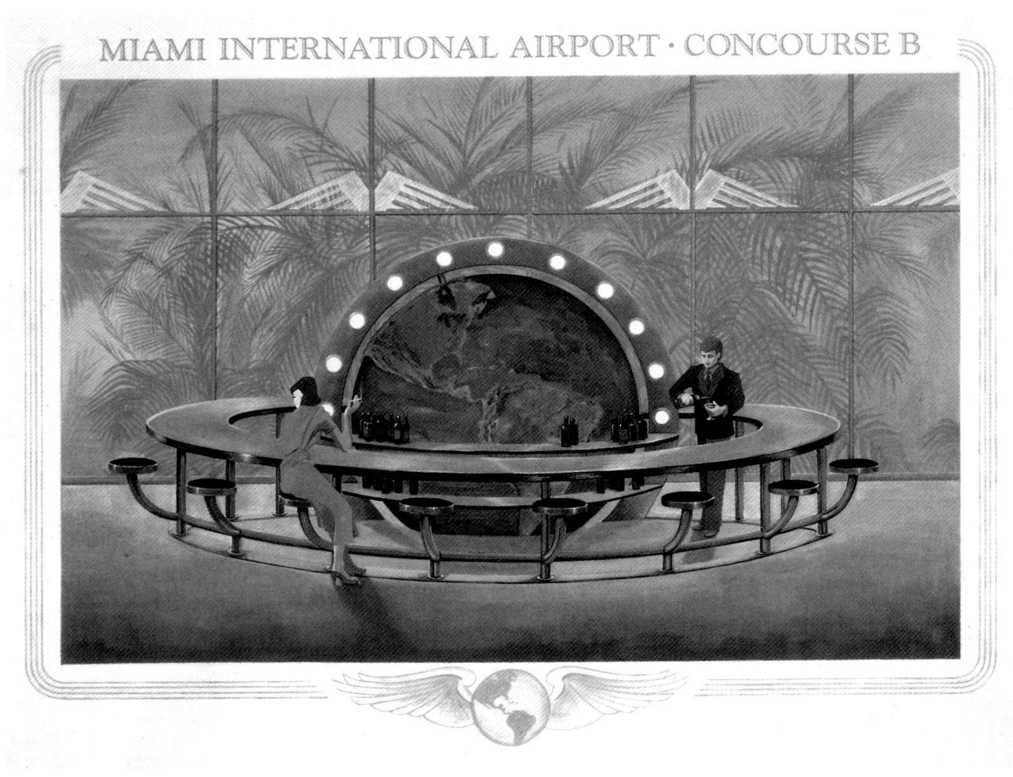

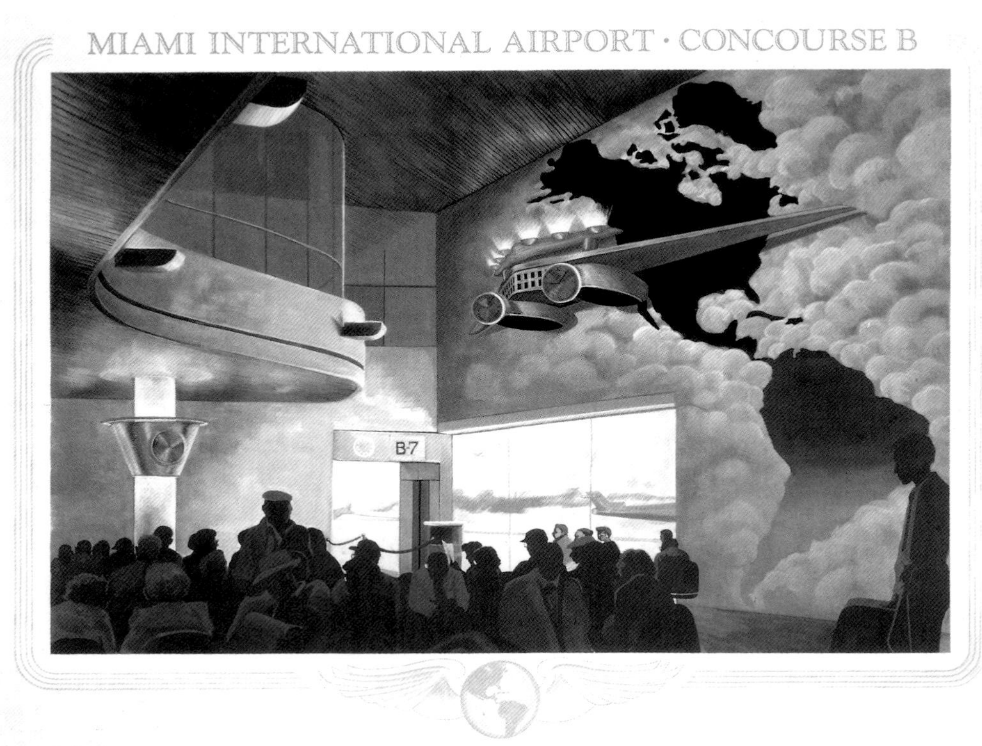

Collaborative proposal with R.M. Fischer for
Concourse B, Miami International Airport, 1988
Renderings by Lucia Vinograd

In the course of proposing and realizing a series of mini-monuments for MacArthur Park in central Los Angeles, Smith met and became friends with R.M. Fischer. His sculptures of reassembled found parts struck a sympathetic chord in collagiste Smith. When she was asked by her friend and former teacher, site-specific sculptor Robert Irwin, to join a team of artists he was leading in redesigning Miami's International Airport, Smith asked Fischer to collaborate. They chose Concourse B as the site of their project. After determining that discrete art objects would be overwhelmed by the visual pandemonium of the airport, they drew up plans to entirely remake the area. Its focal point would be a mural of the geographic outlines of North and South America, contoured by clouds. A metal relief by Fischer suggesting a vintage-1930s airplane would emerge from North America and be embellished with "headlight" clocks. On another wall, they envisioned a circular bar built around an oversize metal globe. Other decorations included glass etched with palm fronds, new wall sconces, carpet, and lighting. Smith's longtime fascination with travel—again as portrayed in the golden years of Hollywood—made this an especially apt project. But bureaucratic disagreements within the sponsoring city agency undermined any chance for the realization of this Smith-Fischer design or a subsequent one—a 220-foot-long metal assemblage that joined arrow and airplane motifs in a long frieze directing traffic to Concourse D.

Smith's repeated use of snakes, as in her mural-size collage *Same Old Paradise*, refers to an Edenic fall from grace. In *Snake Path*, which she planned for the Stuart Collection at the University of California, San Diego, the snake assumes a more benign or at least ambivalent role as coiling conductor of pedestrians to a new bermed entry to the university library. More than 500 feet long and 9 feet wide, it will be made of 1-foot hexagonal pieces of gray, green, purple, and sand-colored slate, laid out in mosaic fashion to mimic snake scales. At the halfway point, pedestrians will come upon a 7-foot-high stone book carved with a passage from Milton's *Paradise Lost*, in which the Archangel Michael consoles Adam and Eve upon their expulsion: "Then wilt thou not be loth/ To leave this Paradise, but shalt possess/A Paradise within thee, happier far." Farther on toward the head, the snake will loop around a circular plot with apple trees and a stone bench. In this project, the iconography and landscaping mark the library as the tree of knowledge. With the help of Milton, Smith reassures students that knowledge can induce an Eden of self-awareness that more than compensates for any loss of innocence. The piece is scheduled to be completed in 1992.

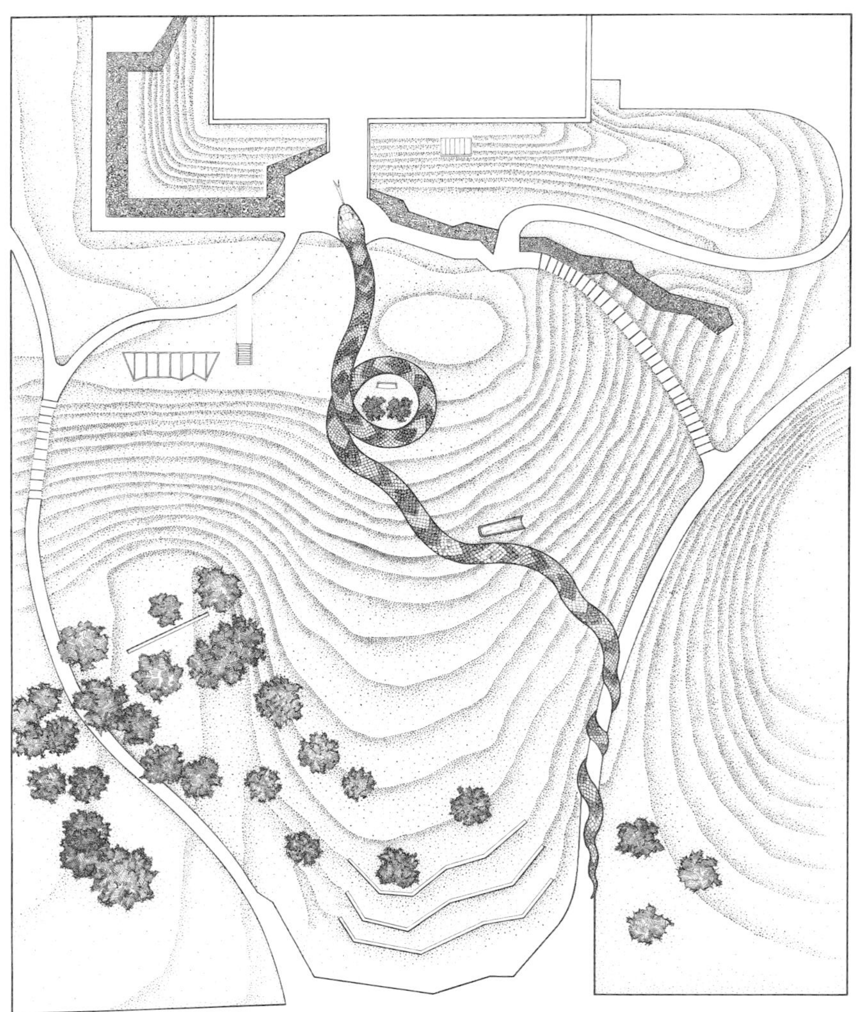

Simultaneous with the planning of *Snake Path*, Smith worked with the New York architect Jim Freed of Pei Cobb Freed and a Los Angeles firm, Gruen Associates, on a plan for a 50,000-square-foot terrazzo floor for the south lobby of an enormous addition to the Los Angeles Convention Center. With a cartographer, she devised a map of the Pacific Ocean and its abutting land masses to commemorate Los Angeles' cultural and commercial ties to the Far East. The new lobby's fan shape and columns prompted Smith's vision of a map of the Pacific rim. The map will be inset with 5-foot-diameter medallions, also terrazzo, that use wheel, wave, or spiral motifs from the various ethnic groups—from Eskimo to Samoan—that inhabit the part of the world depicted. The success of this plan prompted the architects to commission Smith to design a terrazzo floor for the 30,000-square-foot west lobby. Here the map to be executed on two levels is of the night sky. The first floor shows a curved segment of the earth's edge from an aerial view above California, with a crescent hovering at right. Upstairs, a dark blue floor will show a map of the stars, the Milky Way in gray, the other constellations with red lines connecting the white dots of the stars.

Snake Path, 1988–91
Plan for slate pathway
Stuart Collection, University of California, San Diego
Rendering by Lucia Vinograd

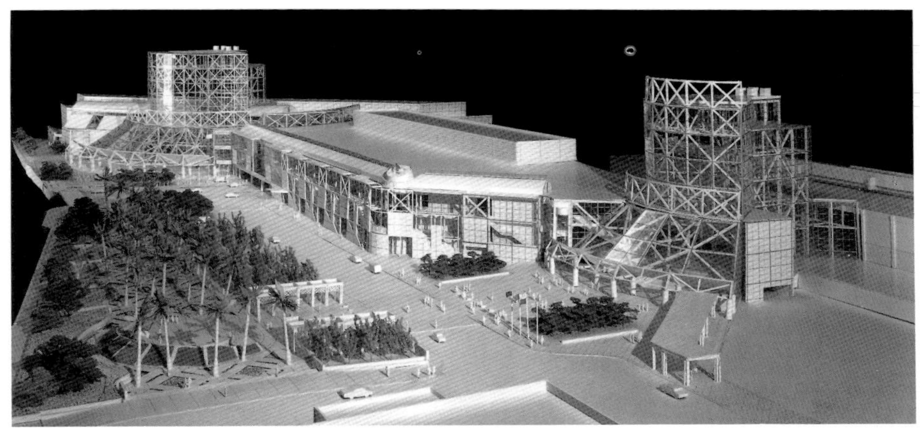

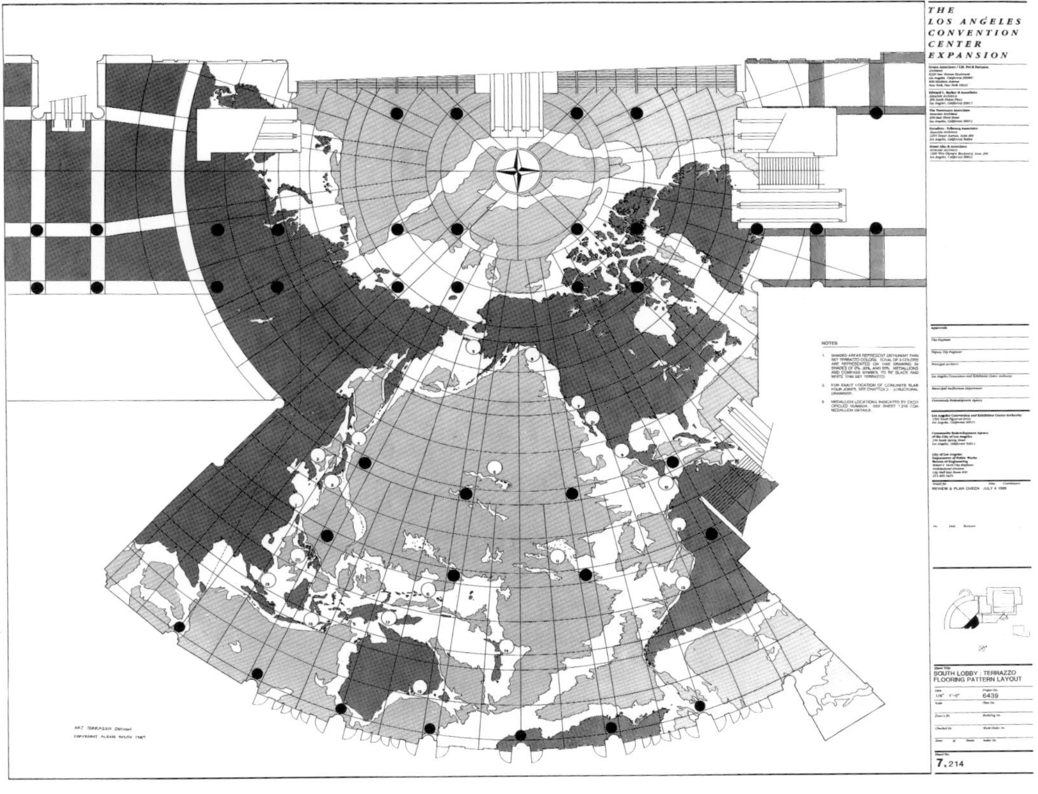

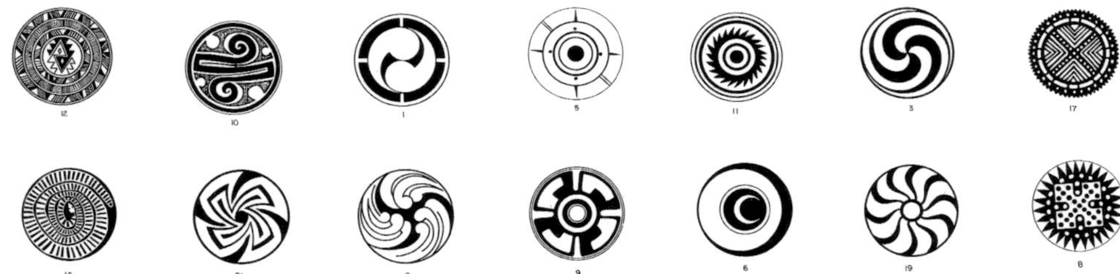

Los Angeles Convention Center Expansion Project, model
Scheduled completion 1994
Pei Cobb Freed, New York, and Gruen Associates, Los Angeles, architects

Plan for 50,000 square-foot terrazzo floor
South Lobby, Los Angeles Convention Center
Design medallions, South Lobby terrazzo floor, 60-inch diameter

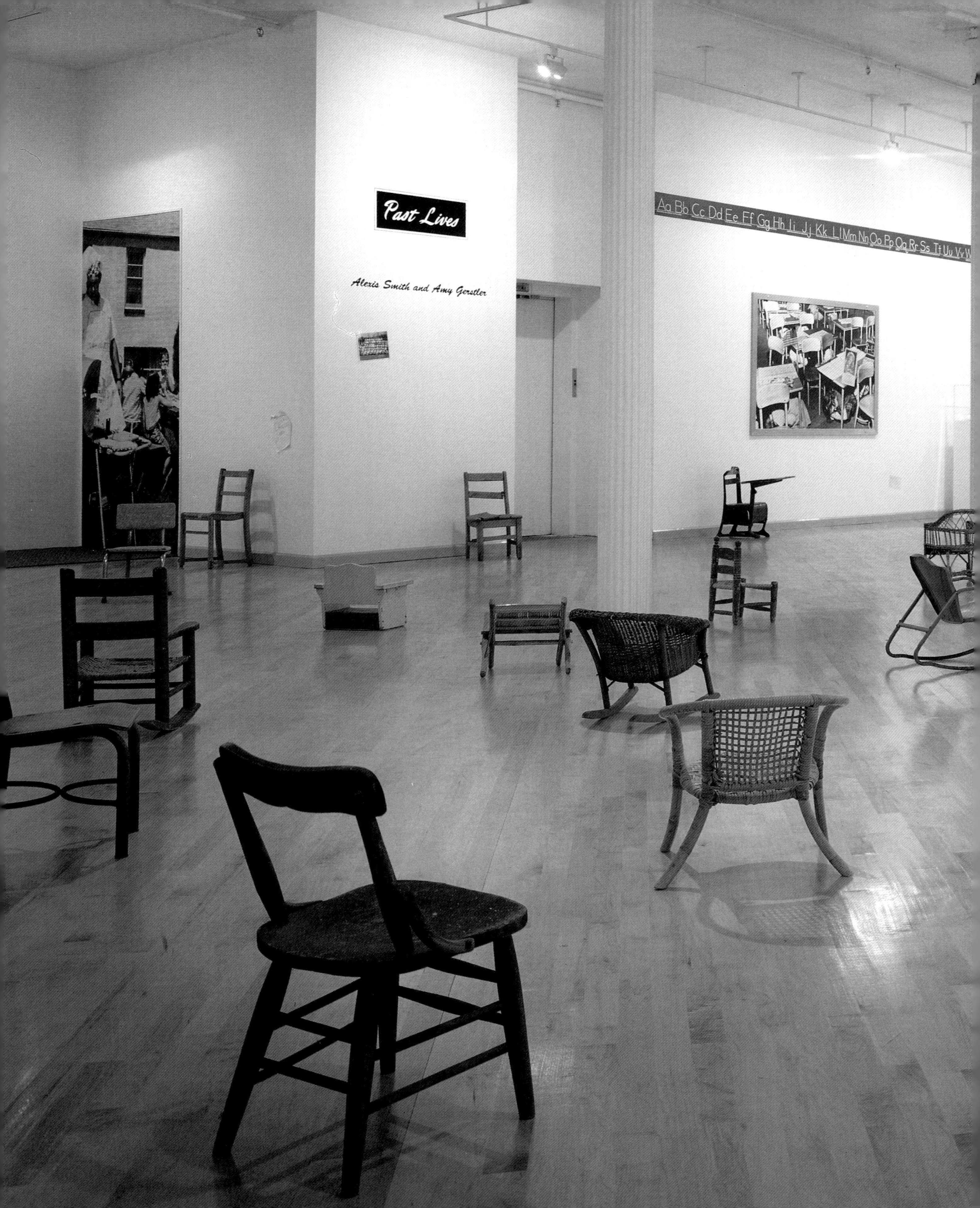
Past Lives
Alexis Smith and Amy Gerstler

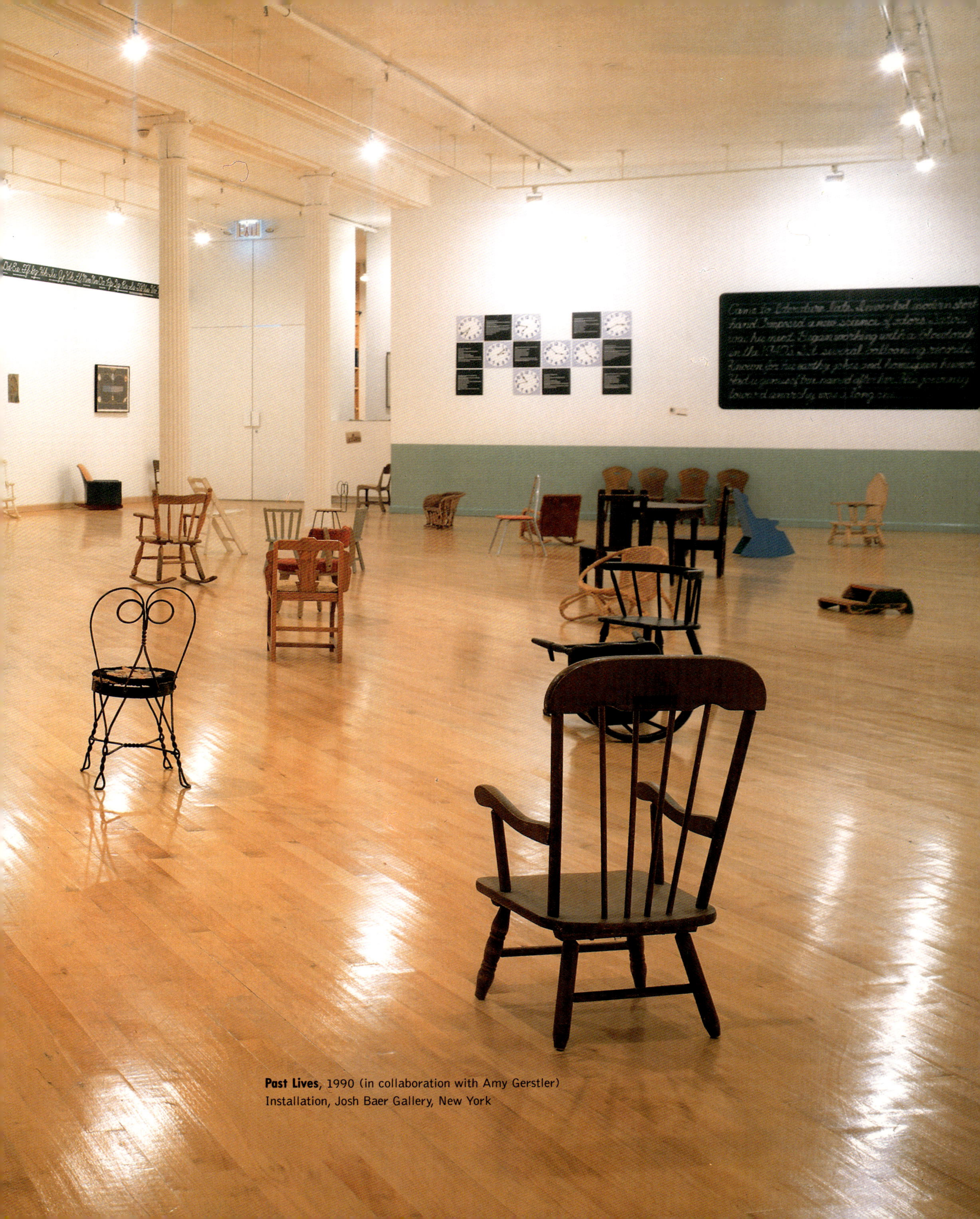

Past Lives, 1990 (in collaboration with Amy Gerstler)
Installation, Josh Baer Gallery, New York

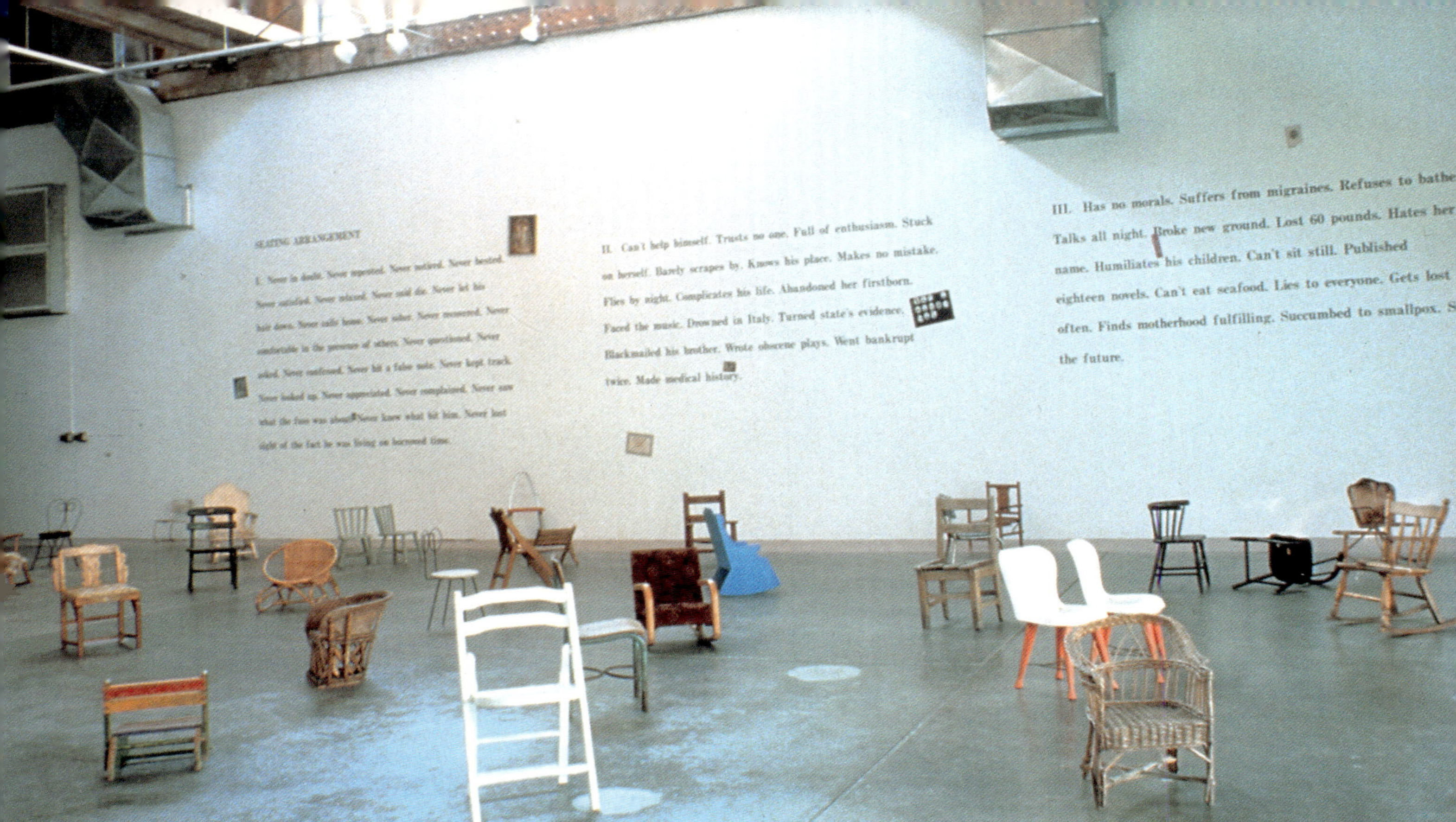

SEATING ARRANGEMENT

I. Never in doubt. Never repented. Never noticed. Never bested. Never satisfied. Never relaxed. Never said die. Never let his hair down. Never calls home. Never sober. Never recovered. Never comfortable in the presence of others. Never questioned. Never asked. Never confessed. Never hit a false note. Never kept track. Never looked up. Never appreciated. Never complained. Never saw what the fuss was about. Never knew what hit him. Never lost sight of the fact that he was living on borrowed time.

II. Can't help himself. Trusts no one. Full of enthusiasm. Stuck on herself. Barely scrapes by. Knows his place. Makes no mistake. Flies by night. Complicates his life. Abandoned her firstborn. Faced the music. Drowned in Italy. Turned state's evidence. Blackmailed his brother. Wrote obscene plays. Went bankrupt twice. Made medical history.

III. Has no morals. Suffers from migraines. Refuses to bathe. Talks all night. Broke new ground. Lost 60 pounds. Hates her name. Humiliates his children. Can't sit still. Published eighteen novels. Can't eat seafood. Lies to everyone. Gets lost often. Finds motherhood fulfilling. Succumbed to smallpox. Sees the future.

Past Lives, 1989 (in collaboration with Amy Gerstler)
Installation, Santa Monica Museum of Art, California

Came to literature late. Invented modern shorthand. Composed a new science of odors. Satire was his meat. Began working with a blowtorch in the 1940's. Set several ballooning records. Known for his earthy jokes and homespun humor. Had a genus of tree named after her. His journey toward anarchy was a long one.

During the 1980s, Smith collected dozens of used children's chairs, sixty of which she included in a large-scale installation she conceived in collaboration with the poet Amy Gerstler. Entitled *Past Lives,* the piece has been presented at two locales—the Santa Monica Museum of Art (1989) and the Josh Baer Gallery in New York (1990). Its essential parts—the freestanding chairs, schoolroom fixtures, photographs, collages, and carefully penned phrases written by Gerstler on the wall—were rearranged at each site. The eerie, depopulated temper of the piece emphasizes the anthropomorphic character of the chairs—their "anatomical" structure of arms, back, and feet. Each of the small chairs is redolent of a past life, a utilitarian monument to the indoor activities of childhood, especially those of the classroom. Gerstler's writings are often cast in a disconcerting past tense that is well suited to this room of empty chairs and seem to be giving a lesson in mortality.

Smith's collages and the bits of illustrated paper and snapshots attached to the wall provide a two-dimensional, "found" population. Mural-scale photographs of a cute infant in a rocking chair or a family at a backyard barbecue establish an idyllic standard of emotional comfort that registers at cross-purposes with both Gerstler's text and the vacant chairs. We are immersed, almost painfully so, in an environment alternately charged with hope and despair, anticipation and regret. *Past Lives* is an ambitiously three-dimensional reprise of the themes of identity and fate that have preoccupied Smith since the beginning of her career. Gerstler's voice, attuned to the richness of Smith's ensemble, tersely articulates the jumble of feelings that erupt in any reconstitution of childhood.

Gerstler and Smith produced an illustrated booklet-souvenir that integrated the poet's words and the artist's imagery. By contrast, the installation separates them into wall-bound words and floor-bound things, as if to admit some irreconcilable schism between thought and action.

Wall-painted blackboard, installation detail, **Past Lives**, 1989

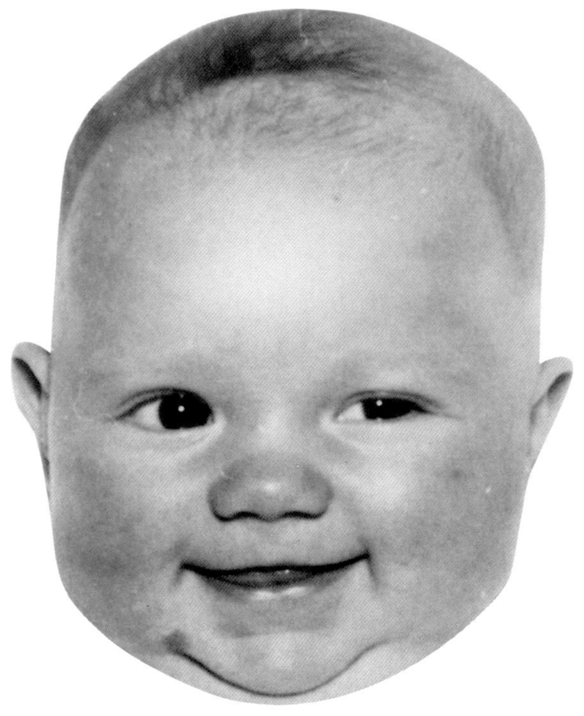

IF YOUR CHILD IS BORN TODAY . . . he or she will have an answer for everything. Hedonistic inclinations will manifest themselves early, which you should neither encourage nor hinder. A strong mechanical bent is indicated. A child born today is likely to suffer from every food-allergy under the sun. Despite many obvious faults, your progeny will demonstrate a warm-hearted and generous nature, full of unfeigned love and pity for humanity, in addition to humor, tenderness, and a charm of style which neither learning nor labor could otherwise bestow.

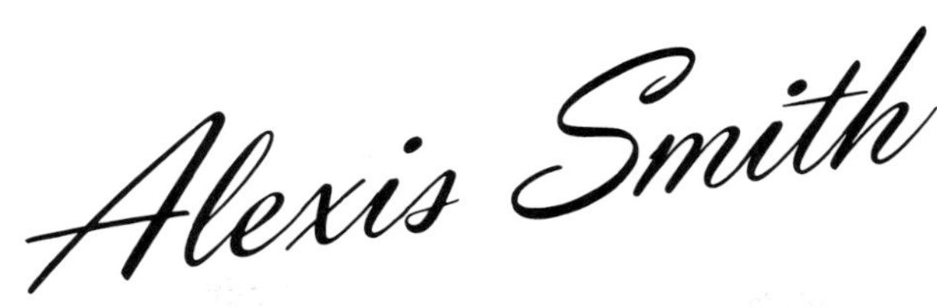

A FICTIONAL BIOGRAPHY, *or* "THE STORY OF THE CENTURY"

CHAPTER I

"Is it to be the Chaste Madonna, or the Messalina, or the Magdalen, or the Blue Stocking?
Where can I find the woman of all these adventures?"
—Isadora Duncan, *My Life*

Just who is this Alexis Smith?
Here are some of the by now old-hat responses
to this much-asked question.

Social historian with a pastepot. Irony-edged archivist of the vernacular. Nurse Smith, aka cultural temperature-taker. Magician who can coax objects to throw their quavering, half-throttled, or overbold voices across great distances, i.e., the expanse of the fruited plain. Distiller of disillusionment, longing, and humor into a potent but sippable visual moonshine, with a marked emotional undertow. Elegant pack rat. Sharp-eyed scavenger. Someone who finds herself facing herself, seated on both ends of the romantic/anti-romantic seesaw. Ms. Smith, concert synthesist, tickler of the ivories of the unexamined American conscience. Slang-slinger. Chandler-ologist. Reliable girl-reporter taking down heartfelt eyewitness accounts in a unique mixture of long- and shorthand. Al Smith, Inc.: road signs collected, curios resurrected, & clichés dissected While-U-Wait. Her oeuvre is the rearview mirror in which the USA, en route to who knows where, frequently checks her freckling complexion.

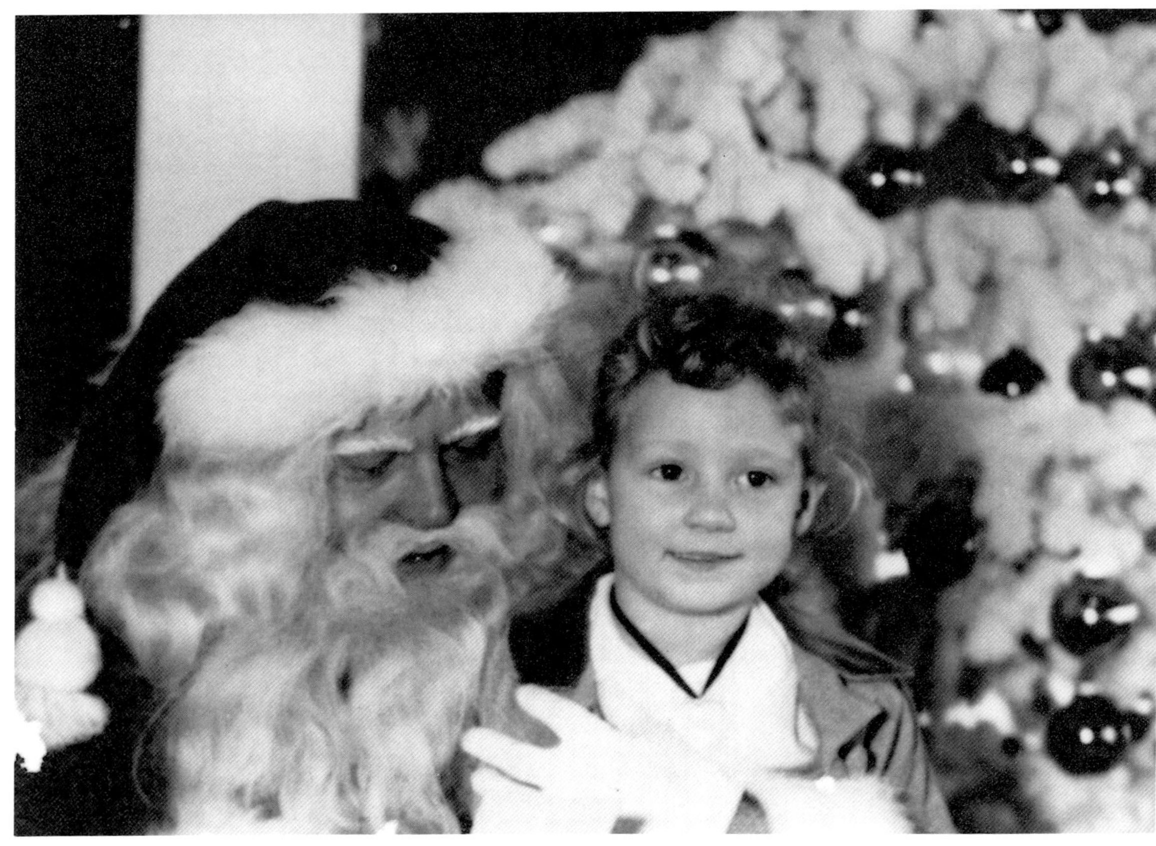

All rhapsodizing aside, available biographical details on Smith are conflicting and sketchy, where they aren't entirely absent or confidential. So it's up to us, the viewing public, to satisfy our own curiosity. Ever mindful that we must respect artists' privacy, if we don't want them to clam up, we can still in good conscience attempt to assemble Smith's puzzle-portrait by imitating her working methods. We can sift persistent bits of data that irritate our brains like mental foxtails, together with phrases culled from cryptic notes we find stuffed into the pockets of a just-purchased second-hand jacket, and add that to the clues Kismet is constantly, teasingly strewing across our path. It's a matter of keeping eyes open and wits ready. What we don't stumble across, we can dream up. Since Smith has a pronounced affinity for print media, especially for use as background material, we might begin our search by leafing through the *Los Angeles Times* (her hometown newspaper) for August 24, 1949 (that red-letter day for American art, the date she was born).

CHAPTER II

"I always wanted to be historical, from almost a baby on. . . ."
—"A Message from Gertrude Stein," 1946

At the library, newspaper pages circa the date in question are lit from behind by an unwieldy microfiche machine. Elongated and made faint by this presentation, the pages can be changed by cranking a creaky flywheel. This issue of the *Times* presents would-be Smith-o-philes with a picture of a city in adolescence, a small-townish locale contemporary Angelenos would hardly recognize. Then again, the place might seem all too familiar.

Full of news from only forty years ago, the newspaper's language and reporting choices seem deceptively quaint and strange, at first. **A DOG, LAST SEEN ALIVE CARRYING A MAN'S HAT IN ITS MOUTH, WAS FOUND MYSTERIOUSLY DROWNED**, the *Times* proclaims. **NEW SHOE SHINE PLAN OUTLINED FOR LA POLICE DEPT** is a front-page story. **A GROUP OF WOMEN BOO ARREST OF LEGLESS BEGGAR** and **NAIL POLISH FIRE FORCES HOTEL GUESTS TO FLEE** appear prominently on page two. Section A contains an update on the peach and pear harvest in the Antelope Valley. Section B features a photo essay on young polio victims. On page 48, section C, an unidentified, black-veiled woman is shown placing roses on Rudolph Valentino's crypt, in honor of the twenty-third anniversary of his death. The main headlines include: **BEL AIR WIDOW VANISHES; FOUL PLAY FEARED. FATHER, LEGALLY DEAD, PAYS NONGHOSTLY VISIT. BRITISH BOY SWIMS CHANNEL; CROSSING TAKES 23 HRS.** In ads scattered throughout the paper, prices quoted provide a smarting reminder of just how much and how quickly times have changed. At Mode O'Day, a sale features dresses @ $3.98, blouses $1.98. Glass salt and pepper shakers sell for a whopping 8 cents a set. A washing machine, which might qualify as a museum piece today, with its four legs, wringer and pump, is priced at $88. Males were encouraged to purchase "suits for college men and other tweedy types." The women's pages advised "college girls should coordinate their make-up with colors in their wardrobe." There's an accompanying photo of a rather repressed, old/young looking coed, holding a selection of lipstick tubes fanned out in front of her. The expression on her face indicates she is *as of this moment* privy to some very important truth. The entertainment section of the paper lists movie titles like *Johnny Stool Pigeon, The Great Sinner,* and *I Was a Male War Bride.*

What's amazing, almost to the point of being scary, is how the items in the newspaper all end up looking and sounding like incomplete Alexis Smith pieces. Trivial, heartrending, or key political stories, the human interest filler and the religious page, for a crazy second all appear to be entirely of Smith's manufacture—concocted to comprise one layer of her rich, complicated work. This illusion occurs because Smith so accurately captures the essence of the way things looked and felt and, weirdly, often still look and feel, in particular areas of American culture. Labels on cans, the cut of clothes, cars and their license plates, the tiny license a beloved pet might wear around its neck, goods and services that advertisements made folks pine for almost without their knowing it, even what was on TV and in educational posters tacked up in classrooms: these things make such powerful appearances in Smith's work, it's as though she constructed them. What's closer to the truth, of course, is that this input played a major role in forming her sensibility.

The carefully chosen fragments of everyday life Smith gives us take on a completeness in her work they rarely possess in their "real-life" contexts—a significance and depth first-time perceptions almost never contain. Old postcards, road maps, smashed cans, and quotes radiate a kind of dignity and heightened meaning in Smith's work that accrues only to survivors. Trash becomes poetic artifact when processed by Smith's acute, organizing vision and exacting sense of distance.

Somehow, for the past twenty years, and on into the dubious future, Smith continues digesting all this history. She keeps making work in which America's soul—its social, material, and emotional past—is shattered and reconstituted, over and over. She relentlessly examines an ideological line that runs through almost all her source material: the assumption of a coherent underlying American mythology. What rises up with the ghost image of the 1949 newspaper is the blind, blanket assumption that what happens in the world can be organized into some kind of ultimate meaning, and Smith provides us golden opportunities to stare down that assumption, in all its dangerous innocence. There is a great deal in Smith's work that addresses the subject of temptation. But while she is a pioneer, she is never a settler for easy solutions. Her materials are the evidence and Smith simply presents her case without calling for any verdict. In her work, the jury is always out.

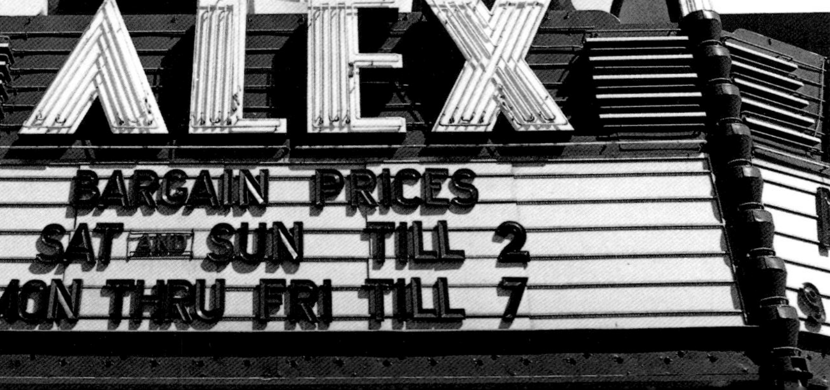

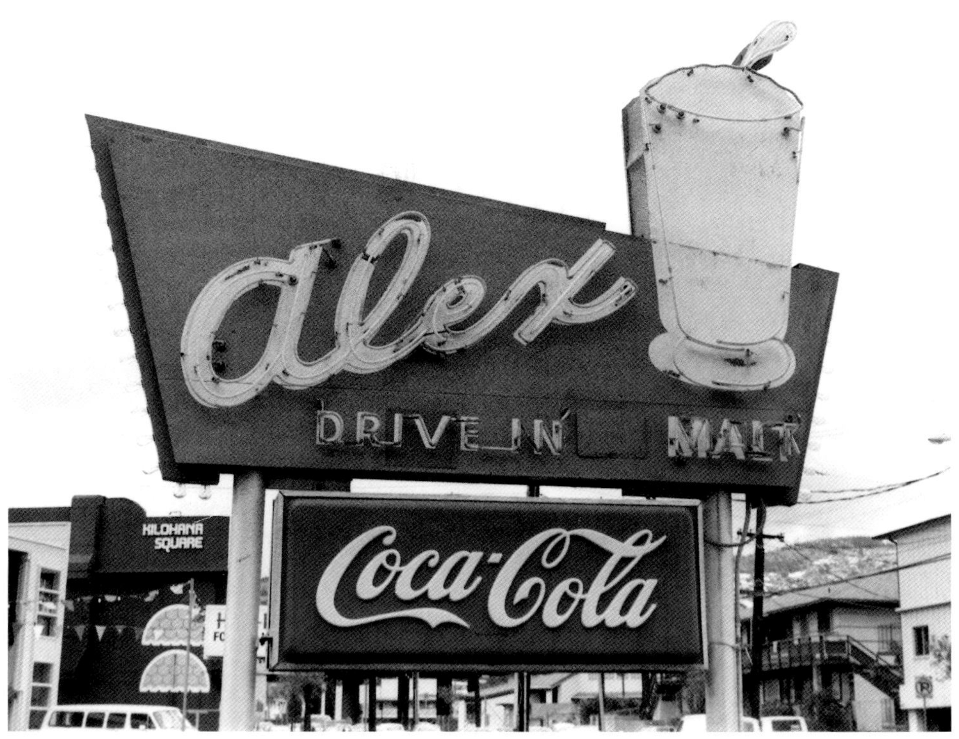

She makes us face the idea that people once thought, and may yet believe, that world events and their aspirations were somehow, perhaps divinely, connected. You might say Smith continues to examine American wistfulness, and its underpinning notions of purpose, destiny, and progress. Whether such notions were/are terrible lies, or components of a viable belief system, or sweet delusion, Smith is too wise to ever try to definitively state. That's not her job, although it might be the self-imposed task of other artists. Smith has her hands full, unerringly coaxing to life much of what shaped many American hearts and minds in the past and, for better or worse, much that continues to influence our development. The excerpt below, from an early poem by a writer she has strong affinities with, Walt Whitman, seems to describe something Smith is unsurpassed at: the bringing to light of images that are trapped in the little house of one's thoughts, pictures that can be traced back to some version of the American psyche:

> In a little house keep I pictures suspended, it is not a fix'd
> house,
> It is round, it is only a few inches from one side to the
> other;
> Yet behold, it has room for all the shows of the world,
> all memories!
>
> —Walt Whitman, "My Picture-Gallery"

CHAPTER III

"No woman has ever told the whole truth of her life."
—Isadora Duncan, *My Life*

Maybe Smith came from a long line of wily, red-bearded inventors, who constructed everything from blenders to time machines out of rusty stuff pilfered from junkyards. Or perhaps her parents were circus folk, stars of an innovative trapeze act. Her uncle could have been elected president of the Mystery Writers of America. Her grandparents might have been German-Jewish immigrants who prospered in the United States; and her parents, prospering too, could have been beguiled by art, languages, and educational theory. It's rumored two of her cousins teamed up to design a line of cookware that was sold door-to-door and became very popular in urban areas, although some called the eye-catching pots and pans fantastic and impractical. Did her great-great-great-grandfather really marry a lady-in-waiting to Queen Victoria—and later, when the couple were down on luck, did they live in the rural South, and raise peacocks? Was it her father who was employed by Pinkerton's detective agency . . . and did her smooth-voiced mother have her own radio show? Wouldn't it have been fitting if her dad rose from a lining cutter in a neckwear factory to become one of the brightest stars in the vaudeville firmament? Would we know more about her if we could say for certain that her ma was a crusading editor who wrote "free verse" . . . or that one of her aunts was the first female American flight surgeon? True or false: Smith's distant uncle was the inventor of that invaluable condiment, Worcestershire sauce. If we began poking around in earnest, wouldn't there be anonymous sources ready to swear, off the record, that her maternal grandpa earned his living making, selling, and repairing bicycles?

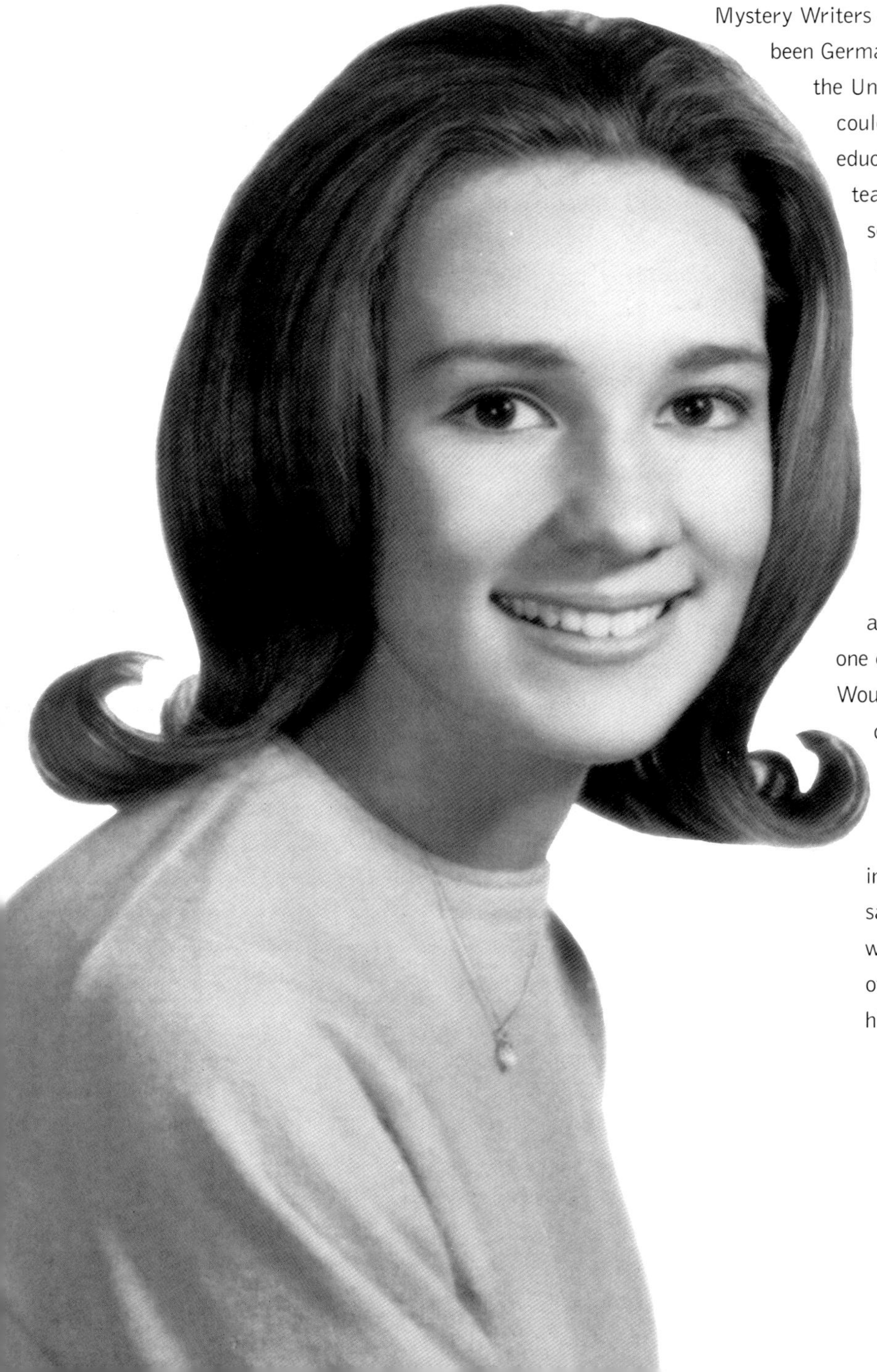

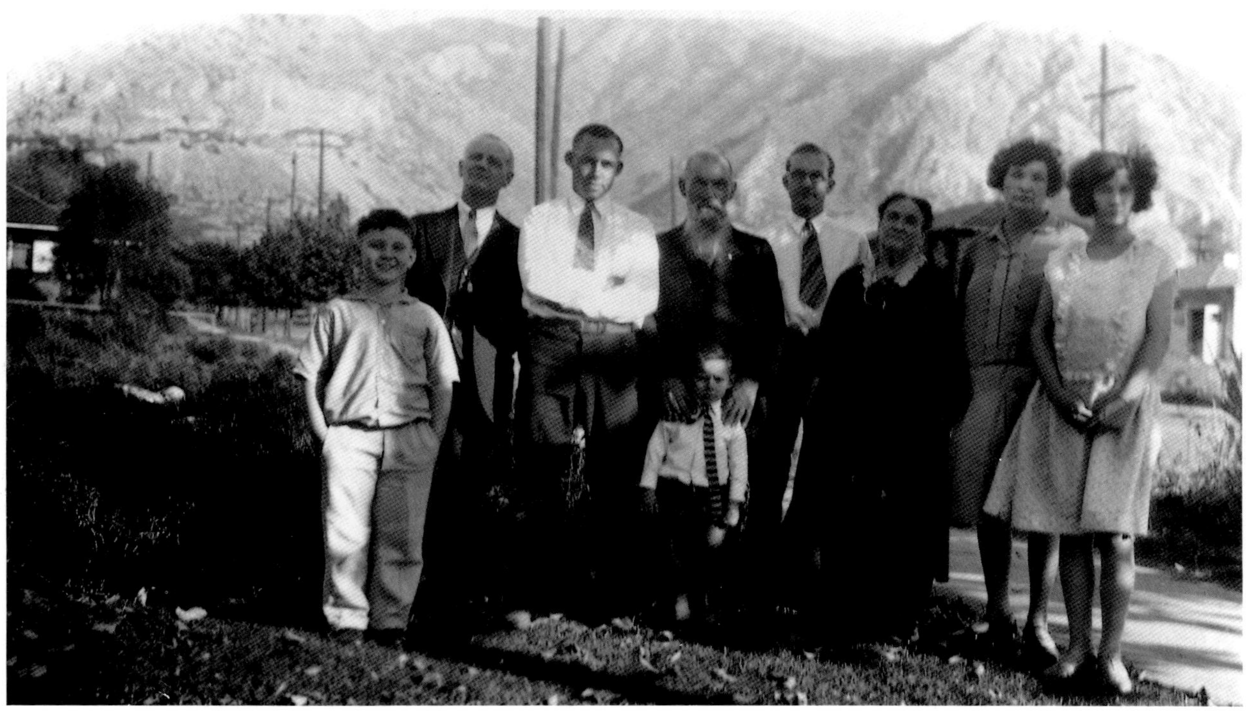

What's invaluable about Alexis Smith is not what we can ferret out or devise about her history. It's what her work continues to reveal about how we think and live, about the collective American unconscious. The biographical snippets in the paragraph above may have been culled from books on the lives of Houdini, Raymond Chandler, Gertrude Stein, Walt Whitman, Wilbur and Orville Wright, Flannery O'Connor, and Frank Lloyd Wright. Some of these facts may even have been tinkered with. Still, who is to say that they don't conjure up a more accurate sense of where Smith "comes from," or paint a truer picture of her *gestalt* as an artist than all the family albums and painstakingly plotted genealogies in the world? Smith is flesh and blood of the quirky American geniuses she admires, because she carries on work in their tradition. There are stronger family ties than mere accidents of birth. Smith can trace her beginnings back to spiritual bonds with artists, like Whitman, who are her relatives in sensibility.

Alexis Smith is necessary; her work, essential. Luckily for us, she sprang into existence somehow. If she hadn't, we would have had to invent her.

—Amy Gerstler

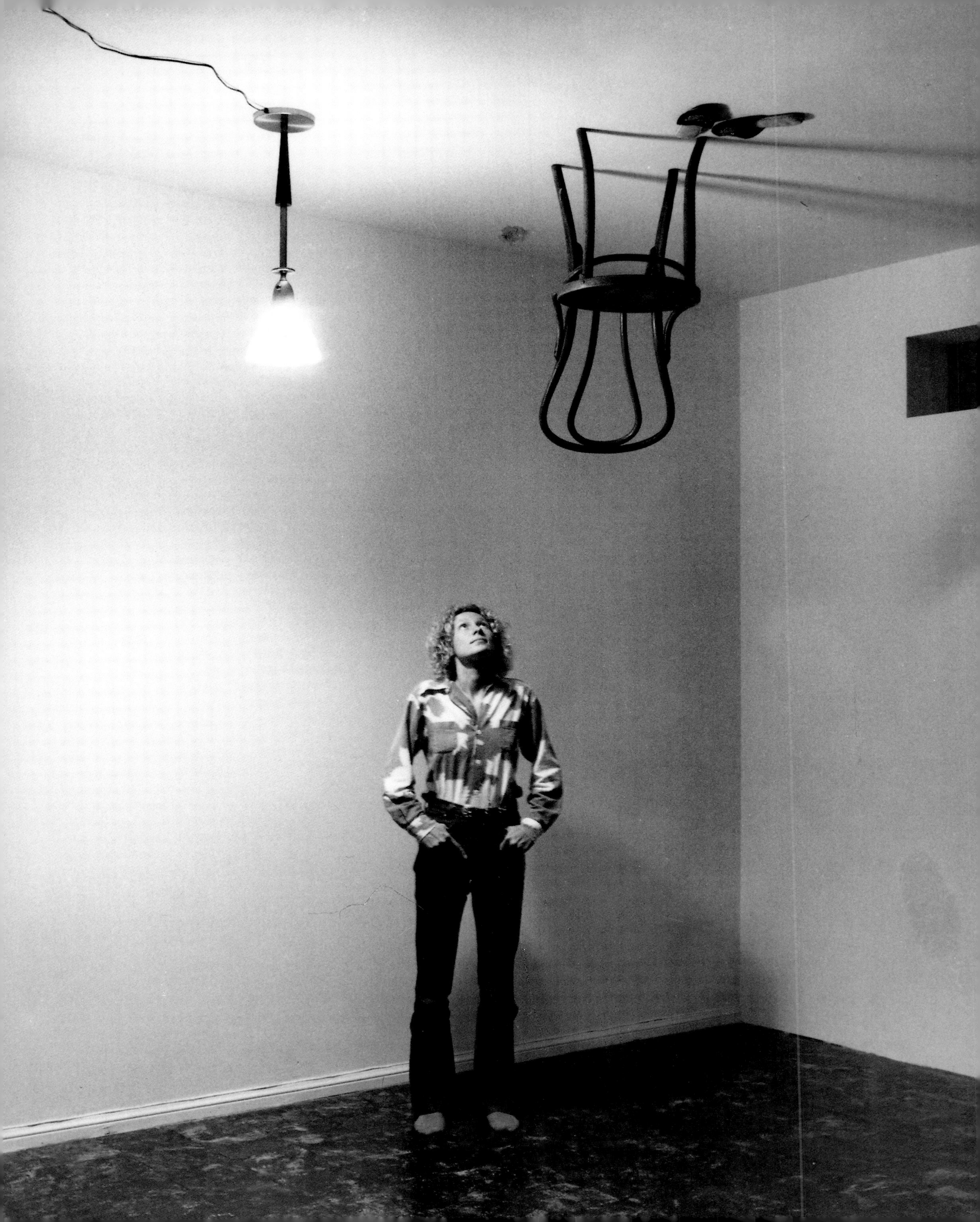

Exhibitions

One-Artist Exhibitions

An asterisk indicates that an exhibition is accompanied by a catalogue, cited in the bibliography.

1974

Riko Mizuno Gallery, Los Angeles, "Alexis Smith."

1975

The Art Galleries, University of California, Santa Barbara, "Rapido."

CARP, Los Angeles, "Anteroom."

Long Beach Museum of Art, California, "Classics Illustrated."

*Whitney Museum of American Art, New York, "Alexis Smith."

1976

CARP, Los Angeles, "Scherherezade the Storyteller" (performance).

Gallery I, San Jose State University, California, "Alexis Smith."

Mandeville Gallery, University of California, San Diego, "Star Material."

1977

Holly Solomon Gallery, New York, "Alexis Smith."

Nicholas Wilder Gallery, Los Angeles, "Tales of Mystery and Enchantment."

1978

Baxter Art Gallery, California Institute of Technology, Pasadena, "The Art of Magic, Close-up" (performance, with Tony DeLap).

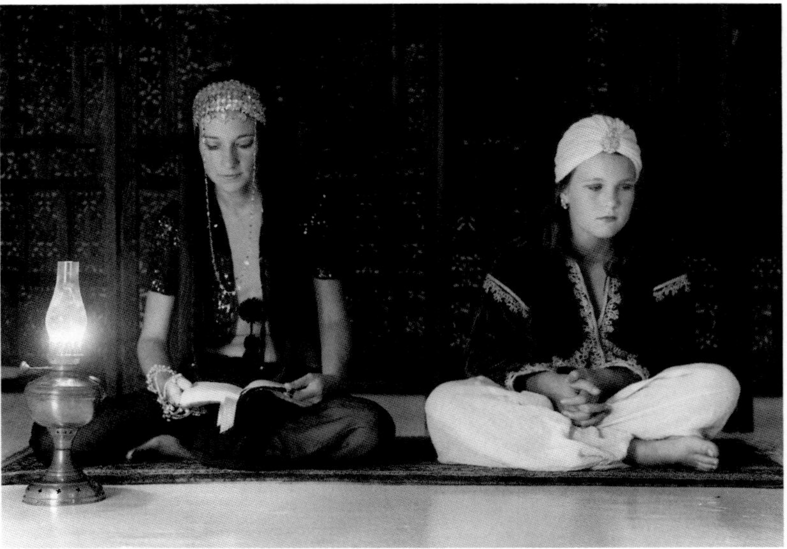

Scheherazade the Storyteller, performance at CARP, Los Angeles, 1976.

Rosamund Felsen Gallery, Los Angeles, "The Magic Mountain" and "Medium" (performance).

Holly Solomon Gallery, New York, "April Foole."

1979

Foundation de Appel, Amsterdam, The Netherlands, "The Room on the Other Side of the Mirror."

The Eastern Columbia Building Downtown Window, Los Angeles (organized by Los Angeles Institute of Contemporary Art), "Autumn Sonata."

Holly Solomon Gallery, New York, "The Magic Mountain."

1980

Rosamund Felsen Gallery, Los Angeles, "Raymond Chandler's L.A."

"Anteroom," installation, CARP, Los Angeles, 1975.

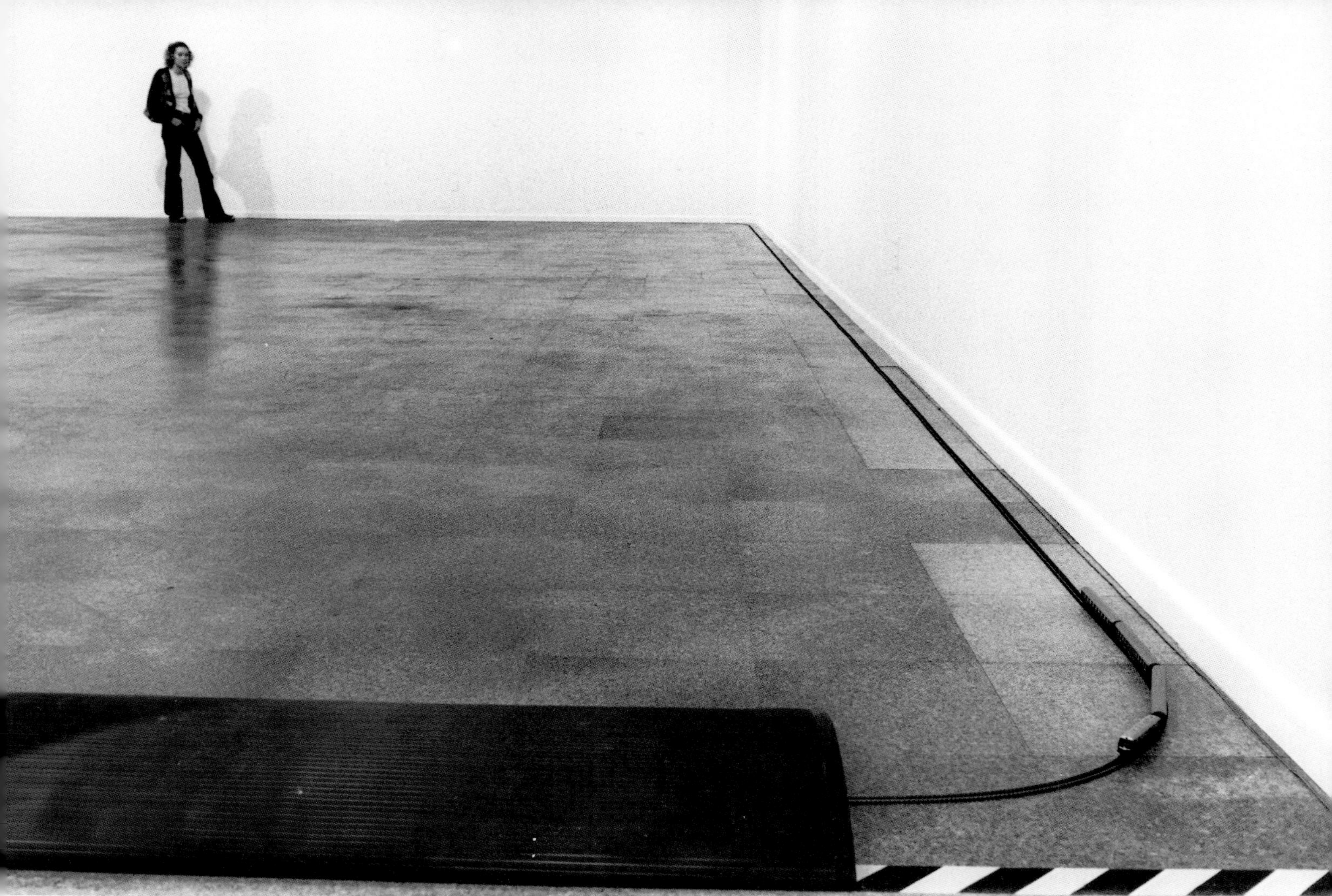

Rapido, 1975
Installation, The Art Galleries, University of California, Santa Barbara

Los Angeles Contemporary Exhibitions (LACE), "Stardust" (performance, with Heidi Hardin). Traveled: Los Angeles County Museum of Art; La Jolla Museum of Contemporary Art, California.

1981

Holly Solomon Gallery, New York, "U.S.A."

1982

The Clocktower, Institute for Art and Urban Resources, New York, "Chinese Junk."

Rosamund Felsen Gallery, Los Angeles, "Satan's Satellites."

Margo Leavin Gallery, Los Angeles, "Christmas Eve, 1943."

1985

*Margo Leavin Gallery, Los Angeles, "Alexis Smith: Jane."

1986

*Institute of Contemporary Art, Boston, "Currents: Alexis Smith."

*Walker Art Center, Minneapolis, "Viewpoints: Alexis Smith."

1987

*Aspen Art Museum, Colorado, "Alexis Smith—Joseph Cornell: Parallels."

*The Brooklyn Museum, New York, "Alexis Smith: Same Old Paradise."

1988
Margo Leavin Gallery, Los Angeles, "On the Road."

1989
Santa Monica Museum of Art, California, "Past Lives" (with Amy Gerstler). Traveled: Josh Baer Gallery, New York.

1990
Margo Leavin Gallery, Los Angeles, "Eldorado (On the Road, Part II)."

1991
* Mandeville Gallery, University of California, San Diego, "Alexis Smith: Public Works."

Group Exhibitions

1972
Art Gallery, University of California, Irvine, "Greater Magic."

Los Angeles County Museum of Art, "Four Women Artists of Los Angeles: Margaret Lowe, Barbara Munger, Alexis Smith, Margaret Wilson."

* Pasadena Art Museum, California, "Southern California: Attitudes 1972."

1974
Art Gallery, University of Nevada, Las Vegas, "Works Selected by Nicholas Wilder."

* Mt. San Antonio College Art Gallery, Walnut, California, "Word Works."

1975
The Art Galleries, University of California, Santa Barbara, "Visual/Verbal."

La Jolla Museum of Contemporary Art, California, "University of California at Irvine, 1965–75."

* Sarah Lawrence Gallery, Sarah Lawrence College, Bronxville, New York, "Word, Image, Number."

* University Art Museum, University of California, Berkeley, "Both Kinds: Contemporary Art from Los Angeles."

Visual Arts Gallery, School of Visual Arts, New York, "Four Los Angeles Artists: Foulkes, Goode, Smith, Wheeler." Traveled: The Corcoran Gallery of Art, Washington, D.C.; Wadsworth Atheneum, Hartford, Connecticut.

* Whitney Museum of American Art, New York, "1975 Biennial Exhibition."

1976
* Long Beach Museum of Art, California, "Southland Video Anthology 1976–77 (Part I, 1976)."

* Los Angeles County Museum of Art, "New Selections: New Talent Award Winners."

Los Angeles Institute of Contemporary Art, "Autobiographical Fantasies."

The Museum of Modern Art, New York, Penthouse Gallery, "Los Angeles."

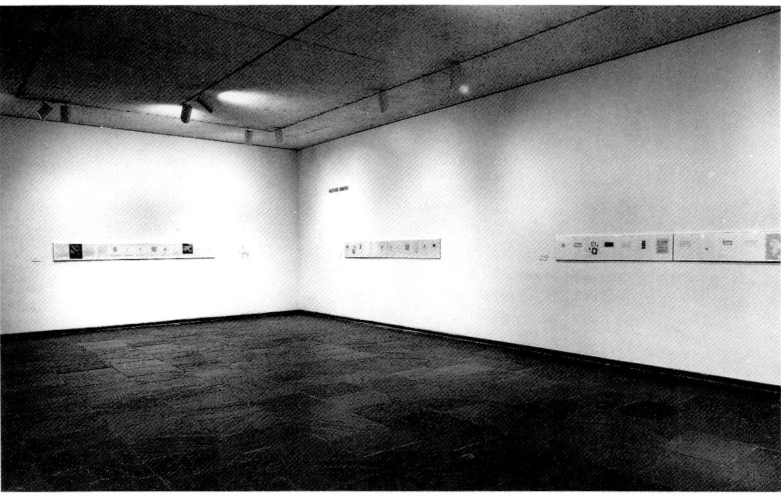

"Alexis Smith," installation view, Whitney Museum of American Art, New York, 1975.

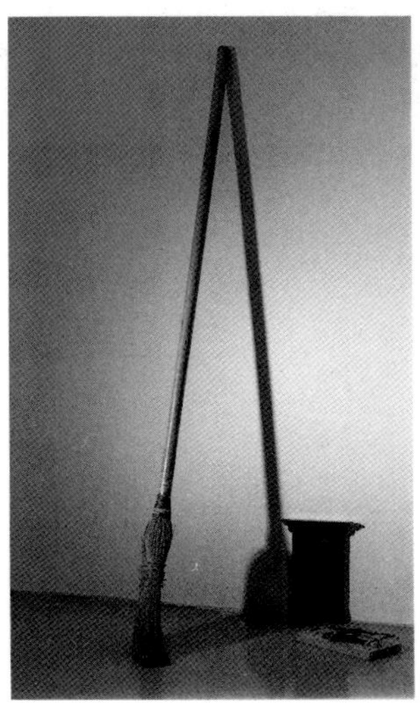

City Mouse, 1980
Mixed-media installation, 48×22×18 inches
"Tableau," Los Angeles Institute of Contemporary Art
Collection of Richard and Jan Baum

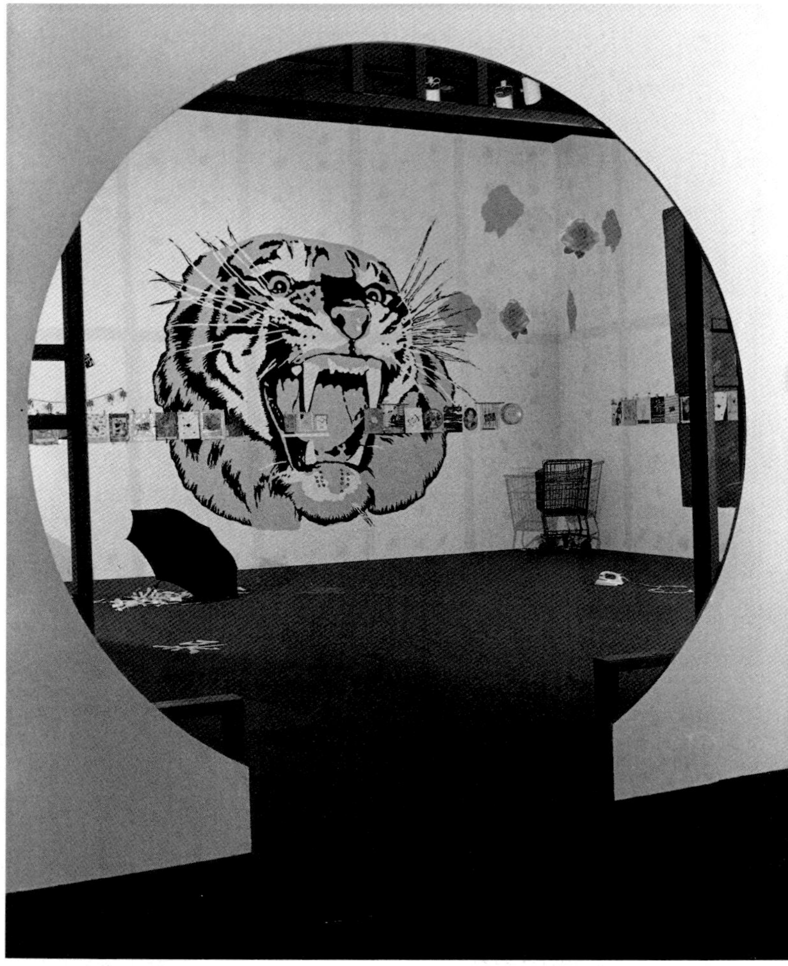

Cathay, 1981
Installation, Los Angeles County Museum of Art

Portland Center for the Visual Arts, Oregon, "Via Los Angeles: Michael Asher, Chris Burden, Bryan Hunt, Channa Horwitz, Allen Ruppersberg, Alexis Smith."

Holly Solomon Gallery, New York, "Summer Group Exhibition."

1977

*Contemporary Arts Museum, Houston, "American Narrative/Story Art, 1967–1977." Traveled: Contemporary Art Center, New Orleans; Winnipeg Art Gallery, Manitoba, Canada; University Art Museum, University of California, Berkeley.

*Fine Arts Gallery, California State University, Los Angeles, "Miniature."

Los Angeles Institute of Contemporary Art, "Narrative Themes/Audio Works."

Mills College Art Gallery, Oakland, California, "Artists' Books."

*Musée d'Art Moderne de la Ville de Paris, "10e biennale de Paris." Traveled: Musée de Nice, France; Musée de Strasbourg, France.

Holly Solomon Gallery, New York, "Artists from the 10th Biennale." Traveled: The Hudson River Museum, Yonkers, New York.

1978

Art Gallery, California State University, Fullerton, "Gallery as Lithography Studio."

*Institute of Contemporary Art, Boston, "Narration."

La Jolla Museum of Contemporary Art, California, "Southern California Styles of the '60s and '70s."

Holly Solomon Gallery, New York, "Gold/Silver."

Holly Solomon Gallery, New York, "The New York Boat Show."

1979

Rosamund Felsen Gallery, Los Angeles, "Christmas in July."

Graz, Austria, "Steirescher Herbst."

The Museum of Modern Art, New York, Penthouse Gallery, "Views Over America."

*San Francisco Museum of Modern Art, "Paper on Paper."

*Whitney Museum of American Art, New York, "The Decade in Review: Selections from the 1970s."

*Whitney Museum of American Art, New York, "1979 Biennial Exhibition."

"Alexis Smith: Jane," installation view, Margo Leavin Gallery, Los Angeles, 1985.

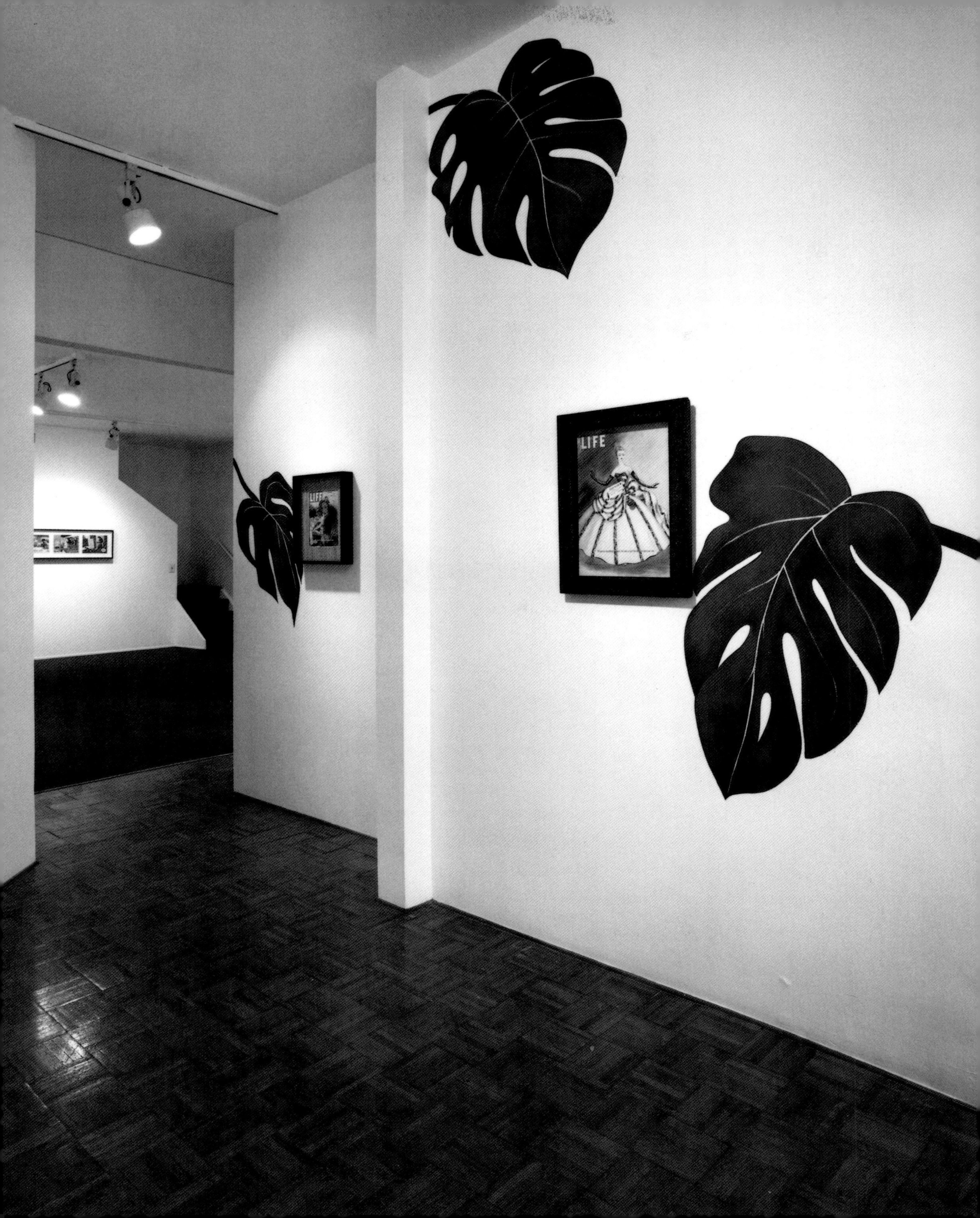
LIFE

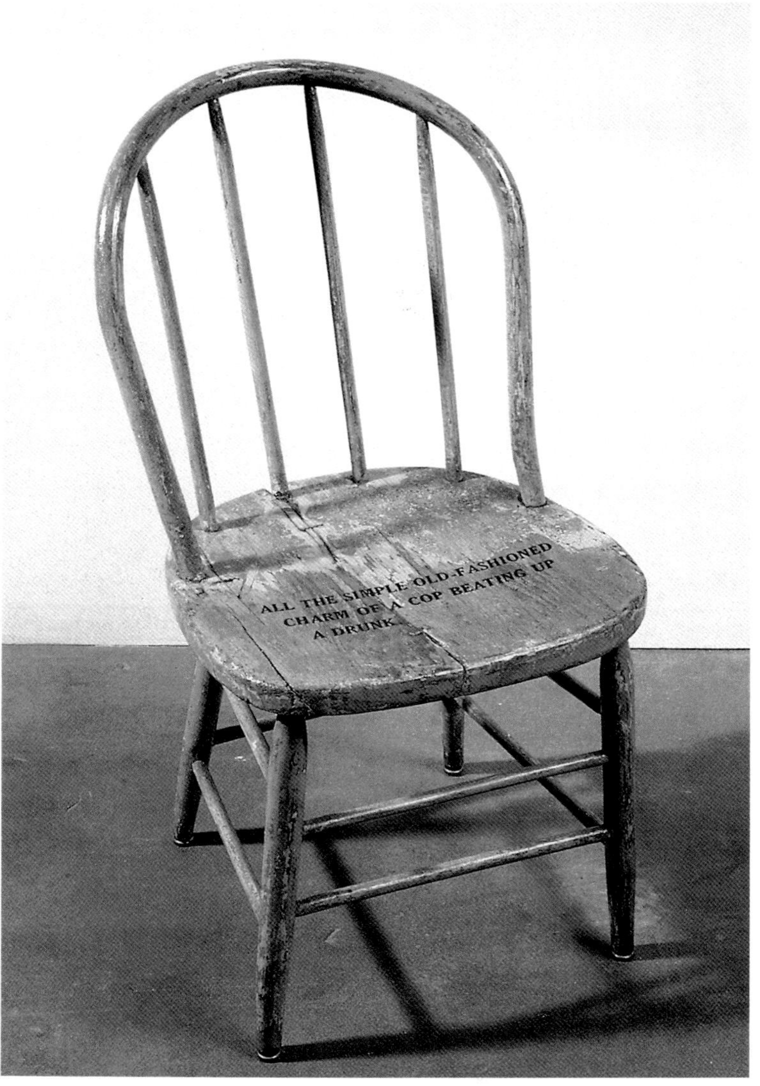

1980

Leo Castelli Gallery, "Drawings."

Joseloff Gallery, University of Hartford, West Hartford, Connecticut, "Southern California Drawings."

Los Angeles Institute of Contemporary Art, "Tableau."

New Jersey Center for Visual Arts, Summit, "Words and Numbers."

Audrey Strohl Gallery, Memphis, Tennessee, "Group Show."

All the Simple Old Fashioned Charm, 1984
Lacquer on wood, 34 × 17¼ × 19½ inches
Margo Leavin Gallery, Los Angeles

1981

*Freedman Gallery, Albright College, Reading, Pennsylvania, "Messages: Words and Images."

*Los Angeles County Museum of Art, "Art in Los Angeles. The Museum as Site: Sixteen Projects."

Los Angeles Institute of Contemporary Art, "Humor in Art."

Otis Art Institute of Parsons School of Design, Los Angeles, "Poetic Visions."

*Philadelphia Art Alliance, "Words & Images: A Contemporary Artists' Book Exhibition."

*The Renaissance Society at the University of Chicago, "Words as Images."

*Whitney Museum of American Art, New York, "1981 Biennial Exhibition."

1982

*Contemporary Arts Museum, Houston, "The Americans: The Collage."

Rosamund Felsen Gallery, Los Angeles, "New Work."

Municipal Art Gallery, Los Angeles, and Nagoya City Art Museum, Japan, "Contemporary Los Angeles Artists."

*Musée d'Art Moderne de la Ville de Paris, "Une expérience muséographique: Échange entre artistes, 1931–1982, Pologne-U.S.A." Traveled: Galeria Foksal, Warsaw; Muzeum Sztuki w Lodz, Poland; Ulster Museum, Belfast; Douglas Hyde Gallery, Trinity College, University of Dublin.

Washington Project for the Arts, Washington, D.C., "Poetic Objects."

1983

Fuller-Goldeen Gallery, San Francisco, "Perspectives of Landscape."

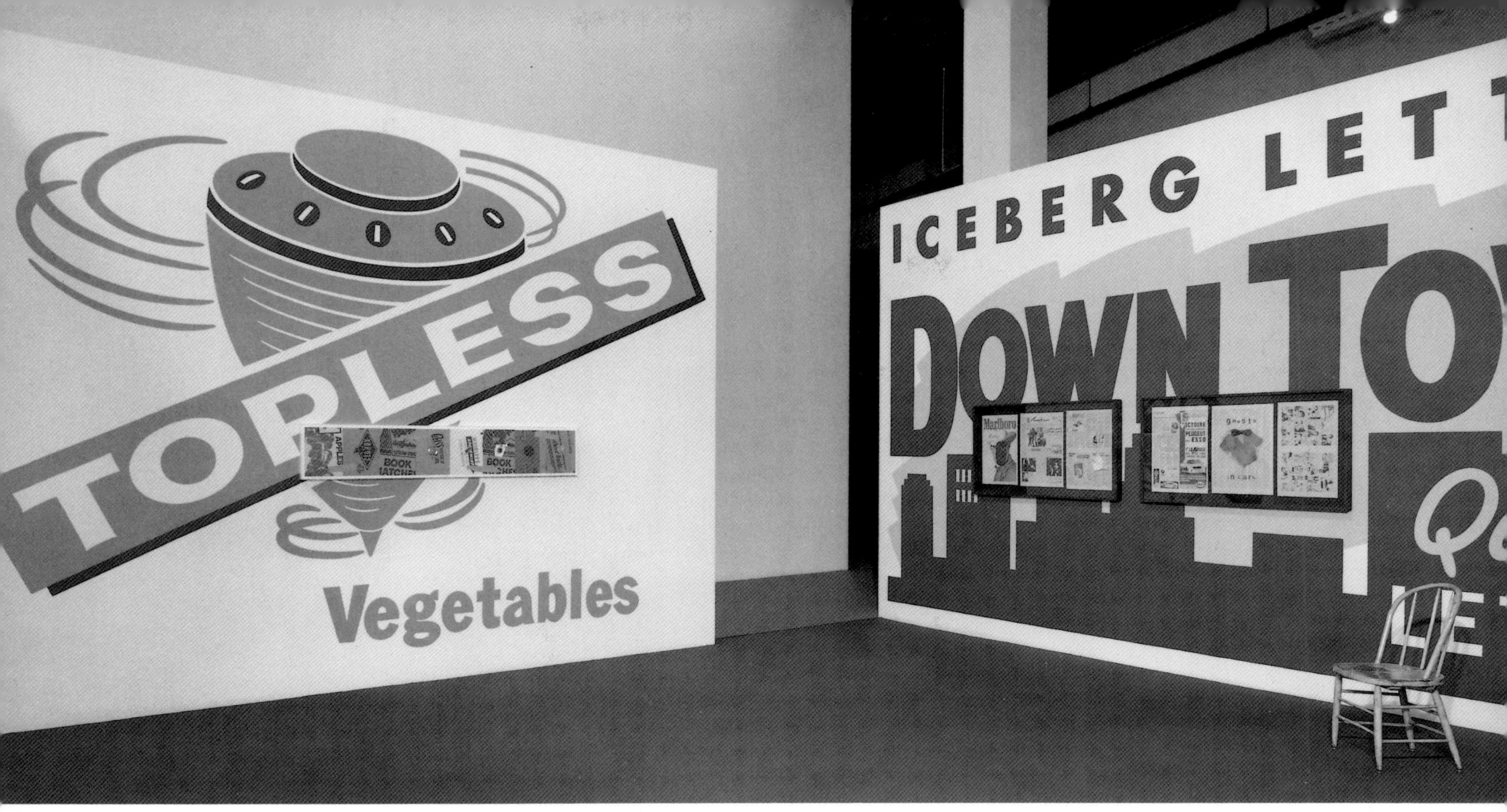

"Individuals: A Selected History of Contemporary Art, 1945–1986," installation view, The Museum of Contemporary Art, Los Angeles, 1986.

*Hirshhorn Museum and Sculpture Garden, Smithsonian Institution, Washington, D.C., "Directions 1983."

*Japanese American Cultural and Community Center, Los Angeles, "Cultural Excavations: Recent and Distant."

*La Jolla Museum of Contemporary Art, California, "A Contemporary Collection on Loan from the Rothschild Bank AG, Zurich."

Los Angeles County Museum of Art, "Young Talent Awards, 1963–1983."

*Montgomery Art Gallery, Pomona College, Pomona, California, "Contemporary Collage: Extensions (Work from Southern California)."

*Holly Solomon Gallery, New York, "Holly Solomon Gallery Inaugural Exhibition."

*Whitney Museum of American Art, Downtown Branch, New York, "The Comic Art Show."

1984

Patty Aande Gallery, San Diego, "Significant Others."

*Fine Arts Gallery, University of California, Irvine, "Selections from the Merry and Bill Norris Collection."

*The Museum of Modern Art, New York, "An International Survey of Recent Painting and Sculpture."

*Queens Museum, Flushing, New York (organized by Independent Curators Incorporated), "Verbally Charged Images." Traveled: University of South Florida Art Galleries, Tampa; University Art Gallery, San Diego State University; Art Gallery, California State College, San Bernadino; Blandon Memorial Art Museum, Fort Dodge, Iowa; Foster Gallery, University of Wisconsin, Eau Claire.

*Triton Museum of Art, Santa Clara, California, "Crime and Punishment: Reflections of Violence in Contemporary Art."

1985

Artemesia Gallery, Chicago, "Critical Messages: The Use of Public Media for Political Art by Women."

*Museum of Contemporary Art, Chicago, "Selections from the William J. Hokin Collection."

Newport Harbor Art Museum, Newport Beach, California, "Selections from the Permanent Collection."

1986

*The Corcoran Gallery of Art, Washington, D.C., "Spectrum: In Other Words."

*Cirrus Gallery, Los Angeles, "A Southern California Collection."

*Long Beach Museum of Art, California, "Remembrances of Things Past."

*Los Angeles Municipal Art Gallery, "Hollywood: Inside and Out."

*The Museum of Contemporary Art, Los Angeles, "Individuals: A Selected History of Contemporary Art, 1945–1986."

Holly Solomon Gallery, New York, "Text & Image: The Wording of American Art."

U.S. Embassy, Helsinki, Finland, "Contemporary Art from Southern California."

*Wight Art Gallery, University of California, Los Angeles, "Teaching Artists: The UCLA Faculty of Art and Design."

The Woman's Building Gallery, Los Angeles, "Gentleman's Choice."

1987

Amerika Haus, Berlin (organized by Los Angeles Municipal Art Gallery), "Los Angeles Today: Contemporary Visions."

*The Baltimore Museum of Art (organized by the Frederick R. Weisman Collection), "Selections from the Frederick R. Weisman Collection." Traveled: Pennsylvania Academy of the Fine Arts, Philadelphia; Walker Art Center, Minneapolis; San Antonio Art Institute, Texas; Birmingham Museum of Art, Alabama; Norton Gallery and School of Art, West Palm Beach, Florida; Colorado Springs Fine Arts Center.

Fresno Art Museum, California, "The Years of Passage 1969–1975."

*The Institute of Contemporary Arts, London, "Comic Iconoclasm." Traveled: Douglas Hyde Gallery, Trinity College, University of Dublin; Cornerhouse Gallery, Manchester, England.

*Los Angeles County Museum of Art, "Avant-garde in the Eighties."

University Art Gallery, Pepperdine University, Malibu, California, "Concept/Reality: Los Angeles Public Art."

1988

Carnegie Mellon Art Gallery, Carnegie Mellon University, Pittsburgh, "Layers: Media and Culture."

*The Museum of Contemporary Art, Los Angeles, "Striking Distance." Traveled: Triton Museum of Art, Santa Clara, California; Fresno Art Museum, California; University Art Gallery, Sonoma State University, Rohnert Park, California.

*Shoshana Wayne Gallery, Santa Monica, California (organized by James Corcoran Gallery in cooperation with Shoshana Wayne Gallery and Pence Gallery), "Lost and Found in California: Four Decades of Assemblage Art. The Second Generation: The Narrative 1959–1987."

1989

*Cincinnati Art Museum, "Making Their Mark: Women Artists Move into the Mainstream, 1970–85." Traveled: New Orleans Museum of Art; Denver Art Museum; Pennsylvania Academy of the Fine Arts, Philadelphia.

*Karsten Schubert Gallery, London, "A Brave New World: John Baldessari, Vernon Fisher, Stephen Prina, Ed Ruscha, Alexis Smith."

*The Museum of Contemporary Art, Los Angeles, "Constructing a History: A Focus on MOCA's Permanent Collection."

*The Museum of Contemporary Art, Los Angeles, "Selections from the Beatrice and Philip Gersh Collection."

*Security Pacific Gallery, Costa Mesa, California, "Art in the Public Eye: Selected Developments."

*Whitney Museum of American Art, New York, "Image World: Art and Media Culture."

*Wight Art Gallery, University of California, Los Angeles, "40 Years of California Assemblage." Traveled: San Jose Museum of Art, California; Fresno Art Museum, California; Joslyn Art Museum, Omaha, Nebraska.

*Wight Art Gallery, University of California, Los Angeles (organized by the Frederick R. Weisman Art Foundation), "Selected Works from the Frederick R. Weisman Art Foundation." Traveled: Joslyn Art Museum, Omaha, Nebraska; Neuberger Museum, State University of New York at Purchase; Akron Art Museum, Ohio.

1990

*Milwaukee Art Museum, "Word as Image: American Art 1960–1990." Traveled: Oklahoma City Art Museum; Contemporary Arts Museum, Houston.

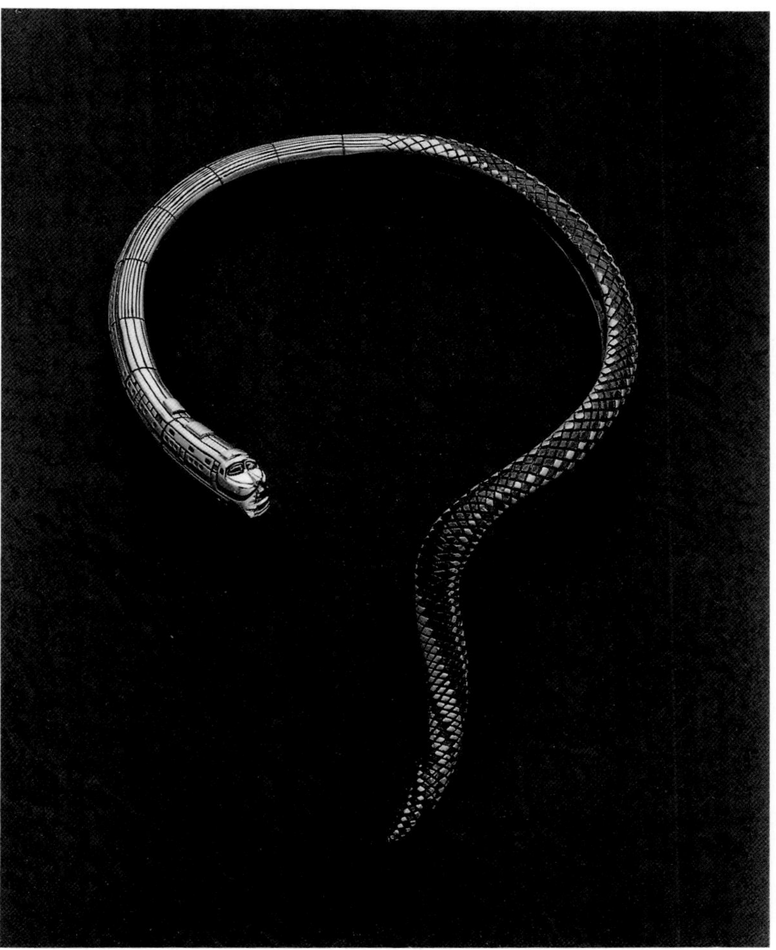

Sidewinder, 1987
Sterling silver necklace with ruby and sapphire, 10 × 7 × ½ inches
Artist Editions Limited, Beverly Hills, California

1991

Margo Leavin Gallery, Los Angeles, "20th Century Collage." Traveled: Centro Cultural/Arte Contemporaneo, Mexico City; Musée d'Art Moderne et d'Art Contemporain de la Ville de Nice, France.

Stephen Wirtz Gallery, San Francisco, "Framed."

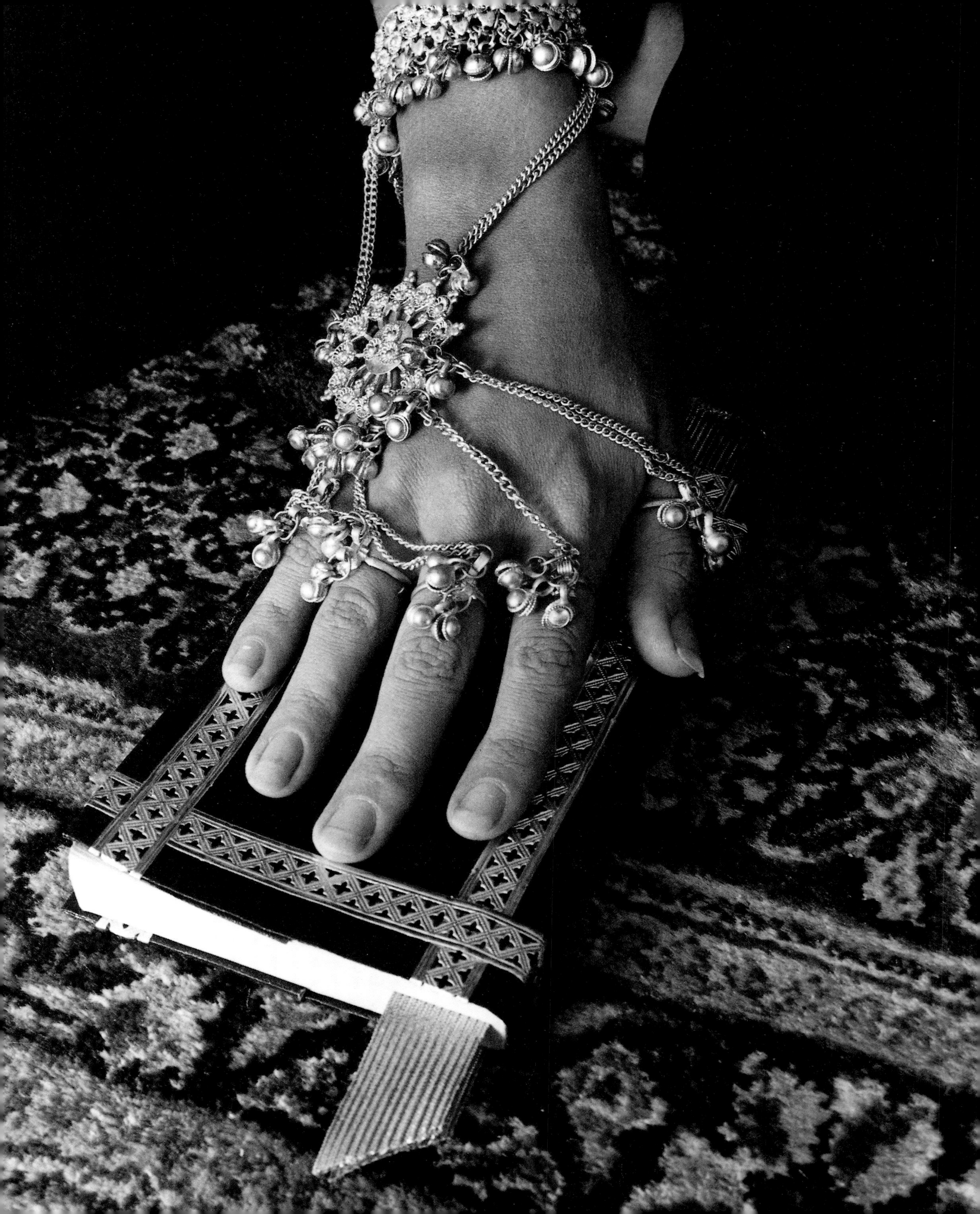

Bibliography

Catalogues and Brochures

Aspen Art Museum, Colorado. *Alexis Smith.* Exhibition brochure by Richard Armstrong, 1987.

The Brooklyn Museum, New York. *Alexis Smith: Same Old Paradise.* Exhibition brochure by Charlotta Kotik, 1987.

Cincinnati Art Museum. *Making Their Mark: Women Artists Move into the Mainstream, 1970–85.* Exhibition catalogue by Randy Rosen and Catherine C. Brawer, 1989.

Cirrus Gallery, Los Angeles. *A Southern California Collection.* Exhibition brochure by Melinda Wortz, 1986.

Contemporary Arts Museum, Houston. *American Narrative/Story Art: 1967–1977.* Exhibition catalogue, edited by Paul Schimmel, 1977.

————. *The Americans: The Collage.* Exhibition catalogue by Linda L. Cathcart, 1982.

James Corcoran Gallery, in cooperation with Shoshana Wayne Gallery and Pence Gallery, Santa Monica, California. *Lost and Found in California: Four Decades of Assemblage Art.* Exhibition catalogue by Sandra Leonard Starr, 1988.

The Corcoran Gallery of Art, Washington, D.C. *Spectrum: In Other Words.* Exhibition brochure by Ned Rifkin, 1986.

Fine Arts Gallery, California State University, Los Angeles. *Miniature.* Exhibition catalogue by Sandy Ballatore, 1977.

Fine Arts Gallery, University of California, Irvine. *Selections from the Merry and Bill Norris Collection.* Exhibition catalogue by Melinda Wortz, 1984.

Freedman Gallery, Albright College, Reading, Pennsylvania. *Messages: Words and Images.* Exhibition catalogue by Marilyn A. Zeitlin, 1981.

Hirshhorn Museum and Sculpture Garden, Smithsonian Institution, Washington, D.C. *Directions 1983.* Exhibition catalogue by Phyllis D. Rosenzweig, 1983.

Independent Curators Incorporated, New York. *Verbally Charged Images.* Exhibition catalogue by Nina Felshin, 1984.

Institute of Contemporary Art, Boston. *Currents: Alexis Smith.* Exhibition brochure by David Joselit, 1986.

————. *Narration.* Exhibition catalogue by Michael Leja, 1978.

The Institute of Contemporary Arts, London. *Comic Iconoclasm.* Exhibition catalogue by Sheena Wagstaff, 1987.

Japanese American Cultural and Community Center, Los Angeles. *Cultural Excavations: Recent and Distant.* Exhibition brochure by Robert L. Pincus, 1983.

La Jolla Museum of Contemporary Art, California. *A Contemporary Collection on Loan from the Rothschild Bank AG, Zurich.* Exhibition catalogue by Lynda Forsha, with text by Robert McDonald, 1983.

Margo Leavin Gallery, Los Angeles. *Alexis Smith: Jane.* Exhibition brochure, with text by Lane Relyea, 1985.

Long Beach Museum of Art, California. *Remembrances of Things Past.* Exhibition catalogue by Connie Fitzsimons, edited by Lane Relyea, 1986.

————. *Southland Video Anthology 1976–77.* Exhibition catalogue by David A. Ross, 1976.

Los Angeles County Museum of Art. *Art in Los Angeles. The Museum as Site: Sixteen Projects.* Exhibition catalogue by Stephanie Barron, 1981.

————. *Avant-garde in the Eighties.* Exhibition catalogue by Howard N. Fox, 1987.

————. *New Selections: New Talent Award Winners.* Exhibition brochure by Betty Asher, 1976.

Los Angeles Municipal Art Gallery. *Hollywood: Inside and Out.* Exhibition brochure by Marie de Alcuaz, 1986.

Mandeville Gallery, University of California, San Diego. *Alexis Smith: Public Works.* Exhibition catalogue, with text by Hunter Drohojowska, 1991.

Scheherazade the Storyteller,
performance at CARP,
Los Angeles, 1976.

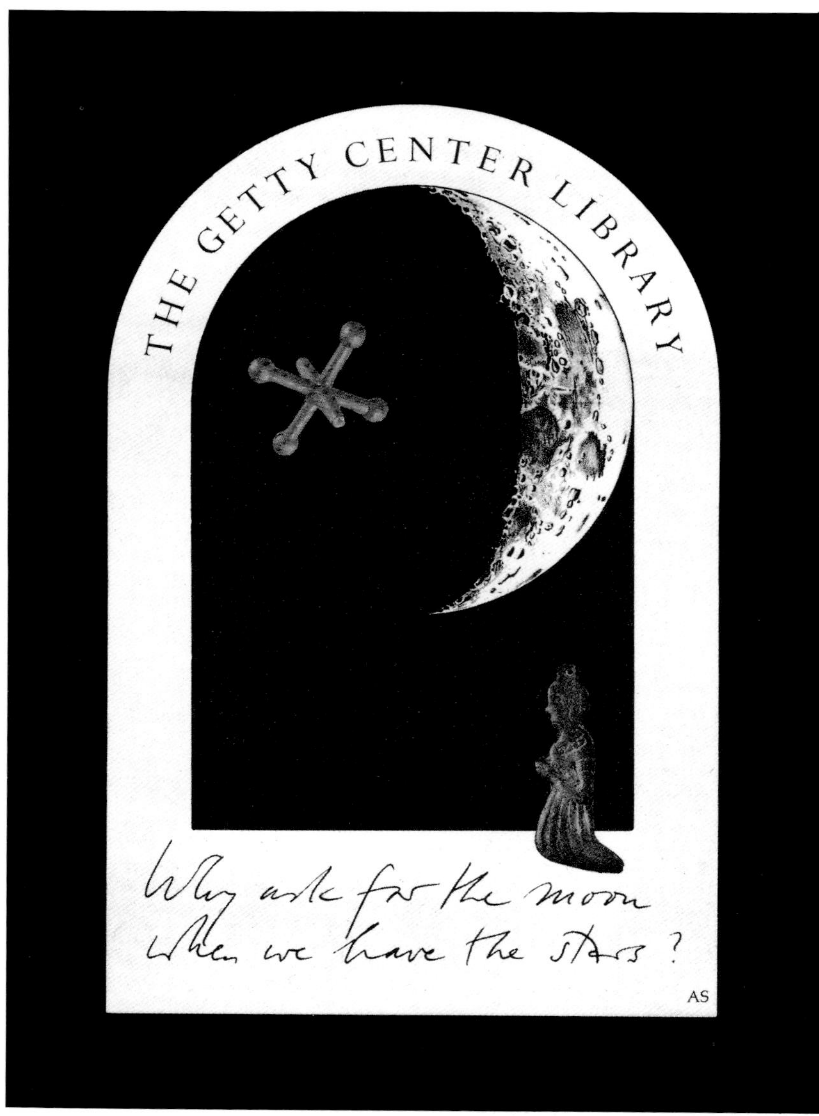

Bookplate for The Getty Center Library, Santa Monica, 1990.

Milwaukee Art Museum. *Word as Image: American Art 1960–1990.* Exhibition catalogue by Russell Bowman and Dean Sobel, with text by Gerry Biller, 1990.

Montgomery Art Gallery, Pomona College, Pomona, California. *Contemporary Collage: Extensions (Work From Southern California).* Exhibition catalogue by Melinda Lorenz, 1983.

Mt. San Antonio College Art Gallery, Walnut, California. *Word Works.* Exhibition catalogue by Jessica Jacobs, 1974.

Musée d'Art Moderne de la Ville de Paris. *Une expérience museographique: Échange entre artistes, 1931–1982, Pologne-U.S.A.* Exhibition catalogue, with texts by Pontus Hulten and Ryszard Stanislawski, 1982.

———. *10e biennale de Paris.* Exhibition catalogue, with texts by Georges Boudaille, Victoria Combalia, Michael Compton, Russell Connor, Jesa Denegri, Nina Felshin, Gerald Forty, Johannes Gachnang, Bernard Lamarche-Vodel, Catherine Millet, Toshiaki Minemura, and Neil Printz, 1977.

Museum of Contemporary Art, Chicago. *Selections from the William J. Hokin Collection.* Exhibition catalogue, edited by Terry A.R. Neff, 1985.

The Museum of Contemporary Art, Los Angeles. *Constructing a History: A Focus on MOCA's Permanent Collection.* Exhibition brochure by Ann Goldstein, 1989.

———. *Individuals: A Selected History of Contemporary Art, 1945–1986.* Exhibition catalogue by Julia Brown Turrell, edited by Howard Singerman, 1986.

———. *Selections from the Beatrice and Philip Gersh Collection.* Exhibition catalogue by Kerry Brougher, 1989.

———. *Striking Distance.* Exhibition brochure by Ann Goldstein, 1988.

The Museum of Modern Art, New York. *An International Survey of Recent Painting and Sculpture.* Exhibition catalogue by Kynaston McShine, 1984.

Pasadena Art Museum, California. *Southern California: Attitudes 1972.* Exhibition catalogue by Barbara Haskell, 1972.

Philadelphia Art Alliance. *Words & Images: A Contemporary Artists' Book Exhibition.* Exhibition catalogue, with text by Peter Frank, 1981.

The Renaissance Society at the University of Chicago. "Words as Images." *WhiteWalls*, 5 (Winter 1981). Exhibition catalogue, edited by Buzz Spector, Reagan Upshaw, and Roberta Upshaw.

San Francisco Museum of Modern Art. *Paper on Paper.* Exhibition catalogue by Constance E. Goldsmith, 1979.

Sarah Lawrence Gallery, Sarah Lawrence College, Bronxville, New York. *Word, Image, Number.* Exhibition catalogue, with texts by Brooks Adams, Dan Carter, Mary Delahoyd, Mark French, Lester Paul Kane, and Kevin Trevillian, 1975.

Karsten Schubert Gallery, London. *A Brave New World: John Baldessari, Vernon Fisher, Stephen Prina, Ed Ruscha, Alexis Smith.* Exhibition catalogue, with text by Colin Gardner, 1989.

Security Pacific Gallery, Costa Mesa, California. *Art in the Public Eye: Selected Developments.* Exhibition catalogue by Mark Johnstone, 1989.

Holly Solomon Gallery, New York. *Holly Solomon Gallery Inaugural Exhibition.* Exhibition catalogue, with texts by Richard Armstrong, Robert Rosenblum, Neil Printz, and Harald Szeemann, 1983.

———. *Holly Solomon Gallery: The First Two Years.* Exhibition catalogue, 1977.

———. *Holly Solomon Gallery: Three More.* Exhibition catalogue, 1980.

Triton Museum of Art, Santa Clara, California. *Crime and Punishment: Reflections of Violence in Contemporary Art.* Exhibition catalogue by Jo Farb Hernandez and Marc D'Estout, 1984.

University Art Museum, University of California, Berkeley. *Both Kinds: Contemporary Art from Los Angeles.* Exhibition catalogue by Peter Plagens, 1975.

Walker Art Center, Minneapolis. *Viewpoints: Alexis Smith.* Exhibition brochure by Robert M. Murdock, 1986.

Frederick R. Weisman Art Foundation, Los Angeles. *Selected Works from the Frederick R. Weisman Art Foundation.* Exhibition catalogue by Nora Halpern Brougher, with text by Donna Stein, 1989.

Frederick R. Weisman Collection, Los Angeles. *Selections from the Frederick R. Weisman Collection.* Exhibition catalogue by Nora Halpern, 1987.

Whitney Museum of American Art, New York. *Alexis Smith.* Exhibition brochure by Barbara Haskell, 1975.

———. *The Decade in Review: Selections from the 1970s.* Exhibition brochure by Patterson Sims, 1979.

———. *Image World: Art and Media Culture.* Exhibition catalogue by Marvin Heiferman and Lisa Phillips, with John G. Hanhardt, 1989.

———. *1975 Biennial Exhibition.* Exhibition catalogue by Barbara Haskell, John G. Hanhardt, James Monte, Elke Solomon, and Marcia Tucker, 1975.

———. *1979 Biennial Exhibition.* Exhibition catalogue by Barbara Haskell, John G. Hanhardt, Richard Marshall, Mark Segal, and Patterson Sims, 1979.

———. *1981 Biennial Exhibition.* Exhibition catalogue by Barbara Haskell, John G. Hanhardt, Richard Marshall, and Patterson Sims, 1981.

Whitney Museum of American Art, Downtown Branch, New York. *The Comic Art Show.* Exhibition catalogue by John Carlin and Sheena Wagstaff, 1983.

Wight Art Gallery, University of California, Los Angeles. *40 Years of California Assemblage.* Exhibition catalogue by Anne Ayres, Andrea Liss, and Elizabeth Shepherd, 1989.

———. *Teaching Artists: The UCLA Faculty of Art and Design.* Exhibition catalogue by Edith Tonelli, 1986.

Newspapers and Periodicals

Andreoli-Woods, Lynn. "Alexis Smith's Dreams, 'On the Road.'" *Los Angeles Reader*, April 13, 1990, pp. 25–26.

Anderson, Michael. "Los Angeles." *Contemporanea*, 3 (March 1990), pp. 44–45.

Armstrong, Richard. "Review of Exhibitions: Alexis Smith, Rosamund Felsen and L.A.C.E./Los Angeles." *Flash Art*, no. 102 (March–April 1981), pp. 44–45.

"Art: Alexis Smith." *The New Yorker*, December 24, 1990, p. 16.

Ashbery, John. "Biennials Bloom in the Spring." *Newsweek*, April 18, 1983, pp. 93–94.

Atlas, Billie. "Alexis Smith: Individualism in Art." *Santa Monica Outlook*, August 28, 1980, pp. 13, 42.

Ballatore, Sandy. "Alexis Smith: Object-Language Collages." *Journal* [Los Angeles Institute of Contemporary Art], no. 7 (August–September 1975), pp. 22–24.

Berman, Avis. "A Decade of Progress, But Could a Female Chardin Make a Living?" *Art News*, 79 (October 1980), pp. 73–79.

Burkhart, Dorothy. "Alexis Smith: A Literary Sensibility." *Artweek*, May 8, 1976, pp. 1, 20.

Carlson, Prudence. "Review of Exhibitions: Alexis Smith at Holly Solomon." *Art in America*, 67 (September 1979), pp. 135–36.

Casademont, Joan. "Reviews: Alexis Smith, Holly Solomon Gallery." *Artforum*, 19 (April 1981), pp. 65–66.

Clothier, Peter. "Art Seen: Alexis Smith at Margo Leavin Gallery." *L.A. Weekly*, October 4–10, 1985, p. 61.

————. "The Next Wave." *Art News*, 89 (December 1990), pp. 112–17.

Danieli, Fidel. "Alexis Smith/Cathay in L.A." *Images & Issues*, 2 (Winter 1981–82), pp. 56–57.

————. "Not So Plain Janes." *Artweek*, October 5, 1985, p. 3.

Doubilet, Susan. "Artists on Architecture." *Progressive Architecture*, 112 (September 1981), p. 47.

Drohojowska, Hunter. "Alexis Smith Rtist." *Artforum*, 26 (October 1987), pp. 86–90.

————. "Geniuses at Work." *Republic Magazine*, April 1986, pp. 22, 25, 28, 30.

————. "Her Artwork Combines the Myths and Madness of Everyday Life." *Los Angeles Herald Examiner*, September 15, 1985, section E, p. 2.

————. "The Nation: Alexis Smith, Margo Leavin." *Art News*, 84 (November 1985), p. 127.

Faust, Gretchen. "New York in Review." *Arts Magazine*, 65 (March 1991), p. 100.

ffrench-frazier, Nina. "New York Reviews: Alexis Smith (Holly Solomon)." *Art News*, 76 (Summer 1977), p. 195.

Filler, Martin. "Puttin' on the Ritz." *House & Garden*, 156 (June 1984), p. 213.

————. "Rediscovering America." *House & Garden*, 153 (February 1981), pp. 114–15, 175–76.

Frank, Peter. "Art Pick of the Week: Alexis Smith & Amy Gerstler; Gary Simmons." *L.A. Weekly*, December 29, 1989–January 4, 1990, p. 122.

————. "Something Old, Something New, Something Borrowed, Something Cerulean." *The Village Voice*, April 10, 1978, p. 78.

Freudenheim, Susan. "Landscape Painting." *Arts + Architecture*, 1, no. 3 (1983), pp. 21–26.

Gamwell, Lynn. "Alexis Smith Interprets Thomas Mann." *Artweek*, November 18, 1978, pp. 1, 16.

Gardner, Colin. "Reviews: Alexis Smith, Margo Leavin Gallery." *Artforum*, 24 (November 1985), pp. 113–14.

Garris, Laurie. "The MacArthur Park Program." *Arts + Architecture*, 4 (July 1987), pp. 16–17.

Gerstler, Amy. "Alexis Smith: Detonated Clichés." *Visions Art Quarterly*, Winter 1988, p. 15.

Glueck, Grace. "Review: Alexis Smith and Mary Heilmann." *The New York Times*, January 23, 1981, section C, p. 19.

————. "Two Biennials: One Looking East and the Other West." *The New York Times*, March 27, 1983, section H, pp. 35, 36.

Gottlieb, Shirle. "Past Makes Its Presence Known at L.B. Museum." *Long Beach Press Telegram*, December 14, 1986, section D, p. 7.

Greenstein, Jane. "Monuments to the Art of Losing." *Los Angeles Times,* December 10, 1985, section 6, p. 2.

Hayes, Mary Eshbaugh. "Alexis Smith Is Storyteller in Collages of Found Things." *The Aspen Times,* July 3, 1987, pp. 7–8.

Johnson, Ken. "Review of Exhibitions: Alexis Smith and Amy Gerstler at Josh Baer." *Art in America,* 79 (March 1991), p. 133.

Joselit, David. "Lessons in Public Sculpture." *Art in America,* 77 (December 1989), pp. 130–34.

———. "Public Art & the Public Purse." *Art in America,* 78 (July 1990), pp. 142–50, 183.

Kandel, Susan. "Alexis Smith and Amy Gerstler." *Art Issues,* no. 9 (February 1990), p. 29.

———. "Los Angeles in Review." *Arts Magazine,* 64 (Summer 1990), pp. 105–06.

Knight, Christopher. "Art Exhibit That's an Event." *Los Angeles Herald Examiner,* October 20, 1982, section C, pp. 1, 2.

———. "Images with No Meaning." *Los Angeles Herald Examiner,* February 1, 1981, section E, pp. 4, 7.

———. "L.A.'s Art Direction." *G.Q.,* 53 (August 1983), pp. 136–39.

———. "Los Angeles: Art on the Move." *Art News,* 82 (January 1983), pp. 72–75.

———. "A Meeting of Media." *Los Angeles Herald Examiner,* October 27, 1981, section B, p. 3.

———. "Paradise Found in New York Museums." *Los Angeles Herald Examiner,* Sunday, November 15, 1987, section E, p. 8.

———. "Reviews: Alexis Smith, 'Satan's Satellites,' Rosamund Felsen Gallery, and 'Christmas Eve, 1943,' Margo Leavin Gallery." *Artforum,* 21 (January 1983), pp. 81–82.

———. "Season-opening Shows May Presage Great Art." *Los Angeles Herald Examiner,* October 6, 1985, section E, p. 8.

———. "Site Seeing at the County Museum." *Los Angeles Herald Examiner,* July 26, 1981, section E, p. 2.

Kornblau, Gary. "Cover: Alexis Smith." *Art Issues,* no. 8 (December 1989–January 1990), p. 40.

Kurcfeld, Michael. "The Artist as Sleuth." *L.A. Weekly,* January 27–February 2, 1989, pp. 75, 89.

Larson, Kay. "Art: Old and New Image-Makers." *New York Magazine,* January 19, 1981, pp. 56–57.

———. "Dying Light." *New York Magazine,* January 7, 1991, pp. 50–51.

Levin, Kim. "The Way It Wasn't." *The Village Voice,* January 14, 1981, p. 87.

Lisi, David. "Jane Gang." *House & Garden,* 158 (February 1986), p. 78.

Livingston, Jane. "MS. L.A.: 3 Women in the City of Angels." *Art in America,* 61 (January–February 1973), pp. 98–101.

Lubell, Ellen. "Arts Reviews: Alexis Smith." *Arts Magazine,* 52 (June 1978), p. 47.

Marks, Richard. "LA's Finest." *Air California Magazine,* December 1980, pp. 42–45.

Marmer, Nancy. "Alexis Smith: The Narrative Act." *Artforum,* 15 (December 1976), pp. 31–33.

———. "Reviews: Alexis Smith, UC Santa Barbara Art Galleries." *Artforum,* 14 (February 1976), pp. 71–72.

McGuigan, Cathleen, and Janet Huck. "Picasso in Lala Land." *Newsweek,* November 24, 1986, pp. 86–88.

McKenna, Kristine. "'Past Lives' Explores the Terrors and Perils of Childhood." *Los Angeles Times,* December 23, 1989, section F, p. 15.

———. "13 Artists Share Their 'Remembrances.'" *Los Angeles Times,* January 3, 1987, section F, pp. 8–9.

Muchnic, Suzanne. "The Art Galleries: La Cienega Area." *Los Angeles Times,* September 13, 1985, section 6, p. 4.

———. "Art/LA89 Mixes Culture, Commerce." *Los Angeles Times,* December 4, 1989, section F, pp. 1, 6.

———. "California Mural Takes Chill Off Brooklyn—But Take Another Look." *Los Angeles Times,* December 24, 1987, section 6, pp. 1, 10–11.

———. "Sizing Up Alexis Smith." *Los Angeles Times,* January 6, 1991, section 6, pp. 3, 74.

———. "'Visions' Has Sense of Humor." *Los Angeles Times,* February 2, 1981, section F, pp. 1, 3.

Nilson, Lisbet. "Alexis Smith: Lost in America." *Angeles,* July 1990, pp. 42, 44.

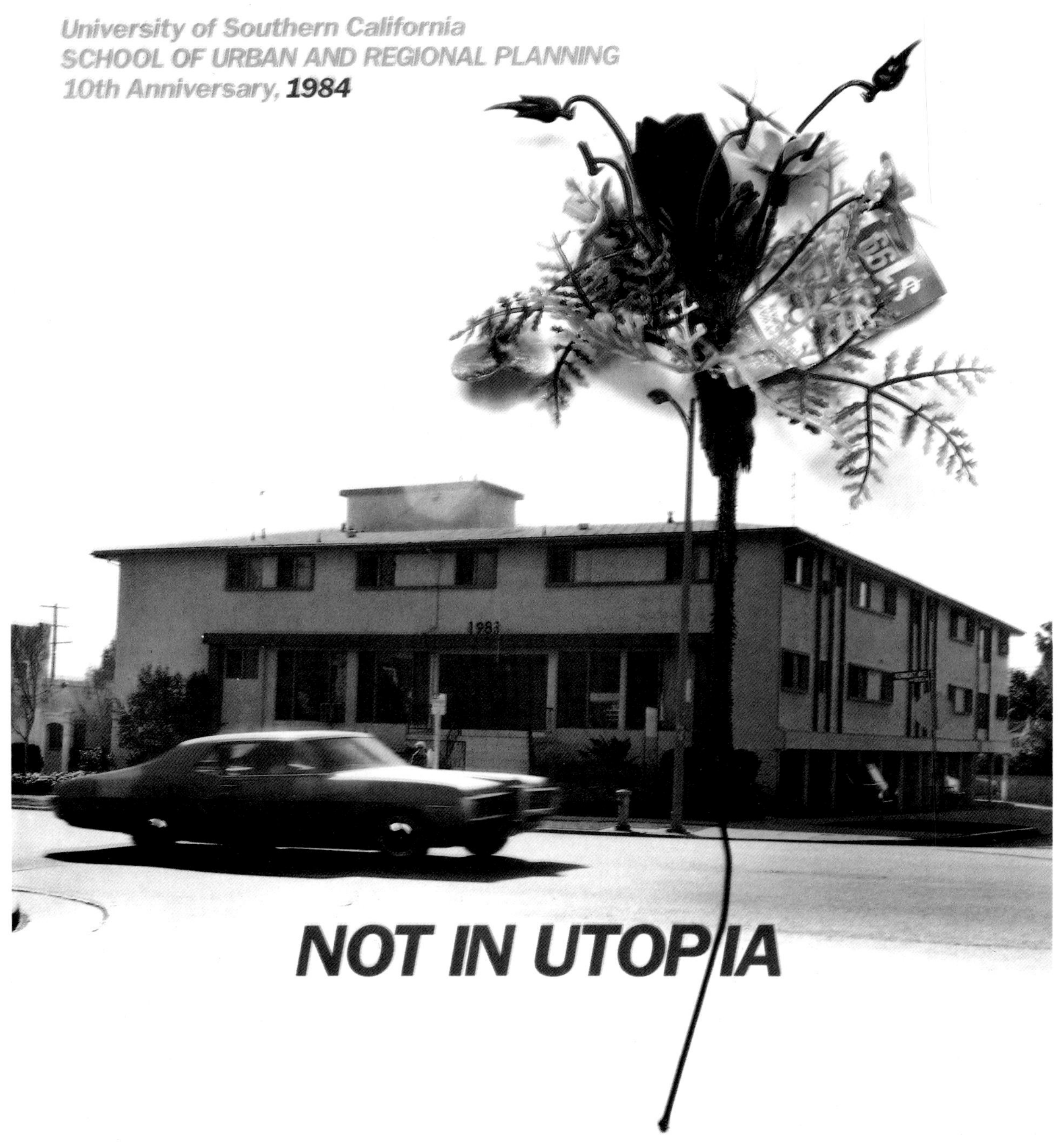

Not in Utopia, commemorative poster, commissioned by the University of Southern California, School of Urban and Regional Planning, Los Angeles, 1984.

Pagel, David. "Alexis Smith at Margo Leavin." *Art Issues*, no. 12 (Summer 1990), p. 32.

Perlmutter, Elizabeth. "The Nation: Salton Sea to Muscle Beach." *Art News*, 75 (April 1976), pp. 66–68.

Perrone, Jeff. "Notes on the Whitney Biennial." *Images & Issues*, 2 (Summer 1981), pp. 46–49.

Pincus, Robert L. "Exhibition Reviews: Alexis Smith at Margo Leavin." *Art in America*, 76 (December 1988), p. 161.

————. "Thirteen Artists Remember the Past . . . in Thirteen Different Ways." *San Diego Union Tribune*, December 25, 1986, section C, p. 10.

————. "Turning a Park into a Park of Art." *Los Angeles Times*, January 26, 1985, section 6, pp. 1, 3.

————. "Two Give Pop Art a New Twist." *San Diego Union Tribune*, October 6, 1985, section E, p. 1.

Plagens, Peter. "Reviews." *Artforum*, 13 (September 1974), p. 88.

————. "Site Wars." *Art in America*, 70 (January 1982), pp. 90–98.

Quinn, Joan. "All American Art: Alexis Smith." *Interview*, 11 (March 1981), pp. 56–58.

Raynor, Vivien. "A Show That Requires Reading, Too." *The New York Times* [New Jersey edition], March 23, 1980, section 1, p. 20.

Rubinfien, Leo. "Through Western Eyes." *Art in America*, 66 (September–October 1978), pp. 82–83.

Rugoff, Ralph. "Alexis Smith." *LA Style*, 2 (July 1986), p. 28.

Russell, John. "Art: Alexis Smith." *The New York Times*, May 5, 1979, section C, p. 23.

————. "Art: Alexis Smith/ Thomas Lanigan-Schmidt." *The New York Times*, April 15, 1977, section C, p. 23.

————. "Art: In Show of New Noland Paintings, Consistency Takes Unexpected Forms." *The New York Times*, November 22, 1975, section L, p. 38.

————. "Whitney Finds This Land Is Its Land." *The New York Times*, February 6, 1975, section L, p. 26.

Saunders, Wade. "Los Angeles." *Bomb*, no. 22 (Winter 1988), pp. 74–84.

Schjeldahl, Peter. "Reviews: Alexis Smith, Rosamund Felsen Gallery." *Artforum*, 17 (January 1979), pp. 68–69.

————. "Spanning Time Zones." *The Village Voice*, September 2, 1981, p. 70.

Selwyn, Marc. "Reviews: Alexis Smith, Margo Leavin." *Flash Art*, no. 141 (Summer 1988), pp. 138–39.

Singerman, Howard. "Reviews: 'Art in Los Angeles,' Los Angeles County Museum of Art." *Artforum*, 20 (March 1982), pp. 75–77.

Smith, Alexis. "Alexis Smith." *Art Présent*, no. 6–7 (Winter 1977).

————. "Alexis Smith." *Flash Art/Heute Kunst*, no. 20 (November–December 1977), p. 33.

Smith, Roberta. "Alexis Smith." *The New York Times*, January 1, 1988, section C, p. 29.

————. "Alexis Smith and Amy Gerstler: Past Lives." *The New York Times*, December 14, 1990, section C, p. 30.

————. "Some Things Old, Some Things New." *The Village Voice*, April 27, 1982, p. 98.

Smith, Valerie de F.D. "Review of Exhibitions: Alexis Smith, Holly Solomon." *Flash Art*, no. 102 (March–April 1981), p. 39.

Stevens, Mark. "California Dreamers." *Newsweek*, August 17, 1981, pp. 78–79.

————. "The Dizzy Decade." *Newsweek*, March 26, 1979, pp. 88–91, 94.

Strini, Tom. "Biography by Inference." *Artweek*, November 22, 1980, p. 3.

Suderburg, Erika. "Watching the Myth Unfold." *Artweek*, April 16, 1988, p. 7.

Tucker, John G. "Designed on the Right Track." *Interior Design*, 55 (April 1984), pp. 200–02.

Weisberg, Ruth. "Alexis Smith: A Forties Escapism." *Artweek*, October 16, 1982, p. 1.

Weissman, Benjamin. "Art Pick of the Week." *L.A. Weekly*, April 22–28, 1988, p. 123.

————. "Reviews: Alexis Smith, Margo Leavin Gallery." *Artforum*, 28 (Summer 1990), p. 173.

Wilson, William. "Alexis Smith: A Treasure in Collage." *Los Angeles Times*, December 15, 1975, section 4, pp. 1, 8–9.

————. "Art Reviews: The Tomboy Laureate." *Los Angeles Times*, March 30, 1990, section F, p. 16.

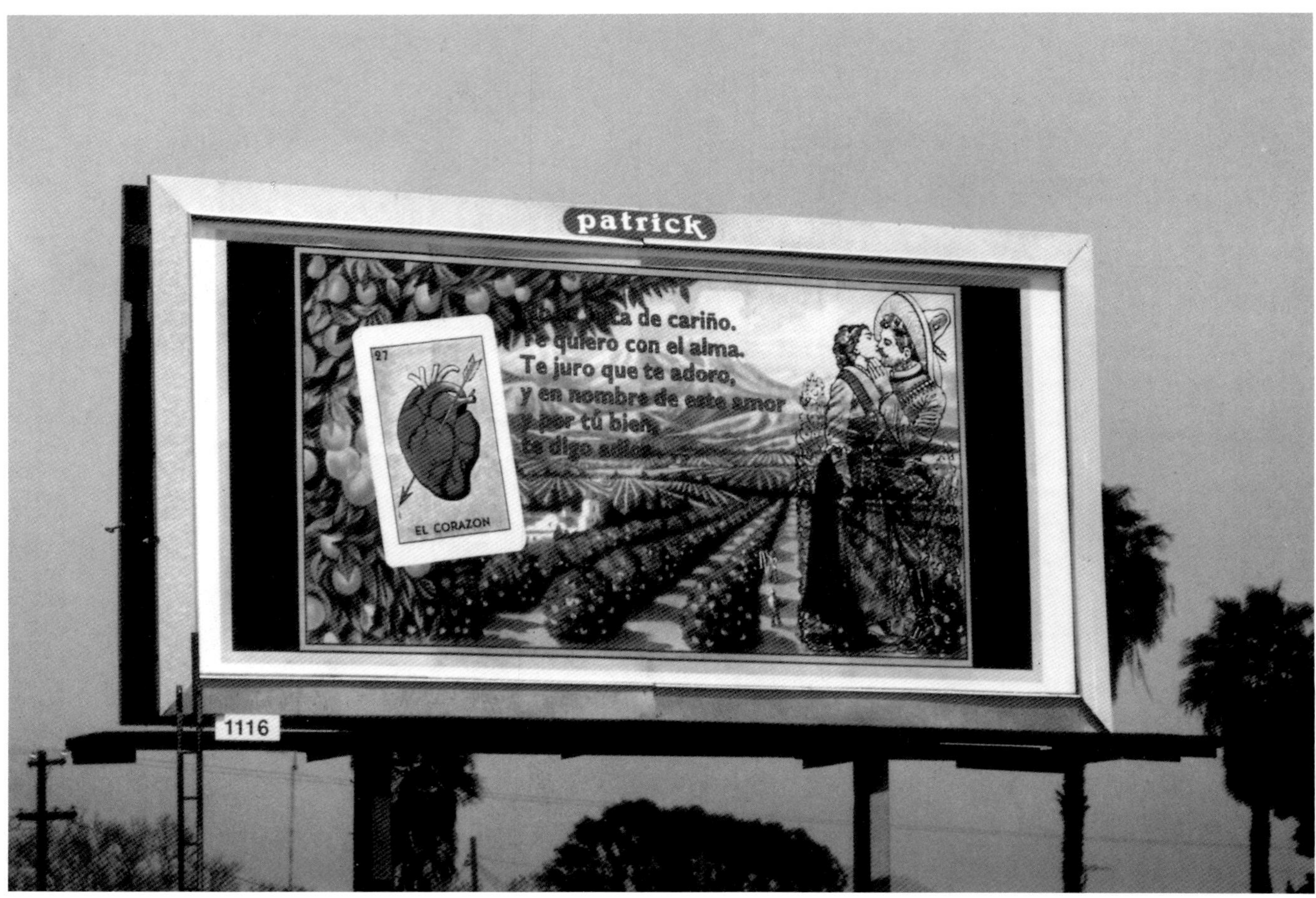

———. "Art Walk: A Critical Guide to the Galleries: La Cienega Area." *Los Angeles Times,* November 3, 1978, section 4, p. 10.

———. "The Galleries: La Cienega Area." *Los Angeles Times,* April 1, 1988, section 6, p. 18.

———. "A Museum Where Art Is a Site to Behold." *Los Angeles Times,* July 26, 1981, section 6, p. 92.

———. "'Tableau': Rooms for Improvement." *Los Angeles Times,* February 24, 1980, section 6, p. 85.

Wortz, Melinda T. "Alexis Smith at Margo Leavin and Rosamund Felsen." *Images & Issues,* 3 (March–April 1983), pp. 59–60.

———. "Alexis Smith—Concepts." *Artweek,* March 30, 1974, p. 5.

———. "Painting: Back to Back." *Journal* [Los Angeles Institute of Contemporary Art], no. 23 (June–July 1979), pp. 62–64.

Published projects

Alexis Smith Playing Cards, Made in USA, commissioned by Otis Art Institute of Parsons School of Design, Los Angeles, for "Poetic Visions," 1981.

Alone. Los Angeles: privately published, 1977.

"Anteroom/Anti-Room." *Avalanche,* no. 12 (Winter 1975), pp. 22–23.

Bookplate for The Getty Center Library, Santa Monica, 1990.

Blue Chip, poster, commissioned by Los Angeles Art Fair for "ART/LA '89," 1989.

"Chandlerism." *Journal* [Los Angeles Institute of Contemporary Art], no. 20 (October–November 1978), pp. 40–43.

"The End." *WhiteWalls,* no. 6 (Summer 1981), pp. 46–51.

"Italics." *The Paris Review,* 20 (Spring 1978), pp. 71–79.

New World, commissioned installation for *House & Garden,* Condé Nast Studio, New York, 1980.

Nosotros, billboard for Dos Cuidades/Two Cities project, San Diego, commissioned by the San Diego Museum of Contemporary Art, 1991.

Nosotros, billboard for Dos Cuidades/Two Cities project, San Diego, commissioned by San Diego Museum of Contemporary Art, 1991.

Not in Utopia, commemorative poster, commissioned by University of Southern California, School of Urban and Regional Planning, Los Angeles, 1984.

Past Lives by Amy Gerstler and Alexis Smith. Santa Monica, California: Amy Gerstler, Alexis Smith, and Santa Monica Museum of Art, 1989.

"Shanghai Express." *Los Angeles Herald Examiner*, November 22, 1981, magazine section, pp. 10–11.

"Tropical Paradise." *Journal* [Los Angeles Institute of Contemporary Art], 5 (Fall 1987), p. 28.

The True Bride by Amy Gerstler. Cover by Alexis Smith. Santa Monica: Lapis Press, 1986.

"Valentine." *Journal* [Los Angeles Institute of Contemporary Art], 4 (Winter 1983), insert.

"Variety—The Spice of Life." *For Members* [Museum of Contemporary Art, Los Angeles], 1 (1984).

Virgin Sacrifice, exhibition poster, commissioned by Los Angeles County Museum of Art for "Young Talent Awards, 1963–1983," 1983.

Watch Your Step, Chicago Transit Authority platform billboard, commissioned by Artemesia Gallery, Chicago, for "Critical Messages," 1985.

"Work." *Spazio Umano/Human Space*, 2 (May 1988), pp. 152–53.

Commissions

Starlight, 1982
Mixed-media collage on painted wall
Unity Savings and Loan,
West Hollywood

There's No Place Like Home, 1982
Mixed-media collage on painted wall
Collection of Aviva and Carl Covitz

The Grand, 1983
Mixed-media installation
Keeler Grand Foyer, De Vos Hall
Grand Rapids, Michigan

California, 1984
Mixed-media collage on painted wall
California State Office Building,
Santa Rosa

Niagara, 1985
Granite monument
Artpark, Lewiston, New York

Proposal for mixed-media collage on painted wall, 1985
The Brooklyn Public Library's Central Library, New York
(not realized)

Mini-monuments
Bronze suitcase, granite headstone, and terrazzo sidewalk inlay, 1986
Proposal for park bench with bronze plaque (not realized)
MacArthur Park, Los Angeles

Proposals for mixed-media installations (in collaboration with R.M. Fischer)
Concourse B, Miami International Airport, 1988 (not realized)
Concourse D, Miami International Airport, 1989 (not realized)

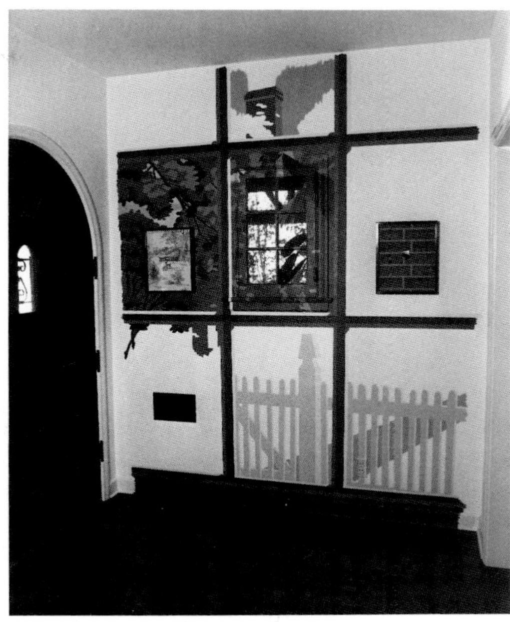

Proposal for plaza design, 1990
Playhouse Square, Cleveland
(not realized)

Snake Path
(scheduled completion 1992)
Slate pathway
Stuart Collection, University of California, San Diego

Terrazzo floor designs for south and west lobbies (scheduled completion 1994)
Los Angeles Convention Center Expansion Project
Pei Cobb Freed, New York, and Gruen Associates, Los Angeles, architects

There's No Place Like Home, 1982
Mixed-media collage on painted wall
Collection of Aviva and Carl Covitz

Works in the Exhibition

Unless otherwise indicated, dimensions are in inches; height precedes width precedes depth.

Colorado, 1971
Loose-leaf book with collage pages, 11×10½ each
Collection of the artist

Ma-chees-ma, 1971
Paper collage, 14×11
Collection of the actress Alexis Smith

The Keynote to Success, 1974
Paper collage, 12½×18½
Collection of James and Linda Burrows

Movies and Dreams, 1974–75
Paper collage, two panels, 14¼×47¼ each
Collection of Bette Hirsh

Madame Butterfly, 1975
Mixed-media collage, two panels, 12½×71 each
Collection of Patricia Faure

The Red Shoes, 1975
Mixed-media collage, two panels, 13½×63; 13½×54½
Collection of the Grinstein Family

Words Cannot Cook Rice–Charlie Chan, 1975
Mixed-media collage, 12×9¼
Collection of
Mr. and Mrs. Eugene D. Brody

Stairway to the Stars, 1977
Mixed-media collage, 12×9
Collection of John Solomon

The Big Sleep (Requiem for Raymond Chandler), 1978
Mixed-media collage, 14½×83¼
Collection of Richard Levine

Card, 1978
Paper collage, 11¾×9¼
Collection of the artist, courtesy Margo Leavin Gallery, Los Angeles

Chandlerism #1, 1978
Mixed-media collage, 12×9¼
Collection of the estate of Nancy Yewell

Chandlerism #9, 1978
Mixed-media collage, 12×9¼
Collection of Lyn and Norman Lear

Chandlerism #10, 1978
Mixed-media collage, 12×9¼
Collection of Judy and Stuart Spence

Chandlerism #12, 1978
Mixed-media collage, 12⅜×9½
The Chase Manhattan Bank, NA

Chandlerism #19, 1978
Mixed-media collage, 12×9¼
Collection of Richard Wiegand

Chandlerism #22, 1978
Mixed-media collage, 12¼×9½
Private collection

Chandlerism #25, 1978
Mixed-media collage, 12×9¼
Collection of Richard Wiegand

Chandlerism #29, 1978
Mixed-media collage, 12×9¼
Collection of Joy and Jerry Monkarsh

Chandlerism #30, 1978
Mixed-media collage, 12×9¼
Collection of Diana Zlotnick

Chandlerism #31, 1978
Mixed-media collage, 12×9¼
Collection of the Grinstein Family

Cannery Row, 1980
Mixed-media collage, 13½×70×1½
Collection of
Anne and William J. Hokin

Downtown, 1980
Mixed-media collage, 12¾×60¾
Private collection

Golden State, 1980
Mixed-media collage on sandpaper, three panels, 14×48; 14×57; 14×48
Collection of Walker Art Center, Minneapolis; Gift of Audrey Taylor Pretorius Gonzales, 1986

Hello Hollywood, 1980
Mixed-media collage, five panels, 9½×21 each
Collection of Raymond J. Learsy

Mean Streets, 1980
Mixed-media collage on aluminum printing plates, 16×72½
Collection of Harold I. Huttas

Newsreel, 1980
Mixed-media collage on aluminum printing plates, 16×41¾
Margo Leavin Gallery, Los Angeles

Stardust, 1980
Mixed-media collage, 12×60
Collection of Martin Sklar

Cathay, 1981
Mixed-media collages, 12×10 each
Collection of the artist

Blonde Venus, 1982
Mixed-media collage, 20¹³⁄₁₆×16¹³⁄₁₆
Collection of Renee Vollen

Bloody Mary, 1982
Mixed-media collage, 20⅞×17⅞
Margo Leavin Gallery, Los Angeles

Bombshell, 1982
Mixed-media collage, 17⅞×12⅝
Collection of Merry Norris

El Cartero Siempre Llama Dos Veces, 1982
Mixed-media collage, three panels, 21⅝×13¾ each
Margo Leavin Gallery, Los Angeles

Christmas Eve, 1943, 1982
Mixed-media collage, two panels, 20½×17½; 20½×17
San Diego Museum of Art; Gift of the Frederick R. Weisman Foundation

Coconut Grove, 1982
Mixed-media collage, 21½×18½
The Capital Group, Inc., Los Angeles

Danger, Curves Ahead, 1982
Mixed-media collage, three panels, 20⅞×17⅞; 21⅛×18⅛; 24×16
Margo Leavin Gallery, Los Angeles

Ebb Tide, 1982
Mixed-media collage, 21×18$\frac{1}{16}$
The Walt Disney Company, Los Angeles

Happy Hunting Ground, 1982
Mixed-media collage, 17½×25¾
Collection of the artist

If Looks Could Kill, 1982
Mixed-media collage, two panels, 15¼×12¾ each
Collection of Jonathan C. Ahearn

It's Lucky When You Live in America, 1982
Mixed-media collage, 21⅜×18½
Collection of Lenore and Bernard Greenberg

Madame X, 1982
Mixed-media collage, 21⅜×18½
Collection of Richard Rosenzweig and Judy Henning

Mustang Sally, 1982
Mixed-media collage, 20⅝×16¾
Collection of Alan Shayne

Satan's Satellites, 1982
Painted wall with hubcaps, 13×13 feet
Collection of the artist

Sea of Tranquility, 1982
Mixed-media collage, 20⅜×17⅝
Collection of the artist

Snapshot, 1982
Mixed-media collage, 21¾×20
Collection of Harold I. Huttas

Tokyo Rose, 1982
Mixed-media collage, 21¼×16
Collection of Lawrence M. Kauvar

All the Simple Old Fashioned Charm, 1984
Lacquer on wood, 34×17¼×19½
Margo Leavin Gallery, Los Angeles

Another World, 1985
Mixed-media collage, 24½×19¾
Security Pacific Bank, Los Angeles

The Ape Man, 1985
Mixed-media collage, 29⅛×21¼
Collection of Douglas S. Cramer

Asphalt Jungle, 1985
Mixed-media collage, two panels, 45⅛×25 each
The Museum of Contemporary Art, Los Angeles; The El Paso Natural Gas Company Fund for California Art

Calamity and Deadwood, 1985
Mixed-media collage, two panels, 24⅝×18⅛ each
Collection of Andres and Vanessa Moraga

Calamity Jane, 1985
Mixed-media collage, two panels, 32×20¾ each
Collection of Anne and William J. Hokin

Days of Our Lives, 1985
Mixed-media collage, 24½×19½
Collection of John Margulies

The Girl Can't Help It, 1985
Mixed-media collage, two panels, 26⅛×18⅞ each
Collection of Merry Norris

Hell on Wheels, 1985
Mixed-media collage, 32¾×21½
Collection of Laila and Thurston Twigg-Smith

Men Seldom Make Passes at Girls Who Wear Glasses, 1985
Mixed-media collage on painted wall: two panels, 27×33×5 each; 10×15 feet×5 inches overall
Collection of the artist

Me Tarzan, You Jane, 1985
Mixed-media collage, two panels, 19×15½ each
Collection of Peg and Chuck Rosenquist

The Perfect Couple, 1985
Mixed-media collage, 38⅜×30½
Collection of Mr. and Mrs. Robert J. Woods

Wild Life, 1985
Mixed-media collage, 18⅜×16⅜
Santa Barbara Museum of Art, California; Gift of Bruce Murkoff

Bob White, 1986
Mixed-media collage, 12⅞×10¾
Collection of Margo Leavin

The Holy Road, 1988
Mixed-media collage, $38\frac{3}{4} \times 31\frac{1}{4}$
Collection of Richard Rouilard

Mercury, 1988
Mixed-media collage, two panels, $43\frac{3}{4} \times 36\frac{5}{8}$ each
Collection of James and Linda Burrows

Miss America, 1988
Mixed-media collage, $36\frac{3}{8} \times 35\frac{7}{16}$
Collection of Nina MacConnel

Rock of Ages, 1988
Mixed-media collage, $54\frac{1}{4} \times 90\frac{5}{16}$
The Capital Group, Inc., Los Angeles

Route 66, 1988
Mixed-media collage, $31\frac{1}{4} \times 21$
Collection of Bernard and Rosalie Kornblau

Running on Empty, 1988
Mixed-media collage, $34\frac{1}{2} \times 74\frac{7}{16}$
The High Museum of Art, Atlanta; Gift of The Eli Broad Family Foundation

Seven Wonders, 1988
Mixed-media collage, $47\frac{1}{4} \times 41$
Margo Leavin Gallery, Los Angeles

Blue Chip, 1989
Paper collage, $14\frac{3}{16} \times 12\frac{7}{8}$
Collection of James and Linda Burrows

Lonesome Traveler, 1989
Mixed-media collage, $20\frac{5}{8} \times 15\frac{1}{4} \times 3\frac{1}{8}$
Collection of Rosamund Felsen

Moonlight Serenade, 1989
Mixed-media collage, $32\frac{3}{4} \times 38\frac{1}{2}$
Collection of Anne and William J. Hokin

Blue Denim, 1990
Mixed-media collage, $44\frac{1}{2} \times 57$
Collection of Mandy and Cliff Einstein

Eldorado, 1990
Mixed-media collage, $51\frac{1}{2} \times 65\frac{3}{4}$
Collection of Maurice Marciano

Fruits 'n' Nuts, 1990
Mixed-media collage, $35\frac{1}{4} \times 24 \times 16$
Josh Baer Gallery, New York, and Margo Leavin Gallery, Los Angeles

Jack, 1990
Mixed-media collage, $71\frac{1}{2} \times 93$
Collection of Laila and Thurston Twigg-Smith

Peaches, 1990
Mixed-media collage, $20\frac{1}{2} \times 20 \times 3$
Collection of the artist

Rocky Road, 1990
Mixed-media collage, two panels, 64×23 each
Margo Leavin Gallery, Los Angeles

Acknowledgments

One of the pleasures particular to museums of contemporary art is that of exhibiting the work of an artist who is also a friend. This exhibition is an extraordinary example of that experience. I salute Alexis Smith both for herself and her art. Her husband, Scott Grieger, has tolerated, with characteristic good will, my many interruptions of their domestic life.

I am indebted to Smith's past and present commercial representatives, the Margo Leavin Gallery foremost among them. At the gallery, Margo Leavin, Wendy Brandow, and Lynn Sharpless have faithfully and accurately replied to countless requests during the organization of this project and I am pleased to acknowledge their invaluable assistance. Likewise, I thank Rosamund Felsen, Holly Solomon, and Josh Baer for providing needed information at several important moments.

Sharon Freedman, my assistant, ably compiled the bibliography and exhibition history for this catalogue. She also made sense of my manuscripts through many transformations. I am very grateful to her for all her good work. Tom Armstrong, director emeritus, lent welcome support at the inception of the exhibition; the help of his successors, Jennifer Russell and, now, David A. Ross, lightened my burden during the project's subsequent stages. My colleague Barbara Haskell, long an admirer of Smith's work, shared her thoughts with me.

For their essential participation in arranging the tour of the exhibition to The Museum of Contemporary Art, Los Angeles, I am beholden to Richard Koshalek, director, Paul Schimmel, chief curator, and Ann Goldstein, curator. I am also appreciative of the sacrifice made by the many lenders to the show, whose collective generosity has made its assembly and presentation a reality.

R.A.

Photo credits

Chris Burden: p. 218, 220
Geoffrey Clements: p. 80, 81 (open magazine)
D. James Dee: p. 64 (left), 71 (bottom left and right, top right), 164 (right)
David Familian: p. 208, 209
Jeffrey Gubbins: p. 219, 228
Nancy Hirsh: p. 214
Coy Howard: p. 77
Leonard Koren: p. 38 (bottom)
Jim McHugh: p. 18
Grant Mudford: p. 199 (bottom), 200, 201
Peter Muscato: p. 194, 195
Patrick Nagatani: p. 72, 73, 83, 98, 99, 102, 196, 197, 222, 237
Douglas M. Parker: cover, p. 11, 14, 17, 18, 21, 27-29, 34, 35, 37, 38 (top), 39-41, 43-45, 46 (top), 47 (top), 48-53, 64 (middle), 74-76, 78, 79, 91, 93 (bottom), 103-115, 117-141, 143-160, 163, 165, 167-193, 223-225, 230, 234
Harry Shunk: p. 221 (top)
Grant Taylor Photography: p. 54-56, 64 (right), 65 (left and middle), 67-70, 71 (top left)
Tom Vinetz: p. 164 (left)
Willard Associates Photography: p. 62, 63
Ellen Page Wilson: p. 206, 207
Tom Yee: p. 80 (installation photo), 85-87

I can't replace our ideals, but I'll buy you a new watch when we get to Shanghai.

This publication was organized at the Whitney Museum by Doris Palca, Head, Publications and Sales; Sheila Schwartz, Editor; Deborah Lyons, Project Editor; Jane Philbrick, Associate Editor; Aprile Gallant, Production Assistant; and Debra Kelvin, Assistant.

Design: Bethany Johns
Typesetting: Trufont Typographers
Printing: South China Printing Company

Library of Congress Cataloging-in-Publication Data

Smith, Alexis, 1949–
Alexis Smith / Richard Armstrong; with a contribution by Amy Gerstler.
p. cm.
Includes bibliographical references.
ISBN 0-87427-076-6 WMAA
ISBN 0-8478-1446-7 Rizzoli
1. Smith, Alexis, 1949- —Exhibitions. I. Armstrong, Richard.
II. Gerstler, Amy. III. Whitney Museum of American Art. IV. Title.
N6537.S58A4 1991
700'.92–dc20 91-18179
CIP